TEACHING THE SOCIAL SCIENCES AND HISTORY IN SECONDARY SCHOOLS

A Methods Book

Developed by the Social Science Education Consortium, Inc.

Wadsworth Publishing Company
I(T)P® An International Thomson Publishing Company

Belmont • Albany • Bonn • Cincinnati • Detroit • London • Madrid • Melbourne • Mexico City
• New York • Paris • San Francisco • Singapore • Tokyo • Toronto • Washington

Education Editor: Sabra Horne
Editorial Assistant: Janet Hansen
Production Editor: Merrill Peterson
Designer: Cynthia Bogue
Photos: Carlye Calvin
Print Buyer: Karen Hunt
Copy Editor: Carole Crouse
Cover Designer: Lucy Lesiak
Compositor: Cecelia Gaytán Morales
Printer: Quebecor Printing Book Group/Fairfield

SSEC STAFF
Project Directors: James C. Schott, Suzanne W. Helburn
Project Editor: Laurel R. Singleton
Production: Cindy A.E. Cook
Project Secretaries: Marcia L. Hutson, Sylvia Thomas

This book was written as part of the SSEC project, Integrating Social Science Knowledge and Pedagogy in the Training of Social Studies Teachers. The project was supported by the National Science Foundation, grant no. TPE-8954727. Any opinions, findings, and conclusions or recommendations expressed herein are those of the writers and do not necessarily reflect the views of the National Science Foundation.

Printed in the United States of America
1 2 3 4 5 6 7 8 9 10—01 00 99 98 97 96 95

For more information contact:
Wadsworth Publishing Company
10 Davis Drive
Belmont, California 94002

International Thomson Publishing
Berkshire House 168-173
High Holborn
London, WCIV7AA, England

International Thomson Publshing GmbH
Konigwinterer strasse 418
53227 Bonn, Germany

Thomas Nelson Australia
102 Dodds Street
South Melbourne 3205
Victoria, Australia

International Thomson Publishing Asia
221 Henderson Road #05-10
Singapore 0315
Tokyo

Nelson Canada
1120 Birchmount Road
Scarborough, Ontario
Canada, M1K 5C4

International Thomson Publishing Japan
Hirakawacho-cho Kyowa Building, 3F
2-2-1 Hirakawacho-cho
Chiyoda-ku, 102, Japan

Library of Congress Cataloging-in-Publication Data

Teaching the social sciences and history in secondary schools : a methods book / developed
    by the Social Science Education Consortium, Inc.
        p.   cm.
    "Written as part of the SSEC project . . . supported by the National Science Foundation,
grant no. TPE-8954727"—T.p. verso.
    Includes bibliographical references and index.
    ISBN 0-534-26526-X
    1. Social sciences—Study and teaching (Secondary)   2. History—Study and teaching
(Secondary)   I. Social Science Education Consortium.
H62.T2875   1996
300'.71'273—dc20   95-12893
                                                                                         CIP

CONTENTS

CHAPTER 3

TEACHING IN THE REAL WORLD 37
John P. Zola

CHAPTER 4

THE PLANNING PROCESS 54
John P. Zola

PART II
THE SOCIAL SCIENCES AND HISTORY IN SCHOOL 71

CHAPTER 5
STUDYING AND TEACHING PSYCHOLOGY 72
Michael Wertheimer, Tina Yeager, and Virginia L. Jones

CHAPTER 6

STUDYING AND TEACHING SOCIOLOGY 105

J. Ross Eshleman and John P. Zola

CHAPTER 7

STUDYING AND TEACHING POLITICAL SCIENCE 137

Stephen L. Schechter with Jonathan Weil

CHAPTER 8

STUDYING AND TEACHING ECONOMICS   171
Suzanne Wiggins Helburn and H. Michael Hartoonian

CHAPTER 9
STUDYING AND TEACHING ANTHROPOLOGY 203
Roger C. Owen and Jack Zevin

CHAPTER 11

STUDYING AND TEACHING HISTORY 273

James R. Giese

CHAPTER 12

INTEGRATING THE CURRICULUM   312

James C. Schott

PART III
PLANNING FOR INSTRUCTION 341

CHAPTER 13
TEACHING STRATEGIES 342
Laurel R. Singleton

CHAPTER 14

USING INSTRUCTIONAL MATERIALS 390

Laurel R. Singleton

CHAPTER 15

CLASSROOM ASSESSMENT 408

Laurel R. Singleton

APPENDIX A

PROFESSIONAL ORGANIZATIONS 434

PREFACE

No pursuit should be of greater interest to students than the study of human behavior. Yet something happens on the way to the classroom, where secondary students often rate social studies courses, including history, as their most boring. The culprits, in students' eyes, are content that seems far removed from their present and future lives and teaching strategies that fail to grab their interest. Clearly, teachers' decisions about what to teach and how to teach it are critical.

Can a methods book help prospective teachers make better decisions on these questions? The authors of this book believe it can. We have chosen to address these issues in the following ways:

- By dealing realistically with the context in which social studies teachers work. The nature of schools and of the social studies curriculum as "officially" represented in curriculum mandates and textbooks all influence what and how teachers teach. Part One of the book deals explicitly with those issues.

- By engaging you with the content of the disciplines that make up the social studies. To that end, Part Two presents chapters on the individual disciplines, as well as on integration of the disciplines. The purpose of the chapters is to intrigue you, to entice you into further study of the subject if you are a novice or to encourage you to think more openly and creatively if you are already familiar with the subject. We are more interested in capturing your interest and communicating the intellectual excitement that each of the disciplines has to offer than in being sure that all aspects of the subject have been covered.

- By modeling strategies that promote engagement with content and development of understanding. Learning is to a large extent a matter of constructing meaning; it is a natural process we all engage in continuously. You, as well as your students, carry around a set of interconnected ideas and beliefs about social studies subjects. These conceptual structures are unique to the individual and are, to varying degrees, accurate and useful. Your job as a teacher is to help students become aware of their own conceptual structures and to provide them with experiences and opportunities to embellish, revise, and enrich those structures so that they will become more powerful tools for understanding the world. We are convinced that these conceptual schemes are revised and restructured only when the student is engaged in meaningful activities. Thus, throughout the book, we have included teaching/learning activities designed to help you construct meaning. Many of the activities can also be adapted for use with secondary students.

- By providing tools for planning. Part Three presents these tools, which include a brief introduction to a wide range of teaching strategies and approaches; insights into the use of a variety of instructional materials; and an overview of issues related to assessment in the classroom.

Because we believe content and pedagogy are inseparable, the book's authors include experts in the disciplines (a geographer, an economist, a historian, and so on), as well as experts in pedagogy (teachers, social studies coordinators, and the like). The authors do not necessarily agree with each other on every issue; indeed, at times they disagree rather violently. We have not tried to temper those disagreements or give all the authors "a common voice," since disagreement is integral to the social sciences and the social studies curriculum.

The book has been field-tested in several settings. We would like to thank the following methods professors and their students, who used all or portions of the text in their classes and provided extremely valuable feedback:

Thomas E. Baker
Austin College

G. Dale Greenawald
University of Northern Colorado

Carole Hahn
Emory University

Larry Herke
Mankato State University

Arthur H. Rice
Queens College, City University of New York

Paul Robinson
University of Arizona

Gregory P. Wegner
University of Wisconsin at LaCrosse

We would also like to thank the many authors and publishers who have allowed us to reprint material from their publications; this source material makes the book infinitely richer than it might have been.

ABOUT THE AUTHORS

Don Bragaw is associate professor of education at East Carolina University. Bragaw was the president of the Social Science Education Consortium in 1989 and is also a past-president of the National Council for the Social Studies.

J. Ross Eshelman is professor of sociology at Wayne State University. He has published textbooks in introductory sociology and sociology of the family and has been actively involved in teacher-training activities and curriculum projects.

James R. Giese, a historian by training, has been executive director of the Social Science Education Consortium since 1986. He has been involved in many aspects of history/social science education, including teacher training, curriculum development, and assessment. He is currently writing an eleventh-grade U.S. history textbook.

H. Michael Hartoonian is Supervisor of Social Studies Education for the state of Wisconsin, Department of Public Instruction, and adjunct professor in the School of Education, Department of Curriculum and Instruction, University of Wisconsin at Madison.

Suzanne Wiggins Helburn is professor of economics at the University of Colorado at Denver and one of the authors of ECON 12 (published as *Economics in Society*). Her scholarly interests include research on the economics of child care and the philosophic foundation of John Maynard Keynes's economics.

A. David Hill is professor of geography, University of Colorado at Boulder. He is coordinator of the Colorado Geographic Alliance and director of the Center for Geographic Education, UC—Boulder. He is currently directing a three-year NSF-funded project to produce instructional materials for secondary-level global geography.

Virginia L. Jones taught junior and senior high school students for fourteen years, then served as the State Social Studies Specialist at the Colorado Department of Education for six years. She recently returned to a high school to once again work with kids.

Roger C. Owen is a professor of anthropology, Queens College, City University of New York. A specialist on urban anthropology and aboriginal Americans, he is the author of professional books, monographs, articles, and curriculum materials. He obtained his Ph.D. at UCLA in 1962.

Stephen L. Schechter is professor of political science and director of the Council for Citizenship Education at Russell Sage College in Troy, New York. He has written extensively on American politics and constitutional history and is the former director of the New York State Commission on the Bicentennial of the U.S. Constitution.

James C. Schott is a senior staff associate at the Social Science Education Consortium. Schott holds a doctorate in social and multicultural foundations of education. He was formerly an assistant professor of education at the University of Wisconsin at Whitewater and taught secondary social studies for ten years.

Laurel R. Singleton is associate director and managing editor of the Social Science Education Consortium.

Steve Wanner has taught geography for twenty-one years in Boulder, Colorado. He is active in the Colorado Geographic Alliance and has been honored twice by the National Council for Geographic Education for outstanding teaching.

Jonathan S. Weil, chair of the History and Social Science Department at Evanston Township (Illinois) High School since 1984, has been involved with a variety of activities to encourage the professional and intellectual development of the staff. His particular interest has been the development of a global studies curriculum that includes study and travel opportunities for students and teachers.

Michael Wertheimer has been a professor of psychology at the University of Colorado at Boulder for almost four decades. He is author or co-author of several textbooks in the field. Long interested in the teaching of psychology at all levels, including high school, he recently received an award for distinguished career contributions to education and training in psychology from the American Psychological Association.

Tina A. Yeager is an author, consultant, and teacher from Boulder, Colorado.

Jack Zevin is currently professor of social studies education at Queens College, City University of New York. His interests include the social sciences, world studies, and curriculum and instruction. He has recently completed a book on *Social Studies for the 21st Century* and is a contributing editor to *The Social Studies* and *The Social Science Record*.

John P. Zola teaches at the New High School in Boulder, Colorado, and has taught social studies methods courses at the University of Colorado at Boulder. Zola has taught grades 7–12 and has experience as a staff developer and curriculum writer.

1

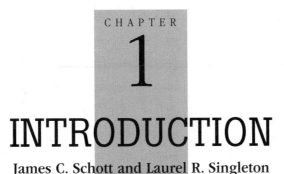

INTRODUCTION

James C. Schott and Laurel R. Singleton

ACTIVITY LIST

• • •

Reflective writing in response to a quotation, p. 1
Journal Writing, p. 6

At the beginning of each chapter, you will find a list like this one, showing the activities in the chapter. You can use these lists when looking for models of teaching strategies you want to use. For more on use of the activities in this book, see page 3.

ACTIVITY

Thinking about the Rewards of Teaching

Read the following quotation from an experienced teacher:

> *. . . what about the impact we have on the kids? Do we as teachers really change lives? It seems presumptuous to say yes, since I feel that many of my students were already remarkable human beings, confronting overwhelming odds with strength and maturity beyond their years. I would say that we can encourage our students and give them a nudge in the direction that each may ultimately choose to take. How many of us know which push got us to where we are? Who knows whose encouragement in my circuitous route got me teaching? But to whoever gave me the nudge, I am very thankful. (Siegel 1990, 67)*

Write your reactions to this statement. What do you think of Siegel's estimation of the teacher's impact? Can you identify the "nudge" that got you into teaching? Do you think a positive view of students is important?

As you continue with this book and, indeed, as you start your teaching career, keep the rewards of teaching in mind. Talk with experienced teachers about their views on students and on the teacher's impact on students. How do the views of teachers who seem happy in the profession differ from those of discontented teachers? How much support do teachers give each other? Do those teachers with a good collegial relationship with other teachers seem happier in the classroom than teachers who are relatively isolated? Also talk with secondary students about why some teachers have greater influence on them than do others.

THE CHALLENGE OF TEACHING

Teaching is not easy. Recent research is now confirming what many teachers have known intuitively for a long time—that teaching and learning are highly complex, interactive processes that include not only the teacher, the content, the school context, and the materials but also the students' preexisting knowledge structures and beliefs. The students to whom we introduce new ideas and concepts are not empty vessels. To teach effectively, the teacher must take the students' construction of the world into consideration.

Our intention in this book is to take seriously the complexity of the teaching task and the importance of meshing knowledge about schools, teaching, learning, subject matter, and content in ways that will provide useful models for you as you prepare to become a social studies teacher. Too often, we compartmentalize subject matter and teaching methods. Thus, a new teacher may possess extensive knowledge in both areas but may not have integrated that knowledge in a way that allows him or her to make good teaching decisions. Lee Shulman has given the name "pedagogical content knowledge" to the "blending of content and pedagogy [teaching methods] into an understanding of how particular topics, problems, or issues are organized, represented, adapted to the diverse interests and ability of learners, and presented for instruction." The importance of this blending can be seen by examining the phases of thoughtful teaching (adapted from Shulman):

- Comprehending the subject matter to be taught, how it relates to other ideas within the subject area, and why it is important to teach this subject matter to young people.
- Transforming knowledge of the subject matter "into forms that are pedagogically powerful and yet adaptive to the variations in ability and background presented by the students." This transformation involves ways of representing the content—for example, explanation, analogies, metaphors,

and examples—as well as instructional strategies for presenting and engaging students with the material.

- Actually performing the teaching tasks, including managing the classroom.
- Assessing their teaching and students' learning.
- Reflecting on the teaching and learning that occurred, with the aim of developing new comprehension of their purposes, of the subject matter, of the students, and of pedagogy.

Acquiring an integrated and accessible understanding of subject matter, students, and teaching methods is a daunting task. The fundamental assumption supporting the creation of this book was that we could, by example, begin to blend those realms. To that end, you will find that every chapter presents not only essential content but also engaging activities critical to developing understanding of that content. The activities are designed to demonstrate how interacting with content can help make the material personally meaningful to the individual learner (in this case, you). The activities are varied; some will require the instructor's assistance to set up, conduct, or both. Others can be done by small groups of students in or outside of class (e.g., in a study group). Still others can be completed on your own.

Some of the activities require classroom observations, interviews with classroom teachers, or other in-school activities. We recognize that making arrangements for such activities at the exact time you are using a particular chapter may be difficult, if not impossible. The activities will not, however, lose their value simply

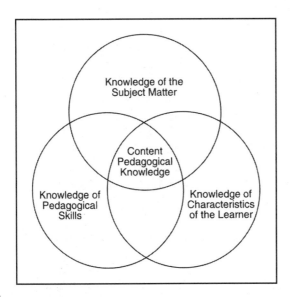

| **Figure 1.1** | Content pedagogical knowledge. What would you add to this diagram if you wanted it to show all the components of successful teaching?

because you cannot implement them immediately. You may find them useful as you begin student teaching or even as you start your first teaching job.

We believe your use of the book will be greatly enhanced by doing as many of the activities as you can. We also suggest reflecting on each activity you take part in, considering such questions as:

- What are the strengths of this activity? What learning objectives did it help me achieve?

- What were the weaknesses of this activity? How might it have engaged me with the content more effectively?

- How might this activity be adapted for use with secondary students? What teaching objectives would it help me achieve?

ORGANIZATION OF THIS BOOK

This book is quite different from most methods texts. First, it is longer than many such texts, primarily because we do not see it as a textbook that you would begin reading on page 1 and continue reading in lockstep fashion to the end. Rather, we see it as a resource book from which your methods instructor can pick and choose material that will help prospective teachers begin to develop understanding of the relationship between content, teaching methods, and students. We also see the book as a resource useful to you long after the course is over. Thus, although your instructor may choose not to use the chapter on anthropology, you may find it very useful when you are assigned to teach a course in world cultures. Similarly, your instructor may not cover all the material on teaching strategies presented in Chapters 13 and 14, but you may find that information helpful when planning lessons.

A second unique feature of this text is its three-part organization. The first part, "Teaching Social Studies," describes the context in which secondary social studies exists. In Chapter 2, "The Social Studies: The Civic Process," Don Bragaw provides a historical and philosophical context in which to understand the current debates about the proper role, content, and purpose of the social studies curriculum. Since you cannot teach all of the content of history and the social sciences, you will have to make choices about what and how you teach and for what purposes. This chapter will help you make those choices thoughtfully in light of decisions others have made in the past.

Many of the problems in social studies education continue to be problems because of organizational and systemic forces at work on the curriculum, teachers, students, and publishers. In Chapter 3, John Zola writes about the social and organizational context of teaching and suggests some choices you will make that will affect what you teach, the way you teach, and how you determine your successes and failures.

These chapters provide a context for considering how you will go about planning social studies courses, units, and lessons that you will teach. John Zola addresses "The Planning Process" in Chapter 4. Zola argues that planning will make your job as teacher less frantic and more effective and provides a variety of planning tools for your use. The information on planning will provide a useful backdrop to Part Two of the book.

Part Two, "The Social Sciences and History in the Schools," explores—in greater depth than most methods books—the seven disciplines that, separately and together, are the wellspring from which the social studies draws its content, concepts, and skills. To be sure, some social studies courses draw from other humanities and natural science disciplines. Such emerging disciplines as social psychology, jurisprudence, world or global studies, American studies, and ethnic or women's studies might also have been considered. We chose history, geography, anthropology, economics, political science, sociology, and psychology because they are the disciplines most commonly used as the foundation for building social studies curriculum, teaching social studies courses, and educating social studies teachers.

Although the chapters in this section, written by teams of academicians and social studies educators, are highly informative, they were never intended to be substitutes for formal study of the disciplines. It is hoped that these chapters will inspire you to pursue more complete and complex understanding of the various disciplines on your own.

To encourage writing that would inspire you to such pursuits, the authors of the discipline-based chapters were directed to "follow your bliss." With those words, we hoped to avoid typical "textbook" writing, which, in the name of being comprehensive, is often dense with meaningless data. We wanted the authors to write about their disciplines from their particular points of view, to write about the things that mattered to them. For example, we asked them: What is it about your discipline that interests you? What are the controversial issues? What is problematic about your discipline? We meant to communicate to the authors that we did not want them to write just another statement of "what students should know about sociology or geography or any of the other disciplines." Nor did we want the chapters to read like a survey-course outline in which every topic was covered, no matter how superficially.

In light of that freedom, what can you expect to find in the chapters in Part Two? You will find that each chapter has its own organizational structure. For example, the anthropology chapter is organized around a set of propositions anthropologists have developed about human existence, whereas the economics chapter is organized around the multiple ways to understand economic phenomena and the value positions upon which each is based.

You can, of course, read the chapters as though they were the final word on the subject. To do so would be a mistake, however. The authors have written their chapters from very particular points of view and with sets of assumptions and value positions built into not only the organization and content of the chapter but also the activities in which they engage you and the questions with which they ask you to cope. As you read, try to state or understand the point of view that is represented by each of the chapters.

However, neither we nor our students experience the world in formal disciplinary terms. None of us goes through the day watching television or reading the newspaper, saying to ourselves that this or that event is an economic event or a sociological event or a political science event. A recent newspaper headline read "Food Airlift to Bosnia Begins Third Year." Surely many of the disciplines would have something to contribute to our understanding of this headline and the following article. The final chapter in Part Two, therefore, deals with curricular integration.

You will note that Part Two does not contain a separate section on multicultural education, an important substantive concern for social studies teachers. The discipline-based chapters do, however, deal with issues related to diversity and multicultural society. The sociology chapter includes a section on racism, for example; the economics chapter deals with the feminization of poverty; the anthropology chapter looks at similarities and differences in child rearing across cultures. All the disciplines offer approaches to creating knowledge and a body of content that is applicable to multicultural issues. In addition, the strategies for integrating content matter presented in Chapter 12 will be useful to teachers in using information and methods of inquiry from several disciplines to develop multicultural units or courses.

Part Three, "Planning for Instruction," addresses questions of how to teach. Here you will find the "nitty-gritty" tricks of the trade. In Chapter 13, Laurel Singleton describes the essential characteristics as well as the appropriate applications of a broad range of teaching strategies. This chapter will make an excellent reference guide for thinking about creative ways to present material. A companion chapter, Chapter 14, looks at potential uses of various teaching materials. The text's final chapter focuses on evaluation, looking particularly at what is meant by authentic assessment and how teachers can move toward more authentic evaluation.

Reflecting on the Chapter

Reflection is a key to developing meaning. Both teachers and students need time to reflect on the classroom experience (Mathison 1994). One way of developing the habit of reflection is to keep a journal. Thus, we are encouraging you as you work through this book to keep a journal in which you comment on the substance presented, activities in which you are involved, issues raised in the course or issues in the news that seem to have relevance to what you are learning in this course, conversations with teachers, observations in classrooms, and so on. At least once in each chapter in the book, we present a specific issue to address in your journal.

Keep your journal in a separate notebook from your class notes. Write in your journal at least once a week; ideally, your instructor will allow some class time for this activity, as well as for discussion of the journals among students. Although your instructor may collect and comment on the journals, your journal belongs to you and is a way for you to explore your own reactions to material and discover your own meanings.

References

Mathison, S. "Critical Reflection on Classroom Practice: Teaching as an Investigative Activity." In *Reflective Practice in Social Studies*, ed. E. W. Ross, 23–28. Washington, D.C.: National Council for the Social Studies, 1994.

Shulman, L. "Knowledge and Teaching: Foundations of the New Reform." *Harvard Educational Review* 57, no. 1 (February 1987): 1–22.

Siegel, J. "It's the Kids Who Keep You Going." *Teacher Magazine* 1, no. 7 (April 1990): 66–67.

TEACHING SOCIAL STUDIES

2

THE SOCIAL STUDIES: THE CIVIC PROCESS

Don Bragaw

ACTIVITY LIST

• • •

Journal writing, pp. 10 and 32
Ranking rationale statements and building consensus, p. 12
Reflecting on personal experience/card sort, p. 17
Comparing/contrasting, p. 19
Designing a course, p. 22
Analyzing a definition, p. 28
Analyzing textbooks, p. 29

ACTIVITY   **Reflecting on the Social Studies Curriculum You Experienced**

Think back to your own elementary and secondary school days. When did you first become aware of social studies as a subject area? What was the focus of your social studies class each year after that point? Do you remember covering any subjects or topics several times? If so, what were they? How did you feel about the repetition at the time? Have your thoughts changed at all since you've been in college? Based on what you remember of your social studies classes, what do you think the rationale for the program was; that is, what were your social studies teachers trying to accomplish through their classes? Write some thoughts on these questions in your journal.

INTRODUCTION

A Personal History

In 1950, as I entered the department office in the school in which I was to do my student teaching, the sign on the door, in bold script, read HISTORY DEPARTMENT. I was to be supervised by Mr. X, whose assignment after almost forty years of teaching was five classes of eleventh-grade American history. The methodology was lecture and recitation. The students were passive and obedient.

Physically, Mr. X reminded me of my college American history professor; the resemblance ended there. Professor Y, who paced around a table in front of his classroom in bedroom slippers, seemed to know Thomas Jefferson, Jonathan Edwards, and William McKinley personally; his presence at the Battle of Vicksburg must have been decisive in winning that clash for the Union. Not only had Mr. X lost the battle, he had also been buried with Robert E. Lee. The classroom was a living mausoleum, and the students and I were all part of a very sad funeral.

The brashness of my youth was a startling contrast for the students, who, but for five years, were my peers. Mr. X never let me forget that—chiming in on my lessons with details that were superfluous and, sometimes, irrelevant. "New-fangled" methods, like debates, role playing, and Socratic discussions, had to be smuggled into my lessons when Mr. X was out of the room.

At my third job, about 1956, the door to the department office read CITIZENSHIP EDUCATION. I was assigned to teach three American history and two world history courses. The courses were chronologically sweeping, with a rush to get to the end for the Regents' (NY) examination that would confront the students and determine my future with the district.

The significance of the department's title was lost in the tacit understanding: History was the key to citizenship. History, it was believed, would provide the right attitudes and display the correct role models for the wise voters of the future. Instruction, however, was geared to memorization of certain bodies of data that were rarely centered on significant, major ideas and only occasionally touched on civic relationships. The guillotine chopped off the heads of nameless, faceless people whose blood spattered no textbook page; no moral or ethical dimensions of the deaths were examined. History was civic-less and bloodless. People moved across pages but did not act or react. Despite the name on the door, citizenship—the active participation of people in their own destinies—was not a part of the program.

By 1960, the sign on the door had changed to SOCIAL STUDIES. The name of our department was now reconciled with those of the Regents' examination and the administrative unit of the State Education Department that influenced social studies programs. The courses remained the same, however: American and world history, with occasional electives in the social sciences or an advanced placement course in history.

The name *social studies* was first coined in 1916. The changing department names I experienced in those early years of my career reflect the conflict over the focus and development of the field that has persisted since 1916:

- Is social studies really the study of university-devised disciplines—history or history and the social sciences—simplified for younger students? If so, why not call it by its true name?

- Is social studies a study of all of the social sciences (history being one of them) to enable people to understand the social nature of the world in which we live?

- Should this curriculum area be called citizenship education, which may include all the social sciences, history, the humanities—in fact, any discipline that helps to inform people of the nature of their relationship to the institutions and operations of the society?

- Is social studies more a process than a substantive area of study? Should it focus on *how* people learn to conduct their lives in association with one another and with distant (both in time and in space) others?

- Should social studies create social critics, passive believers, or compliant voters? Whichever you choose, what should young people study to achieve your goal?

- Is social studies the primary subject by which our society culturally reproduces itself through the schools?

Although the very nature of social studies is at the heart of this heated debate, most teachers have little or no knowledge of the debate. The gulf between university-based professionals and their classroom counterparts is profound and remains a challenge to students just entering the social studies teaching field (Mehlinger 1981; Leming 1989). Before you put on the mantle of social studies teacher, you must understand the origins of the subject and the debates that have marked its existence. You need, also, to take a stand—for how you view social studies will determine how you will help students learn the subject.

ACTIVITY ## Considering Alternative Rationales for Social Studies*

A rationale explains why people are doing what they are doing. The rationale for a school curriculum includes certain assumptions about students. A social studies rationale should include a philosophical statement about the nature of society—past,

---

*Adapted from *Planning a Social Studies Program* (Boulder, Colo.: Social Science Education Consortium, 1991). Rationale statements by Barbara Miller and John Zola.

present, and future—as well as a statement about the nature of the social studies, including the role of the social science disciplines.

This activity is designed to help you begin identifying your own view of the rationale for the social studies. Read the following seven teacher statements below carefully. Then rank them from 1 to 7, with 1 indicating the statement that comes closest to what you believe and 7 indicating the statement that is the furthest from your beliefs.

_____ A. The main task of education in a democratic society is to produce citizens who are neither apathetic nor cynical; that is, who feel that problems can be solved, that wrongs can be righted, and, most of all, that they personally can participate and influence the direction of the society. The social studies curriculum must show students how to participate and convince them that their efforts can really count. We have to demonstrate, maybe through community service and action learning, that individuals and organizations can exert power in ways that improve society.

_____ B. Kids in the U.S. don't know the basic data necessary to live in and understand today's world. In a phrase, they are not "culturally literate." Surveys reveal that the typical 17-year-old can't identify the correct half century in which the Civil War occurred, can't identify key phrases from the Declaration of Independence, and can't even locate basic information on a map or globe. We need an emphasis on "core" curriculum that, when mastered by our youth, will bind us together as a society and a people.

_____ C. Let's face it, we are increasingly becoming a society of "haves" and "have-nots." Racism, homelessness, age and sex discrimination are only a few of our persistent social problems. Social studies must knock down the myths and rationalizations that support discrimination. Every graduate of the public schools should understand why our multicultural society honors equality and human dignity and should express their personal commitment to these democratic values with votes and with their actions.

_____ D. If you're teaching college-bound students, the primary task of the social studies is crystal clear: teach the academic courses that will get your students into college. If you don't, your students will be anxious, their parents will be furious, and you will be (come contract time) superfluous. School is a mobility machine, and the main function of the social studies, like that of every subject, is to do the conventional academic thing. Up the social ladder!

_____ E. Survival is what we need to teach—survival in an impersonal and competitive urbanized society. How to cope with bureaucrats and employers and police and landlords. How to resolve conflicts productively. How to cope with shoddy products, crowded living, aggressiveness. And—not least—how to cope with loneliness. Social studies must be accountable for preparing the new generation to find more satisfying solutions than the distractions of the boob tube and the cop-outs of drugs and alcohol.

_____ F. Our current emphasis on coverage leads to trivializing of knowledge and information. It promotes a mistaken reliance on "objective" testing to assess isolated, sometimes irrelevant, "bits" of information. Instead, social studies teachers must pursue fewer topics in far greater depth. Students must have opportunities to rigorously explore a topic through research, primary source materials, and significant discussions—to process the significance and meaning of information.

_____ G. We live in an increasingly interdependent global society. What we should be doing is developing cross-cultural understandings and building the best radar we can for looking into the future. We have to help students apply social science concepts to the accelerating changes of our own times. Students need to be alerted to developments that are still over the horizon but which will strongly affect their lives. They need to begin thinking about the future in a disciplined way.

● ● ●

After you have completed your rankings, compare them with the rankings of several other students. What are the areas of disagreement? Agreement? Try to write a series of statements on which the members of your group agree; group your statements into three categories: assumptions about students, views about the nature of society, views about the social studies.

You will have a chance to reflect on this exercise again later in this chapter.

A Personal View

In my view, the citizenship or civic process should be the dominant force in social studies education. The process of which I speak is not a series of isolated skills or a particular body of content. Rather, it is the knowledge and capacity to identify needed information, make the connections between that information and the problems that confront society, evaluate the implications of the connections, and then act upon the problem for the individual's and society's good. That is the spirit in which social studies was born; it is the spirit in which I believe it should prevail.

This chapter will provide, in broad strokes, an account of the field of social studies education as it emerged from the history of the country. That history can be highlighted through discussion of a series of special commissions or committees formed at various times to establish goals for social studies education. The responses to those commissions and the reality of what was going on in the schools and universities will also be explored. The focus, however, will be on the development (or lack thereof) of citizenship education—the ways in which history, the social sciences, and all subjects are combined for the purposes of preparing students for a useful and civically responsible life.

TRADITIONS IN SOCIAL STUDIES CURRICULUM

Throughout the history of the social studies curriculum, most educators have agreed that the curriculum is, in fact, composed of the various social science disciplines. One can tick off the disciplines in descending order of importance, depending on who is doing the ordering. The order has generally begun with history, followed by geography and civics. Since the mid-1970s, economics has claimed a significant place in the curriculum; sociology, anthropology, and psychology have received less attention.

Subjects blending two or more of the disciplines have had a modicum of success. For example, law-related education, which combines civics with jurisprudence and a smattering of history, psychology, and sociology, exerts some influence among electives. Career education, consumer education, ethnic studies, environmental education, and similar permutations of subjects have all had surges of prominence, but never dominance.

What accounts for the selection and methods of presenting information and processes from the social sciences? Numerous analysts (Barr, Barth, and Shermis 1977; Morrissett and Haas 1982; Engle and Ochoa 1988) have identified at least three traditions in social studies education, each of which constitutes a guide for curriculum development and implementation. These traditions are (1) social studies as a vehicle for cultural or citizenship transmission, (2) social studies as the study of the social sciences, including history, and (3) social studies as reflective inquiry.

The first of these traditions continues to be the predominant one in classrooms across the country. Often, the actual program in a school taking this approach is defined by textbooks written by one or another historian or social scientist and concentrating on the delivery of predigested information. The program may also involve the deliberate indoctrination of certain beliefs or values (which may change from time to time), using social science or historical generalizations to sustain the position. This tradition does not require the student to engage with information in any way that would stimulate thoughtful citizenship in a democracy.

The second tradition—social studies as the critical study of key concepts or ideas in the social sciences and history—gained prominence in the "new social studies" era in the 1960s and early 1970s. Adherents of this tradition have often advocated use of an inquiry-discovery approach to the examination of data, modeled after the manner in which professional social scientists investigate problems. These advocates thus transcend the boundary between this tradition and the reflective-inquiry tradition.

The reflective-inquiry tradition has focused on thought processes by which knowledge is created, evaluated, and used. Often, those favoring this tradition have recommended an interdisciplinary decision-making curriculum focused on social issues or problems. This approach suggests a need to go beyond the study of separate disciplines, to allow the problem or experience to open up a need to examine all manner of data—regardless of its source. The study would require investigatory, connective, and application skills—again not limited to social science methods. Although the integrationist position has never been ascendant in social studies, it has always had its supporters.

The pendulum of advocacy of one or another of these or other traditions or approaches to social studies swings according to several factors: the political climate in the country; the attention, or lack thereof, given to the precollegiate curriculum by university scholars; the infusion of federal or other dollars; the results of opinion polls; the publication of influential intellectual interpretations; the dedication and enthusiasm of inspired teachers. The line of demarcation is not always easy to detect, and a period of overlapping is sometimes present, as subsequent sections will show.

SOCIAL EDUCATION IN THE EIGHTEENTH AND NINETEENTH CENTURIES

The Early Years as a Nation

The earliest social studies (although not called that) was cultural transmission in the form of patriotic inculcation and blind acceptance of authority. The early Noah Webster texts in history and geography were glorifications of the Constitution and the federal government as it was beginning to emerge in the 1790s. The "social studies" of the day was study of the principles and details of the Declaration of Independence and the Constitution and a celebration of the not-too-distant revolution. As Belok (1981) has reported, this type of text—and concomitant learning—was to continue almost without change throughout the nineteenth century. The history, civil government, and geography that were the mainstays of the early school curriculum bred loyalty to the nation, and there was little room for challenge.

Developments in the Late Nineteenth Century

As public high schools began to emerge alongside the private and semipublic academies that had served the affluent populace, a new concern arose: What was the purpose of education beyond grammar school? Was the purpose of secondary education to prepare students for the university or to prepare young people to take their place in society?

The universities had for some time organized themselves—administratively as well as intellectually—by disciplines. The influence of the German universities was dominant, and that system was very influential in shaping the numbers of private and public schools emerging in the last half of the nineteenth century.

Business interests also sought to influence the direction of education; they had a very real stake in the preparation of young men for work in the rapidly developing American industrial society (the education of young women was not of great concern to most business leaders—or educators—of the time). Preparing an astute and intelligent managerial staff, workers who could do the minimal reading and writing required, and a vast supply of laborers was a daunting challenge to educators.

These two groups shared a belief that students should be carefully nurtured to become good, law-abiding citizens. Much of what emerged as formal civics programs in the late nineteenth and early twentieth centuries derived from the Americanization process instituted to educate immigrants into American traditions of political and social life. Students studied large doses of American history to instill new national identity and create a new patriotism. In "civics" class, the new arrivals unlearned monarchy and learned the structures and functions of American government and democracy. English classes featured essays and poems on patriotic lore and heroism.

This program of indoctrination was incorporated with little change in regular school programs for all students in the United States. If it worked well for the immigrant, then it would serve to initiate the young among the native-born. To meet the needs of the many students who ended their schooling at the end of the eighth or ninth grade, the formal civics program was placed at the early secondary level.

Schools added another citizenship dimension at this time: to encourage students to learn good manners and conduct themselves with civility, thereby proving themselves to be good citizens. Indeed, one of the key sections of the report-card form was a column entitled "Citizenship." This section continued from my mother's school life at the turn of the century, into my own at midcentury; some schools today feature the same notation. The citizenship column had an O (Outstanding), S (Satisfactory), or U (Unsatisfactory). Good marks were frequently rewarded with certificates, medals, or the privilege of carrying the flag or leading the prayer in the opening morning exercises.

In my own elementary class (there were the same fourteen of us from kindergarten through eighth grade), Robert, who was always in trouble, invariably got the U's, while Roger and Leon, who also happened to be the "smartest," usually carried the flag and led the prayer. Girls were seldom thought of as being better than Leon or Roger; indeed, their "good citizenship" was expected and therefore did not need to be rewarded (and wasn't). The rest of us endured our S's and continued to strive for the honor on which Roger and Leon apparently had a monopoly. We all knew our place in the world and acted accordingly.

I have often thought about whether any of those fourteen are carrying flags and saying prayers at civic functions today. How many of them no longer cast a vote in any election? None, to my knowledge, has ever been elected to Congress; but, then again, none has appeared in the national newspapers as a perpetrator of a capital crime. I guess Robert turned out all right!

ACTIVITY ## Reflecting on Implicit Citizenship Education

David Bricker in his book *Classroom Life as Civic Education* (1989) contends that classroom interactions, implicit and explicit rules, and the system of rewards and punishments teach children about what it means to be a good citizen. Think back to your own school interactions. List two experiences in which your school interactions taught you a lesson about being a good citizen. In small groups share your experiences. To what extent were the experiences of your group members similar to one another? Put each experience on a 3-by-5-inch card. In your group, sort the experiences according to the lesson taught. Based upon your sorting activity, report to the class upon the ideas about citizenship that were transmitted by the classroom culture.

Were these implicit lessons applied differently to different groups in your school? Were women or minorities subject to the same set of expectations? What about athletes or student council members or children from low-income families?

The NEA Committee of Ten (1893)

The rivalry between the university and the corporation for control of the secondary school brought about the need to clarify goals for secondary education. To address that issue and provide guidelines to both public and higher education units, the National Education Association (the strongest educational organization of the day) convened a committee in 1893 "to consider the teaching of History, Civil Government, and Political Economy in the schools" (National Education Association 1893). This committee set down a regimen of instruction that was essentially concerned with modern history and gave a tip of the hat to civil government and political economy (economics):

Grade 7: American history and government

Grade 8: Greek and Roman history

Grade 9: French history

Grade 10: English history

Grade 11: American history

Grade 12: Optional studies in depth

The increased emphases on modern history and history as a process were an indication of the influence of James Harvey Robinson, whose "new history" (history that both is selective and clearly relates to the present) was beginning to emerge. This was evident in the report:

History is the study of human character. . . one object of historical study is the acquirement of useful facts; but the chief object is the training of the judgement, in selecting the grounds of an opinion, in accumulating materials for an opinion, in putting things together, in generalizing upon facts, in estimating character, in applying the lessons of history to current events, and in accustoming children to state their conclusions in their own words. (National Education Association 1893)

The committee's statement in reference to civil government is worthy of some attention, since its principles have found their way into present school social studies programs. The committee indicated that instruction in government in the "grammar school" should be "simple and practical," using familiar materials and institutions as examples; in all history classes, the subject of government should be interwoven; and at the high school level, government should be "taught more elaborately." The report indicated that the program should be activity-oriented (though not social action–oriented) and that school interaction with the community was desirable.

The AHA Committee of Seven (1899)

The American Historical Association in 1899 appointed its own committee to study the role of history in the secondary schools. As could be expected, this committee recommended a full four-year program of history as the correct preparation for college (American Historical Association 1899):

> Grade 9: Ancient history, especially Greek and Roman but also including the early Middle Ages, ending in the fourth century
>
> Grade 10: Medieval and modern European history
>
> Grade 11: English history
>
> Grade 12: American history and civil government

Ten years later, another AHA committee (The Committee of Eight) dealt with the program at the elementary grades (K–8) and in like fashion recommended a heavy historical orientation, emphasizing holidays, biography, and mythology, as well as American, ancient, and medieval history. This committee also recommended a separate study of government at two grade levels (American Historical Association 1909).

ACTIVITY

Comparing Contemporary Curriculum with That Recommended by Early Committees/Commissions

In the early 1980s, the Social Science Education Consortium undertook a major project to study the present status of social studies. That project confirmed what most had known for some time: There was a de facto national pattern for the social studies curriculum (Lengel and Superka 1982), one that with minor exceptions persists today:

> Grade K: Self, school, community, home
>
> Grade 1: Families
>
> Grade 2: Neighborhoods
>
> Grade 3: Communities
>
> Grade 4: State history or geographic regions
>
> Grade 5: U.S. history
>
> Grade 6: World cultures or Western hemisphere

Grade 7: World geography or history or Eastern hemisphere

Grade 8: American history

Grade 9: Civics or world cultures/history

Grade 10: World history

Grade 11: American history

Grade 12: American government, economics, or sociology/psychology

What similarities do you see between this pattern and those recommended by the 1893 and 1899 committees? What emphases have persisted? What significant differences do you note? What subjects are no longer taught? Create a diagram or some other graphic that will allow you to keep track of the changes in curriculum organization throughout the twentieth century.

SOCIAL STUDIES EMERGES AS A SUBJECT

The Intellectual Background to the Social Studies

The end of the nineteenth century and the beginning of the twentieth was a tumultuous time in the social and intellectual history of the United States. Industrialization brought serious social and economic inequities. Because of the concentration of people in large urban centers, more people than ever suffered the indignities of poor housing, poor working conditions, poor quality of food and health care. In spite of the "Horatio Alger" success rhetoric of the day, many had the feeling that they could not, in fact, control their destiny. While the poor resigned themselves to hoping for better things for their children, a powerful and wealthy few were amassing huge fortunes, justified by some with social application of Darwin's theory of evolution; that is, the wealthy represented the survival of the fittest.

The combination of the forces of modernization and the principles of evolution as applied to society's operation—social Darwinism—also brought about an intellectual reaction, known as pragmatism. One of pragmatism's founders, Charles Peirce, asserted that evolutionary principles were not fixed and immutable and that science had the ability to modify those principles through human intervention (Cohen 1962). Additionally, Peirce claimed that since all was in a constant state of flux, one had to continually identify and deal with these new conditions or forces. This could be accomplished only by free and unfettered inquiry and the creation of new configurations of knowledge.

Peirce's wide-ranging thought inspired both William James, in his explorations of pragmatism, and John Dewey, in his development of socially focused instrumentalist pragmatism. Dewey's thinking was to greatly influence American education in general and the development of social studies education in particular. Later in his life, Dewey was to describe this new philosophical direction as a *fundamental idea . . . which is the idea that action and opportunity justify themselves only to the degree in which they render life more reasonable and increase its value . . . the unstable character of American life and civilization has facilitated the birth of a philosophy which regards the world in continuous formation, where there is still room for indeterminism for the new and for a real future. (Dewey 1932)*

Dewey's position, when applied to the social world, asserted that the world was in a constant state of development and required the application of human intelligence to solve problems and make decisions vital to that development. This was the *civic process*, giving an activist, or participatory, backbone to what a person needed to know and to do given the changing circumstances of life. Peirce and Dewey emphasized that change and growth, not stability and stasis, were the characteristics of modern society.

The instrumentalism that Dewey gave to education was, for him, key to enabling people to take charge of their lives. Life, like the United States itself, was an ongoing experiment. It was from this philosophical basis that social studies education was derived; social studies became the school subject that would train citizens in the problem-solving and decision-making skills and knowledge of the world around them needed to make their lives more reasonable and valuable. If democracy was to work, and work well, then children needed to know, understand, and use information to solve the problems they encountered. Discipline-focused subject matter was important as a source of data for use in solving problems, not as an end in itself. It was this vision of citizenship that gradually took hold among leading social studies educational thinkers after World War I.

The 1916 NEA Committee on Social Studies

The most powerful influence on the social studies curriculum of today is the 1916 social studies subcommittee report of the National Education Association's Commission on the Reorganization of Secondary Education. The commission singled out citizenship for the first time as a significant outcome of schooling in the United States (Commission on the Reorganization of Secondary Education 1918). The social studies committee, heavily influenced by classroom teachers, reflected the significant influence of John Dewey and other pragmatists, being far more conscious of the need for students to reflect on and try to resolve the issues that were besetting American society and altering the American dream.

The committee report on social studies was highly influential in bringing to the fore the interaction of history, civics, and the social sciences. The committee saw social studies as an overarching educational umbrella designed to help children understand the processes by which people operate in and with society. Their report placed citizenship at the heart of social studies.

The committee report did recommend retaining much of the history endorsed by previous committees—American history at both eighth and eleventh grades and

European history in tenth grade—as well as civics in grade 9 and geography in grade 7. Political and military history were to be downplayed, with greater emphasis on what has since become known as social history.

The emergent social sciences were also included as part of the broad new curricular field called *social studies*. The committee considered recommending separate social science discipline courses for twelfth grade, but opted instead for a totally new approach that would combine the social sciences, including history, in a course dealing with current issues; they entitled the course Problems of American Democracy. The committee asserted that such problems, or issues, would be selected by teachers on the basis of two criteria: their "immediate" interest to students and their "vital" importance to society.

Significant in this report was the clear recognition that "in actual life . . . we face problems or conditions and not sciences. We use sciences, however, to interpret our problems and conditions. Furthermore, every problem or condition has many sides and may involve the use of various sciences . . ." (Committee on Social Studies 1916).

The war and its immediate aftermath delayed the impact of the NEA's efforts; the Problems of Democracy course did not receive wide acceptance until the late 1920s and 1930s (Jenness 1990). Yet the 1916 and 1918 reports unmistakably influenced the direction of social studies education. Much of what the committee recommended has remained in place with but minor adjustments to the present day, and the report stimulated the first of the provocative experiments with social/public issues approaches to social studies education, at both the junior and the senior high school levels.

That experiment was the work of Harold Rugg at Teachers College (Columbia University), who set about the task of meeting the needs of the new Problems course. His work led to the publication of a series of textbooks for both junior and senior high school under the general title *Man and His Changing Society*. The series, which embodied process notions, became extremely popular in the 1930s. The social reconstructionist thinking (i.e., training students to reform society) of Rugg and his colleague at Columbia, George Counts, remains a significant, although far from dominant, influence on social studies education (Nelson 1982).

In the late 1930s and early 1940s, Rugg's books came under attack as leading to socialism (and, possibly, communism). World War II brought not only an end to the Depression but also a resurgence of nationalist feeling that in the schools, once again, took the form of a return to history and a rejection of the problems approach, which was considered a negative approach to intellectual development.

ACTIVITY   ## Designing a Problems Course for the Twenty-First Century

Imagine that you have been appointed to a committee designing a new semester-long Problems of Democracy course for the school district in which you are teaching. The course will be based on the rationale developed by the 1916 social studies subcommittee, but it must also meet the needs of students who will be living their adult lives in the twenty-first century. Discuss the following questions with a group of classmates.

- What are the goals or outcomes for the course?
- What criteria will teachers use in selecting issues or problems to be covered?
- How will the issues be approached?
- How will knowledge from the disciplines be used to illuminate problems?
- How will students demonstrate achievement of the goals of the course?

Use the group's answers to these questions to develop a course description. Explain how a particular issue, such as poverty, race relations, or immigration, would be treated in the course.

THE WAR AND ITS AFTERMATH

World events from 1939 to 1950 restored a strong nationalistic fervor to social studies programs. Postwar confrontations with the Soviet Union challenged the dominance and integrity of the United States and spurred a seeming rivalry in education between the two powers. Some educational Cassandras treated apparent U.S. deficits as dire threats to our strength and commitment as the leading democratic nation.

Critics such as Rudolf Flesch, who wrote the best-seller, *Why Johnny Can't Read: And What You Can Do About It*, attacked the teaching of reading, foreign languages, math, and science; teacher education; and the teaching methods associated with progressive education and "life adjustment education." Historian Arthur Bestor (1953) claimed that the public schools did not value training students' minds in the intellectual disciplines and the power to think. He believed this problem was exemplified in the teaching of such broad fields as science and social studies rather than the "pure" disciplines, such as history, physics, and chemistry. The decennial *New York Times* test of American history knowledge on the part of entering college freshmen proved again, as it had a decade earlier (and would again a decade later), that U.S. students did not know basic information about their nation's heritage.

The result, critics claimed, was that American students lagged behind students in other countries, particularly the Soviet Union. The Soviet Union's launching of Sputnik I on October 4, 1957, appeared to provide the critics with evidence of their claims (Haas 1977).

University-based scholars had, in fact, begun reform efforts in math and science in the early 1950s. In September 1959, many of the leaders in educational reform met at Woods Hole, Massachusetts, to conceptualize the new principles of curriculum development. Jerome Bruner (1960) summarized the conference:

- Students can learn how to learn; massive transfer of learning can be achieved.

- The disciplines have distinctive "structures" that students can learn, or discover, which tie together discrete knowledge so that it can be more effectively gained and retained.

- Mastery of the fundamental ideas of a field involves not only general principles but the development of an attitude towards learning; that is, learning by "inquiry" or "discovery."

- Since intellectual inquiry is everywhere the same, the "school-boy" can learn more easily by behaving as a social scientist.

- Any subject can be effectively taught in some honest form to any child at any level. (Hertzberg 1981)

These principles became key to many of the projects that came into being when vast government support for social studies became available in the 1960s.

SOCIAL STUDIES IN THE 1960s AND 1970s

The "New Social Studies"

In the 1960s, the federal government (and private sources) generously funded an array of projects that became known as the "New Social Studies." The projects were more concerned with development of materials than with the overall organization of the social studies curriculum. As many as forty projects of "national significance" had been funded by the mid-'60s (Fenton and Good 1965). Among them were Our Working World, the High School Geography Project, the Carnegie-Mellon history inquiry project, the Anthropology Curriculum Study Project, Man: A Course of Study, Sociological Resources for the Social Studies, and ECON 12.

The majority of the New Social Studies projects focused on specific disciplines at the secondary level. A number sought to identify and teach the structure of the discipline—that is, its characteristic theories, concepts, generalizations, and modes of inquiry. Others simply organized the curriculum around important concepts and generalizations from social science or history. This emphasis represented a significant shift from the piling on of factual information that had previously characterized much instruction in social studies.

Also significantly different from the norm was the primary method of instruction employed by most of the projects—an inductive or inquiry approach sometimes drawing on the investigative processes of the particular discipline being studied. Through this approach, the projects provided multiple opportunities for critical thinking.

Although incremental changes have occurred because of the influence of the New Social Studies curricula and the innovations initiated by them paved the way for the current emphasis upon critical and reflective thinking, nevertheless the New Social Studies materials have all but disappeared from the educational landscape.

There is no single reason or simple explanation for the demise of the New Social Studies effort. A number of participants in and observers of the New Social Studies movement (Haas 1977; Fenton 1981, 1991; Hertzberg 1981; Anderson 1982; Marker and Mehlinger 1990) have suggested reasons as diverse as inadequate dissemination, failure to attend to K–12 scope-and-sequence issues, overlooking diversity among students and teachers, overemphasis on unidimensional solutions to curriculum problems, raising the hackles of some conservative groups and some educators, and the cost of the curriculum materials.

Perhaps most telling is the charge that the developers of the New Social Studies materials simply did not understand the culture of the schools well enough. They underestimated the tenacity of the traditional scope and sequence of the social studies curriculum and particularly the change-resistant pedagogy of social studies teachers, who tended to cling to textbook- and lecture-centered practices (Cuban 1991). Curriculum developers assumed that teachers should and would use unfamiliar teaching strategies and complex, modular teaching materials and technologies that were incongruent with their customary practices and the culture of the school. Conservative and religious groups often opposed the new curricula. The social science emphasis not only tended to ignore the cultural transmission approach to social studies but also raised troubling social, economic, and cultural value issues. For example, the SRSS materials raised issues about social inequalities based upon race and class, and *Man: A Course of Study* seemed to propose cultural relativism.

An Effort at Synthesis

An effort to develop a process-oriented synthesis of the social sciences was made by the Social Science Education Consortium in 1971. Irving Morrissett and William Stevens, Jr. (1971), invited three eminent social scientists to describe a possible synthesis of the social sciences that might be viable in the schools.

Lawrence Senesh, the developer of the *Our Working World* elementary program, chose the metaphor of "orchestration" to describe his synthesis. In Senesh's vision, social studies curriculum would comprise "units in which different disciplines are called upon to play the dominant analytical role." An orchestral piece, such as a Mozart flute concerto, may feature one instrument, but the instrument is surrounded, assisted, complemented, and supplemented by all the other instruments. Similarly, a social studies unit might feature one discipline, blended with others. For example, a multidisciplinary grade 1 unit on the family, Senesh suggested, would include political science (decision making), economics (producing, distributing, and consuming goods and services), sociology (differing roles in the family), and social anthropology (differences among families and family members). Although sociology would be the central focus of the unit, "family" would have no meaning without bringing the other parts into a unified whole. Senesh's work never really touched upon the secondary program, where the "orchestration" might have more difficulty being achieved.

Alfred Kuhn's contribution was to project a "unified social science" built around analytical tools. Kuhn saw unified and interdisciplinary as two totally different approaches to social science learning. In an interdisciplinary structure, the topic or problem would be approached (or attacked) from the individual disciplines, with each contributing its knowledge and insights; the emerging analysis or response would thus be interdisciplinary. What Kuhn proposed was to center a unified social science approach on an analytical tool, which could then be applied to a multiplicity of problems, real or experimental. The analytical tools might involve communications and information theory, linguistics, semiotics, learning theory, game theory, negotiation, and organizational or management theory. Various social sciences would be involved as appropriate; history would provide insight into the variables that have affected decision making or problem solving on past occasions. The absence of any school-based examples weakened Kuhn's presentation.

The most provocative of the syntheses offered was that of Kenneth Boulding. Advocating a general systems approach, Boulding sounded an educational alarm:

> *What formal education must do is to produce people who are fit to be inhabitants of the planet. This has become an urgent necessity because for the first time in human history we have reached the boundaries of our planet and found that it is a small one at that—the spaceship earth.*

What Boulding proposed in his "total systems" approach was that the world be examined not in disciplinary terms but with respect to problems or threats that confront the need for ecological equilibrium—drawing upon whatever database will aid in clarifying or leading to a solution to a problem. Students, Boulding asserted, should be learning significant factual information as well as where to find information. History and geography should be global in nature; students should realize that civilization is not the unique province of their own heritage, but recognize the difficulty of cultural development wherever it is found.

Boulding's later work on the total systems approach posited seven basic interacting global systems: biological, physical, social, political, economic, communications, and evaluative. The systems are totally interactive with one another, calling upon the full investigative powers of any and all sources of data. The biological system, for example, would involve the widest possible array of databases—genetics, bioethics, biochemistry, botany—but would not call upon the discipline nature of the base, but rather the way in which the database enabled people to deal with whatever problem or situation existed.

Boulding's prime concern was with the ecological condition of the planet; the entire structure of learning, therefore, would be focused on the goal of global survival (Boulding 1985). Such a determination would provide a clear rationale for the goals and objectives for elementary and secondary school programs. Goodlad, writing in 1990, used the Boulding systems as a centerpiece for a recommended return to the "core curriculum" (Goodlad 1990).

The 1971 SSEC effort had no direct effect on schools and teachers; what it accomplished was to provide "fodder" for future thought. Boulding's ideas have greater acceptance today in an environmentally threatened world than they did in 1971.

The 1970s

The response of the schools, and of social studies, to the tumult of the 1960s was, at best, mixed. Some critics charged that high schools had become "shopping malls," in which students could choose from a vast array of courses and minicourses of questionable academic integrity. Despite reports to the contrary, the shopping-mall high school was not a common phenomenon. In fact, very little had changed in most social studies departments, which were still cleaving to the 1916 recommended curriculum.

Yet, by the mid-'70s, the reaction to presumed educational anarchy began to make itself known. Accusations of declining test scores, of students graduating from high school unable to read, of lowering mathematics competence, and of schools producing civically irresponsible or apathetic citizens began to appear in the popular press. The reaction was a call for a return to "basics." Throughout the last half of the '70s and into the '80s, condemnation of the "soft" area of social studies was one rallying cry of those who saw the erosion of education in clear contrasting tones: process versus content, skills versus knowledge, the sacrifice of history to "pseudo–social science" courses. This era can best be represented in the reign of William Bennett as Secretary of Education in the Reagan administration, in the publication of E. D. Hirsch's *Cultural Literacy* (1987) and Allan Bloom's *The Closing of the American Mind* (1987). Reminiscent of Arthur Bestor's arguments in the 1950s, the cycle of a return to pure and unfettered disciplines, especially history and geography, was on its upward swing.

RECENT EFFORTS TO MODIFY THE CURRICULUM

Efforts of the National Council for the Social Studies

Throughout the 1980s and into the 1990s, the National Council for the Social Studies (NCSS), the leading professional organization in the field, undertook a range of efforts to unify and provide direction for the field. In the mid-'80s, NCSS devoted considerable effort to developing alternative scopes and sequences and then endorsing three of those plans ("In Search of a Scope and Sequence . . ." 1989; Hartoonian and Laughlin 1989; Kniep 1989). In this analyst's view, none of the models that emerged made significant changes in the basic scope-and-sequence design. Discipline domination continued in each, although each had its own twist: for example, the global educator prescribed a global conceptual overlay to the usual progression of courses. No evidence suggests that the models have had a significant impact on what is taught.

Also having little impact was the National Commission on Social Studies in the Schools, established by NCSS and the American Historical Association in the mid-80s. Lack of funding severely hampered the commission's work. Its Task Force on Curriculum developed a scope-and-sequence document, which was never discussed or endorsed by the full commission (National Commission 1989). Except for a recommendation for a three-year (ninth, tenth, and eleventh grades) program of world history that would integrate U.S., Western, and non-Western history, the curriculum recommendations did not significantly alter the curriculum as it exists. The most significant omission was the report's lack of attention to citizenship and civic affairs.

At its annual meeting in 1992, NCSS formally adopted a definition of the social studies that acknowledged civic competence as the central purpose of social studies:

> *Social studies is the integrated study of the social sciences and humanities to promote civic competence. Within the school program, social studies provides coordinated, systematic study drawing upon such disciplines as anthropology, archaeology, economics, geography, history, law, philosophy, political science, psychology, religion, and sociology, as well as appropriate content from the humanities, mathematics, and natural sciences. The primary purpose of social studies is to help young people develop the ability to make informed and reasoned decisions for the public good as citizens of a culturally diverse, democratic society in an interdependent world. (Anderson 1993)*

The definition will be used as the basis for all future documents and position statements developed by NCSS.

ACTIVITY   ## Analyzing the NCSS Definition of Social Studies

Carefully reread the NCSS definition of social studies. Identify the similarities and differences between the position taken in the definition and the position you developed in the rationale exercise on page 12. How congruent is your thinking with the NCSS definition?

Think about the implications of the definition for curriculum. Would the traditional social studies curriculum support the definition? If not, what changes would be required to achieve a curriculum that would fit the NCSS definition? Would you support such changes? Why or why not?

Discipline-Based Efforts

As the plans for the National Commission on Social Studies in the Schools were being developed and publicized, a quickly formed group mounted another commission with significant funding. The Bradley Commission's members included historians and history teachers. Its report (*Building a History Curriculum* 1988), which has been distributed and publicized widely, did not support one or another pattern for history/social studies education. Rather, it identified themes to be taught and described several ways in which the curriculum (both elementary and secondary) could be organized to teach those themes.

The report appeals to the history-oriented, but its recommendations (never far from what presently exists in the schools) are conscious of the need to incorporate all of the social sciences. The commission's themes, for example, recognize global interdependence, the multicultural nature of our society, the social science implications of studying such documents as the Constitution and the demographic changes that have occurred, and the fact that history alone cannot explain events.

Continued funding has enabled staff of the Bradley Commission, reconstituted as the National Council for History Education, to maintain an office, publish a monthly newsletter entitled "History Matters," and undertake efforts to change the social studies curriculum throughout the United States.

In 1984, a joint committee of the National Council for Geographic Education and the Association of American Geographers, concerned about the lack of geographic knowledge among young people, published the *Guidelines for Geographic Education: Elementary and Secondary Schools.* With generous financial support from the National Geographic Society, two additional documents have been published to help teachers implement the five themes presented in the guidelines, and a network of state geographic alliances has been developed to provide teacher training. (See Chapter 10 for more information about the geographers' curriculum reform efforts.) The five themes are now widely visible in geography textbooks; whether classroom instruction has changed significantly is less apparent.

ACTIVITY   ## Analyzing the Use of Themes in Curriculum Planning

How useful are recommended themes in planning curriculum? Imagine that your department chair has appointed you to serve on a committee considering how to adapt the eleventh-grade U.S. history course in your district to reflect the Bradley Commission's recommended themes. Traditionally, the course text (your committee of five to six students may choose one from your school's curriculum library for the purposes of this exercise) has provided both the structure and the content for the course. Are the themes, which are listed below,* currently incorporated in the text? If so, how could their development be improved? If not, how could they be incorporated?

- Conflict and cooperation: The many and various causes of war, and of approaches to peacemaking and war prevention. Relations between domestic

---

*From *Building a History Curriculum: Guidelines for Teaching History in Schools,* by the Bradley Commission on History in Schools, 1988. Available from and published by the National Council for History Education, Westlake, OH 44145. Used by permission.

affairs and ways of dealing with the outside world. Contrasts between international conflict and cooperation, between isolation and interdependence. The consequences of war and peace for societies and their cultures.

- Comparative history of major developments: The characteristics of revolutionary, reactionary, and reform periods across time and place. Imperialism, ancient and modern. Comparative instances of slavery and emancipation, feudalism and centralization, human successes and failures, of wisdom and folly. Comparative elites and aristocracies; the role of family, wealth, and merit.

- Patterns of social and political interaction: The changing patterns of class, ethnic, racial, and gender structures and relations. Immigration, migration, and social mobility. The effects of schooling. The new prominence of women, minorities, and the common people in the study of history, and their relation to political power and influential elites. The characteristics of multicultural societies; forces for unity and disunity.

- Civilization, cultural diffusion, and innovation: The evolution of human skills and the means of exerting power over nature and people. The rise, interaction, and decline of successive centers of such skills and power. The cultural flowering of major civilizations in the arts, literature, and thought. The role of social, religious, and political patronage of the arts and learning. The importance of the city in different eras and places.

- Human interaction with the environment: The relationships among geography, technology, and culture, and their effects on economic, social, and political developments. The choices made possible by climate, resources, and location, and the effect of culture and human values on such choices. The gains and losses of technological change. The central role of agriculture. The effect of disease, and disease-fighting, on plants, animals, and human beings.

- Values, beliefs, political ideas, and institutions: The origins and spread of influential religions and ideologies. The evolution of political and social institutions, at various stages of industrial and commercial development. The interplay among ideas, material conditions, moral values, and leadership, especially in the evolution of democratic societies. The tensions between the aspirations for freedom and security, for liberty and equality, for distinction and commonality, in human affairs.

The National Goals for Education

Following an "education summit" in late 1989, then-President George Bush issued a statement enumerating six national education goals. These goals, also endorsed by the National Governors Association, identified history and geography, rather than the curriculum area of social studies, as core subjects. Pressure from various groups resulted in civics and economics being brought into the goals during the first year of President Clinton's administration. Separate groups have developed standards in history, geography, civics, and economics and are planning for national assessments of students' achievement of those standards. In response, NCSS has developed curriculum standards in *social studies*. Whether any of these standards and assessments are, in fact, implemented and have a lasting effect on education may depend on politics more than on any critique of education. It is possible, however, that the standards will be having wide-reaching effects on curriculum as you begin your teaching career.

SOCIAL STUDIES AS THE CIVIC PROCESS

Although some states have experimented with changes to the traditional arrangement of content in social studies, there is little to indicate that schools have moved more than a modest distance from the de facto national curriculum identified in the early 1980s (see p. 19). The curriculum is history-based, Western-oriented, college-oriented, generally narrative in form, and totally dependent on teacher creativity if it is to speak to all students. The curriculum documents issued by state education departments or local districts usually reflect the national curriculum pattern. Special emphases, such as multicultural education, usually end up as add-ons or special inserts. Whereas goals and objectives in curriculum documents bespeak integration and interdisciplinary focus, the syllabus portions do not. The social studies requirements in the fifty states may vary in number of years required, but content has shifted little since 1916 in the vast majority of states.

Why does this pattern persist? Tradition has a great deal to do with it: What exists tends to remain. No crisis has motivated change, no conceptual breakthrough has challenged present thinking or conditions. Perhaps the greatest preserving force comes from the teachers and schools themselves. Schools are, of course, conserving cultures, and the educational milieu would prefer the stability of changelessness— a condition that should be anathema to social studies.

Change in social studies education at the elementary and secondary levels has historically come from the "outside." Changes in demographics and what they mean to the status quo; changes in political philosophy that determine what and who gets encouragement (including funding); strong voices from the academic community, protesting educational goals or creating commissions or committees to formulate new directions; economic pressures that build both internally and externally—these are the kinds of forces that propel change in education generally and social studies in particular. Because of the autonomous nature of the various state and local units of the educational system, however, a concerted message seldom gets conveyed to everyone. Unless an outside change agent takes deliberate and concerted steps to implement its recommendations, the impact will be lost. Although both the Bradley Commission and the coalition of professional geography organizations have obtained considerable financial backing and made plans for extensive implementation of their frameworks, it is too early to tell whether their efforts will have lasting effects. The standards movement may finally tip the balance in favor of a uniform national curriculum. Whether instruction will improve at the same time remains to be seen.

Even though the social studies curriculum still reflects the discipline-based structure that governs the university, with history the dominant discipline, social studies is the subject having the greatest potential for integrating knowledge and thereby enabling students to see the interconnectedness of their world before they start pulling it apart into smaller entities called disciplines. That sense of the whole, combined with problem-solving and decision-making capabilities, is essential if we hope that students will take personal and public responsibility for the "whole earth."

The education of our youth to awareness of the nature of human existence in concert with the environment (broadly interpreted) is a "road not taken" except as it may incidentally occur in each of the separate school subjects. No one helps students "put it all together" so that they see the connections, the interrelatedness of knowledge, and the power that that brings to their lives in taking action—private and public—to sustain themselves and to step forward into the future.

Social studies can perform that role; it can be the enacting process that enables students "to render life more reasonable and increase its value." Somehow, people's lives must be made more meaningful and efficacious when it comes to controlling the society in which they exist. That is the "civic process." The challenge is to find a school structure that will allow that to happen.

Reflecting on the Chapter

Return to the statement you picked as most closely representing your views on the purpose of social studies. Does it still reflect your views? Would you discard it after completing this chapter? Revise it? Retain it? In your journal, reflect on how your views on the purpose of social studies have changed or been reaffirmed as you learned about the history of the social studies curriculum.

References

American Historical Association. *The Study of History in Schools*. New York: Macmillan, 1899.
———. *The Study of History in the Elementary Schools*. New York: Scribners, 1909.
Anderson, C. "President's Message." *The Social Studies Professional* (January/February 1993): 2.
Anderson, L. F. "Barriers to Change in Social Studies." In *The Current State of Social Studies: A Report of Project SPAN*. Boulder, Colo.: Social Science Education Consortium, 1982.
Atwood, V. A., ed. *Elementary Social Studies: Research as a Guide to Practice*. Washington, D.C.: National Council for the Social Studies, 1986.
Barr, R. D., J. L. Barth, and S. S. Shermis. *Defining the Social Studies*. Washington, D.C.: National Council for the Social Studies, 1977.
Belok, D. "Schoolbooks, Pedagogy Books, and the Political Socialization of Young Americans." *Educational Studies* 12, no. 1 (1981): 35–47.
Bestor, A. E., Jr. *Educational Wastelands: The Retreat from Learning in Our Public Schools*. Urbana: University of Illinois Press, 1953.

Boulding, K. *The World as a Total System*. Berkeley, Calif: Sage Publications, Inc., 1985.

Bloom, A. *Closing of the American Mind: Education and the Crisis of Reason*. New York: Simon & Schuster, 1987.

Bragaw, D. H., ed. "Scope and Sequences: Alternatives for Social Studies." *Social Education* 50, no. 7 (1986): special section.

Bricker, D. C. *Classroom Life as Civic Education*. New York: Teachers College Press, 1989.

Bruner, J. K. *The Process of Education*. Cambridge: Harvard University Press, 1960.

Building a History Curriculum: Guidelines for Teaching History in Schools. Washington, D.C.: Educational Excellence Network, 1988.

Cohen, M. *American Thought: A Critical Sketch*. New York: Collier Books, 1962.

Commission on the Reorganization of Secondary Education. *Cardinal Principles of Secondary Education*, Bulletin 35. Washington, D.C.: Government Printing Office, 1918.

Committee on Social Studies. *The Social Studies in Secondary Education*, Bulletin 28. Washington, D.C.: Government Printing Office, 1916.

Cuban, L. "History of Teaching in Social Studies." In *Handbook of Research on Social Studies Teaching and Learning*, ed. J. P. Shaver, 197–209. New York: Macmillan, 1991.

Dewey, J. *Philosophy and Civilization*. New York: Minton, Balch, 1932.

Fenton, E. "What Happened to the New Social Studies: A Case Study in Curriculum Reform." Unpublished paper (1981).

———. "Reflections on the 'New Social Studies'." *The Social Studies* 82, no. 3 (1991): 84–90.

Flesch, R. *Why Johnny Can't Read: And What You Can Do About It*. New York: Harper and Row, 1955.

Goodlad, J. I. *Teachers for Our Nation's Schools*. San Francisco: Jossey-Bass, 1990.

Guidelines for Geographic Education: Elementary and Secondary Schools. Macomb, Ill.: National Council on Geographic Education; Washington, D.C.: American Association of Geographers, 1984.

Haas, J. D. *The Era of the New Social Studies*. Boulder, Colo.: Social Science Education Consortium, 1977.

Hartoonian, H. M., and M. A. Laughlin. "Designing a Social Studies Scope and Sequence for the 21st Century." *Social Education* 53, no. 6 (1989): 388–398.

Hertzberg, H. W. *Social Studies Reform, 1880–1980*. Boulder, Colo.: Social Science Education Consortium, 1981.

Hirsch, E. D. *Cultural Literacy: What Every American Needs to Know*. Boston: Houghton Mifflin, 1987.

"In Search of a Scope and Sequence for Social Studies." *Social Education* 53, no. 6 (1989): 376–87.

Jenness, D. *Making Sense of Social Studies*. New York: Macmillan, 1990.

Kniep, W. M. "Social Studies within a Global Education." *Social Education* 53, no. 6 (1989): 399–403.

Leming, J. S. "The Two Cultures of Social Studies Education." *Social Education* 53, no. 6 (October 1989): 404–8.

Lengel, J. G., and D. P. Superka. "Curriculum Organization in Social Studies." In *The Current State of Social Studies: A Report of Project SPAN*, 81–103. Boulder, Colo.: Social Science Education Consortium, 1982.

Marker, G., and H. D. Mehlinger. "Social Studies." In *The Handbook of Research on Curriculum,* ed. P. Jackson. New York: Macmillan, 1990.

Mehlinger, H. D. "Social Studies: Some Gulfs and Priorities." In *The Social Studies: Eightieth Yearbook of the National Society for the Study of Education,* ed. H. D. Mehlinger and O. L. Davis, Jr. Chicago: University of Chicago Press, 1981.

Morrissett, I., and J. D. Haas. "Rationales, Goals, and Objectives in Social Studies." In *The Current State of Social Studies: A Report of Project SPAN.* Boulder, Colo.: Social Science Education Consortium, 1982.

Morrissett, I., and W. Stevens, Jr. *Social Science in the Schools: A Search for Rationale.* Boulder, Colo.: Social Science Education Consortium, 1971.

National Commission on Social Studies in the Schools. *Charting a Course: Social Studies for the 21st Century.* Washington, D.C.: National Council for the Social Studies, 1989.

National Education Association. *Report of the Committee on Secondary Social Studies.* Washington, D.C.: Government Printing Office, 1893.

Nelson, M. R. "The Rugg Brothers in Social Education." *Journal of Thought* 17, no. 3 (1982): 68–82.

Planning a Social Studies Program. 3rd ed. Boulder, Colo.: Social Science Education Consortium, 1991.

Other Recommended Readings

Armento, B. J. "Research on Teaching Social Studies." In *Handbook of Research on Teaching,* 3rd ed., ed. M. C. Wittrock, 942–51. New York: Macmillan, 1986.

Battistoni, R. *Public Schooling and the Education of Democratic Citizens.* Jackson: University Press of Mississippi, 1985.

Bellah, R. N., et al. *Habits of the Heart: Individualism and Commitment in American Life.* Berkeley and Los Angeles: University of California Press, 1985.

Berelson, B., ed. *The Social Sciences and the Social Studies.* New York: Harcourt, Brace, and World, 1962.

Bragaw, D. H., and M. Hartoonian. "Social Studies: The Study of People in Society." In *The Content of the Curriculum,* ed. R. Brandt. Alexandria, Va.: Association for Supervision and Curriculum Development, 1988.

Butts, R. F. *The Civic Mission of Educational Reform: Perspectives for the Public and for the Profession.* Palo Alto, Calif.: Hoover Institution Press, 1989.

Deledalle, G. *C. S. Pierce: An Intellectual Biography.* Philadelphia: J. B. Publishing, 1990.

Dennis, L. J. *George S. Counts and Charles A. Beard: Collaborators for Change.* Albany: State University of New York Press, 1989.

Engle, S. H., and A. S. Ochoa. *Education for Democratic Citizenship: Decision Making in the Social Studies.* New York: Teachers College Press, 1988.

Epstein, T. L., and R. W. Evans, eds. "Reactions to Charting a Course: Social Studies for the 21st Century." *Social Education* 54, nos. 7–8 (1990): special section.

Foundations of the Social Studies Special Interest Group. *Identifying What Is Unique about the Social Studies.* Washington, D.C.: National Council for the Social Studies, 1989.

———. *A Social Studies Discipline.* Washington, DC: National Council for the Social Studies, 1990.

Gagnon, P., ed. *Historical Literacy: The Case for History in American Education.* New York: Macmillan, 1989.

Gross, R. E. "The Status of Social Studies in the Public Schools of the United States: Facts and Impressions of a National Survey." *Social Education* 41, no. 3 (1977): 194–200, 205.

Hunt, M. P., and L. E. Metcalf. *Teaching High School Social Studies*, 2nd. ed.. New York: Harper & Row, 1968.

Leming, J. S. "Rethinking Social Studies Research and the Goals of Social Education." *Theory and Research in Social Education* 14, no. 2 (1986): 138–52.

Longstreet, W. S. "The Social Studies: In Search of an Epistemology." *The Social Studies* (1990): 244–48.

Marcell, D. W. *Progress and Pragmatism: James, Dewey, and Beard and the American Idea of Progress.* Westport, Conn.: Greenwood Press, 1974.

Morrissett, I. "Four Futures for Social Studies." *Social Education* 48, no. 7. (1984): 511–16.

Nelson, M., ed. *The Future of the Social Studies.* Boulder, Colo.: Social Science Education Consortium, 1994.

Pratte, R. *The Civic Imperative: Examining the Need for Civic Education.* New York: Teachers College Press, 1988.

Project SPAN Staff and Consultants. *The Future of Social Studies: A Report and Summary of Project SPAN.* Boulder, Colo.: Social Science Education Consortium, 1982.

Ravitch, D. "Tot Sociology: Or What Happened to History in the Grade Schools." *The American Scholar* (1987): 343–54.

Rodgers, D. T. "In Search of Progressivism." In *The Promise of American History,* ed. S. I. Kutler and S. N. Katz. Baltimore: Johns Hopkins Press, 1982.

Shaver, J. P. "Commitment to Values and the Study of Social Problems in Citizenship Education." *Social Education* 49, no. 3 (1985): 194–97.

———., ed. *Handbook of Research on Social Studies Teaching and Learning.* New York: Macmillan, 1991. Especially recommended are articles by Armento; Joyce, Little, and Wronski; and Lybarger.

Shaver, J. P., O. L. Davis, Jr., and S. W. Helburn. *An Interpretive Report on the Status of Precollegiate Social Studies Education.* Report to the National Science Foundation. Washington, D.C.: National Council for the Social Studies, 1978.

Stanley, W. B. *Review of Research in Social Studies Education: 1976–1983.* Washington, D.C.: National Council for the Social Studies; Boulder, Colo.: Social Science Education Consortium, 1985.

Tryon, R. *The Social Sciences as School Subjects.* New York: Scribners, 1934.

Turner, M. J., and F. Haley. *Utilization of New Social Studies Curriculum Materials.* Boulder, Colo.: Social Science Education Consortium, 1975.

United States Prepares for Its Future: Global Perspectives in Education, The. New York: Global Perspectives in Education, 1987.

Vincent, W. S., et al. *Building Better Programs in Citizenship.* New York: Teachers College Press, 1958.

Wesley, E. G., and S. P. Wronski. *Teaching Secondary Social Studies in a World Society,* 6th ed. Lexington, Mass.: Heath, 1974.

White, J. *Social Thought in America: The Revolt Against Formalism.* Boston: Beacon Press, 1947.

Wiley, K. B., and D. P. Superka. *Evaluation Studies on "New Social Studies" Materials.* Boulder, Colo.: Social Science Education Consortium, 1980.

Wiley, K. B., with J. Race. *The Status of Pre-College Science, Mathematics and Social Science Education, 1950–1975*, Vol. 3, *Social Science Education*. Boulder, Colo.: Social Science Education Consortium, 1977.

Wong, S. Y. "The Evolution of Social Science Instruction, 1900–86: A Cross-National Study." *Sociology of Education* 64, no. 1. (1991): 33–47.

Wronski, S. P. "Edgar Bruce Wesley (1891–1980): His Contributions to the Past, Present, and Future of the Social Studies." *Journal of Thought* 17, no. 3 (1982): 55–67.

Wronski, S. P., and D. H. Bragaw, eds. *Social Studies and the Social Sciences: A Fifty-Year Perspective*. Washington, D.C.: National Council for the Social Studies, 1986.

3

TEACHING IN
THE REAL WORLD

John P. Zola

ACTIVITY LIST

• • •

ACTIVITY

Role Playing Social Studies Classes

With a group of five or six students, role-play what you think the "ideal" social studies classroom would be like. Think about how the teacher and the students should act, as well as about the subject matter of the lesson. Then role-play the typical social studies classroom. In creating the role plays, draw on your own experiences in social studies classes, as well as on your thinking related to Chapter 2.

Discuss the differences between the role plays. How were teachers' behaviors toward students different? How was their treatment of content different? How did students behave toward the teacher and each other? How did they react to the content?

As you begin this chapter, keep these role plays in mind. Look for reasons that the real so often varies from the ideal.

INTRODUCTION

Mr. Roy listened to the bell ring and gazed at the door. As students straggled in, they talked with one another, seemingly oblivious of the presence of their teacher. Comments could be heard about upcoming sporting events, a recent disturbance by the "senior" lockers, and potential dates for the fall dance. Not a single comment related to the class they were now entering, U.S. History from 1876 to the Present. *Several minutes after the bell had rung, Mr. Roy asked the class to be quiet and get out their textbooks and homework. After he had repeated the directions several times, only about half the class was ready to begin. The others simply went on with their conversations. Mr. Roy read the answers to the questions on the worksheet that he had assigned. After asking "Are there any questions?" and receiving no response, Mr. Roy began to explain the outcomes of industrialism during the late 1800s. Few, if any, students were taking notes or paying much attention. Side conversations continued, and a number of students did homework for other classes. With twenty-five minutes remaining in the period, Mr. Roy assigned a textbook reading and told the class to answer the questions at the end of the section. As he returned to his desk to grade papers, Mr. Roy gave an exasperated sigh and slumped into his chair to await the end of the period.*

• • •

Ms. Rowland had moved the seats into groups of three before school started. As students entered the classroom, she directed them to sit in mixed-gender groupings. Directions on the board told students to consider the following question and jot down their ideas: "If you were a 'Captain of Industry' during the Industrial Era of the late 1800s, what, if any, responsibility would you assume for the quality of life of your workers?" When the bell rang, students were in their seats arguing about what degree of social responsibility an industrialist was likely to feel. Ms. Rowland quickly took roll, allowed several minutes for groups to complete their work, and called the class to order. Answers from groups were posted on the board and briefly discussed. Then students were handed a historical dilemma that centered on factory life during the industrial era. Students were directed to read the situation and take an individual stand on what should be done. Small groups then shared responses and brainstormed possible pros and cons of each. A large-group discussion allowed students to defend their positions. Ms. Rowland raised issues related to the values being presented and pushed students to base their reasoning on sound historical evidence. Before the period ended, students were given a homework assignment to write a brief essay explaining their answers to the dilemma. Students could be heard arguing about the industrial era as they left the room.

Social studies should be exciting and involving. Teaching practices in the social studies should promote interest, engagement, rigor, enthusiasm for learning, and a sense of personal investment and empowerment.

Why, then, do the teacher's lecture and the textbook reading found in Mr. Roy's classroom, rather than the active learning in Ms. Rowland's, predominate in most social studies classrooms? The reasons are many: The organizational realities of school systems reward orderliness at the expense of creativity; secondary schools are based on a turn-of-the-century model of factory education that encourages students to be passive receivers of information; social studies teachers question the value of excitement and intellectual playfulness in the classroom; teacher supervision and evaluation criteria tend to maintain the status quo; preservice social studies education fails to help new teachers understand and become invested in the use of a wide variety of teaching strategies.

Despite those impediments, more involving teaching practices can and should be expected of both new and experienced social studies teachers. Social studies teachers *can* bring artistry, rigor, authenticity, and meaning to the learning process regardless of countervailing organizational and structural pressures.

In this chapter, you will review the current state of social studies teaching and explore a variety of constructs for understanding why social studies education is practiced as it is. Suggestions are offered for improving teaching practices as a way of enhancing the quality of social studies teaching in general, and for beginning teachers in particular. Although organizational changes are necessary for the renewal of social studies education, teachers can implement teaching practices that lead to worthwhile learning experiences.

THE CURRENT STATE OF SOCIAL STUDIES EDUCATION

In a recent review of the research on social studies teaching, Cuban reached the following conclusion:

> *The most common pattern, employed by the vast majority of social studies teachers, is that of teacher-centered instruction. This pattern includes activities using the textbook and teacher as sources of information for assignments, recitation (now commonly called* discussion*), tests, and individual seatwork. Talking by the teacher . . . exceeds talking by students, whose responses are generally confined to answering the teacher's questions. Occasional use of films, videos, and other devices supplements these activities. This core pattern is most frequently enacted when the entire class is taught as a group. Infrequently at the high school level . . . small-group work is a vehicle for classroom activities. (Cuban 1991, p. 204)*

In summarizing three National Science Foundation studies of the status of social studies, Project SPAN (Fancett and Hawke 1982) found that teachers relied on textbooks as a central instrument for teaching and learning. Recent research reveals that textbook use might be less significant than once assumed, but the news is hardly encouraging. Downey and Levstik (1989) report that textbooks are mainly used as references for completing worksheets of lower-level exercises. In place of regular textbook reading, many teachers rely upon lectures drawn from previous college courses as the means of providing students with content. Study after study (see, for example, Goodlad 1984; Sizer 1984; Powell et al. 1985) confirms the absence of enthusiasm, creativity, involvement, controversy, and values-oriented teaching in social studies.

Although students may not rebel against the teaching practices outlined above, Mark Schug and others (1984) have found that students do not perceive social studies to be very important or particularly relevant to their future plans. Students' most frequent comment about social studies was that it was boring. Most often, boredom was tied to the repetitive nature of social studies content and teaching methods.

ACTIVITY   **Analyzing a Cartoon**

Analyze the cartoon by Matt Groening (Figure 3.1). In one sentence, describe what you believe the cartoonist is saying. Share your interpretation with a neighbor.

Once you have done that, list the techniques and images Groening uses to communicate his message. Discuss them as a class. Which techniques are most effective? Why?

Finally, draw a cartoon that communicates one of your perspectives on schooling or on social studies education. Let a classmate interpret your drawing!

CONTROL AS A FACTOR IN TEACHING PRACTICES

Why do so many teachers teach in the constrained and uninvolving fashion illustrated by Mr. Roy? Linda McNeil's (1988) three-part analysis of school organization sheds light on one of the most important reasons: the contradiction between a school's stated goal of educating students and the felt need for control—moving students in an orderly manner toward their diplomas.

McNeil contends that the bureaucratic organization of schools has caused teachers to devalue active learning as they assume an ever increasing burden of controlling student behavior. The goal of many "business manager principals" is to create smoothly running schools that maximize order and the attainment of diplomas. In schools like these, little, if any, value is attached to surprise, innovation, and educational diversity; in fact, such characteristics are frequently seen as either disruptive or counterproductive.

McNeil describes a series of "defensive teaching strategies" teachers use to control knowledge and classroom interactions so as to control student behavior. As you read the list that follows, compare these strategies with the common social studies teaching practices just reviewed.

- *Fragmentation:* Teaching by means of lists of facts, names, dates, etc. Lists convey information efficiently. Using well-planned lectures that transmit

isolated bits of information can circumvent elaboration, divergent thinking, and controversy. Teacher authority—over content and student behavior—is maintained through fragmentation. For students, lists provide unambiguous expectations for classwork and testing.

- *Mystification:* Maintaining the teacher's role as the authority in the subject matter (and in the classroom). Students are expected to be able to identify difficult or controversial topics but not to wrestle intellectually with them. Content mystification, supplemented by the bland coverage in textbooks, leads to the avoidance of messy discussions and challenging questions from students.

- *Omission:* Ignoring topics viewed as too controversial, too complex, or too current. The absence of rigorous examination of the Vietnam War in the U.S. history curriculum is one example of a tendency to self-censor topics or issues that can engender controversy, an unacceptably high level of personal student investment, or discussions so charged that the authority of the teacher or the text is undermined and the pace of instruction slows.

- *Defensive simplification:* Gaining student cooperation and minimizing resistance by assuring students that work will neither be difficult nor take great effort to complete. Based on the need to cover the curriculum, teachers rely on simple readings and single-page worksheets that can be quietly completed in a single class period.

These defensive teaching strategies reflect the organizational structures and values of the modern high school. The culture of the school, the community's expectations that teachers will "cover" certain content regardless of the manner in which it is done, the overall expectation of society that ever more students will attain a high school diploma in an orderly fashion in orderly schools (see, for example, Cuban 1986; Hartoonian 1989), and the survival instincts of individual teachers all conspire to place a premium on highly mechanistic, uncreative, and noninvolving teaching practices.

ACTIVITY **Observing Defensive Teaching Strategies**

With a group of your classmates, develop a checklist to help you determine to what extent teaching reflects McNeil's "defensive teaching strategies." To develop your checklist, think about what evidence would indicate that the teacher is using the defensive strategies listed. Each indicator can be an item on the checklist. Here is an example.

Defensive Teaching Strategy	*Indicator*	*Times Observed or Percentage of Class Time Observed*
Fragmentation	Use of lecture	70% of class time devoted to a 35-minute lecture

Each member of the group should use the checklist in observing one or more classrooms. Keep field notes to supplement the data on the form. If possible, get the teacher's permission to tape the class. If you are currently student teaching, you may want to ask another group member to observe your teaching and tell you whether you employ these strategies.

Discuss the data gathered by your group. How well did the checklist work? Did you observe any indicators of defensive strategies that you had not thought of in advance? To what extent do McNeil's descriptions characterize the classrooms you observed? In classrooms where you did not observe defensive teaching strategies, how was teaching different? Did students behave differently?

THE MIMETIC AND TRANSFORMATIVE TRADITIONS IN EDUCATION

Philip Jackson (1986) describes two broad educational traditions that reveal themselves in varying combinations in all social studies classrooms: the mimetic tradition and the transformative tradition. The mimetic tradition takes its name from the Greek word *mimesis*, from which the words *mime* and *mimic* are derived. This tradition emphasizes transmission of factual and procedural knowledge from one person to another through an essentially imitative process. Such knowledge is second-hand knowledge, in that it must have belonged to someone first before it can belong to anyone else. It is knowledge "presented" to a learner, rather than "discovered" by him or her. Knowledge in the mimetic tradition is also reproducible and thus can be transmitted from the teacher or the text to the student. Success in learning is measured by how accurately the learner's knowledge matches that of the teacher or the text.

The transmission of knowledge or skills in the mimetic tradition consists of a series of orderly steps, which can be summarized as follows:

- *Test.* Students are questioned to see if they already know the material or can perform the skill in question.
- *Present.* The teacher presents or models the knowledge or skill to be learned.
- *Perform/evaluate.* The student repeats what he or she has just witnessed, read, or heard, and the performance is evaluated for accuracy or correctness.
- *Reward/fix or enter remedial loop.* If the performance is judged to be reasonably accurate, the teacher comments favorably on what the student has done and prescribes any necessary repetitions to habituate, or "fix," the material or skill in the students' repertoire. If the performance is judged to be incorrect, the teacher initiates remedial procedures to correct the effort in question.

- *Advance.* Once the unit of knowledge or skill is "fixed," the teacher and the student advance to the next unit of instruction by returning to the first step in this process.

Many social studies teaching practices clearly reflect the mimetic tradition. Lectures and textbook readings are ways of transmitting discrete bits of information from the instructional authority (text or teacher) to students. The ability to mimic that information on standardized or objective tests is the measure of a student's (and a teacher's) success.

Although mimetic teaching practices may be appropriate in transmitting factual information and developing certain discrete skills, the tradition is inadequate when teachers move beyond intellectual mimicry to promoting meaning and student involvement.

Those who teach in the "transformative" tradition seek to accomplish a change in the person being taught. This qualitative change or metamorphosis is typically conceived as being more deeply integrated within the student and more enduring than those changes sought through the mimetic tradition. Whereas cognitive changes in the mimetic tradition have an additive quality, changes sought within the transformative tradition are more likely to be revealed as new attitudes, values, or interests.

The teaching practices associated with the transformative tradition are also different. Teachers in the transformative tradition rely on three "modes of operation":

- *Personal modeling.* Teachers personify the qualities they seek to engender in their students, such as intellectual curiosity and playfulness. According to Jackson, "most teachers already know that no attitude, interest, or value can be taught except by the teacher who himself or herself believes in, cares for, or cherishes whatever it is that he or she holds out for emulation" (p. 124).

- *Soft suasion.* Soft suasion implies a much milder form of pedagogical authority than the showing, telling, reminding, and testing central to the mimetic tradition. The formal roles of teacher and student often become blurred, with the teacher posing questions for students who, in considering answers, appear to be teaching the teacher. Soft suasion involves a set of teaching practices that entice students to become involved in the pursuit of knowledge and meaning.

- *Use of narrative.* The transformative tradition has an inherent moral quality, in that it seeks to change the individual and his or her conceptions of the world. Stories reflect and reinforce this moral quality by presenting narratives about how to live, or not live, our lives. As you are probably aware, the narrative found in textbooks and most student readings is not of this type.

These three modes of operation highlight how the mimetic and the transformative traditions differ. In the mimetic tradition, the teacher occupies the role of content expert, commanding a specified body of information or set of skills and the methodological expertise to transmit knowledge or skills to receptive students.

Within the transformative tradition, the pedagogical superiority of the teacher is not nearly so clear-cut, with teacher and students alternately raising and answering questions. The transformative tradition centers its teaching practices on discussion, demonstration, and argumentation—all powerful tools of reason.

Common practices of social studies teachers appear to overlap little with the transformative tradition. Personal modeling, soft suasion, acknowledgment of the moral quality of the classroom, discussion, demonstration, and argumentation threaten many social studies teachers. The high degree of student participation and active involvement in the learning process that these approaches require raise issues of control for many teachers. Additionally, social studies teachers who are generally unwilling to raise the specter of controversy in the classroom are unlikely to be comforted by talk of the moral nature of teaching. The transformative tradition undermines the hierarchical relationship many teachers establish with their students, requiring that teachers relinquish absolute intellectual control and acknowledge that they might not have all the answers.

To a new teacher, talk of the "transformative nature of teaching" can be quite daunting. Beginning teachers commonly want to assert control over their classrooms and over the content they have been hired to teach. Classroom management is certainly critical to successful teaching. Indeed, having clearly established and understood procedures for how a class accomplishes its work can be critical in making the classroom a vibrant, cooperative community where students can spend the maximum amount of time engaged in learning in a wide variety of ways. Expectations that promote student-student dialogue and a spirit of mutual inquiry can be set and reinforced. Role playing, debates, and other interactive strategies that place a greater degree of the responsibility for learning on the students' shoulders do not need to degenerate into chaos. In fact, once students come to understand that their involvement in the classroom is valued and that events in the classroom will not be monotonous, it is highly likely that discipline problems will diminish. Like many of us, students tend to "act out" when they are bored and disengaged.

In practice, teaching involves both mimetic and transformative outcomes. Although one cannot avoid the knowledge and skill foundations upon which discussion, demonstration, argumentation, debate, and related transformative teaching practices are based, neither can the uncritical acquisition of content be the sole aim of social studies teaching practices.

ACTIVITY Analyzing Outcomes and Teaching Practices

As the section above indicates, outcomes and teaching practices are closely linked. Return to the tapes or field notes your group compiled while observing classrooms. Choose one class for analysis. Construct a chart showing the intended outcomes of the lesson you can infer from the notes. Indicate on the chart whether each outcome is mimetic or transformative. What clues help you answer these questions?

Note on the chart the questions, activities, or other evidence you need to make your determination.

Your chart should look something like the following example.

Outcome	Type	Evidence
Students list examples of music used in social movements.	Mimetic	Teacher presented "minilecture" and checked for factual understanding.
Students develop personal definitions of the functions of music in society.	Transformative	Music was presented, along with a personal narrative from a musician involved in the civil rights movement. Active student involvement was encouraged.

THE EFFECTIVE AND ARTISTIC APPROACHES TO TEACHING

A distinction has often been drawn between the science and the art of teaching, or, in terms more familiar to practicing teachers, between effective instruction and the artistic/craft nature of teaching. *Effective instruction* is a term that has arisen from classroom-based research that has sought to define specific teacher behaviors that correlate with increases on such measures as time on task or student performance on criterion-referenced tests. An extensive body of research exists on effective instruction (see, for example, Cummings 1980; Hunter 1982; Rosenshine 1986; Alvermann 1987; Good and Brophy 1989; Porter and Brophy 1988). Although much of this research has focused on the elementary classroom, it does provide insights for teachers of secondary social studies, especially when the instructional objective is to teach a performance skill or a specified body of knowledge.

Research on *effective instruction* has identified specific protocols or processes for the explicit teaching of concepts and skills (Rosenshine 1986):

- Begin a lesson with a short statement of goals.
- Begin a lesson with a short review of previous, prerequisite learning.
- Present new material in small steps, with student practice after each step.
- Give clear and detailed instructions and explanations.
- Provide active practice for all students.
- Guide students during initial practice.
- Provide systematic feedback and corrections.

- Provide explicit instructions and practice for seatwork exercises, and, when necessary, monitor students during seatwork.
- Continue practice until students are independent and confident.

Note how closely these steps parallel the processes described by Jackson in the mimetic tradition and how the goals of control delineated by McNeil can be accomplished through this control of content and process. Although total reliance on such methods would lead to a sterile and uninviting classroom, they can have a positive effect on some kinds of learning.

Additional benefits of the effective-instruction research lie in the emphasis on careful planning, the identification of instructional objectives, and the provision of opportunities for students to practice new learnings. Adapting instruction to student needs and anticipating and addressing misconceptions during the instructional process can help reduce the chances for paralyzing frustration or creeping boredom.

Finally, research on effective instruction reveals that effective teachers are thoughtful and reflective about their practice. In fact, a significant adjunct to effective-instruction research has been an emphasis on the important contributions to teaching practices of peer coaching. A thoughtful and reflective teacher is more likely to identify those situations that warrant adherence to the specific processes of effective instruction, while also exploiting a wide variety of less-teacher-centered practices.

Teaching also involves artistry (see, for example, Eisner 1979; Rubin 1985; Gage and Berliner 1989). Eisner (1979) contends that teaching "is an art in the sense that [it] can be performed with such skill and grace that, for the student as well as for the teacher, the experience can justifiably be characterized as aesthetic" (p. 153). In essence, the artistic interpretation of teaching addresses many of the complexities and mysteries of what happens in a classroom that truly "works." The descriptor *artistic* is appropriate because expert teaching involves qualities generally associated with artistic endeavors, including awareness of, and attendance to, tempo, tone, climate, pacing, and forward movement.

Much of the artistic nature of teaching involves the subtleties of instruction that cannot necessarily be prescribed in advance. Rubin (1985) states, "A major dimension of artistry, in fact, involves the ability to take advantage of unanticipated opportunities—to capitalize on the ripeness of the moment. While master teachers are, of course, organized in one fashion or another, they are nonetheless able to temper a plan, precipitate serendipity, or exploit chance situations when they occur" (p. 17). This ability to be flexible, to respond and react, to be free of lockstep procedure, is what makes a classroom come alive for both the student and the teacher.

Artistry in a classroom does not happen by accident, however. Mastery of the craft of teaching (e.g., lesson planning, classroom management, questioning skills) is necessary before there can be artistry. A mastery of content knowledge (Shulman 1986) is also required for a teacher to be able to fully plan for and exploit teachable moments. A teacher must thoroughly understand the particular content and must have processed it for himself or herself to be comfortable approaching it from various directions. Flexibility requires comfort with the content, with a broad repertoire of teaching behaviors and strategies, and with "myself as teacher."

Does it seem as though it would be impossible for a novice teacher to be artistic in his or her teaching? In fact, the enthusiasm, creativity, and willingness to challenge traditional boundaries and practice a new teacher brings to the classroom can provide the basis for a great deal of artistry. While as yet unable to confidently "read" a class and the direction it may take, a beginning teacher who has developed a well-thought-out lesson plan based on a highly involving teaching strategy can provide for significant student interaction and strong learning experiences. It's not easy, but it certainly is possible.

A solid structure based on the selection of appropriate and varied teaching practices undergirds artistic teaching. The teacher and the class must have regular and cumulative experiences with discussion, simulation, role playing, debates, and other engaging strategies to be comfortable extending a discussion or pursuing a tantalizing, if somewhat tangential, issue. Students in such classes realize that they play a significant role in setting the direction and intellectual tone of the classroom. Tolerance of ambiguity, respect for the right of all class members to a positive learning environment, and the celebration of serendipity are traits that must be carefully and consistently nurtured. Standards, rigor, and high expectations for student learning are also integral to the artistic nature of teaching.

A teacher's repertoire of teaching practices should include behaviors representative of the literature on both effective instruction and artistry in teaching. Planning, setting of objectives, determining appropriate content, providing for practice, and checking for understanding are practices that should be expected of all teachers. Every teacher should clearly communicate to students the behavior expected of them and the supporting behavior and academic accountability systems (Evertson 1989). It is around these "bottom-line" structures that serendipity and flexibility are nurtured and encouraged.

According to the work of Csikszentmihalyi and McCormack (1986), students described influential teachers as generating enthusiasm for learning through personal involvement with the subject matter and skill in teaching it, as communicating a sense of excitement or contagious intellectual thrill, and as being exceptionally approachable or easy to talk to. Although students projected a sense that memorable teachers presented material in original or creative ways, "to label such behavior as 'creative' could be misleading, because that term implies that only exceptionally gifted teachers have the capability. *It seems more probable that a teacher who presents material in an original manner is not necessarily highly creative but simply more willing to spend time thinking about how best to convey information to a specific audience.* In other words, creativity—like nurturance and involvement—is probably a reflection of a teacher's enthusiasm for teaching" (p. 418, emphasis added).

The value of the teacher's having fun and being enthusiastic in a classroom also cannot be underestimated. What is a student to make of a classroom in which the teacher, who supposedly has the power to decide what will take place, is bored?

Reflecting on Memorable Social Studies Experiences

Reflect on the social studies classes you took in junior high/middle school and high school. Think of two or three of the most memorable experiences you had. Applying what you have learned in this chapter, describe those experiences with respect to:

- The teacher's desired outcome
- The kinds of teaching strategies used to achieve those outcomes
- The students' role in the activity
- The nature of the learning task

Now describe a more typical social studies experience. What do you think is the most important difference between the two? What does this suggest about the needs in social studies education? Discuss your conclusions with your classmates.

AUTHENTIC STUDENT ENGAGEMENT

Given the problems in social studies teaching we have identified, what kinds of changes are needed? The work of Fred Newmann is of particular value in establishing new directions for social studies teaching (see, for example, Marshall 1987; Newmann 1988, 1989; Wiggins 1989; Paul n.d.). Central to Newmann's thinking are two changes: the need to provide for authentic student engagement and placing depth above coverage in teaching social studies.

Student engagement in academic work is defined by Newmann (1989) as "the student's psychological investment in learning, understanding, or mastering the knowledge, skills or crafts that academic work is intended to promote" (p. 1). Engagement, as a form of psychological investment, is thus distinguished from the mere commitment to complete assigned tasks for good grades or social approval. For students to be engaged, the work they are doing must be authentic. Authentic academic work, according to Newmann (1989), "involves disciplined inquiry; the integration of knowledge; and producing outcomes that are meaningful to self and others beyond merely demonstrating success in school tasks" (p. 2). Such goals sharply contrast with the meaningless and mechanistic reproduction of knowledge common in many classrooms.

Lack of engagement is often linked to student boredom, but Newmann (1989) cautions that "as the sole diagnosis, boredom can lead to false remedies: gimmicks to interest and entertain students" (p. 242). Gimmickry will not alter the current state of social studies teaching, but the consistent use of rigorous and involving teaching practices may well accomplish that goal.

Perhaps the greatest reward for promoting engagement is the affective response of students. Body language becomes more animated, the common "glazed-over" look disappears, and comments become more passionate and purposeful. A class often is surprised by the bell, rather than knowing to the minute how much of the period remains. Teachers leave the classroom invigorated, knowing that their students are wrestling with important issues and questions. Students continue discussions into the hallway and even to the dinner table.

A curricular change needed for student engagement in social studies classrooms is a shift from an emphasis on *coverage* to an emphasis on *depth*. Coverage reinforces the fact/list, text- and lecture-based instruction common to current social studies teaching. Coverage, with its emphasis on getting through a body of material, is antithetical to the principles of authentic student engagement. With a shift to depth, engaging strategies can become the core of the instructional experience: The goals will have shifted from knowing a little about a lot to knowing a lot about less.

The transition from coverage to depth will be a difficult one for teachers. A stumbling block is the guilt that accompanies such a transition. Trained within a discipline, teachers experience a powerful desire to include every name, concept, or fact in a semester or yearlong course. Objectively, trying to teach the entire history of the world in 186 days is ludicrous; yet, every year, tens of thousands of teachers try to do just that. Teachers who decide to emphasize fewer concepts or themes must believe that they are developing skills and attitudes that will enable their students to pursue other content on their own. They must also recognize that depth leads to longer-term retention and student investment in social studies topics.

The insights of Newmann and others provide a strong rationale for changing teaching practices in the social studies. Much has been written about engaging teaching practices that should become the core of every social studies classroom. Such practices include, but are not limited to, cooperative learning; analysis of public policy issues; simulations and role plays; use of primary source documents;

Figure 3.2   Do you think the students in this discussion group are engaged in their work? Why or why not?

learning logs, response journals, and other meaningful writing activities; oral histories; community service projects; and inquiry-based field experiences.

These types of strategies, when appropriately implemented, promote the rigorous attainment of a strong content base and provide the potential for both engagement and depth. Teaching practices in the social studies should facilitate learning opportunities that are real, meaningful, useful, and valuable, not simply so that students are compliant and cover identified content, but so that they can achieve important learning goals as well.

ACTIVITY   ## Responding to the Current State of Social Studies

Looking closely at the current state of social studies can be disheartening. One way to counteract the pressures to teach in mechanistic, uninspiring ways is to develop strong collegial relationships with other teachers who value authentic student engagement, creativity, and controversy. Working with several other students, create a poster, a mural, or some other artwork that reflects your views on how collegiality might support successful social studies teaching.

CONCLUSION

Social studies should be the most challenging and involving of subject areas. Yet teacher practices that discourage authentic engagement are rendering the term "social studies" nearly oxymoronic. Teaching practices that allow students to assume authentic and genuine ownership of their learning demand a greater degree of flexibility and artistry from teachers. Those strategies can be taught to, and modeled for, teachers. Once successfully experienced in the classroom, they can become part of an individual's instructional repertoire. Beginning teachers, with their enthusiasm for and commitment to improving social studies teaching, can model strategies that engage students in the learning process and help students take greater responsibility for their learning. Novice teachers who are not yet dependent on a routine of lectures and worksheets can take the risks necessary to bring excitement and energy into their classrooms. Perhaps change, in this case, will be a case of the young leading the way.

Reflecting on the Chapter

Think about the learning activities in which you participated while studying this chapter. Which engaged you? Why? What substance did you find most interesting and important? How will this content affect you as you prepare to be a teacher? Include some thoughts on these questions in your journal today.

References

Alvermann, D. "Strategic Teaching in Social Studies." In *Strategic Teaching and Learning: Cognitive Instruction in the Content Areas,* ed. B. F. Jones, et al., 92–110. Elmhurst, Ill.: North Central Regional Educational Laboratory; Alexandria, Va.: Association for Supervision and Curriculum Development, 1987.

Csikszentmihalyi, M., and J. McCormack. "The Influence of Teachers." *Phi Delta Kappan* 67, no. 6 (1986): 415–19.

Cuban, L. "Persistent Instruction: Another Look at Constancy in the Classroom." *Phi Delta Kappan* 68, no. 1 (1986): 7–11.

———. "History of Teaching in Social Studies." In *Handbook of Research on Social Studies Teaching and Learning,* ed. J. P. Shaver, 197–209. New York: Macmillan, 1991.

Cummings, C. *Teaching Makes a Difference.* Edmonds, Wash.: TEACHING, 1980.

Downey, M. T., and L. S. Levstik. "Teaching and Learning History: The Research Base." *Social Education* 52, no. 5 (1989): 336-42.

Eisner, E. W. *The Educational Imagination: On the Design and Evaluation of School Programs.* New York: Macmillan, 1979.

Engle, S. "Late Night Thoughts about the New Social Studies." *Social Education* 50, no. 1 (1986): 20-22.

Evertson, C. M., et al. *Classroom Management for Elementary Teachers.* 2nd ed. Englewood Cliffs, N.J.: Prentice Hall, 1989.

Fancett, V., and S. Hawke. "Instructional Practices in Social Studies." In *The Current State of Social Studies: A Report of Project SPAN,* 207–64. Boulder, Colo.: Social Science Education Consortium, 1982.

Gage, N. L., and D. C. Berliner. "Nurturing the Critical, Practical, and Artistic Thinking of Teachers." *Phi Delta Kappan* 71, no. 3 (1989): 212–14.

Good, T. L., and J. Brophy. "Classroom Instruction: Quality and Quantity." In *School and Classroom Organization,* ed. R.E. Slavin, 25–68. Hillsdale, N.J.: Lawrence Erlbaum Associates, Inc., 1989.

Goodlad, J. *A Place Called School: Prospects for the Future.* New York: McGraw-Hill, 1984.

Hartoonian, M. "Perceptions of Knowledge and Educational Reform in a Democratic Republic." *Social Education* 53, no. 2 (1989): 93–95.

Hunter, M. *Mastery Teaching.* El Segundo, Calif.: TIP Publications, 1982.

Jackson, P. W. *The Practice of Teaching.* New York: Teachers College Press, 1986.

Marshall, H. H. "Building a Learning Orientation." *Theory into Practice* 26, no. 1 (1987): 8–14.

McNeil, L. M. "Contradictions of Control, Part 1: Administrators and Teachers." *Phi Delta Kappan* 69, no. 5 (1988): 333–39.

———. "Contradictions of Control, Part 2: Teachers, Students, and Curriculum." *Phi Delta Kappan* 69, no. 6 (1988): 432–38.

———. "Contradictions of Control, Part 3: Contradictions of Reform." *Phi Delta Kappan* 69, no. 7 (1988): 478–85.

Newmann, F. M. "Can Depth Replace Coverage in the High School Curriculum?" *Phi Delta Kappan* 69, no. 5 (1988): 345–48.

———. *Student Engagement in Academic Work: A Conceptual Model.* Paper presented at the annual conference of the American Educational Research Association, San Francisco, 1989.

Paul, R. W. *Two Conflicting Theories of Knowledge, Learning, and Literacy: The Didactic and the Critical*. Unpublished paper, n.d.

Porter, A. C., and J. Brophy. "Synthesis of Research on Good Teaching: Insights from the Work of the Institute for Research on Teaching." *Educational Leadership* 45, no. 8 (1988): 74–85.

Powell, A., E. Farrar, and D. Cohen. *The Shopping Mall High School: Winners and Losers in the Educational Marketplace*. Boston: Houghton Mifflin, 1985.

Rosenshine, B. V. "Synthesis of Research on Explicit Teaching." *Educational Leadership* 43, no. 7 (1986): 60–69.

Rubin, L. J. *Artistry in Teaching*. New York: Random House, 1985.

Schug, M., R.J. Todd, and R. Beery. "Why Kids Don't Like Social Studies." *Social Education* 48, no. 5 (1984): 382–87.

Shaver, J. P., O. L. Davis, and S. W. Helburn. "The Status of Social Studies Education: Impressions from Three NSF Studies." *Social Education* 43, no. 2 (1979): 150–53.

Shulman, L. S. "Those Who Understand: Knowledge Growth in Teaching." *Educational Researcher* 15, no. 2 (1986): 4–14.

Sizer, T. R. *Horace's Compromise*. Boston: Houghton Mifflin, 1984.

Wiggins, G. "The Futility of Trying to Teach Everything of Importance." *Educational Leadership* 47, no. 3 (1989): 44–59.

4

THE PLANNING PROCESS

John P. Zola

ACTIVITY

Analyzing Teaching Decisions

To gain some perspective on just how complex the process of planning is, think through a lesson you recently taught or observed. (It would be helpful if the entire class or at least groups of students had observed the same lesson.) List decisions the teacher made in planning for and conducting the lesson. Code the decisions to indicate whether they could have been made in advance or had to be made as the class was occurring.

Now pick an important decision the teacher made in planning the lesson. What do you think were some of the other options the teacher considered before reaching a decision? What factors were probably considered in rejecting those options? For example, if the lesson involved small-group work using information from a text reading assigned as homework, what alternatives might the teacher have considered before assigning the reading as homework? The alternatives might have included presenting the same information as a lecture, showing a film presenting the same information, allowing time in class to read the text materials, or selecting and assigning primary sources that provided a firsthand perspective on the material covered in the reading. Factors that went into the decision might have included a dislike for lecturing, lack of time to find appropriate source materials, a commitment to using class time for interactive activities, and the desire to develop responsibility among students.

What does this exercise indicate about the complexity of a teacher's planning task? How can skills you have used successfully in planning as a student be adapted to the planning you will do as a teacher? Keep these questions in mind as you read the material presented in this chapter.

INTRODUCTION

As a teacher, you will need to do three general types of planning: course planning, unit planning, and daily lesson planning. As a new teacher, it is unlikely that you will have the opportunity to plan an entirely new course. On the other hand, much of your time (during the days and in the evenings) will be taken up by the planning of units and lessons. This chapter is designed to give you practical help and guidance in the skills of planning. Teachers who take planning seriously and engage in the tasks with a combination of rigor and creativity enter the classroom with a reservoir of confidence and a knowledge that what is supposed to take place may actually do so!

PLANNING AT THE COURSE LEVEL

Soon after you are hired, you will learn what classes and courses you will be expected to teach. Nearly every school district has some sort of written curriculum guide for each course it offers. These guides may be current and of great use, or they may be ancient and hardly worth the paper upon which they were printed. In either case, they provide a starting point for your planning.

The guide probably will contain the official course title and an outline of the content to be addressed. For example, a world history guide might explain that the course is designed as a chronological survey of world history from prehistory to the present. A world studies guide might explain that the course is to be a regional study focusing on China, Latin America, Europe, the Soviet Union, and the Middle East. Students are expected to focus on history, geography, and current issues in each region. Although both guides are designed to meet a tenth-grade world history requirement, each would involve planning for significantly different types of learning experiences.

Course guides, when available, can vary in comprehensiveness and in the degree to which you, as a teacher, are expected to follow them. Some guides include specific instructional goals and objectives, suggested teaching activities, sequences of learning experiences, textbook and supplemental reading assignments, and other specifics that can be quite helpful in planning to teach the course. Other guides might include a series of objectives but few concrete details for actually teaching the course.

Some guides may reflect a district's adoption of a philosophy called Outcome-Based Education (OBE). Advocates of OBE argue that education should be focused on agreed-upon outcomes that all students are expected to meet. An outcome is defined as "a successful demonstration of learning that occurs at the culminating point of a set of learning experiences" (Spady and Marshall 1991, 70). If a district has adopted OBE, its guides are likely to specify broad exit outcomes around which the curriculum in all subject areas is to be designed. For example, the Aurora (Colorado) Public Schools have identified five role-based exit outcomes; the roles included are collaborative workers, quality producers, self-directed learners, complex thinkers, and community contributors. Here is one outcome statement:

We will know we are accomplishing our mission when all of our students are:

- *Collaborative Workers, who use effective leadership and group skills to develop and manage interpersonal relationships within culturally and organizationally diverse settings (Spady and Marshall 1991, 71).*

A final consideration in course-level planning involves finding out if the course is designed for a particular population of students, such as those with low reading abilities or advanced placement students. Consider the range of abilities and learning styles likely to be in each of your classes. The best instruction provides meaningful learning experiences for all students and respects each student as a unique learner. Keep that important premise in mind as you structure units and daily lesson plans.

ACTIVITY

Reviewing Curriculum Guides

Ask a teacher with whom you have been working or whom you have been observing for several different course outlines or curriculum guides. If possible, get one for a class that you are observing. Review the guides and answer the following questions:

- What are the specific components of each guide? For example, are there objectives? suggested activities? suggested readings?

- How useful would each guide be for a beginning teacher trying to determine what should be taught in that class?
- What strengths and weaknesses can you identify in each of the guides?
- What is the practicing teacher's opinion of the guides? How does he or she use them when planning instruction?

PLANNING UNITS

Choosing Unit Topics

Students in your classes should expect that they will experience a logical sequence of lessons and activities. That goal is accomplished through careful unit planning. Units in social studies courses generally focus on one concept, theme, or period of time. For example, a U.S. history course might include units on early exploration, the Revolutionary War era, the Constitution, the Civil War, the age of industrialism, and so on. A psychology course might include units on personality types, the brain, and child development.

A unit should present a coherent set of instructional activities that support the defined unit goals, which, in turn, support course goals or outcomes. Unit goals provide focal points for the selection of readings, teaching strategies, and classroom discussions. Units are introduced in some fashion, have a body of instructional approaches, and are most commonly concluded with some form of evaluation. A series of units makes up a quarter, a trimester, or a semester.

As a new teacher, you will spend a great deal of time blocking out and conceptualizing units—deciding what units to teach, roughly how long each will be, and in what order they will be taught. Those decisions can be based on several sources of help and information. If a comprehensive course outline or curriculum guide is available, it will have already broken the course into suggested or required units.

A second, and often most helpful, resource is colleagues who are teaching, or have taught, the course. They can give "real-life" answers to your questions and suggest options that have worked for them. You will want also to take these suggestions with the appropriate grains of salt, because each teacher has his or her biases and idiosyncrasies. Always keep in mind that, though a rookie, you have been hired because of your demonstrated competence. With a contract comes a degree of empowerment to begin making the professional decisions you believe are in the best interests of your students.

One word of caution is in order: Many social studies departments decide as a group how they will structure courses that are being taught by several teachers. This practice eliminates some problems for students who must make schedule changes and switch teachers. For example, all of the U.S. history teachers in a department may agree to end the first semester of a yearlong survey course at a common point, such as 1898. It is a matter of professional courtesy as a newcomer to the department to participate in and respect those sorts of decisions.

A third resource for deciding upon unit topics and themes are existing resources in the field of social studies. This text will be extremely helpful in beginning the process of unit identification. *Social Education*, the journal of the National Council of the Social Studies, frequently has articles and special sections devoted to suggestions as to how to teach various courses and topics. Numerous other social studies resources, such as commercially produced curriculum guides and publications of scholarly and professional organizations, have useful suggestions for teachers. These resources often go beyond the mere suggestion of unit topics and themes to provide suggested teaching activities and other resources. Don't ignore the role of the textbook as a significant resource in structuring your unit plans. Texts already have an organizational structure that can provide guidance for your planning process. Beware, however, of the "tyranny" of the textbook. Use the text as a resource, not as a bible!

Finally, your own common sense and academic preparation should be helpful in determining unit topics and themes. Although you would not want to recreate a college course, don't ignore information from your own course work. For example, the dominant themes explored in a college U.S. history course would most likely find their way into a high school U.S. history course. Though the level of conceptual understanding might differ, the underlying conceptual principles would not. College courses, however, often have the luxury of an entire semester to explore relatively narrow topics; such is rarely the case in secondary schools.

ACTIVITY Identifying Unit Topics

To practice thinking about unit planning, identify units that might be taught in each of the following secondary social studies courses: U.S. history, world history, world geography, government/civics, U.S. foreign policy. Use information from Chapters 5–11 in identifying the units. Analyze your choices. Are they primarily topical, chronological, or thematic, or could they be characterized in some other fashion?

Compare your choices with those of your classmates. Discuss how you determined your selection of unit topics. Do some choices make better sense than others? Why? What might you do to determine unit topics if you were assigned to teach a course about which you knew very little?

Creating a Course Calendar

Once you have explored these resources, it is time to roughly block out the quarter, trimester, or semester. From your list of the topics, themes, and concepts you might want to include in the course, sort, and combine some potential topics, and eliminate others; the result will provide the basis for your sequence of units. Put together an initial listing of unit topics, and either compare them with the district course guidelines or ask colleagues in your department to evaluate them.

With this information, you are ready to make a tentative outline. Take a calendar and determine how many weeks you have to "play" with; begin to assign approximate lengths of time to each unit topic. As you do so, you will want to begin sequencing the units. For some courses, such as a chronological history class, the sequencing is almost automatic. What is more difficult is deciding what to emphasize and what to ignore. (See Chapter 3 for discussion of depth as opposed to coverage.) For other courses, such as a thematic U.S. history course or a world regions or sociology course, the sequencing of units becomes more difficult. What themes should go earlier and later in the course? What themes or topics will serve to engage students or to help them better organize the themes and concepts that follow? Those decisions should be based upon course expectations, suggestions of colleagues, other resources, and your own good thinking.

Decisions at this point should be seen as extremely flexible. Many factors, ranging from your own inexperience in determining how long it takes to teach a particular aspect of a course to snow days and pep assemblies, will throw your schedule off. What is important is that you begin the process of lesson planning within a "best case" framework of the concepts, topics, and themes you want to address.

You now have a skeleton outline of units for the quarter, trimester, semester, or year. While reading this, you may have been wondering exactly when such planning takes place. If you are fortunate, you will have the summer to leisurely consider these issues and to engage in planning the courses you have been assigned. Planning takes time and is best done when you can think about and reflect on the decisions you are making. Unfortunately, many of you will not have an entire summer to work on course outlines. If that is the case, it is still vital that you engage in the process of determining the scope and sequence of units for each course you will be teaching. It is through this process that you can anticipate and make connections throughout the year. It is also one of the only ways to avoid having your courses resemble a smorgasbord rather than a well-planned banquet. Students deserve learning experiences that fit within a carefully planned context. So . . . much of this thinking is likely to take place in the evening, on weekends, and over holiday breaks. Such is the life of a teacher!

Writing the Unit Plan

Before writing daily lesson plans, you will need to take the unit you are preparing to teach and flesh it out more thoroughly. An important first step in this process is identifying more specifically the goals of the unit. You will probably find it easiest to write knowledge goals, but skill and affective outcomes are also important. In fact, since most text materials address knowledge goals more effectively than skill and affective goals, writing good skill and affect outcomes will be a key to developing a unit that goes beyond mere factual acquisition. You may be able to find models for affective and skill goals in district curriculum guides, in statements from such professional organizations as the National Council for the Social Studies and the National Council on Geographic Education, or in exemplary curriculum materials. For example, an excellent supplementary program, *Reasoning with Democratic Values: Ethical Problems in United States History*, lists the following goals:

1. [Students will] develop more complex and systematic reasoning about decisions involving democratic values.

2. [Students will] gain a deeper understanding of important events, people, and issues from the American past.

3. [Students will] increase their ability to identify ethical values and to analyze situations involving them.

4. [Students will] demonstrate increased respect for individual rights and responsibilities.

5. [Students will] improve their ability to express clearly reasoned judgments, both orally and in writing.

6. [Students will] become more effective participants in productive group discussions of ethical issues. (Lockwood and Harris 1985, p. 5)

Fleshing out the unit also involves selecting teaching strategies and materials and deciding in what order they will be used to develop the content, concepts, attitudes, and skills the unit will focus upon. When you have completed this process, you will have a concrete picture of what you are going to teach during the unit, the strategies and activities you plan to use, and the estimated length of time for addressing each component of the unit. This process also involves important thinking about how you will evaluate student learning during and after completion of the unit. Knowing your intended instructional outcomes and some of the means you will use to measure them helps to focus planning and ensure that each classroom activity has a clear purpose.

ACTIVITY   **Planning a Unit**

Now it is time for you to try applying what you have just read. Using the guide in Figure 4.1, begin planning a single unit. The process will appear to be somewhat "lockstep," but it does mimic the process a teacher must use to put together a well-planned and teachable unit. To do this, form a small group with other students and work through the steps together. Be creative and realistic. Push one another to explain reasons for choices of objectives, goals, content, strategies, and so on. At the end, you should have the beginning of a unit you could teach—and greater familiarity with how to plan units.

Planning a Unit

1. Pick a social studies course and write its title.
2. List three broad unit topics you might teach in this course.
3. Select one of the topics by circling it. Now, write three supporting themes that might be included in that particular unit.
4. Brainstorm a list of the *content, skills,* and *attitudes* you might include in a unit built around these themes.
5. Write five *unit* objectives for this unit. These should include knowledge, skill, and attitude objectives.
6. List possible materials you could use to teach this unit. If you know of none, list places where you might find out about available materials.
7. Brainstorm 7–10 activities you might use to teach this unit. Consider a variety of learning styles and a mix of strategies. Arrange the activities so that students
   - Are engaged in the topic or issue. Engagement activities should help students connect the topic with what they already know.
   - Explore the topic or issue through common experiences in which they examine available information, look for relationships and patterns, and identify questions to be answered.
   - Develop an explanation of the topic or concept based on their common experiences in the exploration phase.
   - Have opportunities to elaborate on their understanding of the topic by gathering additional information, applying their explanations to new situations, and the like.
   This sequence may be repeated several times within the unit.
8. How might you evaluate student learning from this unit? What essay questions could you ask to evaluate student learning? What performance-based tasks would demonstrate student achievement of the unit objectives? How would you encourage students to reflect on and assess their own learning?

Figure 4.1 Unit-planning guide

PLANNING LESSONS

The Role of Lesson Planning

Daily lesson plans are central to your thriving as a teacher. Daily lesson plans list the goals and activities for the day's instruction. They include such mundane information as a reminder to take roll and more significant information, such as the content and instructional steps to accomplish the day's objectives. While observing classrooms, you might have seen teachers who seem to be "winging" instruction. Although such a lesson might be successful, it is folly to expect to be able to "wing" your lessons. Imagine a builder attempting to "wing it" when constructing a building. Blueprints give a builder a clear sense of which elements are to be built first, second, third, and so on. Lesson plans are blueprints for a class period, just as your unit plans are like the architect's rendering of the finished building.

Before discussing how to put together daily lesson plans, we must address a common concern: When does a teacher do all of this lesson planning? If, during the process of unit planning, you have begun to identify potential teaching strategies, supplemental materials, simulations, debates, and so on, you will have saved yourself time and effort at the daily-lesson-planning stage. Daily lesson planning takes place, for most beginning teachers, each evening and over the weekend. Many teachers work hard to have a clear conceptualization of what the upcoming week will entail in each of their courses. Again, careful unit planning will help you to develop this conceptualization.

By the weekend, you should know whether there will be schedule conflicts from assemblies or field trips during the upcoming week. Figure out as much of the coming week's daily plans as possible. Unexpected events might change plans, but it is still extremely useful to project what you intend to happen over the next five days. Obviously, Monday's plan should receive the greatest attention over the weekend. Plans for the subsequent days might be a bit less detailed at this point. Weekend planning also allows you to plan ahead for photocopying needs, reserving supplemental or audiovisual materials, and related logistical concerns. One of the best feelings for a new teacher is going to bed on Sunday evening with carefully developed plans for Monday and a clear vision of the plans for the week ahead. Unfortunately, this rewarding feeling is often diminished by the fact that you went to bed around 1:00 in the morning!

Writing Objectives

The first step in developing a daily lesson plan is to determine your objectives. This decision should not be seen as restricting your creativity or as limiting the sort of learning that might take place. Instead, determining instructional objectives helps you to narrow your focus for each class period. In a world history class, you may decide that your central objective is that at the end of the class students will be able to take a stand on whether a particular ancient culture was representative of a "great" civilization. With that goal in mind, you should center your planned activities on developing a definition of or a list of criteria for a "great" civilization and evaluating the particular ancient culture according to those criteria. Your instructional strategies might include small- and large-group work, some form of collaborative learning, a debate format, or use of a reading before a teacher-led discussion.

It should be clear that determining instructional objectives for a class period need not restrict the sorts of teaching approaches used that day.

If you have not had the opportunity to learn how to write useful and measurable instructional objectives, seek information on how to do so from your methods instructors. A self-instruction booklet on writing instructional objectives that you might find useful is Robert F. Mager's *Preparing Instructional Objectives* (1984).

ACTIVITY   ## Examining Instructional Objectives

Instructional objectives receive "mixed reviews" from classroom teachers. Some believe objectives have an important and central role in planning and teaching. Others believe they are just another layer of "bureaucratic nonsense," having little to do with what actually takes place in the classroom. To become more familiar with opinions on instructional objectives and their role in the planning process, interview three teachers about their use of and opinions on instructional objectives. Ask to see examples of instructional objectives. Compile your information and bring it back to class for discussion with classmates. What generalizations can you draw about the role of instructional objectives in teaching and planning in secondary schools?

Choosing Instructional Strategies and Materials

Once you have determined your objectives for the day, the next step is choosing the specific instructional strategy and content to accomplish your objectives. Again, careful unit planning should assist you in determining the materials and teaching approaches you want to use. Students should be exposed to a variety of instructional approaches that actively involve them in their own learning. A variety of approaches also allows more students to succeed: Some like to write, others to draw, others to debate and engage in role plays. Evaluate your planned teaching activities with the following list of criteria for quality learning experiences.

1. The experience is meaningful. It provides an opportunity for students to discover meaning, to make sense of their experience, to integrate knowledge.

2. The experience is involving. It seems likely to involve all students in the active processing of experiences.

3. The experience is diverse and multiple. It requires the use of many learning styles, modalities, and talents.

4. The experience is ethical. It does not require the use of deception by students or teachers and in no way diminishes the dignity of participants.

5. The experience is challenging. It requires the students to acquire new information and also to process that information: to synthesize it, apply it, and create new forms.

6. The experience is appropriate. It is appropriate for the context (the classroom or the community) and the participants (the teachers and the students).

7. The experience is relevant. It relates to and contributes to the unit objective. (Glatthorn 1987)

Before planning for instruction, it would be useful for you to review Chapters 3, 13, 14, and 15 of this book.

Selecting an instructional approach and the materials to be used in class often entails searching through the resources in your social studies department, asking for ideas from more experienced colleagues, getting in touch with publishers of supplemental teaching materials, and allowing your own creativity to run loose. For example, your colleagues might have useful ideas for teaching about the draft during the Vietnam War. If not, the Center for Social Studies Education in Pittsburgh has a number of strategies for accomplishing that goal. Or you might put together an activity on your own, in which you establish some arbitrary cutoff birth date; all the students born after that date are "drafted" and must complete some additional assignment or face a specified consequence. This idea was spawned in a casual discussion among colleagues about how to teach about the Vietnam War draft experience to middle school students. Now, the entire eighth-grade class is subjected to the draft with a number of additions to heighten the reality of the experience. This sort of "shoestring curriculum development" is what creative and hardworking teachers do. Push your imagination to figure out how to make learning rigorous, involving, and active.

ACTIVITY

Brainstorming Teaching Approaches

To practice generating creative teaching ideas, form small groups and quickly brainstorm at least two ways of teaching each of the following topics, concepts, skills, or values:

- The Underground Railroad
- Black Power
- The Chinese concept of "barbarian"
- The concepts of supply and demand
- Tolerance of diverse views
- Respect for the democratic value of equality
- The skill of judging the integrity of a source
- The skill of classifying artifacts based on observations

Compare your ideas with those of the rest of the class. Begin to develop the self-perception that you are, in fact, a social studies curriculum developer. Your ideas might not be published (at least not right away), but they will enliven your classroom and help you develop the confidence to make exciting things happen.

Writing the Lesson Plan

Once you have determined what materials and strategy you are going to use, combine that information into a usable and teachable lesson plan. To meet these two criteria—utility and teachability—a lesson plan should include several components: a lesson opener, often called the "anticipatory set" or engagement activity; a series of instructional steps you will follow to accomplish your lesson objectives; and some sort of lesson closure that might include an evaluation of student learning or assigning homework for the next class period.

Each lesson you plan should have a clear and distinct beginning point. Many teachers find it helpful to write their instructional objective on the chalkboard so that students know "where they are going" during the class period. An opening can be quiet and thought-producing (asking each student to write down the constitutional right he or she most treasures as a citizen) or more active (having students join with a neighbor to brainstorm all of the rights they think are contained in the U.S. Constitution). Both of these openings focus students on the theme of constitutional rights and would support an instructional objective related to listing, defining, and evaluating the relative importance of rights found in the U.S. Constitution. Both also tap into the students' existing knowledge of the topic, a key factor in developing new understandings.

A lesson opener acknowledges the strange lives of junior and senior high school students. They spend roughly fifty minutes in one class and then have five minutes to see friends, go to the bathroom, flirt, and get to their next class, where they spend another fifty minutes on a single topic, only to repeat this madness six or seven times each day. Given that reality, a lesson opener helps students make the transition from their previous class and the excitement of the hallways to your lesson. A carefully structured opening activity also allows you a moment or two to take roll, deal with the student who needs to know what happened yesterday, and other "administrivia." While you are attending to business, the class is beginning to focus on the topic at hand.

A word of caution: The scenario just described won't happen automatically. Take the time to communicate and establish your expectations regarding the first few minutes of class time. This is part of the management of student behavior that parallels the management of instruction. For help in this area of teaching, see Emmer et al. (1989).

An effective lesson opener begins the instructional steps that make up the bulk of the lesson plan. A useful daily lesson plan is really a protocol for what should happen during your time with the class. The step-by-step instructions help you present a logically sequenced lesson that incorporates what you know about how students learn. These instructions also help you stay on track if the lesson strays without purpose.

In your step-by-step instructions, include the specific content you expect students to learn. This might include definitions, lecture content, names, dates, and so on. Including this information forces you to consider in advance what you intend to present to students.

Your plan should not simply be a list of content. It should also have the instructions you plan to give for group work, debates, role plays, simulations, and any other strategies you will be using. It should include questions you plan to use to guide a discussion. Although you will certainly think of questions on your feet and in response to student answers, a well-thought-out questioning sequence increases the chances that the class will examine the issues you feel are worth exploring, while in no way limiting the opportunity for discussion of issues raised by students. Thinking of questions in advance also makes it easier for you to check periodically for student understanding, as well as to ask higher-level questions that will promote critical thinking and reflection. The best discussions often begin with planned questions, then move to issues raised by the students and the teacher in the context of the discussion itself, and finish with summary questions from your list. (See Chapter 13 for a more detailed discussion of questioning strategies.)

The third component of any lesson plan is a designed ending for the lesson. Too often, a teacher suddenly recognizes that the bell is going to ring in ten seconds and shouts hurried instructions for a homework assignment as the students are packing their books and heading for the door. A carefully constructed lesson has a planned closure that allows students to reflect on what they have learned and helps the teacher get a quick reading of whether the expectations for the day were accomplished. Lesson closure ideas include asking students to jot down three things they learned during the period and then report them to the class, going around the room and having each student complete such sentence stems as "Today, I learned . . ." or "Regarding the day's topic, I had never really thought about . . . ," or asking students to write three or four sentences on a topic related to the day's activities. If assigning homework, plan time to give and review directions.

The steps in your lesson plan should be clearly listed. How you write your lesson plans will be a matter of personal preference. Some teachers find an outline format most useful, whereas others create more of an expanded "to do" list of the steps needed to implement the day's lesson. Many teachers highlight the most important elements or key transitions in their lesson plans with highlighter pens or use various colors of ink to make critical elements stand out. Play with different styles and adopt one that is most comfortable for you.

Recognize that some plans will be relatively brief (when you have planned to view a videotape and only expect students to take limited notes). Other plans (those used when conducting a more elaborate simulation or providing information through a lecture/discussion format) will most likely be longer and more complex. Although a single activity might stretch over several days, as in the case of a lengthy simulation or role-play activity, you will still need a plan of action for each day's segment.

As the school year progresses, develop a filing system for saving lesson plans. This is not so you can duplicate the plan the next year but, rather, to maintain a record of what you taught, how you attempted to teach it, and how successful it was. On the plans, jot down ideas for how to teach the lesson better or differently the next time around. Many teachers have lesson plans from dozens of years; these plans serve as an archive of ideas for improving their teaching.

Finally, use your lesson plan—carry it as you teach! You did the thinking and the work to craft a plan of action for the day's instruction; it is foolish to let the plan languish on the desk while you flounder, wondering what to do next.

An experienced teacher recounts how he insisted that his student teacher write well-defined lesson plans for each day's instruction. The cooperating teacher then sat in the back of the room and realized that the student teacher was trying to steal sideways glances at the plan sitting on a desk in the front of the room. It came as both a shock and a relief to the student teacher when the cooperating teacher explained that it was all right to walk around the room and teach from the lesson plan. Plan carefully, and then use the plan to increase your odds of conducting a successful class period.

ACTIVITY   ## Planning a Lesson

Many of the activities in Part Two of this book, although designed to help you understand key ideas in the disciplines that make up the social studies, are also intended as teaching ideas you can use with secondary students. Figure 4.2 presents one such activity, originally written to be part of the chapter on history.

Do the activity in Figure 4.2 as a learner. When you have finished, reflect on what you learned about history as a result of completing the activity.

Next, think about how you would use the activity with students. Where would it fit in the curriculum? How would it need to be adapted?

Working with a partner, identify the objectives the activity would help you achieve. Then consider how you would open the lesson. How would you prepare students for the mind-walk activity? Develop a series of steps for implementing the lesson and a means of bringing closure to the lesson. In devising your plan, consider what you know about how students construct meaning. Estimate how long each component should take to implement, and be sure that you will be able to complete the plan in a single class period. If your idea goes longer than one class period, plan for the transition between day 1 and day 2.

Once finished, exchange lesson plans with another pair of students and provide constructive criticism to the authors. As a class, discuss the process of constructing these lesson plans.

Activity: Mind Walk

To get a sense of the immensity of the possible facts or events of the past and to understand the possible limits of the historical record, do the following activity.

At the end of the day, conduct a mind walk of all the activities in which you engaged in one period of the day. List as many facts or events as you can recall about this period of time.

After you have completed your mind walk and have listed all the activities in which you were engaged, think of what traces those activities have left. What kinds of records are those activities reflected in or captured by? Are any of those records created consciously (e.g., a diary or journal)? What records might your activities appear in that are indirect (i.e., created by someone else, as, for example, a telephone directory), or for which other agents are responsible (e.g., census returns)? Which of your activities are most and least likely to leave traces? Which of those traces might be most likely to be preserved? least likely? Why? What biases may therefore be likely in the potential record of your activities?

Other aspects of the historical record are not records per se but nevertheless offer clues about our lives. Think, for example, of the trash you throw away—the soft drink cans, juice bottles, razor blades, food packages, and the like. Think about other items you commonly use—coins, paper money, stamps, and so on. Think about other material items in your life—the layout, construction, and other characteristics of your home or public buildings. What might those things contribute to understanding of your life?

What might a historian, working a thousand years from now and perhaps having little else to go on, infer from those items about your life, your history?

Which of your activities would you consider significant? What sorts of traces and records would the significant activities leave as compared with the more mundane? How might the historian's sense of significance be different from your own?

Now think of a more public event or episode currently happening. What kinds of traces might this sort of event leave? Who creates the traces or records? What purpose is each record intended to serve?

Figure 4.2   History activity

CONCLUSION

Instruction should be a conscious act, a fact made real in the development of lesson plans. To return to the analogy of the builder, a novice carpenter will look a bit more carefully at the plans for the building and be a bit more hesitant in making on-the-job adaptations. Experience in construction frees the carpenter to work more comfortably with the plans of the architect and to improvise when and where appropriate. Although the highly experienced builder might be able to take a single look at a set of blueprints and then spend the day framing with abandon, he or she will still refer to the plans to ensure that what is desired comes about in the end. Recognize that, for a novice, it is additionally important to come to each class period with a carefully considered set of plans for instruction. These plans will boost your self-confidence as a teacher and provide the structure from which you can more confidently follow the worthwhile tangents that inevitably arise in a well-run social studies classroom.

Reflecting on the Chapter

What was the most difficult aspect of developing a lesson plan? Why do you think that part of the process was difficult for you? In your journal, reflect on steps you might take to make that part of the process easier for you.

References

Emmer, E., C. Evertson, J. Sanford, B. Clements, and M. Worsham. *Classroom Management for Secondary Teachers*. 2nd ed. Englewood Cliffs, N.J.: Prentice Hall, 1989.

Glatthorn, A. A. *Curriculum Renewal*. Alexandria, Va.: Association for Supervision and Curriculum Development, 1987.

Lockwood, A. L., and D. E. Harris. *Reasoning with Democratic Values: Ethical Problems in United States History, Instructor's Manual*. New York: Teachers College Press, 1985.

Mager, R. F. *Preparing Instructional Objectives,* 2nd rev. ed. Belmont, Calif.: D. S. Lake Publishers, 1984.

Spady, W. G., and K. J. Marshall. "Beyond Traditional Outcome-Based Education." *Educational Leadership* 49, no. 2 (1991): 67–72.

THE SOCIAL SCIENCES
AND HISTORY IN SCHOOLS

5

STUDYING AND TEACHING PSYCHOLOGY

Michael Wertheimer, Tina Yeager, and Virginia L. Jones

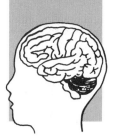

ACTIVITY LIST

• • •

ACTIVITY

Drawing a Typical Psychologist

Sketch your idea of the typical psychologist. Show something about the psychologist's personality and work. Post your drawing with those of other class members.

Make a class list of positive and negative stereotypes reflected in the drawings. On what are these views based? How might they affect your responses to this chapter? your teaching of psychology? your application of the results of psychological research?

INTRODUCTION

Psychology addresses questions that are universally appealing: Why are we the way we are? When is personality established? How do genetics and the environment influence us? Why are some people mentally ill? Should the mentally ill be held responsible for their behavior? If what we do is a product of genetics and environment, should any of us be held responsible for our behavior? Why are some people overweight? Why do others diet to the point of endangering their health? Why do we sometimes do things in a crowd that we wouldn't think of doing alone? Why do teenagers and their parents often interpret a teenager's behavior differently? Where do ethnic stereotypes and prejudices come from? Why are some people strongly attracted to members of the opposite sex and others strongly attracted to members of the same sex?

Psychologists consider evidence, data, and empirical observations when formulating questions about human and animal behavior. The questions with which psychologists deal are incredibly diverse. Yet the basic methodology—an evidential approach—is what all psychologists have in common.

Psychologists' common methodological orientation leads them to question every assertion about behavior and experience, and to think about how the validity or truth of that assertion could be assessed. Endorsement of an assertion is always tentative and depends upon the amount, objectivity, and quality of the evidence that can be brought to bear upon the validity of the assertion.

The commitment to this evidential or empirical approach, though, does not mean that there is unanimity about what issues are worth raising, what domains of behavior or experience are the most interesting or important, what kinds of questions to ask, or what sorts of research strategies (experiments, surveys, interviews, etc.) are the most appropriate. There have always been differences, and undoubtedly there will always be differences, in psychologists' theoretical perspectives. These frames of reference profoundly affect how different psychologists go about their work. Perspectives influence the kinds of problems they consider worth investigating, how they go about investigating the problems they choose to study, and how they make sense of their findings.

Psychology's evidential, empirical approach is based on the assumption that human behavior—and animal behavior—is not haphazard or capricious; dispassionate observation can discover regularities in behavior. The "behavioral science approach" can be used to discern such regularities in one's own as well as in others'

Figure 5.1   Psychologists study human and animal behavior. How would you define behavior? What questions would you ask about the behavior of the people in this photo?

behavior, and the resulting insights can be used to enhance one's own and others' welfare. We need not be the hapless victims of an impersonal, incomprehensible fate, but can discover, and use, principles of behavior in helping to construct a more ideal world in which human potential is realized, in which people support one another in worthwhile endeavors, and in which there is more social justice. Psychology, the dispassionate search for regularities and for predictability in behavior, holds substantial promise for the enhancement of human welfare, both individual and collective.

The aim of this chapter is to present some key concepts in the field, to show how psychologists approach various questions, and to suggest ways in which the discipline may be effectively taught in the high school. We begin by briefly describing the history of psychology as a discipline. We then provide an overview of the field today. Finally, we address questions related to teaching psychology in high school classrooms.

ACTIVITY

Testing the Variability Hypothesis

Early in the twentieth century, many psychologists in the United States believed that the "variability hypothesis" explained gender differences in both eminence and abnormality. Why are there far fewer female than male composers, musicians, scientists—and also criminals and residents of mental hospitals? Women are inherently less variable than men, it was argued; since variability along almost any dimension is greater in males, there will be more male than female "outliers" at both the top and the bottom of any distribution. This ingenious hypothesis provided a satisfying explanation for the observed difference between the genders: Men, on average, deviate more from one another than do women.

Develop a set of measurements with your classmates that could be used to test the variability hypothesis. Pick measures that can be done in the classroom (e.g., the distance from the right elbow to the tip of the right index finger, how long it takes the student to count the number of words on a standard page of text, the number of anagrams each student can complete in a given period of time).

Record scores on the selected measurement for all members of the class. Determine the mean for males and the mean for females. Is the average deviation of individual males' scores from the mean of male scores greater than the average deviation of individual females' scores from the mean of female scores? In other words, do your data support the variability hypothesis?

Psychologist Leta Stetter Hollingworth pursued a study of variability between genders. She collected statistics from physical and psychological dimensions on large groups of U.S. men and women and found that there was, in fact, no reliable difference in the average variability between the sexes. Her pioneering research definitively refuted the variability hypothesis. Given this information, how would you interpret the evidence gathered through your class measurements?

• • •

Would you use this activity with a group of secondary students? What objectives would it help you achieve? What adaptations would you make to ensure its success?

HISTORY OF PSYCHOLOGY

Precursors of Psychology

Psychology's roots can be found in philosophy (MacLeod 1975). Although psychology did not emerge as a separate discipline until fairly late in the nineteenth century, interest in the kinds of questions that concern modern psychology was already evident twenty-five hundred years ago, during the Golden Age of Greece. Plato and Aristotle pondered how it is that we obtain knowledge through our senses. They recognized the quandary humans face in attempting to obtain certain knowledge through the senses because the senses are subject to illusions.

Aristotle also speculated on the nature of memory, proposing several "laws" of association. In trying to determine why one idea makes us think of another, he suggested that ideas tend to be associated if (1) they are similar, or (2) they contrast with one another, or (3) they have occurred to us together in space and time, or (4) they have frequently been associated in the past. Aristotle also wrote a book about the "psyche," in which he summarized the thoughts of some of his predecessors.

The next two millennia produced, with few exceptions, relatively little progress in the sciences or in technology. The rebirth of science, as well as of general intellectual and artistic endeavor, occurred during the Renaissance (literally, "rebirth") in the fifteenth, sixteenth, and seventeenth centuries.

The methods of experiment, of careful dispassionate measurement, and of rigorous rational thought about the results of measurements and experiments became preferred as avenues to truth over the almost exclusive reliance on faith and scripture that characterized the preceding centuries. Human beings began to be seen less as creations in the image of God and more as objects in the natural world that could be studied just as easily as could inanimate objects, plants, and animals. Discovery of the circulation of the blood, dissection of the nervous system, chemical analyses of digestion, and other physiological endeavors made it clear that the body functions in many respects like a machine—and that the regularities in how the body functions can be discovered by careful empirical work. Not surprisingly, this empirical orientation soon spread to study of the human mind as well as of the human body.

The British empiricists (John Locke, George Berkeley, David Hume, and especially James Mill) tried to generalize Aristotle's laws of association into an entire theory of mind. What is the content of the mind, and how does it get to be what it is? They argued that all ideas come from experience, and that association is, in effect, a principle like gravitation or attraction that makes simple ideas compound into more complex ideas. Ultimately, all ideas are based on sensations, and the process of association of ideas that are contiguous in space and time generates the entire rich content of complex ideas that are, as it were, the furniture of the mind. Prominent European intellectuals took this theory of mind for granted during much of the eighteenth and nineteenth centuries.

Associationism led to general interest in the process of sensation. E. H. Weber's experiments early in the nineteenth century led G. T. Fechner later in the century to establish the new field of psychophysics; that is, study of the relationships between physical, objective quantities and mental, subjective quantities. Weber determined how much a physical stimulus (a lifted weight, a line of particular length) must be changed for a person to notice that it had changed; he discovered what can be called the first "law of relativity" in psychology. How much the stimulus must be changed so that the change is noticeable is not constant over the range of stimulus intensities from slight to great, but is generally proportional to the stimulus intensity already present. That is, a strong stimulus must be changed more than a weak one if a person is to notice the change. An ounce added to a two-pound weight might be just enough for a noticeable difference, but a four-pound weight would have to be changed by two ounces to be noticeably different, an eight-pound weight by four ounces, and so on.

Fechner systematically elaborated on Weber's work, rigorously specifying a number of "psychophysical methods" that can be used to establish the value of subjective intensities by setting physically measurable stimuli equal to them and generalizing Weber's law to a logarithmic mathematical equation: Subjective quantities increase in proportion not to the actual increase in the stimulus intensity but much more slowly; subjective intensities increase in proportion to the *logarithm* of the objective intensity. This general psychophysical law, propounded by Fechner in 1860, is one of the oldest and most robust empirical laws in psychology.

Many developments in physiology during the nineteenth century were also important to the development of psychology. The finding that the back part of the spinal cord carries sensory messages (its destruction leads to loss of sensation) while the front carries motor messages (its destruction leads to paralysis) demonstrated a striking relationship between anatomical structures and behavioral functions. The reflex (muscle twitches in response to specific local stimulation) in frogs and later in many other animals provided a convenient mechanical model for how sensations can lead to actions. Much work was devoted to the anatomy and function of the nervous system.

Psychology's Emergence as a Separate Scientific Discipline

By 1879, Wilhelm Wundt, who had sought to create a recognized new science of psychology, had a functioning Psychological Institute for the conduct of experimental studies in psychology at the University of Leipzig, Germany. Wundt conceived of psychology as the science of immediate experience. He proposed systematic introspection by trained observers in experimental settings where the stimulus input could be controlled as the method of choice for the new science. By systematic introspection he meant the careful analysis of the content of subjective experience into its constituent elements, and study of how the various elements compound to form the rich content of subjective experience. Although this experimental method is, according to Wundt, the preferred method for study of the basic mental processes, such as sensation, the higher mental processes, such as thinking and social interaction, require a different method: observation without experimentation. He prepared a huge ten-volume work on sociocultural psychology to begin to achieve this aim, devoted to the psychology of myth, of language, of religion, of art, and of moral and legal codes. This work epitomized for him the highest and most interesting problems of psychology.

Yet sociocultural psychology must be built on a thorough understanding of the basic mental processes as well. Accordingly, Wundt championed careful quantitative experimental work on sensation, perception, association, attention, reaction time, and what he called feeling. The voluminous experimental work undertaken at his laboratory attempted to reduce human consciousness to its elements. Students soon flocked to Leipzig from many parts of the world, including the United States, to learn the new experimental psychology from the master himself; experimental psychology laboratories were established throughout Europe and North America and in other parts of the world as Wundt's students returned home, inspired by his example.

Development of Alternative Viewpoints

Wilhelm Wundt was the personification of the new field, but alternative frameworks soon emerged. One of Wundt's prominent pupils, Edward Bradford Titchener, elaborated further on Wundt's experimental psychology at Cornell University. Titchener developed a system that he called *structuralism*, since he believed that psychology must be devoted to study of the structure of the mind's contents. Others proposed a system called *functionalism*, since they believed that, consistent with Darwinian evolutionary theory and other nineteenth-century scientific developments, psychology should concentrate on what functions are served by psychological processes: In contrast to structuralism's concentration on the "what" or "is" of the mind, the functionalists advocated concentration on the "how" or "is for" of the mind. Among the early American proponents of functionalism, which flourished especially at the University of Chicago and at Columbia University, was William James at Harvard University, a prominent American philosopher and psychologist.

During the first half of the twentieth century, several different orientations coalesced, each with a number of enthusiastic adherents. The paradigms, attitudes, opinions, and perspectives shared by such groups of people came to be called *schools*. The members of a particular school had a shared theoretical orientation that permeated the way in which they defined the problems they considered worthy of study, specified the research methods they believed were appropriate, and generated the techniques of analysis used to draw conclusions. For several decades, interschool controversy and even acrimony were intense.

One of the earlier schools, *psychoanalysis*, arose out of the medical and psychiatric tradition. Sigmund Freud, its most prominent proponent, argued that the mentally healthy and the mentally ill are not qualitatively different, but differ only in the degree to which they display various mental mechanisms. All of us are driven, he argued, by intense primordial drives for pleasure. Since society cannot function if all its members seek their own selfish ends without regard to others' welfare, young children early begin to learn ways to satisfy their needs that are acceptable to the society—and to keep themselves unaware of those many aspects of their own intense desires that are not considered socially acceptable. As a consequence, most human motivation stems from the unconscious, which Freud and his followers considered the most important aspect of the psyche. Buried deep in the unconscious is the *id*, the part of personality with which we are born, which contains the *libido*, or the spring of all action. Soon the young child develops an *ego*, an agent that tries to mediate between the libido's desires and the unresponsive, sometimes repressive real world, as well as a *superego*, a kind of oppressive conscience that is largely an unforgiving internalization of the society's values as reflected in parents' efforts to socialize the child.

The seething internal turmoil among these three aspects of personality, most of which remains in the unconscious, leads to such *defense mechanisms* as repression, projection, and regression, as the ego works to keep us from becoming aware of the intense unacceptable impulses that actually motivate us while also attempting to achieve some degree of satisfaction of those impulses. The internal turmoil can also lead to various forms of psychopathology. Freud and his followers devised a form of psychoanalytic psychotherapy, to help patients overcome neurotic symptoms largely by becoming aware of the unconscious striving and mechanisms that the psychoanalysts believed were their source.

An entirely different school, *Gestalt theory,* became prominent in Germany and then in the United States. Gestalt theorists objected to the elementism (breaking consciousness down into its components) of the prevailing views in psychology. Most psychological units or wholes, they argued, are not the sum total of their parts, nor even is the whole *more* than the sum of its parts; rather, most wholes are dynamic, integrated structures that are totally different from a mere sum of their parts or from a sum of their parts plus a "whole quality" (such as squareness or a melody). In an important sense, wholes and their characteristics are *prior to,* and determine, the nature and characteristics of their parts. The characteristics of many wholes determine the nature of their parts, and the place, role, and function that the parts fulfill in the whole. Parts are not inert, connected atoms that are indifferent to one another. The front right leg of a four-legged chair is not just an indifferent piece of wood but a piece of a certain size, strength, length, and location in the whole without which the chair would not even be able to stand.

The Gestalt theorists did extensive experiments on Gestalt phenomena in problem solving, thinking, perception, memory, and other fields, showing that the

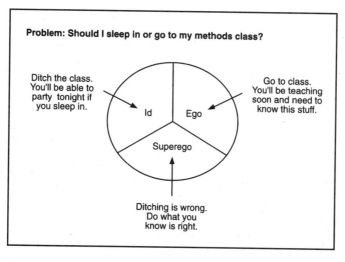

Figure 5.2   This diagram shows the operation of the three aspects of personality in addressing a problem you may have faced.

dynamic principles of organization and systemic integration characterize most psychological phenomena. Gestalt research was soon expanded to include personality and social psychology as well. The typical personality, for example, is not just the sum of traits, but a dynamic, integrated system, the separate constituents of which are not indifferent to each other but are dynamically interrelated.

Yet another school, one that dominated the American scene during much of the first half of the twentieth century, emerged at about the same time as Gestalt theory. *Behaviorism* held that if psychology is to aspire to the status of a science, it must give up all reference to subjective experience, because no one can measure or observe someone else's mental events. Psychology must be the science of behavior, because only behavior is directly observable; psychology's task is to do experiments on what people—and animals—do. Introspection can play no role in this endeavor.

This orientation led to concentration on how behavior changes with experience, that is, on the psychology of learning. The most prominent spokesman for the school, John B. Watson, soon discovered the work of a famous Russian scientist, Ivan P. Pavlov, on what has since been called classical conditioning; Watson made this kind of learning the keystone of the behaviorist system of psychology. In classical conditioning, repeated paired presentation of a previously neutral stimulus (such as a bell) with a stimulus (such as food) that leads regularly to a particular response (such as salivation) will eventually make it possible for the previously neutral stimulus (the bell) alone to elicit the response (salivation); once the bell can elicit the salivation, conditioning has occurred. Watson and his followers believed that this mechanism can explain the great bulk of human behavior; behavior is essentially a chain of conditioned reflexes. This strong emphasis on the role of learning led him also to an extreme environmentalism: If one had sufficient control over a child's environment, then one could mold that child to become any kind of adult one wishes—beggar, doctor, lawyer, thief.

Later versions of behaviorism included emphasis on a different form of learning, instrumental or operant conditioning. The basic principle of operant conditioning is that the probability of a given response is increased any time that emission of the response is followed by a reinforcing stimulus (i.e., a reward). Responses, in effect, are instrumental in achieving certain desirable consequences in the environment; they operate on the environment. B. F. Skinner used a variant of this principle to account for virtually all behavior in all species; Skinner and his followers applied their notions to educational technology, to maintaining order in prisons, mental hospitals, and school classrooms, and even to the design of utopian communal living. A quite different version of behaviorism, a social learning theory advocated by Albert Bandura, argued that much behavior is learned by noticing the consequences that others' behavior leads to and by imitating those behaviors that lead to desired end states and avoiding those behaviors that lead to unpleasant consequences.

By about the middle of the twentieth century, a self-styled "third force" (contrasting itself with psychoanalysis and behaviorism) emerged: *humanistic psychology*. Its proponents, such as Abraham Maslow and Carl Rogers, argued that the other schools were too mechanistic and deterministic in their approaches to human nature. If you consider human conduct as nothing more than the expression of vile unconscious urges or chains of automatic reflexes, you are losing what is distinctively human—and noble—about human nature. Humanistic psychologists emphasized human growth and the tendency toward mental health and the achievement of human potential. Their opposition to the negative and purely mechanical view of human nature brought them a large popular following, but the impact of the humanistic orientation on professional and academic psychologists has been minimal.

Probably the "school" that has become the most popular among research psychologists in the United States since about 1970 is a product of what has been called the "cognitive revolution." Sparked partly by the advent of the high-speed computer, partly by the demise of strict Watsonian behaviorism, and partly by reemphasis on problems in the psychology of thinking, an "information-processing" orientation to sensation and perception, to learning and memory, and to problem solving and thinking has become widely prominent. The writing of computer programs that display "artificial intelligence" in such domains as chess, medical diagnosis, and weather prediction, the effort to simulate human problem solving with computer programs, and the analysis of what happens when people "catch on" to something they did not understand before are all instances of the endeavors of the *cognitive school.*

Nevertheless, throughout the twentieth century and today as well, a large number of psychologists have remained eclectic, not identifying themselves strongly or exclusively with any one of the schools. They may use a Skinnerian behaviorist approach when that appears appropriate for dealing with a particular problem, a psychoanalytic one for trying to make sense of some baffling issue in the psychology of personality, or a Gestalt orientation in trying to analyze what happens when a pupil gains insight into a difficult intellectual problem. Eclecticism does not generate a unified, integrated system of psychology, but it at least acknowledges that a number of schools have proposed ideas that have some utility.

ACTIVITY ## Defining Psychology

Based on what you have read so far, try to develop a definition of *psychology* that will encompass all the various "schools" described in the previous section. Include in your definition an indication of *what* psychologists study, *why* they study it, and *how* they study it.

Don't be discouraged if you find this task difficult. Psychologists and others have debated for many years whether psychology is a natural science, a social science, both, or not a science at all. In 1979, eminent psychologist Amedeo Giorgi said, "It is clear to most astute observers of the field that psychology's disciplinary status is ambiguous at best and chaotic at worst. . . . Its precise meaning and its place among the other sciences are still to be determined in a manner acceptable to the majority of psychologists. . . . While from time to time there has been agreement with respect to a label—study of mind, consciousness, psyche, experience, or behavior—a common in-depth understanding of each of those terms was never achieved. . . . I believe that psychology's disciplinary status cannot be solidified until we clarify the meaning of psychology, however difficult that may be" (Giorgi 1985).

What difficulty might lack of clarity in defining a field pose to you as a teacher? What opportunities might the diversity in the field offer? Discuss these questions with other members of your class.

OVERVIEW OF THE FIELD

Although modern psychology is not a unified field or discipline, psychologists share the conviction that human conduct can be explained by laws about human behavior. This conviction that conduct is lawful is based on the philosophical assumption of determinism; that is, what people (and animals) do, think, and feel is at least to some extent caused and predictable. All psychologists make the determinist assumption that regularities in behavior and experience can be discovered—and that, at least in some cases, such discoveries can be used to help solve real problems of real people. Once the causes of certain phenomena are known, manipulation of those causes may be able to provide at least some control over these phenomena.

The Broad Diversity of Psychology

People who call themselves psychologists pursue many different kinds of careers, careers that fall roughly into two large categories: those concerned with developing and teaching psychological knowledge and those centered on applying psychological principles and techniques. Psychologists in both categories also work in widely diverse occupational settings.

Careers in the first category involve teaching, research, administrative responsibilities, or, most typically, all three. Experimental psychologists apply the scientific method of the natural sciences to problems of human and animal behavior to try to discover general laws that apply in any of psychology's many subject-matter subfields. Social psychologists apply either natural-science or social-science methods to trying to enhance knowledge about intergroup relations and about both how the individual is influenced by the group and how the individual can influence the group. The developmental psychologist's concern is how behavior changes over the individual life span from before birth to old age. Personality psychologists are interested in how individual differences among people come about, in how they are best described, and in what enduring characteristics individual people display in a variety of situations to which various humans react differently. The biopsychologist or physiological psychologist studies relationships between behavioral events and correlated events in the body.

Other psychological specialties include psychometrics (the technology of how to create effective and trustworthy tests or measurements of individual differences), gerontology (the study of behavior in old age), sociocultural psychology (study of how human behavior and experience are affected by ethnic, linguistic, and cultural diversity), the psychology of women (dealing with issues that specifically concern the behavior and experience of women, and more.

Diversity is comparable among applied psychologists. Engineering psychologists or human factors specialists see to it that the devices, settings, and systems with which people interact when they work and play are appropriate to human characteristics and limitations; they are concerned with such issues as human–computer interaction, the design of the displays and controls in airplane and spaceship cockpits, and the safety of toys for infants. Counseling psychologists are trained to help clients with important life decisions, such as selecting educational goals and how to achieve them. Clinical psychologists diagnose problems in individuals' adjustment to their life circumstances, ranging from minor annoyances to severe disturbances, and engage in interventions intended to alleviate those problems. Industrial and organizational psychologists help businesses and industrial organizations with such practical problems as employee selection, employee training, and enhancing employee morale and reducing accidents and absenteeism. Educational psychologists serve similar functions in school systems, in addition to applying psychological principles to enhancing the effectiveness of learning and teaching and to the preparation of appropriate instructional materials.

Other kinds of applied psychology include survey research (doing public opinion polls), media psychology and the psychology of advertising, and applied psychopharmacology (study of the behavioral effects of particular drugs intended to be therapeutic).

ACTIVITY   ## Gaining a Personal Perspective on Psychology

Interview several professors in the psychology department at your university. What are their specialties? What research questions do they pursue using what methodologies? What do these psychologists see as the discipline's unique contribution to knowledge? What potential do they feel psychology holds for enhancing human welfare? Conduct similar interviews with applied psychologists working in settings such as industry, the media, or advertising.

Write profiles of the psychologists you interviewed, including your own thoughts on their work.

• • •

How might you structure an interviewing activity for secondary students? What assistance might they need in framing questions or analyzing the answers given?

Psychology and Its Sociocultural Context

Psychology, like all other intellectual disciplines and human-service practices, is a product of its particular time and place. It has not existed in a vacuum, but its emphases and foci have been changed as the political, cultural, and economic settings within which it has been pursued have changed. Thus, for example, clinical psychology received a substantial boost when vast amounts of federal funds were made available at the end of the Second World War through the Veterans Administration to help returning veterans cope with the traumatic events many of them had experienced during combat and with the stress of returning to civilian life. The recent AIDS epidemic has generated national concern and has resulted in the funding of research and intervention programs intended to deal with AIDS at the individual, regional, national, and international levels. Numerous other instances of the effect of federal priorities on psychological research and practice can be identified.

Psychology and Ethical Issues

Concern about individual human rights also generated a subtle but profound change after 1970 in how the participants in psychological research are viewed. They used to be called "subjects"; now they are called participants, for that is, of course, what they really are. They are not the researcher's victims who should be ready to submit to any treatment that an experimenter wishes to subject them to; instead, the researcher is indebted to the participants for their contribution to the research project. Hence, obtaining the informed consent of participants is now recognized as necessary before they actually engage in the procedures of a study; any procedures that may hurt participants or be otherwise detrimental to their welfare are deemed unethical. This general principle extends, of course, beyond participants in research projects. Teachers of psychology courses must protect their students from exploitation or any other infringements on their individual rights, and practitioners of psychology must make the welfare of their clients their paramount concern. Codes of ethics in psychological research, teaching, and practice developed since the mid-1960s have become the official positions of such major professional organizations as the American Psychological Association.

Some of the most useful information psychologists have acquired has come from research that involved subjecting animals to pain. A case in point is an understanding of learned helplessness—a condition in which people or animals act as though they have no control over what happens to them, so they do not attempt to control their destiny.

The work of Martin Seligman illustrates the principle of learned helplessness. In one experiment, dogs were restrained and given a series of shocks from which they could not escape. After many such trials, the dogs were released from the harness. During a second series of shocks, escape was possible by jumping over a barrier.

Most of the dogs did not learn to escape the shock. On the other hand, a second group of dogs that had not been harnessed and shocked previously, but that had been able to turn off the shock by rotating a wheel in front of them, learned to escape such shocks.

Research on learned helplessness has provided insight into the functioning of the immune system. After animals repeatedly experienced inescapable shock, samples of their blood were analyzed. Such studies revealed an impairment in the functioning of the immune system of dogs that had experienced inescapable shock. Control dogs that had received the same amount of shock but been able to control it (i.e., turn it off) did not suffer such an impairment. Consequently, researchers understand that there is a strong relationship between the experience of perceived uncontrollable stress and health.

Historically, animals have been used in research to advance human understanding of anatomy, physiology, and behavior. Scientists have removed and stimulated portions of animal brains to study physiological and behavioral consequences. Animals have been shocked, deprived, and injected. Such research techniques have been labeled by some as cruel and unethical, yet they have provided significant knowledge that will reduce further suffering—both human and animal.

Figure 5.3   Much of the knowledge psychologists have gained has been learned at the expense of animals. To what extent do you think animals' comfort and even lives should be sacrificed for the sake of advancing scientific understanding? *Source: Bettmann Archive.*

Ethics and Research on Human Behavior

Philip Zimbardo of Stanford University conducted a fascinating landmark study in social psychology. His famous "prison experiment" offers insight into how powerfully people can be influenced by their social roles. Zimbardo randomly assigned volunteer paid participants to the roles of prisoner or guard. The participants took these roles to heart. Guards became obsessed with their power, treating their prisoners with disrespect and contempt. Prisoners became dehumanized and helpless. Zimbardo called his experiment off prematurely because he was horrified at what was taking place; it appeared unethical to continue the study.

Another landmark social psychology experiment is the work of the late Stanley Milgram on obedience to authority. Volunteer paid participants believed they were assisting with research on the influence of punishment on learning. They were told to shock confederate learners who made errors in the recall of learned material. Each time an error was made, the voltage on the shock was increased. Milgram found that the majority of participants would have shocked people at dangerous levels. Obedience to authority seems to be more important than sensitivity to others' well-being.

Divide your class into three groups. One group will play the roles of members of a congressional committee considering whether the federal government should establish regulations to be followed by psychologists conducting research. During the preparation period, the members of this group will develop questions to ask those who testify for and against regulation.

The second group will represent citizens opposed to such regulations. The members of this group, who may assume the roles of psychologists and people who have benefited from psychological research that others consider unethical, should develop arguments for allowing the psychology profession to govern itself, weighing the costs and benefits of particular research practices.

The third group of students will represent citizens supporting regulations. Members of this group may include psychologists, people who feel they were harmed through participation in psychological studies (such as participants in the Milgram and Zimbardo studies), and animal rights advocates. This group should argue that outside regulation is necessary.

Each advocacy group should provide three witnesses to testify before the committee. Each witness should make a two-minute prepared statement and then answer questions from the committee. Other members of the groups may assist in answering questions. Following the testimony, the committee members should discuss the issue and then vote.

• • •

Develop a lesson plan on these issues. Include a set of questions that could be used to stimulate discussion among high school students.

Psychologists' Research Methodology

What characterizes the general research orientation of all modern psychologists is their dedication to rigor and to objectivity in the evidence that they accept as relevant to the evaluation of any statement about human and animal behavior and experience. Opinion, intuition, unsupported speculation, and creative but untestable interpretation are not acceptable, nor is vague innuendo. For an assertion about a psychological topic to be taken seriously, that assertion must be translated into a form in which empirical evidence can be brought to bear upon it. If, for example, it is asserted that moderate degrees of motivation (not too little, not too much) tend to be associated with optimal performance, that statement may be viewed as a wise generalization that probably has some validity, but it is not to be taken seriously as a testable psychological law until its terms are specified much more precisely. What is motivation, and how is it to be measured? What is "moderate," rather than "too little" or "too much"? What kind of performance does it refer to? How is the quality of that performance to be determined, and just what does "optimal" mean?

Once such questions have been answered, one can evaluate the validity of the assertion empirically, and it enters the domain of psychology. One way to turn this assertion into a form in which empirical operations can be performed on it is to specify motivation, for example, as the hours since an animal has last eaten food (an "operational specification" of hunger) and to measure as performance the time it takes the animal to get from one end of a long alley in which it has been placed to the other, at which the animal has frequently previously been given food. Now, "moderate degrees of motivation" could mean twelve to twenty-four hours (and one hour might be "little" and one week "much"), and "optimal performance" could mean the shortest running time. The general assertion can be tested in this operational form by seeing whether, in fact, animals that have been deprived for a moderate amount of time run the alley faster than those that have not been deprived (and are perhaps sated) or those that have been severely deprived (and are perhaps too weak to run very fast).

Other ways to "operationalize" the terms in the general assertion are, of course, possible. The methodological point on which psychologists agree, though, is that until and unless the terms in an assertion are stated in an operational form so that observations or measurements can be made to evaluate the terms and the assertion as such, the assertion is not within the realm of psychology.

Another strategic principle that psychologists accept from general scientific methodology is that although the goal of research is to make generalizations that apply to all of some population of people or animals, an appropriate strategy is *not* to make observations or measurements on *all* the members of that population, but rather, to select a small, representative subgroup or sample of the population, make observations or measurements on that sample, and then generalize the findings from the sample to the entire population from which the sample was drawn. This is, of course, a far more efficient procedure, but it works only if the sample is indeed an unbiased, representative subgroup of the entire population.

Psychologists and statisticians have developed elaborate, sophisticated techniques for selecting samples that maximize the likelihood that the samples will indeed be typical in all important respects of the populations from which they are drawn. What is important to sample carefully so as to assure repesentativeness varies with the issues being studied, but it can include gender, age, situation, and even different ways of measuring a variable. At any rate, the general strategy is to draw a sample from a population of interest so that the sample is truly representative of the population, make appropriate measurements on that sample, and then conclude that if the sample does indeed represent the population, the findings obtained on the sample should hold for the entire population as well.

Statistics are used in psychological research for two purposes: to describe findings obtained in observations of a sample and to draw inferences from findings on a sample about characteristics of the population from which the sample was drawn. Descriptive statistics fall into three classes: those describing the central tendency of some variable (averages such as the mean, median, or mode); those describing how typical the central tendency is (that is, the dispersion or variability of the sample measurements around the central tendency, such as the average deviation, the standard deviation, or the variance); and those describing the extent to which measurements of two or more variables tend to covary (that is, the extent to which values along one variable dimension in the sample can be predicted from knowledge of values along another variable dimension, such as a correlational coefficient). Statistics of inference are then used to infer what the central tendency, the variability, and the correlation are likely to be in the population at large from which the sample was drawn; they are also used to estimate the likelihood that a particular difference or correlation obtained in the sample is characteristic of the population as a whole.

Various strategies are available for psychological research. Which one is most appropriate in a given instance depends upon the particular question being studied. All have as a goal the scientific aim of replication; that is, if someone other than the original investigator were to repeat the study, the second researcher should obtain the same results as the original investigator. Hence, every psychological research project must be reported in sufficient detail that someone else could repeat it.

What is typically of interest is a relationship between some cause (the *independent variable*) and some effect (the *dependent variable*).

ACTIVITY

Designating Variables and Selecting Samples

Designate the independent and dependent variables in the following ideas for empirical studies. Then consider how each researcher should go about selecting a sample for the study. What process would you use if you were doing each study? How large a sample would you select?

Buzz Wheels wants to know if drivers of red cars get more tickets than drivers of cars of other colors. He gives 500 red cars to one group to drive for a year. Controlling the GPA, age, sex, and other factors, he gives 500 cars of other colors (same make) to a sample of 500 from the same population as the first group. After a year, he compares the number of tickets received by the two groups.

Jacqui Serious wants to know if students who are anxious during a lecture and follow-up quiz will perform differently on the quiz than students who are relaxed during a lecture and quiz.

Rocker Hollowmind wants to know if students are influenced by music when they are studying. Rocker designs an experiment to have students complete some reading comprehension tasks while listening to various types of music. Rocker will test the participants on the material they studied. He will control potentially confounding variables to make sure the study is valid.

Research Strategies and Control

Different research strategies differ in their ability to generate convincing evidence about the validity of a cause-effect relationship, largely because they differ in the degree of *control* possible. Among the available strategies are naturalistic observation (where there usually is almost no control at all), systematic assessment or survey research (where there usually is *some* degree of control), and formal experiment (in which there *is* control). These strategies vary in other ways, too, but the extent to which it is possible to draw *causal* conclusions is probably the most important difference.

The basic purpose of controls is basically to eliminate the possibility of alternative (usually trivial) explanations of results. If one treatment (say intense motivation) is always used in a study with one kind of participants (say males) and another (say moderate motivation) is always used with another kind of participant (say females), better performance under moderate motivation is inconclusive because level of motivation is confounded with gender; it would be impossible to tell whether the better performance of the females is due to the lower level of motivation or to other factors characteristic of the female gender. The obvious solution to such problems is to assure comparability of the gender composition of the treated groups, to counterbalance the order in which different tasks are performed by various groups (so that the order of presentation of tasks alone could not confound differences produced by the tasks themselves), and so on.

Naturalistic observation is watching or observing phenomena or events without any effort to intervene or to manipulate those phenomena or events in any way. Thus, one could, for example, examine behavior at a stop sign by recording the drivers' compliance as well as the apparent age of the car (or of the driver), to see if there is any relationship between the independent variable (the age of the car or of the driver) and the dependent (degree of compliance). There is no *manipulation* of the independent variable, nor any control over driver motivation (such as the urgency of the driver's getting to the trip's destination), but it is still possible to observe whether there is any relationship between the two variables (though the *reasons* for any observed relationships would remain obscure).

Systematic assessment involves explicit probes intended to measure two or more variables and to determine whether there is a relationship between them. That is what most questionnaires and surveys aim to do. Are Republicans more likely to vote for support of the elderly than are Democrats? To answer that question, one has to measure two variables: political affiliation or preference, and attitude toward social support for the elderly. If a relationship *is* obtained, it is impossible to draw any conclusion about the cause-effect relationship: Which is the independent, which the dependent variable? Systematic assessment or survey research can establish whether two or more variables are related, but it cannot determine what is cause, and what is effect.

Manipulation of the independent variable can, however, establish whether that variable makes a difference in some dependent variable. This manipulation is the defining characteristic of a true experiment. In a *formal experiment,* the investigator decides the value of the independent variable for a given participant (such as a high level of anxiety, a moderate level of anxiety, or no anxiety), and then measures the value of the dependent variable (number of items answered correctly on a test) at each of the settings of the independent variable. As a consequence, if all other potentially relevant factors have been controlled, average differences in test scores measured in the study can indeed be attributed to the independent variable (levels of anxiety).

<table>
<tr><td>ACTIVITY</td></tr>
</table>

Designing a Research Study

Social psychologists have often studied the effects of competition. Think of a question about the effects of competition on learning that you would like to answer. Develop a hypothesis—your best guess as to the answer to your question. Write the hypothesis in operational terms (so it can be measured concretely). Design a research study that would test the hypothesis.

What research method will you use? What population will you study? Where will you find participants? How will you persuade them to take part? Are there ethical issues to be considered? What will you use for your control and experimental group(s)? How will you collect your data? How accurate is your measure? Is your research study valid? How do you know? Can your study be replicated?

Discuss designs with another student, exploring how each study might be improved. If possible, conduct your research study.

• • •

Could high school students be asked to design an experiment? What additional structure might this activity need to be useful with secondary students?

TEACHING HIGH SCHOOL PSYCHOLOGY

One of the beauties of teaching psychology is that psychological principles can be taught and modeled simultaneously. You will quickly recognize that it is impossible to cover all areas of psychology in one course—whether one or two semesters. The teacher must therefore have a clear view of the goals and objectives of teaching psychology to high school students. The motivated teacher may translate a high school psychology course into one of the most meaningful life experiences secondary students have. This section is designed to assist you in thinking about how to teach psychology effectively in the high school.

Introducing the Course

At the beginning of the semester, it may be useful to introduce the subject matter of psychology by presenting information from several of the vast number of subfields in psychology. To excite students about psychology, the teacher should select high-interest subjects.

Most students find social psychology engaging, and it is certainly replete with controversy, as the activity on page 86 demonstrated. The subfield of biopsychology is also apt to be captivating. Students typically enjoy learning about endorphins—the opiate-like chemicals that naturally occur in the brain, relieve pain, and induce a feeling of well-being. Other naturally occurring brain chemicals known as neurotransmitters provide equal fascination. Neurotransmitters are linked with mental illnesses, suicide, memory, mood, perception, and pain.

Many disorders are caused by an inadequate supply of neurotransmitters. Alzheimer's patients do not manufacture enough of the neurotransmitter acetylcholine. Students may enjoy debating whether brain cell transplants should be conducted to relieve patients of symptoms. Is it acceptable to take cells from aborted fetuses and transplant them into the tissue of needy adults?

The importance of attitude is illustrated by Rosenthal and Jacobson's studies on self-fulfilling prophecy. Students are likely to find these research findings interesting. Classroom teachers were told that some of their students were intellectually gifted, whereas others were identified as dull. Students were not informed of this labeling. At the end of the year, the students who had been designated (at random) as gifted had higher grades than those who were randomly labeled dull. These studies highlight the power of self-fulfilling prophecy (expectations influence the outcome of events).

The high school teacher might give background information on the study and ask students whether being labeled gifted or dull would affect students. How do teachers treat those they think are smart? Do teachers treat "smart" students differently from the way they treat "dull" students? What are the implications of such labeling? To what extent do people's perceptions of us influence what happens to us?

Clinical psychology is also interesting to many people. A teacher might introduce abnormal behavior by briefly explaining schizophrenia. The teacher might differentiate between schizophrenia and multiple personality. A discussion about whether mentally ill people should be held responsible for their behavior might follow. Should there be legal pleas of innocent by reason of insanity or guilty but mentally ill?

In choosing topics to open a psychology course, teachers should remember that active student involvement is important, as is setting the proper tone for a successful course.

<table>
<tr><td>ACTIVITY</td><td></td></tr>
</table>

Designing an Introductory Lesson

Choose a topic from psychology that you think would be interesting to secondary students. The topic should also be one that can be taught using an active approach and that provides an avenue for helping students understand the value of studying psychology. Create a lesson plan on the topic that will serve as an introduction to your course in psychology.

Teaching about the Nature of Psychology

An early focus in a psychology course could be the development of the discipline. Students who learn about the historical roots of psychology learn where it has come from and are apt to understand better where it is going.

Students can gain a variety of perspectives by understanding the various schools or theoretical orientations in psychology outlined earlier in the chapter. Understanding the philosophies of psychologists helps students realize that typically there is not only one definitive answer to a general question. Students must recognize that sciences, including psychology, do not have all of the answers. Even when there are answers, the answers are tentative, and some will turn out to be wrong. The key to theories is not whether they are right or wrong. Theories are significant if they are useful in advancing knowledge and provide a fresh perspective.

After students have learned about the origins and philosophies of psychology, it may be appropriate for them to study research methods and tools of psychology. Students should learn about the strengths and weaknesses of various research methods. A culminating experience for this unit might be having them design and conduct research studies of their own.

<table>
<tr><td>ACTIVITY</td><td></td></tr>
</table>

Analyzing How You Think

Think of an accomplishment of which you are proud. How did you sort through your memory store to find that accomplishment? What steps did you take while thinking? Did you visualize the situation? Did you hear things? Did you sort through emotions?

What is thinking? How do you think? Try to think about nothing for two minutes. What happens?

Teaching about Learning, Memory, and Cognition

An important area of study directly relevant to student experience is the study of learning and memory. What are thinking and learning? How does language influence them? Do bilingual people think differently when thinking in different languages? Do humans learn and think differently from other animals? How do we account for animals learning and using computers and sign language? Figure 5.4 presents an outline for considering these topics in a high school course.

Many students enjoy applying principles of learning and memory to their own lives. Ask how many of them understand classical conditioning. As they raise their hands to signify an understanding, you might point out that raising their hands is an example of conditioning. Ask students to provide other examples from their lives.

Classical and operant conditioning can overlap. This overlap becomes evident in a discussion of using "grounding" as a punishment. A teacher might ask students if grounding is an effective punishment. Typical responses on the part of students include "It just makes me mad if I'm grounded" or "If I'm grounded, I'll just sneak out anyway." Grounding may be ineffective if it relieves people of the responsibility for their behavior. It may signal children to become angry with their parents. Rather than weakening the likelihood that an undesirable behavior will occur, grounding may relieve the child of guilt and responsibility. The consequent emotional irritation can be discussed as an example of conditioning.

Behavior is characterized by regularities. Yet not all people understand how to meet other people's needs. In some cases people are more interested in controlling behavior than in motivating behavior. Consider the fictitious case of Erica's father:

Erica has a midnight curfew. The curfew is one of the ways her father attempts to control her behavior by using a kind of operant conditioning. If Erica is late, her designated punishment is being grounded. Punishment is intended to decrease the likelihood that a behavior will occur again. Erica came home late two Wednesdays ago. Her father told her that she was grounded. Erica was infuriated. Rather than feeling sorry for being late or guilty for worrying her father, Erica became angry. She associates grounding with her father's inflexibility. Every night since she has been grounded, Erica has left the house. Thus grounding was not a punishment for Erica—rather it increased the likelihood that her lateness will occur again.

Erica has a plan. The next time she is allowed to go out on a week night, she will borrow her father's car. She will drive around, running it out of gas. She will return home with an empty tank and wait to enter the house until five minutes before midnight. She intends to do this the night before her dad has a court case 25 miles away. When he expresses his irritation with her for leaving him in a bind, Erica plans to tell him smugly that she couldn't get gasoline because she couldn't break her curfew.

Learning and Memory

A. Defining learning

B. Types of learning
1. Classical conditioning
a. Process of classical conditioning
b. Ivan Pavlov and dogs
c. John Watson and emotional conditioning
d. Extinction, spontaneous recovery, systematic desensitization
2. Operant conditioning
a. Process of operant conditioning
b. Reinforcement and punishment
c. Types of reinforcers
d. Schedules of reinforcement

C. Obstacles to learning
1. Learned helplessness
2. Learned laziness
3. Learning disabilities and attention deficits

D. Memory
1. Information processing
2. Short-term and long-term memory
3. Retrieving information
a. Recall
b. Recognition
c. Relearning
d. Cue-dependent memory
e. Emotional and physical state–dependent memory
4. Steps to improve memory

Cognition

A. Units of thought
1. Image
2. Symbol
3. Concept
4. Rule

B. Kinds of thinking
1. Directed thinking
2. Nondirected thinking
3. Problem solving
4. Creativity

Figure 5.4   Course Outline: Learning, Memory, and Cognition

Cases like this can generate lively discussions. Students almost invariably find it interesting to consider how parents and teachers try to control their behavior. What a teacher views as punishment (being expelled from class for the day) may actually function as reinforcement. Operant and classical conditioning typically generate much student interest. Test anxiety, incidentally, can serve as a good illustration of classical conditioning.

People sometimes learn important ideas or strategies that have a significant negative impact on their lives. Such is the case of learned helplessness. Learned helplessness, as mentioned earlier, is a state that exists when individuals believe they cannot control their destiny, so they give up trying. Learned helplessness is important because it influences self-esteem, motivation, confidence, stress levels, success, and health. The ways in which people evaluate themselves can dramatically influence their emotional responses and future behavior. When students study learned helplessness and attribution theory, they learn important principles of psychology they can apply to themselves.

Think of a time when you did poorly on a midterm or final exam. If you have never done poorly, think of a time when a friend or an acquaintance did poorly and pretend you are that person. Why was the performance poor? Where a person places credit or blame for what happens in life is called attribution. To what can a person attribute failure on an exam? In general, failure (or success) can be attributed to one of four causes: ability, effort, task difficulty, or luck (fate).

Specific reasons for failing a test might be that you didn't study, it tested the wrong things, the teacher can't teach, you are stupid, or the test was unfair. These attributions fit into one of the aforementioned categories. They can also be classified according to locus of control (whether the control over what happens is internal or lies outside the person). Ability and effort are internal, whereas task difficulty and luck (fate) are external.

Researchers have further categorized these behavior determinants according to stability (whether they remain fixed or can change). Ability and task difficulty are stable. Effort and luck (fate) are unstable. If people attribute their failures to internal stable factors, the likelihood of failure increases. If they attribute failure to their abilities, they will expect to fail again in the future.

Helplessness can be seen as universal (individuals believe that anyone would have difficulty in a particular situation) or personal (individuals believe they cannot solve problems that others can solve). Additionally, helplessness can be categorized as global (will occur in many situations) or specific (is limited to specific situations).

Research indicates that girls are more apt to attribute helplessness to a lack of ability, whereas boys tend to attribute it to a lack of effort. Of particular potential utility is the finding that people who seem likely to develop helplessness can be "immunized" against it by learning to attribute success and failure differently: Success is due to their ability and effort, and failure is due to chance or inherent task difficulty.

Students of learning theory acquire principles that will assist them with daily living. Likewise, understanding principles of memory helps people develop strategies to improve their memories. Much of what we remember did not happen as we recall it. Memory is a constructive process that is influenced by values, attitudes, judgments, expectations, hopes, and past experiences. Our perceptions shape our memories. Additionally, we all have the tendency to confabulate (fill in memories with things that aren't true).

Short-term memory typically lasts only a few seconds. People can hold only about seven pieces of information in their short-term memories. Teachers can illustrate these points by having students learn a list of words. People who try to learn auditorily will limit their retention to about seven items. The list must be rehearsed to keep it in short-term memory. If people wish to increase the capacity of short-term memory, they can use chunking (grouping pieces of information together into larger units).

After a while, information can be transmitted from short-term memory to long-term memory. The process is not fully understood. The laying down of permanent memories ("consolidation" or "elaborative processing") takes a number of hours. For that reason, it is often efficient to study difficult material before going to sleep at night. That way, consolidation takes place during sleep, when competing information is less likely to replace the information which we wish to commit to memory.

Using mnemonic devices (learning strategies that involve mental associations) helps to improve memory. Memory is also improved when people use more than one learning modality: visual (viewing things or reading), auditory (hearing), and kinesthetic (doing or feeling). Students who use all three modalities store information in more ways than students who use only one modality.

An interesting learning and memory demonstration involves intentional and incidental learning. The psychology teacher requests six volunteers to learn a list of twenty words in front of the class. The class is instructed (while the six learners are in the hall) to note the facial expressions and gestures learners use while trying to commit words to memory. The six learners go to the front of the class. They remind the class of their names so that students can take notes on learning techniques.

The teacher reads twenty words, pronouncing each word twice. When the list is complete, *all* students in the class are asked to write the words on paper (they need not be in order). Students will be surprised at the amount of incidental learning that took place. Interestingly, students often recall seven words without trying very hard. The six learners will typically remember more than that, showing that the intent to learn is a powerful determinant of the amount retained.

A discussion of learning strategies could follow. Chunking and mnemonic devices are worth looking at closely. Students who remember the most words will probably have made up stories to link the various words together. Students will also probably report that they were not able just to repeat the words and remember them. After about seven words, they probably became confused and tried to adjust their learning strategies.

Cues in the environment influence learning and recall as well. A primary reason for forgetting is that people do not have access to information that is actually stored in their memories. Cues can be developed to assist people in recalling information.

Reflecting on Learned Helplessness as a Teacher

When students do poorly on a test, the teacher must also analyze that failure. How will you analyze such failures in a way that will lead to improved performance? How can you avoid learned helplessness, on your students' part and your own? Write your thoughts about this issue in your journal.

Teaching about Personality and Social Psychology

Learning theory helps explain the process of acquiring new behaviors and thoughts. The entire life span consists of learning stages that help people cope with the changing challenges that life entails. Developmental psychology examines ages and stages of growth; it traces the development and change of an individual from before birth until death.

Development and personality theory have interesting implications for human behavior. (See Figure 5.5.) The famous behaviorist John Watson claimed that he could mold a child to be anything—doctor, lawyer, thief. Can people mold their children using conditioning principles? Other psychologists stress the importance of biology over conditioning. Many physical and psychological problems result from faulty genes. We have the technology to use genetic engineering to alter genes and replace missing enzymes. Should we use genetic engineering to alter people, thus avoiding or solving problems? Such issues pose interesting questions. When does life begin? When does mind begin? Such questions may seem to fall in the realm of philosophy. Yet insurance companies want definitive answers—to determine when they are responsible for paying prenatal bills.

When teaching developmental and personality theories, teachers can take advantage of small-group discussion and role-playing techniques. Sometimes, students enjoy preparing and giving class presentations on the various developmental and personality theories. Further, to help students learn about stages of development, one could prepare a number of statements that correspond with stages of development and have students decide what stage of development each statement reflects. Encourage students to evaluate the theories they are studying. Are the theories useful? Do they seem to be accurate? This realm provides an excellent opportunity to pursue topics that interest students and do not necessarily fit elsewhere—giftedness, prejudice, aggression, resilience, and coping strategies in the context of personality.

Social psychology may be discussed together with personality, or it may be studied independently. Certainly, in a yearlong course, plenty of attention may be given to social psychology, particularly if it is not studied in sociology. Many excellent

Personality

A.   Development
    1.   Attachment
    2.   Stage theories
        a.   Psychosexual—Freud
        b.   Psychosocial—Erikson
        c.   Cognitive—Piaget
        d.   Moral—Kohlberg and Gilligan
    3.   Life-span development
    4.   Gerontology

B.   Socialization and sociocultural context

C.   Adjustment, self-esteem, anxiety

D.   Role theory

E.   Theories of personality
    1.   Trait
    2.   Psychoanalytic
    3.   Social psychoanalytic
    4.   Behaviorist (learning)
    5.   Humanist

F.   Introversion and extroversion

G.   Gender differences, roles and norms

Social Psychology

A.   The person in the social environment

B.   Social perception

C.   Attitude formation and change

D.   Social behavior
    1.   Conformity
    2.   Roles
    3.   Prejudice, labeling, stereotyping
    4.   Relationships and attraction
    5.   Aggressions and violence
    6.   Gender roles

E.   Cultural diversity and intercultural relations

Figure 5.5   Course Outline: Personality and Social Psychology

classroom activities included in the three volumes of the American Psychological Association's *Activities Handbook for the Teaching of Psychology* are relevant to these topics.

Teaching about the Brain and States of Consciousness

More has been learned about the brain since the mid-1960s than in the previous history of humanity combined. Technology is helping increase knowledge about the brain and behavior at a remarkable pace. The key to successful coverage of this area is apt to be enthusiasm on the part of the teacher. (See Figure 5.6.) The teacher could make use of high-interest print materials, such as *The Three Pound Universe* (Hopper and Teresi 1986), that supply anecdotes likely to be intriguing for students. Students typically enjoy learning about endorphins, split-brain research, electrical stimulation of the brain, frontal lobotomy, psychosurgery, multiple personalities, and the brain profile of people with various mental illnesses.

The Brain and Behavior

A. Communication in the brain
   1. Neurons and glial cells
   2. Parts of neurons
   3. Electrical and chemical messages
B. Geography of the brain
   1. Studying the brain
      a. Lesions
      b. Stimulations
      c. Recording
      d. EEG and PET
   2. Two hemispheres
      a. Split-brain research
      b. Major brain features
      c. Specialization in the brain
   3. Differences between brains of males and females
C. Mind–body interaction
   1. The placebo effect
   2. Pain
   3. Psychosomatic and somatopsychic disorders

Altered States of Consciousness

A. Sleep and dreams
B. Hypnosis
C. Drug states
D. Biofeedback
E. Meditation

Figure 5.6   Course Outline: The Brain and States of Consciousness

The study of the brain and behavior is difficult for some students. Their learning becomes more worthwhile if they can apply the new information to a study of material that is intrinsically interesting to them. For that reason, it is often motivating to go on to the topic of altered states of consciousness after discussing the brain. Students are almost universally interested in learning about sleep and dreams, hypnosis, and drug states. When planning teaching materials on altered states of consciousness, it is sensible to check with the health curriculum and teachers in an attempt to minimize curriculum overlap or inconsistency.

Teaching about Psychological Testing and Psychopathology

Two topics that tend to generate almost universal student interest are psychological testing and clinical psychology or psychopathology. (See Figure 5.7.) Psychological testing is particularly relevant to student experience. Students take numerous tests and may find an understanding of the dynamics of testing particularly useful.

Much information about testing can easily be learned independently. Take the case of intelligence testing. The teacher might ask the students to form groups and

---

Psychological Testing

A. Characteristics of tests
B. Intelligence tests
C. Personality tests
D. Assessing abilities and interests
E. Ethics of psychological testing
F. Test-taking strategies
G. Test reliability and test validity

Psychopathology

A. Meaning of "normal" and "abnormal"
B. Defining mental disorders
C. DSM III R
D. Biological and psychological components of mental disorder
E. Intervention
    1. Types of psychotherapy (psychodynamic, behavioral, cognitive, humanistic)
    2. Psychopharmacology
    3. Electroconvulsive therapy
    4. Psychosurgery
    5. The effectiveness of intervention

Figure 5.7 Course Outline: Psychological Testing and Psychopathology

define the various forms of intelligence, including their components. For homework, students might read their text or other print material to learn about intelligence and intelligence testing. Students might then take the Dove Counterbalance IQ Test. This test, written by social scientist Adrian Dove, stresses the influence of culture on intelligence-test performance. People of certain cultural backgrounds would do well on Dove's test, and others would get low scores. The test includes questions about "handkerchief head," chitlings, and so on. Use of this test can highlight the fact that test items are embedded within a particular sociocultural context and that it is inherently impossible to generate any genuinely "culture-free" tests or test items.

The construction of tests of individual differences has become a highly technical field, concentrated especially on efforts to assure test reliability and test validity. Yet most teachers construct tests and quizzes for their classes without a thorough grounding in this technical field. What consequences might that have for the validity of the grades they assign their students?

Most people have taken several achievement and aptitude tests throughout their lives. Many have taken interest inventories. Fewer take personality tests. Should employers be allowed to require personality tests for analysis as a criterion for employment? Are SAT scores a good criterion for determining who should be accepted to a college?

When considering personality, the issue of normality becomes particularly important. What is normal? Is it that which most people do? What is abnormality? Does normality transcend cultural or ethnic boundaries? Or is normality inevitably related to a particular sociocultural context?

It has been estimated that from 5 to 20 percent of the U.S. population suffers from mental disorders, but diagnosis of mental illness is not always reliable. It is difficult to know precisely the extent of the incidence of mental illness. Many people who suffer from psychopathologies are undiagnosed and untreated, and some who are reasonably healthy are misdiagnosed as mentally ill.

When teaching psychopathology, it is important to be aware that many students will be inclined to think about various symptoms and say, "Hey, that sounds like me." Explain to students that such identification is typical and usually entirely unfounded. Medical students tend to identify with various symptoms and diseases they study as well.

Students should understand that the differences between normal and abnormal are not always clear-cut. Diagnostic categories are useful, but they also have their drawbacks. Labeling can lead to unfair treatment and self-fulfilling prophecy. Furthermore, psychiatry is not an exact science. Psychologists and psychiatrists are subject to human error. Errors in diagnosis of psychopathology are not uncommon.

Students studying various psychopathologies should be aware of the complex role of the mind and the brain in producing mental illness. Some mental disorders are predominantly biological. Freud recognized that when he asserted that psychoanalysis is not very useful for schizophrenic patients. Students can become increasingly sensitive to people who are different from them.

The two basic kinds of treatment of mental disorders are psychological therapy and biological therapy. Antipsychotic drugs have proven to be effective and useful in controlling some of the symptoms of some psychotic and some depressive disorders. Such drug therapy revolutionized the treatment of the mentally ill and led to a deinstitutionalization movement. Society has not, though, developed and maintained widespread successful programs for the deinstitutionalized mentally ill. Various programs and community mental health centers have developed around the country. Nevertheless, the United States does not care adequately for its mentally ill. As a result, society is faced with some fascinating questions. Should mentally ill people be forced to have treatment against their will? Who is to decide who would benefit from biological intervention? Another question has to do with psychotherapy: How effective is it? How might one go about finding out how effective it really is?

ACTIVITY

Preparing a Course Outline

Compare the suggested course outline provided in the previous section with the tables of contents of several psychology texts. How are they alike? different? Given what you believe to be the purposes of teaching psychology to secondary students, what are the strengths and weaknesses of each outline?

Use the various outlines to create your own outline for a semester-long psychology course. Provide an explanation of your reasoning in selecting unit topics and ordering the units. Also describe how you would evaluate student learning.

Reflecting on the Chapter

What should be the role of knowledge generated by psychologists in the preservice education of teachers? Do you think your understanding of psychology is adequate? Why or why not? In what areas would more information be useful?

References

Bandura, A. *Social Learning Theory.* Englewood Cliffs, N.J.: Prentice Hall, 1977.

Benjamin, L. T., and K. D. Lowman, eds. *Activities Handbook for the Teaching of Psychology.* Vol. 1. Washington, D.C.: American Psychological Association, 1981.

Diagnostic and Statistical Manual of Mental Disorders. 3rd ed., rev. Washington, D.C.: American Psychiatric Association, 1987.

Dove, A. "Taking the Chitling Test." *Newsweek,* July 15, 1968, 51–52.

Giorgi, A. "Toward the Articulation of Psychology as a Coherent Discipline." Reprinted in *A Century of Psychology as Science,* ed. S. Koch and D. E. Leary. New York: McGraw-Hill, 1985.

Hollingworth, L. S. "Comparison of the Genes in Mental Traits." *Psychological Bulletin* 15 (1918): 427–432.

Hopper, J. and D. Teresi. *Three Pound Universe*. New York: Dell Publishing, 1986. Videotapes.

MacLeod, R. B. *The Persistent Problems of Psychology*. Pittsburgh: Duquesne University Press, 1975.

Makowsky, V. P., et al. eds. *Activities Handbook for the Teaching of Psychology*. Vol. 2. Washington, D.C.: American Psychological Association, 1987.

————. *Activities Handbook for the Teaching of Psychology*. Vol. 3. Washington, D.C.: American Psychological Association, 1990.

Milgram, S. *Obedience to Authority*. New York: Harper & Row, 1964.

Rosenthal, R. and L. F. Jacobson. *Pygmalion in the Classroom: Teacher Expectation and Pupils' Intellectual Development*. New York: Holt, Rinehart & Winston, 1968.

Seligman, M. E. P. *Helplessness: On Depression, Development, and Death*. San Francisco: W. H. Freeman, 1975.

Seligman, M. E. P., et al. "Attributional Style and Depressive Symptoms among Children." *Journal of Abnormal Psychology* 93, no. 2 (1984): 235–238.

Weiss, M. *Double Play: The San Francisco City Hall Killings*. Reading, Mass.: Addison-Wesley, 1984.

Wronski, S. P. and D. H. Bragaw, eds. *Social Studies and Social Sciences: A Fifty-Year Perspective*. Washington, D.C.: National Council for the Social Studies, 1986.

Zimbardo, P. G. "The Mind Is a Formidable Jailer: A Pirandellian Prison." *New York Times*, April 8, 1973, 38.

Teaching Resources

American Psychological Association, Inc. (750 First Street NE, Washington, DC 20002-4242). Publishes many journals, including *American Psychologist* and *The Psychology Teacher Network*; clearinghouse for psychology materials; also curriculum materials, projects, special-interest groups.

Benjamin, L. T. and K. D. Lowman, eds. *Activities Handbook for the Teaching of Psychology*. Vol. 1. Washington, D.C.: American Psychological Association, 1981.

Brain, The. South Burlington, Vt.: The Annenberg/CPC Collection, 1984. 8 videotapes or videodisc; teacher's guide and study guide available.

Brown, F. and D. A. Conforti. *Advanced Placement Psychology: A Practical Guide for Teachers*. New Bedford, Mass.: DAC Educational Publications, 1991.

Cameron, S. M. and P. D. Barsky. *Teacher's Guide to Advanced Placement Course in Psychology*. New York: College Entrance Examination Board, 1990.

Careers in Psychology. Washington, D.C.: American Psychological Association, 1993.

Checklist for a New Course in Psychology. Washington, D.C.: American Psychological Association, 1985.

Conforti, A. *Ten Short Research Reports for A.P. Psychology*. New Bedford, Mass.: DAC Educational Publications, 1991.

Discovering Psychology. South Burlington, Vt.: The Annenberg/CPC Collection, 1990. 26 videotaped programs; teacher's guide and study guide available.

Goldberg, E. *Discovering Psychology Study Guide*. New York: Holt, Rinehart & Winston, 1989.

Greenstone, J. L. *The Curriculum Guide: High School Psychology*. Bloomington: ERIC Clearinghouse for Social Studies/Social Science Education, University of Indiana, 1975.

In-service Training Guidelines for Secondary School Teachers of Psychology. Washington, D.C.: American Psychological Association, 1981.

Johnson, M. and M. Wertheimer, eds. *Psychology Teacher's Resource Book: First Course.* 3rd ed. Washington, D.C.: American Psychological Association, 1979.

Makowsky, V.P. et al., eds. *Activities Handbook for the Teaching of Psychology.* Vol. 2. Washington, D.C.: American Psychological Association, 1987.

————. *Activities Handbook for the Teaching of Psychology:.* Vol. 3. Washington, D.C.: American Psychological Association, 1990.

Mind, The. Alexandria, Va.: PBS Video, 1988. 9 videos.

Psych Lab. Pleasantville, N.Y.: Human Relations Media, 1987. Computer program.

Psychology 94/95: Annual Editions Series. Guilford, Conn.: Dushkin, 1994. Teacher guide available.

Reference Sheet on Psychology and Sociology. Bloomington: ERIC Clearinghouse for Social Studies/Social Science Education, University of Indiana, 1982.

Restak, M. *The Brain.* New York: Bantam, 1984.

Slife, B. and J. Rubinstein. *Taking Sides: Clashing Views on Controversial Psychological Issues.* 7th ed. Guilford, Conn.: Dushkin, 1992.

Vattano, F. J. *Faculty Guide: General Psychology Teaching Modules.* 2 vols. New York: Worth, 1988, 1990.

World of Abnormal Psychology, The. South Burlington, Vt.: The Annenberg/CPC Collection, 1992. 13 videotaped programs; teacher's guide and study guide available.

STUDYING AND
TEACHING SOCIOLOGY

J. Ross Eshleman and John P. Zola

Describing Sociology

Before reading this chapter, use the following process to determine your current level of understanding of the discipline of sociology.

1. Spend a maximum of three minutes writing a brief description of what a sociologist studies.

2. Join with a partner and spend five minutes combining your thinking and writing one description of the role of sociology as a social science discipline.

3. As a class, compare and discuss your descriptions. What are the critical elements of the descriptions? In what ways are they similar and different?

4. Reflect on your class discussion and then post a list of questions about sociology that you hope this chapter will address.

INTRODUCTION

Are you in favor of peace over war, equality over inequality, justice over injustice, and knowledge over ignorance? Assuming most of us would agree in favoring peace, equality, justice, and knowing, why do we find

- War and the stockpiling of weapons for war?
- Inequality between the sexes, the races, and social classes?
- Injustices in arrests, convictions, and punishments?
- Illiteracy in all societies and among all age groups?

Sociologists contend that if answers to such serious questions exist, they will be found at levels beyond individual views and experiences. They will be found by seeing the general in the particular, by seeing the strange in the familiar, and by depersonalizing the personal. What this sociological perspective means is that the behavior of people is patterned and organized. Your personal interests and behaviors, although seemingly unique, are widely shared and influenced by others in the groups and the society in which you exist. It means that social forces act on everyone, making our individual lives far less distinctive than we may imagine.

The nature of sociology is to study social life and the social causes and consequences of human behavior. "Social life" encompasses all interpersonal relationships, all groups or collectives of people, and all types of social organizations. The "causes and consequences of human behavior" encompass how those relationships, groups, and organizations are interrelated; how they influence personal and interpersonal behavior; how they affect and are affected by the larger society; how they change or why they remain static; and what their consequences are. This definition reflects the belief that people can be understood only in the context of their contacts, associations, and communications with other people.

In this chapter, we first examine three areas sociology investigates and the principal orientations (theories) used to focus those investigations. We then turn to the methodology that sociologists use. The chapter ends with a more in-depth examination of selected issues and topics sociologists study. Because only a small proportion of social studies teachers will have the opportunity to teach an elective sociology course, the sociological perspective on issues covered in a wide range of courses may be the discipline's most important contribution to your preparation as a teacher.

SOCIAL INTERACTION AND SYMBOLIC INTERACTION

Social Interaction and Socialization

Sociology looks at the interactions of people, including how they are socialized—that is, how they learn the rules of society, how they learn to live with other people, and how they learn what behaviors are rewarded or punished. Socialization is thus a lifelong process of social interaction.

Is social interaction necessary? Humans are born with the muscles, bones, vital organs, and other biological parts needed to live. Otherwise, they are utterly helpless and cannot survive without human interaction. Babies not only need food and warmth to survive physically, but also need physical stimulation to grow. When they are handled physically by an adult, they are stimulated by touch, tones of voice, and facial expressions, which make them aware of their environment and stimulate them to respond to it. Observations of infants who were comparatively isolated from human contact have shown that lack of social interaction can have serious consequences.

Just how serious lack of social interaction can be was seen in a classic study by Rene Spitz in the 1940s. Spitz (1946) observed children who had apparently been healthy when they were born and who had been living in a foundling home for two years. Nutrition, clothing, bedding, and room temperature in the home were suitable, and every child was seen by a physician weekly. A small staff took care of the physical needs of the children, but other interaction was very limited. Despite their excellent physical care, 34 percent of the ninety-one children in the home died within two years of the study, and twenty-one others showed slow physical and social development.

Spitz compared these children with infants brought up in another institution, where their mothers were being held for delinquency. Physical care was basically the same as in the foundling home, but the mothers enjoyed playing with their children for hours. The infants received a great deal of social stimulation, and their development was normal. Spitz concluded that the difference was the amount of attention the children received, illustrating the crucial importance of social interaction.

Is your socialization complete? If socialization occurs in interaction with others, as long as you interact with parents, siblings, teachers, and friends, or read newspapers and watch TV, your socialization is a lifelong process. Who you are, the language you speak, the sports, music, and dances you enjoy, and the people you like

| **Figure 6.1** | Describe the socialization that is occurring in this scene. |

or dislike are not in-born or "natural" but are products or consequences of your interaction patterns and socializing experiences. Perhaps you are not convinced that you are primarily a product of your interaction and socializing experiences but believe your biological makeup and genetic inheritance are what makes you what you are. This issue is sometimes framed in terms of nature (inherited—biological) versus nurture (learned—in interaction and socialization). Today, the accepted view is that genetic inheritance and learned abilities combine in very complex patterns. Neither nature nor nurture is a sufficient explanation by itself.

Symbolic Interaction Perspective

The approach most widely used in sociology to investigate the topics of social interaction and socialization is *symbolic interaction*. Symbolic interaction directs our attention to the details of everyday life and the interaction between individuals. The approach was introduced to sociology in the 1920s by George Herbert Mead (1863–1931), an American philosopher who emphasized how people assign meanings to each other's words and actions. The perspective implies that (1) people do not respond directly to physical "things" but, rather, to their own interpretations of them; and (2) because people constantly make interpretations—of the world in general, of other people, of themselves—and then act according to those interpretations, human behavior is always changing. How we act is constantly being altered by how we interpret other people's actions and their reactions to our own behavior.

Symbolic interactionists therefore pay very close attention to what people do; they try to determine what meaning people are giving to their own actions and to those of others. Looking at drug use, for example, symbolic interactionists focus far less on *why* people use drugs than on *how* drug use exists and the meanings it has for the persons involved. That is, they study the interactions between users or between users and suppliers, examining how the users and the suppliers define or interpret their behaviors. What happens at the symbolic level is of central concern.

Perhaps the "symbolic level" can be explained this way. Suppose you are driving down the road and come upon a brick wall running across the road. You stop, of course, because you have learned you cannot pass through a physical object. If, however, you perceive the brick wall to be a mental picture, a mirage, you won't "of course" stop. Or suppose you come to a stoplight. Once again you stop—but why? There is nothing physical to keep you from progressing. Your reason for stopping is that you have learned that the red light is a *symbol* that means stop. The world around us can be said to consist of these two elements: physical objects and abstract symbols. Language is a system of symbols. It serves to represent physical objects as well as to communicate ideas (abstract symbols).

It is humans' ability to use symbols that sets us apart from animals and allows us to create social institutions, societies, and cultures. People in a society share an understanding of certain symbols (the stoplight, for example). In interactions, we learn to share meanings and to communicate symbolically through words and gestures. As humans, we can interact at both a physical (a slap) and a symbolic level (showing a fist or making a verbal threat). The fact that others share similar expectations makes life patterned and relatively predictable.

The interactionist perspective examines patterns and processes of everyday life that are generally ignored by macrosociological perspectives. It raises questions about the self, the self in relationships with others, and the self and others in the wider social context. Why do some of us have negative feelings about ourselves? Why can we relate more easily with some people than with others? Symbolic interactionists try to address such questions by examining the social setting in which an individual is born and the interactions he or she has with parents, siblings, teachers, neighbors, and others. From those interactions, we learn what is proper or improper, whether we are "good" or "bad," who is important, and so forth.

ACTIVITY

Identifying Symbolic Hand Gestures

Working in small groups, brainstorm a list of uses of the hands to convey information symbolically. Examples might include clapping of hands, and the "V" for victory.

Next, create a "retrieval chart" with the six columns shown here:

Gesture	Origin	Meaning(s)	Gender Differences	Cultural Differences	Consequences of Misinterpretation

From the brainstormed list of gestures, select four you find interesting and write them in the first column. As a group, complete the retrieval chart.

Compare information from the charts as a class. Questions to discuss might include the following:

- How are these gestures learned?
- What might be the potential impact of not knowing appropriate gestures, or using the wrong gestures, when in a cross-cultural situation?
- Of what practical value are gestures as means of symbolic communication?

Conclude the activity by listing generalizations on the relative power and role of these and other types of symbolic representations in human interactions.

• • •

Into what secondary social studies classes might this activity fit? What objectives would it help you achieve? How would you adapt it for use with secondary students?

SOCIAL GROUPS AND SOCIAL CONFLICT

Social Groups

As just shown, humans are social beings. Even those of us who think of ourselves as loners participate in many groups, and, for most of us, groups are a great source of satisfaction. You may eat with a certain group of friends every day, belong to a drama club, or play tennis every week with your gym class. You probably depend on social groups for most of your psychological and physical needs. Social groups are generally viewed as a collection of people who share some characteristics, interact with one another, and have some feeling of unity.

Social groups vary widely in their size, purpose, and structure. Some are short-lived, such as a group that gathers at the scene of an accident. Others, such as family groups, last a lifetime. Membership in one type does not preclude membership in other types; in fact, it is not unusual for a single group to fall into several categories.

Perhaps the most fundamental distinction is that made between primary and secondary groups. The term *primary group* refers to small, informal groups of people who interact in a personal, direct, and intimate way. Primary groups involve intimate face-to-face association and interaction, and their members have a sense of "we-ness" involving mutual identification and shared feelings. For most of us, our family is our number one primary group, followed by our friendship and peer groups. We have a strong sense of loyalty to these groups that is based on tradition and personal feelings.

In contrast, a *secondary group* is a group whose members interact in an impersonal manner, have few emotional ties, and come together for a specific practical purpose. Like primary groups, they are usually small and involve face-to-face contacts. Although the interactions may be cordial or friendly, they are more formal than primary-group interactions. However, they are of equal importance. Most of our time is spent in secondary groups—committees, classrooms, or neighborhood groups. The key difference between the two is in the quality of the relationships and the extent of personal intimacy and involvement. Primary groups are person-oriented, whereas secondary groups tend to be task- or goal-oriented.

One of the key characteristics of a group is the members' sense of belonging. Those who belong think of one another as forming a social unit. This unit has boundaries that separate "us" from "them," that differentiate those who are "in" from those who are "out." An *in-group* is one in which people feel they belong. They feel they share a common fate, adhere to a common ideology, come from a common background, or otherwise resemble the other members. Conversely, an *out-group* is one to which people feel they do not belong. If you are a member of the in-group, the out-group is everyone else. It is made up of those who do not share an awareness of kind. We do not identify or affiliate ourselves with members of out-groups, and we feel little allegiance to them.

The difference between in- and out-groups is sociologically important for several reasons. First, the in-group tends to stereotype members of the out-group. Although we may notice individual differences among members of the in-group, most of us notice only similarities in the out-group, and we label them accordingly.

Primary Groups	*Secondary Groups*
• Family	• Speech class
• Friends	• Chess club
• Couple	• Political party
• Gang	• Coworkers
•	•
•	•
Can you think of other examples?	

Figure 6.2   Primary and secondary groups

Within the United States, whites (in-group) may label blacks (out-group) as lazy, and blacks (in-group) may label whites (out-group) as racist. A second reason that the two groups are important is that any threat or attack, whether imaginary or real, from the out-group tends to increase the cohesion and solidarity of the in-group. When U.S. citizens are captured and held hostage by terrorists, for example, ideological and political differences among Americans often fall by the wayside.

One type of group from which in- and out-groups draw their members is the *peer group*. A peer group is an informal primary group of people who share a similar status and usually are of similar age. One unique factor in peer groups is their equality. Although leaders emerge and certain members may have more prestige than others, peer groups share similar life experiences. With peers, we can validate our self-concepts with others who share common concerns. Here we learn social roles and values that adults cannot or will not teach—such as sexual behaviors or weekend partying.

Reference groups are the groups we identify with psychologically. They, like peers, serve as sources of self-evaluation and influence how we think and act and what we believe. A grade of B, for example, may be a source of pride to students if their peer reference group did worse, but it may be a source of disappointment to a family reference group if they expected an A.

The size of a group has a dramatic effect on member interactions. The smallest group, called a *dyad,* consists of two people. When just two people are involved, each has a special responsibility to interact—if one person withdraws, the group no longer exists. With the addition of a third person, the dyad becomes a *triad* and the interactions change drastically. With increasing size, it may be more difficult to choose a leader, arrive at an agreement or a consensus, or decide who will perform certain tasks.

Several other characteristics change with increasing size. First, as size increases, so does the division of labor. If the group is small, all the members may engage in the same activities. As size increases, however, activities tend to become specialized. Second, as the size of a group increases, its structure becomes more rigid and formal. Whereas small groups are likely to operate informally according to unwritten rules, large groups usually conduct meetings in accordance with Robert's Rules of Order or some other standard formula. Third, as the size of a group increases, so does the need for a more formal type of leadership.

Fourth, as the size of a group increases, communication patterns change. In large groups, the leaders tend to dominate the discussions. They talk the most and are addressed the most, since the comments of other members are directed at them. In small groups the members are more likely to address one another. And fifth, as size increases, cohesion decreases. A group is considered cohesive when members interact frequently, when they talk of "we," when they work together to achieve common goals, and when they are willing to give up personal preferences in favor of those of the group.

Groups in the High School

Write a first-person description of your own experiences as a high school student with any of the following: primary and secondary groups, in- and out-groups, peer groups, or reference groups. Discuss the values and behaviors that made these groups cohesive units. Also describe the size of these groups and the relative importance attached to membership in them.

Form small groups to compare your experiences with different groups while you were high school students.

• • •

Compare your own experiences in high school with what you are now observing in high schools as prospective teachers. What similarities and differences do you see? In what ways do the concepts of primary/secondary groups, in-/out-groups, peer groups, and reference groups help you to better understand the social lives of the students you will be teaching? In what ways would your descriptions of these groups differ from descriptions written by current high school students?

Social Conflict Perspective

Social groups are commonly investigated from the perspective of *social conflict* theory. The social conflict perspective originated largely from the writings of Karl Marx. His work sensitized sociologists to the existence of inequalities in the amount of power and resources held by participants in any social group or system, from education to entire societies. Marx believed that in a capitalist society the holders of the means of production have more resources and power than do the workers. These opposing groups of owners and workers, those who dominate and those who are dominated, are thus engaged in a continuous struggle over scarce resources. As a result, inequality, competition, and conflict are at the heart of all social relationships and are characteristic of all social structures. This conflict brings about change that is often abrupt and revolutionary rather than gradual and evolutionary.

Conflicts in contemporary society are assumed to involve a broad range of groups or interests: young against old, male against female, one racial group against another, as well as workers against employers. These conflicts result because things like power, wealth, and prestige are not equally available to everyone. Conflict theory also assumes that those who have or control desirable goods and services will defend and protect their own interests at the expense of others.

In this view, conflict does not mean the sort of event that makes headlines. It is instead the struggle that occurs day after day as people try to maintain and improve their positions in life. Neither should conflict be regarded as a destructive process that leads to the breakdown of society. Some writers have focused on the integrative nature of conflict, its value as a force that contributes to order and stability.

How can conflict be constructive? One possible answer is by stimulating people with common interests to join together to seek gains that will benefit them all. By the same token, conflict among groups focuses attention on inequalities and social problems that might never be resolved without conflict. Racial conflicts, for example, may bind people with common interests together and lead to constructive social change.

<table>
<tr><td>ACTIVITY</td></tr>
</table>

Conflict Posters

Using a piece of poster paper and markers or crayons, draw a picture of what you think is a significant conflict. Post your picture when completed.

Circulate around the room and note on a piece of paper the following data: the picture you think portrays the most important conflict, the picture you think portrays the least important conflict, and the causes of conflict portrayed in the various pictures. Note those conflicts that are specific to the school environment.

Discuss the relative importance of the various conflicts portrayed. Next, consider the following causes of conflict: values, misperceptions, tension between unlimited wants and limited resources, the quest for power. Which pictures portray each of these causes? Which cause is most relevant to school-based conflicts? Conflicts can be intrapersonal, interpersonal, intergroup, or international in nature. Which pictures illustrate each of these types of conflict?

Conclude the activity by discussing how conflict can be viewed as a constructive force. If conflict is, in fact, constructive, why is it so often avoided?

• • •

Spend a moment considering ways of using this activity in a secondary classroom.

SOCIAL SYSTEMS AND STRUCTURAL FUNCTIONALISM

Statuses, Roles, and Social Systems

Social systems, unlike social groups, are abstractions composed of interrelated statuses. *Status*, a central concept within sociology, refers to socially defined positions: female, student, lawyer, Buddhist. Some of these are *ascribed statuses*, that is, given to us at birth (age, sex, race), whereas others are *achieved statuses* (high school graduate, father, teacher). All of these statuses have expectations for behavior (roles) associated with them.

Statuses (positions), roles (expectations for behavior), and social systems (interrelated statuses) exist independently of you or me as individuals. Through the process of socialization, we obtain ideas or expectations for the behavior of teachers, for example, even if we are not teachers. If our teachers do not conform to those expectations, we may define them as eccentric, strange, or even deviant. Our expectations may shift as we add other statuses to the position: female teacher; young female teacher; young female chemistry teacher; young, Hispanic, female, unmarried chemistry teacher. To know one's status set (the combination of multiple statuses we or others occupy) enables us to become increasingly aware of our own behaviors—what we do or don't do that is acceptable or unacceptable—as well as to predict what others will do.

At a societal level, we can note statuses that are interrelated and study a given social system. A marital system, for example, is made up of the statuses of husbands and wives. A school system includes the interrelated statuses of administrators, teachers, and students, who may be further classified by the status of freshman or senior. Social systems, like family systems, political systems, military systems, or medical care systems, are said to provide certain functions or tasks that enable society and the people who make up that society to exist. The educational system, for example, is intended to provide literacy and technical skills.

ACTIVITY

Analyzing the Teacher Status

On a sheet of paper, list ten role expectations for the position (i.e., status) of social studies teacher. Once this list is complete, put a "+" beside those expectations you support and/or are looking forward to assuming and a "−" beside those you question and/or are not looking forward to assuming. Reflecting on this list, answer the following questions:

- Do you know whether these are the role expectations others will have for you as a teacher? How might you find out?
- What ten role expectations do you want to fulfill? How could you bring about this desired state?
- How is the role of teacher different from your current role as a methods student?

Form groups of three and discuss your responses. Work to clarify each other's thinking as to the role expectations that follow from the status of social studies teacher.

• • •

How might secondary students complete this activity focusing on the status and role of "student" as opposed to that of "friend"?

Structural Functional Perspective

The *structural functional approach* has its roots in the work of early sociologists, especially Emile Durkheim in France, Herbert Spencer in England, and Robert Merton and Talcott Parsons in the United States. These scholars were interested in social phenomena that have distinctive social characteristics and factors that place constraints on individuals but are external to them: customs, laws, norms, values, and the rules that people accept without question. Durkheim, in particular, believed that individuals are more the products of society than creators of it. Even something as personal as taking one's own life (suicide) is a social phenomenon directly related to the individual's involvement in group life and the extent to which he or she is part of some cohesive social unit. His central thesis was that the more a person is integrated into intimate social groups, the less likely he or she is to commit suicide. Thus, people who have a low level of social integration and group involvement, such as the unmarried and those without strong religious convictions, would be expected to have higher suicide rates. Durkheim found that this was true.

Within the structural functional approach is the assumption that society is composed of many different systems, parts, or elements. These parts, these *social structures*, include institutions, social organizations, statuses, and so forth that are linked to each other and to the whole. Each component acts and reacts upon other components. In addition, each part or component of society—the family, the school, the economy, or the state—contributes something. Likewise, prostitution, crime, and drugs exist because they contribute something or fulfill functions for individual persons or society as a whole. Moreover, all the parts of a system or of a society are interdependent. The family, for example, depends on the school to educate its children, and the school, in turn, depends on the family or the state to provide financial assistance. The state, in turn, depends on the family and the school to help children grow up to become law-abiding citizens.

If something disrupts the existing social order, its parts will adjust in a way that produces a new stability. Suppose the economy is in bad shape, with high rates of inflation and unemployment. The family would adjust, perhaps by spending less and saving more. The school would probably offer fewer programs and emphasize vocational training. The state might cut its budget. The result is a new and different social order.

Each component (structure) of the social system has consequences. Those consequences may be manifest or latent, functional or dysfunctional. Manifest functions are intended and recognized; latent functions are neither intended nor recognized. One manifest function of education systems is to teach literary and technical skills. They also perform the latent functions of "sitting" for children while parents work and of providing contacts for dating.

Robert Merton recognized that not all consequences of systems are functional—that is, they do not all lead to the maintenance of the system. Some lead to instability or the breakdown of a system. Those consequences he termed *dysfunctions*. Families have a manifest function of rearing children. The intensity of family interactions, however, can lead to the dysfunction, or negative consequence, of violence and child abuse.

Note the significance of these ideas in initiating change. If certain consequences or outcomes (functions or dysfunctions—whether intended or not) are the result of a particular type of structure or organization, we can get different outcomes by changing the structure. If a family has no father, ten children, or poverty status, the consequences of such structural arrangements will influence and affect the behaviors of its members. Concerns about crime (including white-collar crime), tax evasion, excessive consumption, pollution, corruption in government, substance abuse, poverty, unwed parenthood, or school dropouts can now be approached, not by addressing the persons per se, but by modifying the structure or organization of the system: different rewards, job opportunities, education, availability of contraceptives, changes in the law, and so forth. Sociologists investigate the wide range of social groups and social systems that exist within society and the outcomes of variations in structures.

| ACTIVITY | **Problem Solving** |

The following social concerns are listed in the text of this chapter: crime (including white collar crime), tax evasion, excessive consumption, pollution, corruption in government, poverty, unwed parenthood, school dropouts, and substance abuse. In pairs, select one of these social concerns, and define the nature of the social concern as you understand it. Then do the following:

- Propose structural and/or organizational changes that could serve to resolve or ameliorate that particular social concern. For example, legalizing marijuana and similar substances would be an example of a structural change that might address problems related to substance abuse or crime.

- When finished, present your plans to the rest of the class. Troubleshoot the potential efficacy of the proposed solutions. What sorts of changes in society would *really* address these sorts of social concerns? Why aren't such suggestions being used in the "real world"?

• • •

Could this activity be used with secondary students? What changes would you make to increase its effectiveness?

Formal Organizations

Formal organizations are another principal component of the social order. Up to this point, social organization has been used to refer to the way society is organized: its norms, roles, values, institutions, and the like. *Formal* organizations are one form of social organization. A formal organization is deliberately constructed and organized to achieve specific and clearly stated goals. Formal organizations tend to be stable, often keeping the same structure and existing for many years. Those who belong to an organization generally feel a sense of membership. Industrial corporations, professional sports, country clubs, trade unions, schools, churches, prisons, hospitals, and government agencies are formal organizations created to meet specific goals.

The importance of formal organizations in modern complex societies can hardly be overestimated. Every day, we deal with some sort of formal organization in connection with food, travel, health care, police protection, or some other necessity of life. Organizations enable people who are often total strangers to work together toward common goals. They create levels of authority and channels of command that clarify who gives orders, who obeys them, and who does which tasks. They are also a source of continuity and permanence in a society's efforts to meet specific goals. Individual members may come and go, but the organization continues to function.

The administrative structures of formal organizations are known as bureaucracies. A *bureaucracy* is a formal organizational structure that directs and coordinates the efforts of the people involved in various organizational tasks. It is simply a hierarchical arrangement of an organization's parts based on the division of labor and authority. A hierarchical structure is like a pyramid—the people at each level have authority over the larger number of people at the level below them (see Figure 6.3). The authority resides in the office, position, or status, not in a particular person.

ACTIVITY   Bureaucratic Hierarchy and Schools

Analyze the bureaucratic hierarchy of a middle, junior high, or senior high school—preferably one in which you have been observing or student teaching. Illustrate this hierarchy with some sort of diagram or illustration. In a brief paper, discuss who holds power, who is responsible to whom, what happens to the structure when someone leaves, and so on. Sources of information for completing this

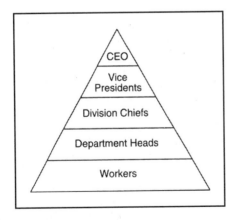

Figure 6.3   A bureaucracy

task might include your own observations, interviews with teachers and other staff members, and discussions with students in a variety of informal settings.

As a class, compare your insights into the schools you analyzed. Can you identify any generalizations that would help you as you enter the teaching profession? In what ways can the tools and insights of sociology help you to analyze bureaucratic structures and hierarchies?

METHODS OF STUDYING SOCIETY

Sources of Knowledge

People arrive at what they know, their beliefs and their opinions, by a number of different routes. We derive some from everyday experiences and common sense. We get other ideas from "authorities," people assumed to be knowledgeable because of their experience or position. A third source of ideas or knowledge is revelation. Revelation may be thought to result from divine experiences, prayer, or magic. A fourth source of ideas is tradition. Much of the information we know, read, and hear from sources such as these does not correspond to reality, facts, or "truth."

A fifth source of knowledge is *research* that uses empirical or scientific methods. Empirical methods focus on observable phenomena, which means that others should be able to observe the same situation and check our observations for accuracy. Empirical methods strive for objectivity, meaning that in the study of any issue, social or nonsocial, the personal biases and values of the people doing the research should not influence the data reported or the interpretation of results. The political, religious, racial, or other beliefs of the investigators should in no way determine the findings of a study. Empirical methods stress replication, which suggests that research should be reported in such a way that someone else can duplicate it. Finally, empirical methods strive for a standard precision of measurement. The more accurate our measurements, the better we are able to test our ideas about the social world.

Qualitative and Quantitative Social Research

Social research involves methods of two types, qualitative and quantitative. *Qualitative* methods are used to study conditions or processes that are hard to measure with numbers, such as self-image, manners, or how police make a decision to arrest someone. This type of research often involves case studies and participant observation in which the observer takes part in the activity being observed. *Quantitative* methods are designed to study variables that can be measured in numbers: age, income, years married, or crime rates, for example. This type of research usually involves surveys or experiments.

One qualitative method of obtaining information about social processes is through *observational research*. The researcher or research team watches what is happening and makes no attempt to control, modify, or influence the ongoing activity. Systematic observation may take several forms. One is the *laboratory observation*, in which the sociologist controls the environment in which a particular activity takes place. Sometimes one-way mirrors are used to reduce the chances that the activity will be influenced by the researcher. This technique might be employed to study how aggression in children's play is influenced by their watching violence on television.

A second type of observation takes place in a natural setting rather than a laboratory. Often termed *field observation*, this research is done "on location." One might observe student behavior in a classroom or the interactions between salespersons and customers at a store, for example.

A third observation technique is *participant observation*, in which the researcher is an active participant in the event being studied. Anthropologists frequently use this method to study a particular community or subculture. Sociologists have been participant observers in studies of nudist camps, bars, prisons, the drug trade, and entire communities. Unlike laboratory or field observers, the researchers become directly involved in the group or community activities.

Most participant observation research takes the form of a case study, in which an individual person, a group, a community, or an activity is observed. Although case studies and participant observation generate new insights and hypotheses for testing, they also present serious difficulties. Generalizing on the basis of observations of a single group may be impossible because an examination of a single case or example may not prove or illustrate anything. Furthermore, a researcher who is also a participant can have difficulty remaining objective and making unbiased observations.

The procedure used most frequently by sociologists to obtain information about the social world is *survey research*. This quantitative technique involves systematically asking people about their attitudes, feelings, ideas, opinions, behaviors, or anything else. Usually, the researcher uses a questionnaire to guide the questioning and standardize the responses.

Surveys have a number of advantages. They are usually easy to administer and often permit researchers to gather data on identical variables from many people simultaneously. Unlike most participant observation studies, which may take months or years, surveys provide a great deal of information in periods ranging from a few minutes to several hours. When highly structured, survey responses are uniformly categorized, which makes tabulation easier. Finally, the precise categorical data provided by surveys are highly amenable to statistical quantitative analysis.

A third procedure for obtaining information about the social world is the *experimental design*, a classic scientific procedure used to determine cause-effect relationships in carefully controlled situations. In an ideal experiment, it is possible to control all relevant factors and manipulate one variable, statistically or in the society itself, to determine its effect. To carry out an experiment, two matched groups of subjects are selected. An independent variable is introduced in the *experimental* group, and the effect of this variable is tested. The *control* group is identical to the experimental group in every respect, except that the variable is not introduced. If we were studying the effects of dim lighting on social interaction, for example, we might randomly choose two groups of students. The experimental group would be placed in a dimly lit room, whereas the control group would be in a normally lit room. The researcher would note differences in the behavior of the two groups: frequency of interaction, level of noise, number of subgroups formed, and other behaviors considered germane. Differences in the social behavior of the two groups would presumably be due to the influence of the independent variable, dim lighting.

ACTIVITY   **Designing a Research Project**

Plan a small-scale sociological research project. You will need to *identify a topic, form a research question,* and *develop a research strategy.*

Identify a topic that is of interest to you—that is what happens in the "real" world of research. Some possible topics might include cars and stop signs, smoking behavior of different types of individuals, male-female differences when walking down a city sidewalk, classmates' views on a contemporary issue, who writes letters to the editor of your local newspaper about what sorts of topics, messages related to violence on children's television programs, voter preferences as related to specific social roles.

If time allows, you may want to implement your plan—that is, actually conduct the research and report your results to the class. What new insights did this process provide into the research activities of sociologists?

ISSUES OF INEQUALITY

Inequality is a fundamental characteristic of contemporary human society. Although we may claim that all "men [and women, too] are created equal," inequality is built into our family structure, with wealth or poverty being transferred from one generation to the next; built into our economic structure, with extreme differences in pay for different jobs; built into our political structure, with differential access to power; built into our educational systems, with great variation in resources and prestige. In short, inequality is a highly patterned aspect of most social systems.

Does it matter that some people are born into families having vast amounts of wealth and others are born into impoverished families? Does anyone care that certain racial and ethnic groups are discriminated against solely because of their skin color, speech, or country of origin? Should we be concerned that certain groups or categories of people have no access to health care or a place to live? If we do care, whose responsibility is it to change or reduce inequalities?

One starting point for a sociologist is to examine what is—to understand the existing institutions, social structures, and inequalities—and to present alternative theories and strategies for change. This section briefly examines inequality by class and race.

Social Stratification and Class Inequality

Social stratification refers to the grouping or differential ranking of persons in a hierarchy of unequal positions. Sociologists often use *social class* to refer to aggregates of individuals who occupy broadly similar positions on scales of wealth, power, and prestige. These three bases of stratification—wealth, power, and prestige—usually go together, but possession of one does not guarantee the others. Many garbage collectors may make more money than teachers, but they have less power and prestige.

Two of the theoretical orientations discussed earlier, the functionalist and the conflict, provide contrasting perspectives and assumptions about stratification. A *functionalist* perspective views stratification as both an inevitable and a necessary feature of society. The assumption is that all societies have a wide range of tasks that need to be performed. These tasks are necessary for the stability and maintenance of the society, but they carry with them differential levels of prestige and rewards. Someone must collect the garbage, repair faulty plumbing, and perform the labor to assemble automobiles; others must teach students, plan defense strategies, and perform heart surgery. Some tasks require greater levels of skill and training, and these are likely to be more highly rewarded. This unequal distribution of social rewards is viewed as functional for society because it enables all roles and tasks to be completed.

In contrast, *conflict theorists* see a stratified society as the key source of dissatisfaction, alienation, and exploitation. The differentiation of economic rewards that exists in capitalistic countries is viewed as leading to major strife and conflict between those who have and those who don't and between those who control the means of production and those whose labor is the instrument of production.

In family terms, it means conflict between those families who own and control the wealth and means of production and the families who are forced to work for wages and produce the products or provide the services that make the owners wealthy. In gender terms, it means conflict between the males, who are most likely to be employed, receive higher wages, and are the order givers, and the females, who are less likely to be employed, who receive lower wages, and who are the order takers. In political terms, it means conflict between those who want to establish policies and tax laws that favor the wealthy and those who favor policies and tax laws that assist the poor, provide health care for all, or insist on a more equitable distribution of wealth.

The class system in the United States lacks clear boundaries. Conflict theorists tend to establish a two-class system—rich and poor or owners and workers. Many of us think in terms of a three-class system of upper, middle, and lower. Other studies divide the classes into four, five, or six strata. Irrespective of the specific number, clear patterns of social inequality exist in the United States.

Inequality and Life Chances

One of the most consistent findings in sociology is that social class is correlated with how people live. People in the higher classes or strata have better *life chances*—a greater likelihood that they will obtain desirable resources and experiences and have more opportunities for living a good, long, or successful life. Research clearly shows that people in the lower classes tend to live shorter and less healthy lives than those above them in the social hierarchy. An infant born into a poor family is at least three times more likely to die during its first year than an infant born into a nonpoor family.

For adults, too, the mortality (death) rates differ among the classes. The lower classes are more likely to die from heart disease, syphilis, tuberculosis, stomach ulcers, diabetes, influenza, and many other diseases. They are also more likely to obtain their medical care in emergency rooms or public clinics than from a private doctor.

Class also shapes lifestyles—tastes, preferences, and ways of living. People in different classes tend to prefer different magazines, newspapers, books, television programs, movies, music, and sports.

Do these class inequalities matter? Are these issues of concern? If so, where does the responsibility lie?

ACTIVITY   ## Analyzing Portrayals of Social Classes on Television

Identify three television programs that portray the lives of different social classes. Watch the programs and keep track of the specific ways in which they present the values and behaviors of different social classes and individuals within different classes.

Using the data gathered from watching the various television programs, discuss these questions:

- How accurate do you feel these portrayals of social classes are? What aspects of stereotyping can you identify?

- What do you think each of these programs is teaching the audience about the status, roles, expectations, behaviors, and values of different social classes? Are these messages consistent or do some programs contradict the messages of other programs? Explain.

- How could you, as a sociology teacher, help students better understand and evaluate the messages regarding social class found in the media today?

• • •

Discuss ways of adapting and using this activity with secondary students. In what classes could it be used? What objectives would it help students meet?

Race and Ethnic Inequalities

Race and ethnic inequalities are closely linked to class inequalities. A disproportionate number of racial or ethnic minorities are poor. This point is extremely important because differences often defined as or believed to be caused by race or ethnicity are due to class. First, let us clarify what we mean by racial, ethnic, and minority groups and note how they differ.

For many years, race was regarded as a biological concept, referring to a large category of people who share certain inherited physical characteristics. Today, however, we know that there are, in fact, no clear-cut biological distinctions—in physical characteristics or genetic makeup—between racial groups. Sociologists therefore define race as a *social* rather than a biological phenomenon. Defined sociologically, a race is a group of people who are *perceived* by a given society as biologically different from others. This definition suggests that the people of a given society define what biological differences are significant (eye color and size of feet are generally excluded, for example).

The word *ethnic* is derived from the Greek word *ethnikos*, which translates as "nations" in English. The word was initially equated with national origin and applied to European immigrants such as the Italians, Germans, Poles, and other national groups who came to the United States in large numbers between 1900 and 1925. Today, ethnicity is given a wider definition and may also refer to group membership based on religion, language, or region. Using the word in this sense, Jews, Mormons, Latinos, and white Southerners can be considered ethnic groups.

Whereas race is based on selected physical characteristics such as skin color, hair texture, or eye shape, ethnicity is based on cultural traits that reflect national origin, religion, and language. Cultural traits may be apparent in manner of dress, speech patterns, and modes of emotional expression.

Defining racial and ethnic relations in terms of minorities and majorities can be misleading. A *minority group* is subordinate in power and privilege; such groups are usually but not always smaller than the dominant group. Women, for example, are a numerical majority in American society, yet they have minority status.

African Americans or black Americans are the largest racial and ethnic minority group in the United States, constituting 12 percent of the total population. Because of such unique historical experiences as slavery, legal and social segregation, and economic discrimination, many African Americans have lifestyles and value patterns that differ from those of the white majority. The relations between white and black have been the source of a number of major social issues in the past several decades: busing, segregation, job discrimination, and interracial marriage, to mention a few.

The inequality between black and white Americans is evident whether one looks at income, education, or percent in poverty. These types of inequality have significant implications for interaction between racial groups in the United States.

The Hispanic population is second to the black population in size, constituting approximately 9 percent of the population. As of the 1990 census, there were about 22.3 million people in the United States who claimed Hispanic origins. The Hispanic origin classification overlaps with other racial and ethnic categories and includes those who classify themselves as Mexican, Puerto Rican, and Cuban, and those from Spain or the Spanish-speaking countries of Central and South America. It includes recent immigrants and people who have lived in what is now the United States for hundreds of years. As with the African-American population, relations between the Anglo majority and the Hispanic minority have been a source of a number of major issues: immigration, bilingual education, and farm workers or migrant labor, to mention a few. Geographically, these issues have been heavily centered in Florida and the Southwest, particularly in states that border Mexico. The inequalities between the Hispanic minority and the Anglo majority are also clear.

The third largest group, representing 2.9 percent of the U.S. population in 1990, is the Asian-American community, which includes Chinese, Filipinos, Japanese, Asian Indians, Koreans, Vietnamese, and people with historical roots in other Asian countries. Given the diversity in numbers, languages, country of ancestry, and historical circumstances that led to their arrival in the United States, it is difficult to categorize Asian Americans into one racial, ethnic, or minority group. The Chinese were the first Asians to enter the country in large numbers; unlike the Japanese, for example, the Chinese tended to resist assimilation and to uphold traditional values such as filial duty, veneration of the aged and of deceased ancestors, and arranged marriages. Today, Chinese Americans live in large urban enclaves in Hawaii, San Francisco, Los Angeles, and New York. Tourists who visit the Chinatowns of various cities are likely to notice only the exotic sights, smells, and sounds; the problems are less evident. There are often overcrowding, poverty, poor health care, run-down housing, and inadequate care for the elderly. Inequality is again evident.

Although census data show a more positive picture for Asian Americans than for other minority groups, the figures mask extreme inequalities within the group, with Japanese Americans at the upper income levels and those of Vietnamese origin at the lower levels.

Following the Asian Americans in size are the Native Americans, categorized in the U.S. Census as American Indians and grouped with the Eskimos and Aleuts. These Native American groups include about 1.9 million people, less than 1 percent of the U.S. population. This population of Americans is actually a varied group of tribes having different languages and cultures. Today, about half of all Native Americans live on or near reservations administered fully or partly by the Bureau of Indian Affairs (BIA). Many other Native Americans have moved to urban areas or have been relocated there by the BIA to help in their search for jobs and improved living conditions.

Inequality with the dominant racial group is dramatic. Their unemployment rate is twice that of whites. Most hold jobs at lower occupational levels and have incomes below the median for most other groups mentioned. Housing is often severely crowded, and two-thirds of the houses in rural areas have no plumbing facilities. The life expectancy is about two-thirds the national average. Teenage suicide, alcoholism, and adult diabetes are more common among reservation Native Americans than any other group in the country. In addition they have the lowest school enrollment rates of any ethnic or racial group in the United States. This extreme inequality has contributed to stereotyping, prejudicial attitudes, and discriminatory behavior.

Prejudice and Discrimination

A *prejudice* is a preconceived judgment, either good or bad, about another group. It is an attitude that predisposes people to think, perceive, and act in favorable or unfavorable ways toward a group or a member of that group. The concern in intergroup relationships tends to focus on the unfavorable or negative feelings and behaviors of one group toward another.

A variety of theories have been offered to explain prejudice. Early theories were often based on the premise that prejudiced attitudes are innate or biological, but today most explanations attribute them to learned behavior. What seems clear is that racial and ethnic differences and the inequalities that exist between them contribute to prejudices. Regardless of the reasons for prejudice, it is sustained through *stereotypes*, which are widely held beliefs about the character and behavior of all members of a group. Stereotypes are usually based on readily discernible characteristics, such as physical appearance, and are oversimplifications that seldom correspond to the facts.

Prejudice is a judgment, an attitude. *Discrimination*, on the other hand, is overt behavior and actions. It is the categorical exclusion of members of a group from certain rights, opportunities, or privileges. From a conflict perspective, the dominant group in a society practices discrimination to protect its advantages, privileges, and interests.

Although we may think of discrimination as operating solely at a personal or an individual level, *institutional discrimination* occurs as well. This type of discrimination occurs when a policy or some criterion is established that continually excludes or oppresses members of a group. In this form of discrimination, individual prejudice is not necessarily a factor, and laws or rules are not necessarily applied with the intent of preventing people of a certain race or ethnic group from belonging.

Suppose, for example, that a certain club requires a $10,000 annual membership fee. In such cases, no bias against any particular racial or ethnic group may be intended—anyone who meets the criterion can be admitted. But the result is the same as if the discrimination were by design. Fewer members of minority or ethnic groups could meet the requirements for admittance to the club, and the benefits of belonging would accrue only to groups that already belonged, thereby continuing existing patterns of deprivation from one generation to the next.

SOCIAL INSTITUTIONS

Although society should not be personified by suggesting that it, like people, has wants, needs, and goals, it is essential to recognize that a society cannot survive unless certain conditions are met. For example, no society can exist unless it has some way to replace its members, socialize its children, transmit the cultural heritage and knowledge from one generation to the next, produce and distribute goods and services, and so forth. These conditions are met by what sociologists call social institutions.

A *social institution* is a system of norms (expectations for behavior), values (what is important), statuses (positions), and roles (expected behaviors appropriate to a given status) that develop around a basic social goal. In the context of the examples given in the preceding paragraph, the family is the institution that reproduces the population and socializes its children. Education is the institution that transmits the cultural heritage and knowledge from one generation to the next. The economic institution produces and distributes goods and services. Other basic goals focus on social leadership and protecting individuals from one another and from forces outside society (political institution); affirming values and providing answers to nonempirical, nonobservable questions (religious institution); caring for the sick and dealing with illnesses and diseases (health care institution); and so forth.

These institutions should not be confused with social groups and social organizations described in prior sections. The concept *institution* is an abstraction that exists independently of any particular person or group. Groups and organizations, like institutions, exist to meet some goal. But groups and organizations are deliberately constructed bodies of individuals, whereas institutions are systems of norms and values. Thus, education is an institution, your university is an organization, and your methods class is a group. Your group may disband and your school may consolidate and exist no more, but the institution persists. Groups, organizations, and any given institution like the family or religion are courses of study in themselves; at this point we will look briefly at one of them: the educational institution.

In the broadest sense, all societies have an educational institution. Schools are the vehicle or organization by which some of the goals of the educational institution are carried out. What are these goals? Why do schools exist?

According to the functionalist perspective, education performs many functions for us as individuals and for society as a whole. The most obvious function of education is to provide a new generation with the *knowledge and skills* necessary to maintain the society. Beginning in primary school, children learn the basic language and mathematical skills indispensable to an industrial society. This learning is gradually expanded throughout secondary school and, for some, in college as well. Because industrial societies change rapidly, formal education teaches students not only facts (which may become obsolete) but also how to learn so that they will be able to adapt to unanticipated changes in the future.

Second, schools *transmit cultural values and norms*. In some cases, students receive explicit instruction in the American way of life (in civics classes, for example). In other cases, values are taught in more subtle ways, as when teachers foster the value of competition by challenging students to get the highest score or finish first. Norms are also learned in schools, which place considerable importance on punctuality, displaying respect for teachers or persons in authority, and generally obeying the rules.

A third function of schools is that of *social placement*. Formal education helps to channel young people into culturally approved statuses and roles that contribute to the ongoing life of society. The purpose of this screening and selection process is to identify and develop the varying talents and abilities of individuals. That is why, ideally at least, schools evaluate students' performance according to achievement rather than social background. This suggests that the "best and brightest" are encouraged to pursue the most advanced studies, whereas students of lesser abilities are guided into programs and occupations more suited to their talents. Education, therefore, supports the American ideal of meritocracy: the idea that your social position and advancement reflect personal ability and effort.

A fourth function of schools might be called *cultural innovation*. Education systems create as well as transmit culture. Schools (some, at least) stimulate intellectual inquiry and provide an environment in which new ideas develop. Today, for example, most college professors not only teach but also engage in research that leads to discoveries and reevaluation of conventional ideas. Sociologists and others may be unpopular with conservative politicians or local school boards because their ideas and research findings challenge the existing values and patterns of behavior. Others, like medical researchers, gain prestige and stature because their research prolongs life and discovers cures for diseases. In both cases, formal education fosters cultural innovation.

In addition to these functions of education that are intended and recognized (manifest functions), educational institutions have functions that are neither intended nor recognized (latent functions). One such function is *child care*. Because of the rising number of one-parent families and two-career marriages, schools function to relieve parents of some custodial responsibilities.

A second latent function of education, particularly in industrialized societies, is to *prolong adolescence*. Students often attend schools well into their twenties. This has the effect of keeping unemployment rates down by keeping many young people out of competition for jobs.

A third latent function of schools is to establish *social relationships* that can have lasting importance. High schools and colleges bring together people of similar age. It is no surprise that many people meet future business contacts or their spouses in school.

In sum, the functionalist perspective views education (and all institutions) as fulfilling both manifest and latent functions (see Figure 6.4). Although the list is not intended to be inclusive, educational institutions reinforce the socialization process that starts with the family, prepares children for work in a complex industrial society, and guides them into the occupations most appropriate to their abilities and society's needs. Child care supports employed parents, prolonging adolescence supports the economy, and establishing social relationships supports future peer interactions.

A conflict perspective on education tends to see schools as agencies that reproduce and legitimate the current social order, benefiting some individuals and groups at the expense of others. In America, schools are viewed as reflecting the needs of capitalist production. They are social instruments that convince the population that private ownership, competition, and profit are just and in the best interests of the entire society. The authoritarian structure of the school, like the bureaucratic hierarchy of the corporation, rewards diligence, submissiveness, and compliance. The grades employed to motivate students parallel the wage system for motivating workers.

Similarly, the *hidden curriculum* of schools requires students to learn, albeit subtly, how to behave appropriately for their position in society. This learning is not a part of the stated, published curriculum but is a part of the hidden curriculum, in which students learn such things as obedience, responsibility, reliability, self-control, thoroughness, conscientiousness, efficiency, and patriotism. No one announces that these qualities are being taught. Nevertheless, if students are to be educated for a job, they must learn to obey rules, to be quiet, to line up, to be punctual, to conform, to do whatever a superior orders them to do, to work as hard as they can, and to be loyal to their superior, the organization, and the nation in which they live. In all cases, the interests of the dominant groups, the owners, the powerful, or the elite are being served.

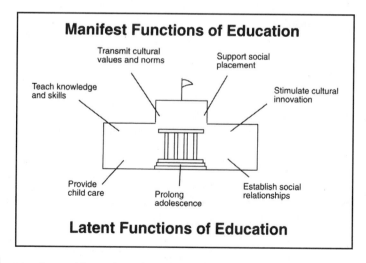

Figure 6.4   Manifest and latent functions of education

Conflict theorists argue as well that the credentials, diplomas, and degrees given by schools represent learning that is not essential to doing most jobs. This is *credentialism*, the requirement that a worker have a degree for its own sake, not because it certifies skills needed for the performance of a job. Since education functions more as a certification of class membership than of technical skills, it functions as a means of class inheritance. Many of these credentials can be obtained only by those who have the time and money to pursue them. As more obtain the credentials (that is, the degrees), the occupational and income return for each year spent in school declines. Whereas at one time a college degree brought an elite occupational position, today it brings a middle-class status with middle-class pay. In brief, as a population gains more education, the relative position of different groups in the stratification system remains basically the same.

ACTIVITY

The Purpose of Schooling

Assume that you have been asked by aliens to answer this question: "Why do schools exist?" You have become familiar with some of the outlooks of sociology and you have your own ideas about the nature and purposes of schooling. Write a one- or two-page response to this alien's question.

Exchange papers with classmates as a means of comparing responses. Discuss your answers and post significant ideas on the chalkboard. Compare your ideas with those in the chapter. Specifically, which of the different functions of schooling, both real and latent, do you agree and disagree with? What agreement or disagreement is there with the conflict perspective on education?

Expand the discussion by focusing your attention on the "hidden curriculum" in schools. In what ways does the hidden curriculum help to reinforce your ideas about why schools exist? How will you, as a classroom teacher, support or challenge this hidden curriculum?

Inequality in Education

Most of us have learned to place a high value on education, to remain in school and obtain those degrees. We have been taught that education is the path that leads us from rags to riches. Yet any number of studies have shown (1) that the higher a student's socioeconomic status, the further up the educational ladder he or she will go; and (2) that equal education has not produced equal incomes for blacks, women, and other minorities. Why do children from white, middle- and upper-class backgrounds profit more from an education than other children?

One possible explanation is that children from these backgrounds are more intelligent. Test results show they do achieve higher scores on IQ and other intelligence tests and receive better grades in school. But does that mean they are smarter? Could they perform as well on the streets of an urban ghetto or on an isolated rural farm? Many critics feel that IQ and similar tests measure a limited set of cognitive skills and are biased against creative children as well as those from minority backgrounds.

A second explanation is that lower-class and minority parents do not prepare their children for school as well as parents from higher-class backgrounds. Existing evidence shows that parents of all classes or socioeconomic backgrounds want their children to do well in school and go on to college. The critical difference seems to be that whereas lower-class parents hope their children will continue their educations, middle- and upper-class parents know how to help their children achieve their goals.

A third explanation for unequal performance in school is that middle- and upper-class children attend better schools. Public schools in this country are financed primarily through local taxes. Hence, schools in wealthy areas tend to be newer, better equipped, and better staffed than those in low-income districts. It seems reasonable to assume that the better the school and the better the education that children receive, the further they will go. Several studies show that schools do make a difference. In the most successful schools, teachers take education more seriously, have higher expectations for student performance, treat students with more respect, and provide a more pleasant learning environment.

A fourth possibility for unequal performance is that not all students are treated equally in school. Evidence exists to show that assignment to college-preparatory or "general" tracks in high school is based to some degree on subjective evaluations and social-class background. *Tracking* results in unequal treatment of students. Students in the college-bound track are assigned more experienced teachers, given better classroom materials and laboratory facilities, and exposed to more field trips. The kind of instruction that students receive also differs. With "slow" learners, teachers tend to emphasize basic skills and memorization of facts, making frequent use of drills. With high-ability students, teachers are more likely to emphasize conceptual learning and to encourage independent projects.

There is no easy or simple answer to the question of why children perform differently in school. The relationship between academic achievement and social and personal characteristics is complex. Children bring different resources to school, they come from different socioeconomic backgrounds and have different abilities, aspirations, and preparation for occupying the status of student. The schools respond differently to different individual and social characteristics. The result of these interacting factors is both unequal education and unequal achievement.

SOCIAL DEVIANCE AND SOCIAL CONTROL

Deviance means different things to different people. The definition we use influences our explanations of its causes and our attempts to control it. Does deviance reside in the individual? Is it a particular act or behavior? Is it defined socially? Are certain groups immune from being labeled deviants? Our answers to questions such as these will influence how we analyze deviance and whether we ultimately understand it.

We will define *deviance* as variation from a set of norms or shared social expectations. It involves a social audience that defines certain people and behaviors as going beyond the tolerance limits of social norms. Social norms, rules, and expectations about appropriate and inappropriate behavior exist in all societies. People everywhere have social controls to enforce the rules and punish those who do not conform. Deviance consists of these norm violations; the norm violators are the deviants.

As you might guess, there are many explanations as to why people engage in deviant behaviors. Some, by biologists, place the focus of attention on the body, or on genes, hormones, or chromosomes. Other explanations, by psychologists, place the focus of attention on personality types or mental disorders.

Sociologists tend to look at sociocultural processes and organizational structures. They may focus on value conflicts between culturally prescribed goals and socially approved ways of achieving them (anomie theory). They may examine who makes the rules that people violate, noting that groups in power define the acts of the weaker groups as deviant to exploit or profit from them (conflict theory). They may focus on how people interact and learn deviance (sociocultural learning theories).

Some look at the meanings, definitions, and interpretations applied to people and acts (labeling theory). Others may concentrate their attention more on conformity than on deviance and on the internal and external controls that inhibit people's involvement in deviance (control theories). Traditional views of deviance are described next.

Traditional Views of Deviance and Deviants

An *absolutist view* of deviance is based on the assumption that everyone agrees on certain norms and that certain behaviors are clearly deviant regardless of the social context in which they occur. Thus, prostitution, homosexuality, and the use of drugs might be assumed to be deviant at all times and in all cultures, whereas chastity, heterosexuality, and abstinence from drugs might be regarded as nondeviant.

A *moral view* shares with an absolutist view the idea that behaviors are deviant in and of themselves but assumes as well that deviance is bad or evil and that people who commit deviant acts lack morals and are depraved and antisocial. Like the absolutist, the moralist assumes that there are just two kinds of people and two kinds of behavior: the moral nondeviant and the immoral deviant. Deviant people are regarded as inherently different from others, innately antisocial and evil, and harmful to others and to society. Entire groups, such as atheists, homosexuals, or socialists, may be viewed as innately evil and harmful to society. Today, these views are rejected by sociologists and most social scientists.

Another approach to deviance is a *medical view*, in which deviance is assumed to be essentially pathological, evidence that society is sick or at least unhealthy. Just as healthy humans function efficiently without pain or discomfort, healthy societies are thought to function smoothly without problems. The prevalence of child abuse, rape, robbery, mental disorders, and alcoholism are thought to indicate that a society has a sickness. Like the moral view, the medical view is absolutist. It assumes that people are either deviant or not deviant—there is no gray area—but this polarity is expressed in terms of health or illness. This view is also rejected by most social scientists.

A fourth view of deviance relies on statistics. Any behavior that is atypical, that varies from the average or mode, is considered deviant. This view is not absolutist: Deviance is assumed to be a variable characteristic that increases the further a behavior is removed from the average. According to the *statistical view*, any variation from a statistical norm is deviant. Thus, a person who is left-handed, who has red hair, or who belongs to a minority group is defined as a deviant. Everyone fails to conform to the average in some respect, however, so according to this definition, we are all deviants.

Like the other views described, this view fails on several counts. It does not take into account the meanings people attach to behaviors, and it ignores situations in which deviance is defined by a powerful group that is a numerical minority. Variations in the enforcement of rules are not considered, nor are interpersonal interactions, societal standards, or public awareness of or response to the deviance. Although much socially defined deviance falls outside of the average, the degree of variation may be less significant than the social definitions and social judgments attached to the variation.

The Relative Nature of Deviance

Many sociologists advocate a relativistic model of deviance. This view assumes that behaviors, ideas, and products can be understood or evaluated only within the context of the culture, society, and situation in which they happen or of which they are a part. Is a seven-foot-tall person a deviant in the context of professional basketball? Is a person without clothes or a bathing suit a deviant at a nudist beach? Context influences these determinations.

By assessing deviance in a particular social context, the relativist model avoids the problems of the absolute, moral, medical, and statistical models. If deviance is relative rather than absolute, an act that is deviant in one context may not be deviant in another. Thus, deviance does not consist merely of acts or behaviors that are right or wrong, deviant or nondeviant per se, but of group responses, definitions, and the meanings attached to behaviors. Therefore, we can expect definitions to vary with circumstances. Some of the most important variations that affect these definitions concern time, place, situation, and social status.

Planning a Unit on Social Deviance

Using the previous discussion, plan a two- to three-week unit on social deviance for a high school sociology course. Work either individually or in pairs. Use the following suggestions to engage in the planning process. (You may also want to look at Chapter 4 for some useful ideas on planning units.)

- Review both college and high school sociology texts to gain a greater understanding of the concept of social deviance and to see how others have organized units on the topic.
- With high school students in mind, determine and list instructional objectives and/or learning outcomes for the unit.
- Select the specific concepts, skills, and content that will help students accomplish these objectives/outcomes.
- Identify teaching activities you would use to teach your selected content, skills, and concepts. Use the activities found in this chapter as models that you can adapt, as well as ideas contained in Chapter 13.

In the exercise, keep in mind certain issues or questions:

- The relative nature of deviance. Do behaviors exist that do not vary over time, place, situation, or social status?
- The theories or "causes" of violation of existing norms. How much is biological, psychological, or social?
- The goals of a society that are viewed as desirable and the existing means by which they can be obtained. How do anomie, conflict, or labeling theories contribute to our understanding of deviance?
- The social consequences of deviance. What positive (functional) outcomes result from having deviance and deviants in a society?
- Deviance and crime. What is the relationship between the law and deviant behavior? Is most deviance illegal?
- Deviance and social control. How much of conformity to norms is explained by an individual's learned social codes of behavior (internal controls) and outside forces such as parents or peers (informal external controls) or police, courts, and prisons (formal external controls)?

Compare plans with others in the class, and identify areas of strength and places where you might want to adapt what you have planned. What concepts of deviance did each of you decide to emphasize, and how did you go about creating learning activities that would help students understand those concepts? Discuss the successes and problems you encountered in the planning process.

How could your ideas about social deviance be related to other social studies courses? That is, could some of the material from your unit on deviance be used in a government or history course? Discuss such uses with the class.

Reflecting on the Chapter

Review the description of sociology you wrote at the beginning of the chapter, as well as the questions you wanted to have answered. Would you change your description of sociology now? If so, how? What questions remain to be answered? How might you pursue those answers? What is sociology's principal contribution to the social studies curriculum? Write some thoughts on these questions in your journal.

References

Berger, P. L. *Invitation to Sociology: A Humanistic Perspective*. Garden City, N.Y.: Doubleday/Anchor Books, 1963.

Eitzen, D. S. with M. B. Zinn. *In Conflict and Order: Understanding Society*, 7th ed. Boston: Allyn & Bacon, 1995.

Eshleman, J. R. "Sociology: From Theory to Social Action." In *Social Studies and Social Sciences: A Fifty Year Perspective,* ed. S. P. Wronski and D. H. Bragaw, 111–23. Washington, D.C.: National Council for the Social Studies, 1986.

————. *The Family: An Introduction*, 7th ed. Boston: Allyn & Bacon, 1994.

Eshleman, J. R., B. G. Cashion, and L. A. Basirico. *Sociology: An Introduction,* 4th ed. Glenview, Ill.: Scott, Foresman, 1993.

Fine, G. A. *Talking Sociology*, 3rd ed. Boston: Allyn & Bacon, 1993.

Hewitt, J. P. *Self and Society*, 5th ed. Boston: Allyn & Bacon, 1991.

Kennedy, R. E., Jr. *Life Choices: Applying Sociology*, 2nd ed. New York: Holt, Rinehart & Winston, 1989.

Mills, C. W. *The Sociological Imagination*. New York: Oxford University Press, 1959.

Nock, S. L. and P. W. Kingston. *The Sociology of Public Issues*. Belmont, Calif.: Wadsworth, 1990.

Oliver, D. W. and F. M. Newmann. *Cases and Controversy*. Middleton, Conn.: Xerox Corporation, 1967.

Parsons, T. and R. F. Bales. *Family, Socialization and Interaction Process*. New York: Free Press, 1955.

Reiss, I. L. "The Universality of the Family: A Conceptual Analysis." *Journal of Marriage and the Family* 27 (November 1965): 443–53.

Sowell, T. *The Economics and Politics of Race: An International Perspective*. New York: Morrow, 1983.

Spitz, R. A. "Hospitalization." *The Psychoanalytic Study of the Child* 1 (1945): 53–72.

————. "Hospitalization: A Follow-Up Report." *The Psychoanalytic Study of the Child* 2 (1946): 113–17.

Walton, J. *Sociology and Critical Inquiry*. Belmont, Calif.: Wadsworth, 1990.

Teaching Resources

Aging, Corrections, Drugs, Ethnic Groups, Family, Women, Youth. Boca Raton, Fla.: Social Issues Resource Series, 1975–1995. CD-ROM or 3-ring binders.

American Social Issues: A Teacher Resource Unit. Dubuque, Iowa: Center for Learning, 1988.

ASA Teaching Resources, Teaching Resource Center, American Sociological Association, 1722 N Street Northwest, Washington, DC 20036.

Campbell, F. L., H. M. Blalock, Jr., and R. McGee, eds. *Teaching Sociology: The Quest for Excellence*. Chicago: Nelson Hall, 1985.

Conforti, D. A. *10 Model Lessons in Sociology*. New Bedford, Mass.: DAC Educational Publications, 1992.

Decisions, Decisions: Prejudice. Watertown, Mass.: Tom Snyder Productions, n.d. Computer simulation.

Goldsmid, C., and E. Wilson. *Passing on Sociology*. Belmont, Calif.: Wadsworth, 1980.

Hometown: A Local Area Study. Midland, Mich.: Active Learning Systems, 1985. Survey software.

MacKeachie, W. J. *Teaching Tips: A Guidebook for the Beginning College Teacher*. Lexington, Mass.: D. C. Heath, 1990.

Rose, S. *Social Stratification in the United States: The American Profile Poster*. New York: W. W. Norton & Co., Inc., 1992.

Sociology 94/95: Annual Editions. Guilford, Conn.: Dushkin, 1994.

Switzer, T. J. "Teaching Sociology in K–12 Classrooms." In *Social Studies and Social Sciences: A Fifty-Year Perspective,* ed. S. P. Wronski and D. H. Bragaw, 124–38. Washington, D.C.: National Council for the Social Studies, 1986.

Teaching Sociology. Washington, D.C.: American Sociological Association, quarterly.

USA Toolkit and *World Toolkit*. Watertown, Mass.: Tom Snyder Productions, n.d. Database software.

Whitehead, F. *Culture Wars: Opposing Viewpoints*. San Diego: Greenhaven Press, 1994.

STUDYING AND TEACHING POLITICAL SCIENCE

Stephen L. Schechter with Jonathan S. Weil

ACTIVITY LIST

• • •

ACTIVITY | **Political Science and Teaching Social Studies**

In Chapter 2, Don Bragaw made a passionate plea for education of citizens, in the broadest sense of the word, as the goal of social studies. Political science, as the scientific study of politics, deals with one of the primary domains in which citizens must act. Reflect on the relationship betwen the education of citizens and political science, given what you know about political science. Then write a paragraph in your journal that begins: The contribution political science can make to the social studies curriculum is . . .

INTRODUCTION

Political science is often defined simply as the scientific study of politics. But what is politics and how should it be studied? Each century of modern life has supplied its own answer to these questions.

In the seventeenth century, politics centered on the creation of the modern state. Political science, influenced by Thomas Hobbes and John Locke, focused on philosophical inquiry into the nature of the state in modern times, the relationship between the individual and the state, and the nature of the sovereign power within the state. In the eighteenth century, politics centered on the establishment of republican government. James Madison and Alexander Hamilton spoke of a "new science of politics" concerned with the study of how a free people can create a constitutional system of government based on popular sovereignty. In the nineteenth century, politics and its study shifted from the founding of political systems to their maintenance and inner workings. In the latter half of the century, changing political priorities once again redirected politics and political science—this time toward the need to reform and empower government in response to the challenges of the new urban-industrial social order.

In the twentieth century, both politics and political science have experienced a profound shift in emphasis from government to the individual. Politics and political science became increasingly separate and specialized pursuits. Political leaders no longer spoke of themselves as political scientists practicing the new science of politics. Political science became a social science guided by the behavioral question posed by Harold D. Lasswell in the subtitle of his book *Politics: Who Gets What, When, How?* The large shift in political science from the study of government to the study of the individual was followed by another shift in emphasis from the study of political institutions to the study of political behavior.

On the threshold of the twenty-first century, political science has experienced yet another shift in emphasis—this time, from the study of political behavior to the study of political decision making. In Lasswellian terms, this shift is characterized by an emphasis less on "who gets what, when, and how" and more on "why and with what consequences." Political scientists in the so-called post-behavioral age are beginning to accept the concern for values, qualitative judgments, and the ends of politics as legitimate considerations of political science.

All these waves of change in modern politics and political science are part of the same great sea of modern Western thought and its preoccupation with the need to balance human freedom and the good of society. Each successive shift in emphasis has built upon, not replaced, the ones that have preceded it. As a result, political science is a diverse discipline of fields and approaches including political philosophy, constitutional law, American government, public administration, political behavior, and public policy, all arrayed as equal approaches and fields of inquiry in their own right.

The purpose of this chapter is to provide social studies educators with an introduction to the study of politics that is both true to that study and relevant to social studies education. Toward those ends, we define *politics* as the making of public choices, and *political science* as the study of how public choices are made, by whom, for what purposes, and with what consequences. Our approach is *conceptual* in nature, focusing on three core concepts in the study of politics: public choice, power, and justice. We then examine the relationship of those concepts to constitutional government and its institutions. Finally, we discuss the applications of those concepts to three enduring issues of politics and their corresponding public policy choices: the allocation of scarce resources (distributive policy choices), the regulation of human behavior (regulatory policy choices), and the preservation of the national interest (foreign policy choices).

Most social studies educators will not teach a course on political science per se. Instead, they will teach courses in history, government, or civics. We believe the concepts presented in this chapter provide a vehicle by which political science may inform the teaching of these related subjects.

Concepts are one of the great organizers of the mind. Concepts are of special relevance to the social studies because of its intrinsically abstract and comparative nature; students are constantly presented with information about different times and peoples, and then asked to make connections to their own lives. Concepts like power and justice can provide some of the connecting links that enable students to make comparisons between different historical periods and cultures.

The concept of public choice is of double relevance to the teaching of history and civics. Not only is it a powerful organizing tool for understanding and comparing political behavior and political institutions across time and across cultures, but it is also a "life skill" that students are expected to acquire in school. This chapter stresses the criteria that can be used to evaluate the decisions of others and to improve the decision-making skills of students.

ACTIVITY   ## Identifying Public Choices

Indicate whether you think each of the choices described below is a public choice. Analyze your responses and develop a definition of *public choice* that embodies the criteria you used in responding.

_____ Governor Smith calls out the National Guard to quell a riot.

_____ John Washington decides to join the Crips.

_____ United Airlines decides to lower airfares by 30 percent.

_____ Roxanne Cole decides to cast her vote for Bill Clinton.

_____ The NRA decides to hold a rally on the steps of the state capitol.

_____ MacDonald's decides to use more recyclable materials.

_____ Congress passes a family leave bill.

_____ The Smith family decides not to watch television for a year.

PUBLIC CHOICE

Defining Public Choice

Who makes public choices is one factor in understanding politics. Certainly, public policy decisions made by public officials acting in their official capacity are public choices, but public choices can be made by a much wider range of actors. Citizens make public choices when they vote for their elected representatives, but individuals can also make public choices when they are not acting in their official capacity as citizens or other public officials. Corporate entities also make public choices: Political parties make public choices when they nominate candidates for public office;

| **Figure 7.1** | Can family purchasing decisions be public choices? If so, when? |

pressure groups make public choices when they seek to influence public officials or public opinion; and private corporations can make public choices when they significantly affect the public purse, as when oil companies increased the price of gasoline immediately following the Iraqi invasion of Kuwait in 1990.

How public choices are made is also an important element in the definition of politics. Politics involves human decisions, whether individual or collective. Public disasters like Hurricane Andrew or the 1994 California earthquake are not politics, but politics is clearly involved in the responses to such disasters. Economic developments such as inflation are not politics, but the public choices creating inflation and responding to it certainly do involve politics.

Why public choices are made brings us to the two great ends of politics: *power* and *justice*. Political power is the ability to change the public choices made by others. Justice is the fairness of public choices, with respect to both process and outcomes. A central point of this chapter is that seeking power and justice are the motivating factors explaining why most individuals enter politics and remain in it. These two concepts form the boundaries (or axes) of that field of human action we call politics. Therefore, we devote an entire section to each concept later in this chapter.

The *consequences* of a decision are perhaps the ultimate test of its "publicness." Ultimately, we think of choices as "public" not because public officials make them or because those decisions are "made public" (i.e., publicized) but because those decisions or choices affect "the public." But what is "the public"?

In classical terms, *a public* refers to all members of a body politic. In ancient Greece and Rome, the identification of the public and the public good (*res publica*, later "republic") was relatively simple: Each city (including its outlying farmland) was a complete *polis* (that is, a polity, civil society, or country). The polis had one government, and this component of the polity could be based on the rule of one, a few, or the many. The polis had a relatively homogeneous population, numbering several hundred thousand residents. However, the polis would have far fewer *citizens*, since that political segment of the population was typically limited to adult, native-born, free men. For all practical purposes, this small and homogeneous citizenry constituted "the public" in a society that relied upon slavery and tolerated political discrimination against women and foreigners.

The modern polity is far more complicated. In the U.S. system, the authority to govern resides with the people, who, in turn, allocate governmental powers to separate national, state, and local governments. Together, these governments constitute the public sector of the country, but there are other sectors and a variety of communities and groups. Within a complex political system like this, there can be many publics. Hence, we can define *a public* in modern terms as "all members of a polity or of a local community or politically significant constituency group within the polity." We can then define *public choice* as any choice affecting the public well-being.

Public Choice and Citizens

All of us make *personal* choices about how we want to live our lives. We decide how we want to appear to others, how we want to face life's obstacles, how seriously we want to take our schooling, how we choose to deal with crises and temptations, and how we choose to relate to others.

Some personal choices also have *public consequences*. As consumers, our individual decisions have a cumulative effect on much more than the prices of and profits on the goods we buy or reject. Individual decisions to conserve the purchase of fuel for automobiles and home heating play an important role in the implementation of energy conservation policy. The types of homes we are able to buy or rent shape the community of the future; that shaping of our social space significantly affects the future need for public goods and services in such areas as crime control, water supply, waste disposal, transportation design, and the design of public parks.

We also make wide-ranging and far-reaching *public choices* in our capacity as citizens. Immigrants elect to become citizens; youth decide whether to take citizenship seriously; voters decide whether to cast their vote.

In recent decades, many public policy issues have been placed on the public agenda as a direct result of citizen pressure. The impact of concerned mothers organized as Mothers Against Drunk Driving (MADD) on highway safety policy is but one example of the ways in which citizen choices are translated into public policy.

What makes a good citizen has been a subject for debate and discussion since at least Aristotle's time. The following section examines Aristotle's thinking on this question.

Aristotle on Citizenship in Western Political Thought*

Over twenty-three centuries ago, Aristotle devoted Book III of his *Politics* to "The Theory of Citizenship and Constitutions." Ever since, this work has been the starting point for any serious study of citizenship.

Aristotle set out two basic questions: What makes a citizen? and What makes a good citizen?

Aristotle answered the first question in three parts. The first was definitional. A citizen is a member of a political society; a democratic citizen shares in the judicial and deliberative functions of that society. The second part of the answer concerns the origins of citizenship. Here, Aristotle relied primarily on *jus sanguinis* (law of the blood), which gives children the citizenship of their parents. Aristotle raised but did not fully answer questions regarding three alternative sources of citizenship: How did the founders of the polis become citizens? Should naturalized citizens be

---

*Adapted from Foundations of Freedom: Citizenship Education, by Stephen L. Schechter (Albany: Law, Youth and Citizenship Program of the New York State Bar Association, 1989). Used by permission of the publisher.

full-fledged citizens? How are old and new citizens to be treated in the wake of a revolution? The third part is the functional or cautiously teleological (ends-oriented) approach so often identified with Aristotle. Here, as earlier, Aristotle maintained that a citizen is one who enjoys constitutional rights of sharing in judicial and deliberative office. At the same time, Aristotle supported slavery as a necessary and natural condition of society. As a result, citizenship and politics were exclusive domains.

Aristotle's second question was "What makes a good citizen?" He answered this question, in part, by comparing the relationship between a citizen and his polis to the relationship between a sailor and his ship. Sailors compose a ship's company, just as citizens compose a polis. Sailors differ from one another by virtue of the different capacities in which they act (e.g., rowers, pilots, and lookouts). So, too, citizens may differ from one another in the political functions they perform within the polis. Nonetheless, all sailors work toward the common end of safety in navigation. Therefore, it is possible to judge a good sailor by how well he or she performs his or her particular task and how well he or she contributes to the common end of safety. Likewise, it is possible to judge the good citizen by the particular function served and in terms of the overall contribution to the good of the polity.

Because Aristotle maintained that the ultimate purpose of every polis is human excellence, he established two additional requirements for good citizenship. The good citizen will be committed to pursuing excellence within and for the polity and will be willing to pursue excellence within the bounds of the law. In sum, then, the good citizen is the patriotic, law-abiding person who strives to pursue excellence by performing his or her role in society to the best of his or her ability.

ACTIVITY   **What Constitutes a Good Citizen?**

Think of an event in your life that was related to citizenship.

- When did it happen?
- Who was involved?
- What happened?
- Was it a positive or a negative event?

Record the basic information on a sheet of newsprint; post it on the wall with the papers of the other members of the class.

Meet in a group of five students. Using only the information on the posting sheets, arrive at a common statement of what constitutes a good citizen.

Write your group's conclusions on a piece of newsprint. Post your conclusions and compare them with those of other groups.

- What were the similarities and differences among the conclusions reached by the several groups?

- How similar was your group's definition of good citizenship to the definition you would expect to find in a civics textbook?
- What are the implications of this exercise for teaching social studies?

Abraham Lincoln on the Morality of Civic Duty

The conflict between being a good citizen and being a good person arises when the obligations of one conflict with the obligations of the other. For example, a particular law or regime may be in conflict with a universal standard of justice. In such a situation, the civic obligation to obey the law comes into conflict with the ethical obligation to follow one's conscience.

A clear and moving example of the conflict between civic duty and personal conscience is described in a letter written by President Abraham Lincoln on August 22, 1862. The letter was written in response to Horace Greeley's communication of August 19, printed in the *Tribune* of August 20, 1862, under the headline "The Prayer of Twenty Millions." Greeley expressed disappointment with "the policy you [Lincoln] seem to be pursuing with regard to the slaves of Rebels." Lincoln's response is printed in full below. No finer statement of the "morality of civic duty" can be found. Lincoln's duty as president is to preserve the Union at all costs. Lincoln would compromise his "personal wish" to free the slaves to any length so that his duty would remain uncompromised.

For Aristotle, the obligation of the statesman (or democratic ruler) is to guide the polity toward the end of human excellence where the demands of a good citizen and a good person are identical. Aristotle relies on the wisdom of the statesman to reconcile the demands of being a good citizen and being a good person.

ACTIVITY

Analyzing President Lincoln's Letter to Horace Greeley

Read Lincoln's letter. In your class, discuss the following questions: What is Abraham Lincoln's view of being a good leader and a good person? Does he agree or disagree with Aristotle's definitions of a good citizen and a good person? Do you agree with Artistotle? Lincoln?

Write a brief response to Lincoln, explaining your views on these questions.

Hon. Horace Greeley: Executive Mansion,
Dear Sir   Washington, August 22, 1862.

I have just read yours of the 19th. addressed to myself through the New-York Tribune. If there be in it any statements, or assumptions of fact, which I may know to be erroneous, I do not, now and here, controvert them. If there be in it any inferences which I may believe to be falsely drawn, I do not now and here, argue against them. If there be perceptible in it an impatient and dictatorial tone, I waive it in deference to an old friend, whose heart I have always supposed to be right.

As to the policy I "seem to be pursuing," as you say, I have not meant to leave any one in doubt.

I would save the Union. I would save it the shortest way under the Constitution. The sooner the national authority can be restored; the nearer the Union will be 'the Union as it was'.* If there be those who would not save the Union, unless they could at the same time *save* slavery, I do not agree with them. If there be those who would not save the Union unless they could at the same time *destroy* slavery, I do not agree with them. My paramount object in this struggle *is* to save the Union, and is *not* either to save or to destroy slavery. If I could save the Union without freeing *any* slave I would do it, and if I could save it by freeing *all* the slaves I would do it; and if I could save it by freeing some and leaving others alone I would also do that. What I do about slavery, and the colored race, I do because I believe it helps to save the Union; and what I forbear, I forbear because I do *not* believe it would help to save the Union. I shall do *less* whenever I shall believe what I am doing hurts the cause, and I shall do *more* whenever I shall believe doing more will help the cause. I shall try to correct errors when shown to be errors; and I shall adopt new views so fast as they shall appear to be true views.

I have here stated my purpose according to my view of *official* duty; and I intend no modification of my oft-expressed *personal* wish that all men every where could be free. Yours,

A. Lincoln

POLITICS AND POWER

People go into politics for two reasons: power and justice. The desire for political power is the desire to affect public decisions. The quest for justice is the pursuit of one's conscience and fairness in public policy.

Together, these two concepts form the matrix of politics and the conceptual boundaries of political science as a discipline.† Political power forms one boundary (or axis) and one set of coordinates of politics, and justice forms the other. In this section, we examine the concept of power; in the following section, we turn to justice.

Generally speaking, *power* can be defined as "the ability to get what you want." Since everyone else in politics is also trying to accomplish what he or she wants, *political power* boils down to, and can be defined as, "the ability to change the public choices of others." In this sense, power is one of the most basic ends of politics.

---

*At this point, Lincoln crossed out the following sentence: "Broken eggs can never be mended, and the longer the breaking proceeds the more will be broken."

†This conceptualization of power and justice is adapted from the work of Daniel J. Elazar (see, for example, Elazar 1984a, 112–14).

However, it is not an end in itself unless one becomes so involved in the "power game" that one loses sight of the reasons for seeking to change the decisions of others.

Typically, political scientists distinguish between two sides of the power equation: the capacity or potential to influence others and the interactional situation in which power is actually exercised. Social scientists attempt to identify and measure the former in the belief that the latter will become less elusive.

Power Resources

Political scientists consider several categories of resources in assessing the power potential of political actors. These categories include positional, reputational, and intellectual resources, as well as access and the support base of the actor.

Positional resources are a function of the position held. They include formal powers, financial resources, and staff. In a system of constitutional government, the formal powers of the actors set the game in motion. The president and the Congress of the United States must come to a budget agreement each year because each of these institutions possesses formal budget-making powers. In a very real sense, governmental institutions function in a system guided not by a separation of powers but by "a government of separated institutions sharing powers" (Newstadt 1976, 101). Of secondary importance are the financial and staff resources political actors can direct toward the achievement of their goals.

Reputational resources refer to the actor's reputation for success, credibility or trust, and style. Politics is governed by the halo principle, "nothing succeeds like success," by which political actors build up their reputational capital. Of additional importance are the credibility of political actors to deliver upon the promises they make and their style, ranging from cooperative to confrontational. Deservedly or undeservedly, for example, President Ronald Reagan secured a reputation for success during his first inauguration ceremony as the hostages were released from Iranian captivity.

In the world of politics, *intellectual resources* are the actor's capacity for strategic planning and tactical maneuvering. A political strategy might entail an overall plan for a large-scale operation, such as a political campaign for winning an election. The overall strategy and the day-to-day maneuvering must be adjusted to changing circumstances and alliances while maintaining the goal of winning and the integrity of the objective sought. This is a major subject of both study and practice by political scientists.

Access is the proximity of political actors to political leaders capable of making a final decision. Hedrick Smith relates a political story on this point by Robert Strauss:

"You know, power is an interesting thing," Strauss said . . . "I used to think political power was going to a political dinner. And then I thought political power was helping put on a political dinner. And then I thought it was being invited to stay at the

candidate's hotel in a convention city. And then I used to stand in the hall outside of Sam Rayburn's suite at the political convention, and I thought that was something. And then I got to go into the living room of the candidate's suite, and I thought that was something. And then I found out there that the decisions were all made back in the bedroom. And finally, I was invited in the bedroom with the last eight or ten fellas, and then I knew that I was on the inside—until I finally learned that they stepped into the john. In the end, just me and Jimmy Carter and Hamilton Jordan made the final decision in the john." (Smith 1988, pp. 70–71)

Constituencies and coalitions are the ultimate resources in a representative democracy; hence, their analysis is an important field of political science: public opinion and voting behavior. In the American system, most political actors are representatives, and their political clout is measured largely by how many votes they can deliver on a particular decision. In an electoral decision, the question is how many voting constituents can be delivered.

Legislative issues are decided by how many legislators can be mustered to vote one way or another. At this level, the political strategy (and field of political science) is one of *coalition building*. In this process, constituencies still count. For example, lobbyists visit legislators and tell them how many of their constituents are also members of the lobbyist's interest group, and the president (or governor) may take his or her case directly to the people, urging them to write to their legislators.

The totality of power resources a political actor can bring to bear in a particular situation is his or her *clout*. In certain situations, a political decision can be obtained from only one political decision maker. In most situations, however, the final decision comes in the form of a vote cast by one's voting constituents or legislative colleagues. In those situations, the test of clout is that final vote, and the results are measured by political scientists and players alike.

| ACTIVITY | **Evaluating Power** |

Choose a local or state political actor. Develop a research plan for assessing this actor's power. What questions would you ask? What data would you gather? From what sources? How would you analyze the data?

Is a high level of power necessarily either good or bad? Explain your answer.

The Exercise of Power

Turning to the other half of the power equation, the situation in which power is actually exercised, we find that public policy fields are multiplying as society becomes more specialized. Thus, political actors may be involved in only a few of these fields.

During the late 1970s, Governor Daniel J. Evans of the State of Washington coined the term "iron triangles" to refer to the policy fields he encountered in Washington, D.C. In each policy field—whether transportation, health, human services, or natural resources management—Governor Evans found a relatively independent and separately functioning power subfield. For example, a higher-education subfield is one of several subfields in the educational field. Like other subfields, higher-education policymaking is composed of three sets of actors for each government: (1) leaders of relevant legislative committees and subcommittees, (2) heads of relevant government agencies, and (3) representatives of relevant interest groups. On noncontroversial issues, these players will deal with one another on a regular and increasingly routine basis, resolving issues and making decisions as they arise. Few political actors cross over from one policy field to another, and few political leaders have the time to become involved in noncontroversial policy fields.

To summarize, there are various resources of power and principles for exercising political power. There is, however, no simple formula for acquiring, using, and maintaining political power in a complex, democratic society.

| Figure 7.2 | Most people perceive the presidency to be a very powerful office. Yet presidents from Truman to Bush have complained about their inability to get things done. Which view of the presidency do you think is more accurate? *Source: Bettman Archive.* |

JUSTICE AND THE ROLES OF GOVERNMENT

Justice, as we shall see, is the end of government and the civil society of which it is a part. That means that every decision or action of government is evaluated first and foremost against the cardinal principle of justice. Justice means *fairness*; in a just society, people come to expect fair treatment and fair decisions from their public institutions. But what is fairness, and how is it defined and implemented in a society that values liberty?

Liberty and Justice Distinguished

The Declaration of Independence proclaims that "Governments are instituted among Men, deriving their just powers from the consent of the governed" to secure "certain unalienable Rights, that among these are Life, Liberty and the pursuit of Happiness." The U.S. Constitution of 1787 goes beyond the rights-directed purpose of government set out in the Declaration and proudly announces its establishment: "in order to form a more perfect Union, establish Justice, ensure domestic Tranquility, provide for the common defence, promote the general Welfare, and secure the Blessings of Liberty to ourselves and our Posterity." In the Pledge of Allegiance, citizens are expected to swear their allegiance to the republic "with liberty and justice for all."

Carefully review these often-confused passages. Which principles are most frequently mentioned? Why? Is there any order or relationship among these principles?

Two sets of political principles recur throughout the founding documents of the American polity. The first set includes those two previously discussed principles by which government is founded and maintained—namely, *republicanism* (popular consent) and *constitutionalism* (the rule of law). The second set of political principles has to do with the ends toward which government is directed. Included in this set are the two terms most frequently mentioned in those documents—*liberty* and *justice*.

Liberty, in its political context, can be defined as "the freedom *from* the arbitrary and capricious limits of others *to* act, think, express oneself, and make choices as one wishes, so long as the exercise of freedom does not unlawfully restrict the freedom of others." In the U.S. system, the most precious freedoms are understood to be those contained in the Bill of Rights and subsequent amendments to the U.S. Constitution.

In a nutshell, then, the American concept of liberty is procedural in that it seeks to free individuals to pursue their own ends; however, this conception is rarely extended to guarantee the substance of the ends themselves. In other words, liberty enables the *pursuit* of happiness, *not* happiness itself. Hence, liberty is a "first principle" because it is instrumental to other human ends that cannot be obtained without it.

If liberty is the instrumental end of *individual* action, then justice is the instrumental end of *governmental* action. James Madison concludes his discussion of the structure of government in *The Federalist* papers with this observation: "Justice is the end of government. It is the end of civil society. It ever has been and ever will be pursued until it be obtained, or until liberty be lost in the pursuit" (*The Federalist* 51).

The relationships among power, liberty, and justice can be explained this way: In civil societies, governments possess the ultimate power, namely, the legitimate authority to coerce others to act. In fact, this is precisely what distinguishes governments from other institutions. The result of any coercive governmental action is an encroachment upon individual liberty. Justice is the first principle or criterion against which such action is judged. Liberty, in this context, is not an absolute right. It can be limited by governmental action, but only if such action is just. It is in this sense that the Declaration of Independence puts justice and power together into the idea of "just powers." But what are just powers? That brings us to the concept of justice.

Justice Defined

Justice, like power and liberty, is a complex and elusive concept essential to political science and susceptible to scientific definition. *Justice* can be defined as "fairness determined on the basis of due process of law and a due regard for proportional equality." This definition has three facets: fairness as proportional equality, in which decision makers must assign benefits and burdens to different people; due regard, in which decision makers must take into account a diversity of circumstances affecting one person's actions; and due process, in which decision makers must carry out their decisions in compliance with the law.

Proportionality, which is at the very heart of justice, means that two persons who act alike under comparable circumstances should be treated alike. This general rule applies to determinations of guilt and sentencing in criminal law, adjustment of claims in civil law, allocation of scarce resources by public policy, distribution of tax burdens and incentives by fiscal policy, and the provision of rights by constitutional design. On some questions, proportional equality *is* absolute equality. For example, all citizens (whether born or naturalized) should be entitled to the right to vote. However, in most cases, proportional equality requires the assignment of different burdens or benefits. The awesome challenge of *just* politics is to determine a reasonable basis for granting each person his or her *due* burden or benefit relative to others of like condition.

Consider the case of *Plyler v. Doe* (1982), in which a suit brought before the U.S. Supreme Court challenged a provision of the Texas Education Code that denied free public education to illegal immigrant children, namely, children who were not "legally admitted" into the United States. The equal protection clause of the Fourteenth Amendment directs that all persons similarly circumstanced should be treated alike. At the same time, government can impose classifications that serve important governmental objectives or substantial government interests especially in situations where a right at issue (i.e., education) has been previously determined by the Supreme Court not to be a fundamental right. In this particular case, the

Supreme Court overturned the state provision on the grounds that the state's primary concerns were financial ones and did not represent a sufficiently substantial interest "to deny a discrete group of innocent children the free public education that it offers to other children residing within its borders."

Due regard reflects certain expectations about the decision-making process. First is the Hamiltonian belief, expressed in *The Federalist* No. 1, that public decisions should be made on the basis of "reflection and choice," not "accident and force." The second expectation is that reflection will be part of a reasoning process in which all sides will receive a fair hearing and consideration. The final element of due regard is the expectation that the deliberative process will yield a final decision that at least meets the standard of reasonableness.

Due process of law is guaranteed by the Fifth and Fourteenth Amendments to the U.S. Constitution as a protection against the arbitrary deprivation of "life, liberty, or property" by national and state governments, respectively. At minimum, due process suggests that judicial proceedings will be guided by a sense of fairness, to borrow from Daniel Webster, "which hears before it condemns, which proceeds upon inquiry, and renders judgment only after trial." As Justice Felix Frankfurter emphasized in his opinion in *Joint Anti-Fascist Refugee Committee v. McGrath*, due process represents "a profound attitude of fairness between man and man, and more particularly between the individual and the government." Justice Frankfurter continued: "Due process is not a mechanical instrument. It is not a yardstick. It is a process."

Seeing justice defined makes it somewhat easier to understand justice as, to quote Madison, "the end of government [and] the end of civil society." Other political principles, such as advancing equality, promoting the general welfare, assisting the needy, providing law and order, and maintaining world peace, are all defined in the context of justice and as touchstones of justice. In relative terms, each society must determine for itself the just mix of those and other political principles. As a result, justice also becomes, as Alexander Hamilton put it in *The Federalist* No. 17, the "great cement of society."

ACTIVITY

Simulating a Legislative Hearing

Should families be allowed to choose the schools students will attend? This question is currently being debated at all levels of government. The public education system in the United States has historically provided choice to those families having the necessary resources. For example, parents with financial resources have been able to send their children to private schools. Similarly, parents with adequate resources have been able to choose to live in neighborhoods or districts with good schools or to persuade policymakers to support their views on how the schools should be operated or what programs should be offered. In addition, special programs within schools, such as programs for the gifted or performing arts programs, have provided some degree of choice in the kind of education a child receives.

So, to some degree, parents, students, and teachers have always had and made choices. Generally, however, school districts have no set policies to maximize choice and no rationales to support the goal of maximum choice of schools, programs, courses; and the public has yet to demand a formal set of policies for promoting choice.

Make an initial assessment of where class members stand on this issue by constructing a human graph. Designate a place along the wall to represent each of the following positions: unlimited choice among private and public schools (with financial aid), unlimited choice among public schools (with transportation or other aid provided as needed), no aid provided to support choice. Each student should stand in front of the position that most nearly represents his or her views on the issue. Three people representing each position should be chosen to serve on the legislative committee in the simulation described below.

The members of the legislative committee will be hearing testimony on the issue of school choice and will then formulate a policy on the issue. The committee should choose a chairperson to run the meeting. The members should conduct research that will allow them to question witnesses and develop a sound policy.

The remaining class members should be divided into six groups, with each group taking one of the roles provided below. Each group is to gather information in support of their role's position and prepare a two-minute opening statement. They should also be prepared to answer questions from committee members.

Professor Goodwrench

Choice is not like the other school reforms and should not be combined with them as part of a reformist strategy for improved public schooling. Choice has the capacity by itself to bring about the kind of transformation that reformers have tried to engineer in myriad other ways. Choice must be adopted without other reforms since the latter are based on democratic control and implemented by bureaucratic means.

Mr. Charles B. Leader

The greatest predictor of school effectiveness is that schools have autonomy and internal, bureaucratic control. Politics are ruining America's public schools. As headmaster of a private school, I am directly accountable to my parent constituency and board. This requires strong leadership, clear goals, ambitious academic programs, teamwork, and professionalism among teachers. We need to establish some form of tuition-tax credit or voucher system in this country.

Ms. Bee Free

I want to be able to choose the school for my own children. There is nothing more precious to me than the health and education of my children.

Mr. Wilson Woodrow

Look at the savings and loan associations. When you get substantial deregulation, there are unanticipated consequences. I question whether parents should choose a school for its superior academic program or for other reasons. It would be almost impossible to create an information system that would enable people to make informed choices among schools. I doubt whether a complacent citizenry would really take advantage of a system of choice to move children from one school to another.

Mr. G. T. Washington

Choice is largely an unproven strategy that could destroy the public school system. We need a system of rewards and punishments based on educational outcomes that would be more likely to focus innovations on improved learning. As professional educators, we are best informed about how children learn. What is needed is greater commitment on a federal and state level to support our schools and teachers.

Ms. Abby Link

Choice is misguided. Parental choice is an elitist wolf wrapped in egalitarian sheepskin. Ultimately, it will deny millions and millions of students access to equal opportunity. *And* the present public school system is dull-witted by lack of competition. What is needed is to give more authority to parents and local school councils, elected by the community, and give them the authority to set budgets, and to hire and fire principals and teachers. This is the only way to address the problem of low-income students.

When the research has been completed, conduct the hearing, allowing two minutes for the opening statement of each witness and three minutes for questions. Following the testimony, committee members should attempt to reach consensus on a proposed piece of legislation related to school choice.

Debrief the activity by considering the following questions:

- How is the concept of liberty related to this activity?
- Did the simulated process conducted by your class give due regard to all sides of the issue? Did it provide due process of law as you understand it?
- Does the policy developed by the committee provide for proportional equality?

• • •

- How might you adapt this activity for use with secondary students?
- What questions would you use to debrief the activity with secondary students?

THE CONSTITUTIONAL FRAMEWORK

Constitutions set the rules by which other choices are made—the goals, the actors and their powers and limits, the boundaries of the field, and the ground rules.

Constitutional Rules: The Goals

The first constitutional goal is constitutionalism or the rule of law—that is, an agreement among the actors to play by the rules. A second goal in democratic societies is popular consent and the freedom of political choice (often termed *republicanism*). The preamble of a constitution typically reflects goals or purposes. Hence, the U.S. Constitution states:

> *We the People of the United States, in Order to form a more perfect Union, establish Justice, insure domestic Tranquility, provide for the common defence, promote the general Welfare, and secure the Blessings of Liberty to ourselves and our Posterity, do ordain and establish this Constitution for the United States of America.*

The goals stated in a constitution are, of course, not the only public goals of a free society. Rather, they are the *fundamental* goals of a free society—those goals too precious to leave to chance. In the foreseeable future, it is unlikely that Americans would choose to alter the goals set out in our national Constitution; however, from time to time, Americans use the opportunity provided by their state constitutions to add goals considered fundamental to the citizens of that particular state. For example, the constitution of Montana, adopted in 1972, constitutionally enshrines the right of its citizens "to a clean and healthful environment" (art. 2, sec. 3), and the New York State Constitution provides that "Labor of human beings is not a commodity nor an article of commerce" (art. 1, sec. 17).

Constitutional Rules: The Actors

In the U.S. system, public policy is democratic, but it is not completely open to all individuals. Its authority is the people; that point is underscored in our state and national constitutions. However, not all people are equally entitled to the enjoyment of all rights set out in those constitutions.

The most appropriate example is the right to vote. This right is granted neither to all individuals nor to all citizens, but rather only to those citizens who are eighteen years of age or older (U.S. Constitution amendment 26, sec. 1).

The point is that the Constitution defines the actors and their roles. "The people" as a collectivity is the authority for the Constitution and its change. "Persons" are the beneficiaries of certain fundamental rights; other rights, such as political rights, belong to the citizenry; certain segments of the population have fought successfully for their rights to be constitutionalized (e.g., the provision for worker rights in the New York State Constitution); however, no person may be denied basic rights because of his or her race or gender.

Constitutional Rules: Distribution of Powers

The Constitution also defines those actors empowered to hold government office. The rule of *federalism* provides for two sets of constitutional governments—national and state—each with its own representatives drawing their authority directly from the people, who are sovereign. Equal partners in their respective spheres, both governments are subject to the U.S. Constitution and to the laws and treaties of the national government passed in pursuance of that Constitution. The resulting structure is a federal system that resembles a nonhierarchical matrix of power. Figure 7.3 displays this matrix view of the American system and two commonly drawn yet constitutionally inaccurate views. The pyramid view, for example, shows a hierarchical, command-and-control system, in which commands flow down and obedience flows up. This view is inaccurate because the Civil War determined the supremacy of the Union, not the sovereignty of the national government over the states. The centrist view displays a center-periphery system in which all roads lead to the national capital. Such a system exists in France, where Paris is quite literally the center of the

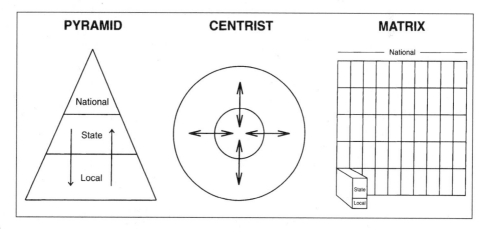

Figure 7.3   Three views of the American system. *Source: From "The American System as a Federal Democracy," by Daniel J. Elazar, in* Teaching about American Federal Democracy, *Stephen L. Schechter ed. (Philadelphia: Center for the Study of Federalism, 1984), p. 10–11. Used by permission.*

universe. However, the American system is composed of a variety of capitals, from the financial capital in New York City to the music capitals of Nashville and Detroit.

The *separation-of-powers* rule provides that national and state governments are, in turn, divided into branches—a legislative branch granted powers of lawmaking, the executive responsible for administering the law, and the judiciary empowered to decide cases involving conflicts arising under the law. Taken together, the rules of federalism and separation of powers are designed to confine the actors to their own turf. At the same time, the players are governed by a third and pragmatic rule of *power sharing,* providing common areas within which various players can (and in some instances "must") cooperate to complete a particular task. Hence, national, state, and local governments have the power to tax, while within each government both legislative and executive branches are required to enact a tax measure.

Constitutional Rules: Boundaries and Ground Rules

The discussion of actors suggests two basic operating rules. First is the rule of limited government; that is, each of the governments in our federal system and each of the actors within those governments has limits and boundaries defining what it can do and where it can do it. Put differently, every power has its limits. John F. Kennedy once described the president "as a man of extraordinary powers. Yet," Kennedy continued, "it is also true that he must wield these powers under extraordinary limitations" (quoted in Sorensen 1963).

At the same time, American constitutions recognize the rule of power-sharing arrangements, not only in the name of checks and balances, but also in the belief that public things are best done by a variety of actors, each bringing a unique perspective to politics and learning how to accommodate individual perspective and interests to those of the other actors. In this sense, the rule of power sharing becomes the political equivalent of the social rule of pluralism and its expectation that actors will play by the rules with a healthy respect for diversity.

For students interested in critical constitutional choices today, we can draw several important lessons from these constitutional rules. First, our national and state constitutions set out broad goals, such as promoting the general welfare and protecting individual liberty, and some state constitutions also formulate public policy. Rarely does one seek a solution to a public problem by amending the U.S. Constitution itself. The Prohibition Amendment (amendment 18) clearly demonstrates the difficulty of regulating social behavior and solving social problems by constitutional amendments.

Second, constitutional goals, such as the general welfare and individual liberty, can result in a clash of rights when one set of actors (whether that be governmental or individual) attempts to pursue a goal at the expense of or without regard for another goal. Behind each constitutional goal is an actor or a group of actors with interests and rights.

Third, the American constitutional tradition typically sees the role of constitutions in public policy making as procedural and not substantive. When facing a public problem like the spread of AIDS or drug abuse, one looks to national and state constitutions for an understanding of where the solutions can be found and not what they might be. Again, constitutions set out the actors, their powers, and their limits.

Fourth, the nature of the constitutional process involves an element of power separation in the name of liberty and power sharing in the name of governance. Virtually every public policy problem—from national defense to waste disposal—simultaneously involves national, state, and local governments as well as the actions of nongovernmental organizations and individuals on national, state, and local planes.

The hard case for this point is constitutional policy itself, normally thought to be the special preserve of the U.S. Supreme Court. In fact, nothing could be further from the truth. Increasingly, state courts, led by the New York State Court of Appeals and the high courts of other innovative states, have relied upon their own state constitutions to extend individual rights beyond those guaranteed by the federal Constitution and its Burger-Rehnquist interpretations. Additionally, both the U.S. Congress and the state legislatures play an important role as constitutional policymakers through their respective powers in amending federal and state constitutions. Finally, though indirectly, constitutional policy is made every time individuals, whether they be public officials or private individuals, seek to act constitutionally by making choices within constitutional limits set by the Constitution itself.

The previous discussion points toward one final lesson: The U.S. Constitution, in the words of one scholar, is an "incomplete document." The U.S. Constitution was intended by its framers to join, not replace, existing state constitutions. That is why the U.S. Constitution could be so brief and could focus entirely on "fundamentals." State constitutions and their governments were then and remain today the workhorses of the American federal system. Together, the fifty-one federal and state constitutions complete the American constitutional system.

ACTIVITY

The Federalist on Limited Government*

Read the excerpts from *The Federalist* provided below. As you read, contrast Hamilton's and Madison's views on the subjects of limited government and rule of law.

NUMBER 51: MADISON

. . . the great security against a gradual concentration of . . . powers in [the government] . . . consists in giving . . . the necessary constitutional means and personal

---

*Adapted from *Lessons on the Federalist Papers*, by John J. Patrick and Clair Keller (Bloomington, Ind.: Social Studies Development Center and Organization of American Historians, 1987). Used by permission of the authors.

motives to resist encroachments. . . . It may be a reflection on human nature that such devises should be necessary to control the abuses of government. But what is government itself but the greatest of all reflections on human nature? If men were angels, no government would be necessary. If angels were to govern men, neither external nor internal controls on government would be necessary. In framing a government which is to be administered by men over men, the great difficulty lies in this: you must first enable the government to control the governed; and in the next place oblige it to control itself. A dependence on the people is, no doubt, the primary control on the government; but experience has taught mankind the necessity of auxiliary precautions [limited government based on the supreme law of a written constitution]. . . . Publius

NUMBER 70: HAMILTON

Taking it for granted, therefore, that all men of sense will agree in the necessity of an energetic executive, it will only remain to inquire, what are the ingredients which constitute this energy? How far can they be combined with those other ingredients which constitute safety [provisions for limited government] in the republican sense [government in the name of the people by their elected representatives]? And how far does this combination [energetic government that is also limited by law] characterize the plan which has been reported by the convention?

The ingredients which constitute energy in the executive are unity [a single chief executive or President]; duration [a long enough term of office]; an adequate provision for its support; and competent powers. [Hamilton argued that these ingredients were included in the Constitution of 1787.]

The ingredients which constitute safety in the republican sense [provisions for limited government and the rule of law] are a due dependence on the people, and a due responsibility. . . . Publius

Questions

Discuss the following questions with your class or in small groups.

1. According to Hamilton and Madison, what are limited government and the rule of law? How do they justify their ideas on limited government and the rule of law?

2. What are the role of the people and the uses of a written constitution in achieving limited government and the rule of law? How does the Constitution of 1787 provide means for balancing powers needed for an "energetic" government and limitations on those powers needed to protect individual rights and liberties?

3. Describe the characteristics of a government that is both energetic and limited. Does the current government of the United States fit your description?

APPLICATIONS TO CONTEMPORARY POLITICS

In a world of rapid change, the present becomes an increasingly important part of the knowledge base for making decisions. In this section, we use the concepts of power and justice to analyze three enduring issues of politics and public policy: the allocation of scarce resources, the regulation of human behavior, and the protection of the national interest. Readers should look for examples of these three enduring issues in the news taking place when this chapter is read.

Enduring Issues: The Allocation of Scarce Resources

There is no better example than the budget of how government allocates resources. October 1 marks the beginning of the federal fiscal year, always a good time for stories of stalled budget negotiations, legislative-executive disagreements, and partisan wrangling. The budget-making process captures the most important policy choices a government can make. For the social scientist, a federal or state budget is not only an instrument of public policy but also a manifestation of political power and the resulting sense of justice. The reason is that public budgets are society's answer to the allocation questions—who will get what and who will pay for it.

How will funding priorities for a particular category of programs (such as higher education) fare relative to other categories of spending elsewhere in education and in other fields, such as transportation, health, human services, and military defense? Should federal funds for higher education be awarded to students, colleges and universities, or some combination of the two? Should regional balance be a factor? What distinction, if any, should be drawn between funding for public and for private institutions? What should be the relative importance of merit and need in determining student assistance? These policy questions draw out lobbyists and other interest-group advocates from all segments of society: state colleges and universities, private colleges and universities, parent associations, teacher associations, student associations, minority groups, conservative groups, liberal groups, union organizations, regional groupings, and coalitions of congresspeople themselves.

On the revenue side, the question "who will pay?" is complicated by the fact that any single budget is only part of the total funding picture, which includes a mix of federal, state, and local public funds with corporate, nonprofit, and self-contributing dollars. Every proposal to increase tax revenues contains a particular burden for a group of individuals. Hence, tax-increase battles are fought not only on the economic grounds of the relative impact of tax hikes but also on the political grounds of the relative influence of affected groups and their advocates in the Congress.

The foregoing examples suggest two ways of addressing the allocation question.* The first is *distributive,* in which expenditure resources (or tax burdens) are

---

*This discussion is adapted from Ripley and Franklin (1987).

allocated on the basis of contributions made. The distributive philosophy is disaggregative and pluralistic, based on the assumption that resources should be widely distributed in small denominations so that there is something for everyone, with the most distributed among the middle (and largest) class. The organizational principle of the distributive philosophy is decentralization or noncentralization based on the belief that the role of government should be limited to translating individual contributions to public services.

By contrast, the *redistributive* answer seeks to allocate expenditure resources and tax burdens based on *need*. The principle of the redistributive philosophy is aggregative, based on the assumption that public resources should be consolidated and then targeted where they are needed most. The organizational principle of the redistributive philosophy is power centralization based on the belief that the proper role of government is to take from those who have more and give it to those who have less. Typically, this added function requires the centralization of power, not only because of the government agencies often created to administer these programs, but also because of the political power needed to resist or persuade "the haves."

These choices can produce a great debate over fairness, especially when students realize that "the haves" are the middle class, "the have-mores" include those who create jobs for the middle class, and "the have-nots" include those who dream of getting a job and entering the middle class. U.S. policies reflect a mix of distributive and redistributive philosophies; however, in comparison with other economically developed countries, our domestic policies of spending and taxing are more distributive in nature.

There is also a power side to the decision over how best to allocate scarce resources in society. According to Ripley and Franklin (1987), the politics of distributive policymaking tends to be characterized by logrolling relationships, stable political relationships, low decision-making visibility, low presidential involvement, high bureaucratic involvement, low involvement by Congress as a whole, high involvement by congressional subcommittees, and high involvement by vested interest groups. As a result, the structure of distributive politics takes the form of an "iron triangle" composed of congressional subcommittees, executive bureaus, and small interest groups; most decisions tend to be noncontroversial and rather routine.

By contrast, the politics of redistributive policy is characterized by political relationships of ideological and class conflict, stable political relationships, high decision-making visibility, high presidential involvement, moderately low bureaucratic involvement, high involvement by Congress as a whole, moderately low involvement on the part of congressional subcommittees, and high involvement of "peak associations" representing clusters of interest groups. That means that the importance of subgovernments is very low, with major decisions made by the executive branch interacting with peak associations. The degree of conflict between the Congress and bureaucracy is potentially high, based on partisan and ideological differences.

ACTIVITY

Designing a Bulletin Board

Select a current issue that involves allocation of scarce resources. Design a classroom bulletin board display that shows students how the concepts of justice and power are reflected in the issue. The bulletin board should show policy options (indicating whether they are distributive or redistributive) and who is involved in policymaking.

Enduring Issues: The Regulation of Behavior

The regulation of human behavior is one of the great functions of government because government possesses the legitimate power to direct public resources to induce or coerce human beings to behave in a particular way. The allocation function of government can be used as an instrument to regulate behavior by inducing certain kinds of behavior with incentives or by controlling other kinds of behavior through criminal sanctions. For example, a tax deduction for property taxes and the interest on mortgage payments provides an incentive to home ownership, valued by many political theorists as the greatest stabilizing force of democracy. At the same time, in power terms, this decision is an attempt to satisfy the political demands of the homeowning middle class.

Regulation is at the very heart of the relationship between the individual and civil society. Some political cultures are based on a fundamental distrust of human nature, which leads them to use government regulations as a means of narrowing the bounds of human discretion. Others seem to place their distrust on government and the very use of regulation to control behavior. Traditionally, American political culture falls into the latter category.

In the U.S. system, the legal source of governmental regulatory power is the *police power*. The purpose of this power is to protect and advance the public health, safety, and morals of the people. Constitutionally and historically, the police power resides primarily in the states. Over time, the federal government has acquired a police power; however, the states possess the lion's share of laws (from criminal law to family law) regulating behavior, the administrative agencies responsible for enforcing those laws, and the courts where suspected lawbreakers are tried and punished.

Every year, thousands of lobbyists and other policy advocates attempt to persuade state legislatures and Congress to pass or block legislation. In the last section, we saw that many of these competing interests are structured as "iron triangles," especially when the pending legislation is noncontroversial and distributive in nature. The politics of regulatory policy is comparable to distributive policy in this way: Positive or protective regulations (such as regulation of the professions) tend to follow the distributive model of subgovernment-dominated politics, whereas negative or social regulations (such as limiting a woman's right to an abortion) tend to follow the redistributive model, in which the stakes are higher, the policy differences more intense, and the players more powerful.

In either case, whether the regulation sought is positive or negative, the political culture and the process of legislative politics and compromise tend to produce incremental results. On returning to their constituents, disputants may celebrate the half they won or mourn the half they lost, but they will undoubtedly return to the legislature next session for more. This is why, over time, most of the bills passed are not new laws but amendments to existing legislation.

Increasingly, decisions affecting government regulation are made in courtrooms as well as in legislative chambers. This field of "public law litigation" increasingly involves suits brought by private parties challenging the legality of a government regulation. Actions such as these touch every quarter of government regulation and range widely from parents seeking public school admission for their mentally ill child to artists seeking to overturn a law banning their artistic work.

| ACTIVITY | **Debating the Regulation of Behavior** |

Choose one of the issues below or another currently in the news. Conduct a class debate on the issue.

- Does William Tennent High School in the Centennial School District, Pennsylvania, have the right to refuse to lease its auditorium to Campus Crusade for Christ and its subsidiary, Student Venture (an outside organization), when school district facilities are used by other community groups?

- Does a federal agency have the power to prohibit the granting of public funds on the basis of obscenity or to require that grant recipients certify in writing that they will not create "obscene" work?

- How should the courts resolve the custody claims of a biological parent and the genetic parents whose fetus was carried by the biological parent?

- Does state government have the power to prohibit live animal research by medical colleges in the name of animal rights?

- Does a city council have the power to pass an ordinance creating a "drug-free" zone around city schools providing for increased sentences for those convicted of selling drugs within, say, 1,000 feet of school property?

- What should be the role of community residents in determining whether a group home of mentally handicapped persons should be located within their neighborhood?

Enduring Issues: Preservation of the National Interest

American politics is played out within a global context. In many policy areas, that context is not an important factor. In others, the international environment can produce significant political factors as a result of (1) the globalization of domestic politics or (2) the domestication of international politics. In still others, ongoing issues of foreign policy and national defense are played out in an international arena in which U.S. political actors must remain sensitive to American public opinion and other domestic political forces. A variety of domestic factors can influence and be influenced by foreign policy. Consider the following examples.

Public opinion, which is a critical factor, tends to run in cycles. For example, public opinion favored nonintervention in the 1920s after the diplomatic failures following World War I, intervention following the diplomatic failures of appeasement and Pearl Harbor, nonintervention when confronted with the no-win situation in Vietnam, and intervention in the Middle East when both oil and honor were threatened. Within these cycles, there can be wide differences between, say, the general public and opinion makers.

Ethnic lobbies can be an important political factor when foreign policy is directed toward the home country of a large, articulate, or otherwise potentially powerful ethnic group. For years, the Taiwan lobby had been a powerful force against recognition of Communist China. As new immigrants began arriving from mainland China, the Chinese-American community became more diversified and the Taiwan lobby lost its strength. To cite another example, the Israeli lobby draws upon the resources of the American Jewish community, and the Arab lobby has more recently come to include resources from within the Arab-American community.

Congressional–presidential relations are critically important in most foreign policy situations owing to the congressional expectation of presidential leadership and the presidential dependence upon congressional approval, whether in the form of Senate ratification of treaties, appropriation of funds, or authorization of actions. Open rivalry between Congress and the president, as in the case of Senate opposition to President Woodrow Wilson's League of Nations, can become highly divisive and debilitating. The shared responsibility of the president and Congress in foreign policy is, as Edward S. Corwin (1940) put it, an "invitation to struggle."

State and local politics can become part of international politics in several ways: Local communities can create international incidents, border states must deal with one another on shared problems, state and local officials promote their markets abroad, and states and localities dependent upon defense dollars lobby for a strong defense. For example, New York State, Quebec, and Ontario have agreements on the management of hydroelectric power. New York State and Poland have an agreement on cultural and educational exchange programs. New York State courts have decided issues with international ramifications ranging from the outcome of an America's Cup race to the freezing of Iranian assets. Governors travel to foreign countries to promote trade and tourism.

International factors and global forces can influence the politics of a particular foreign or domestic policy. Consider the following examples.

International incidents can mobilize entire communities and pit neighbor against neighbor. The "Red scare," Japanese internment, and recent anti-Arab sentiments are examples.

Foreign trade and investment can significantly influence the local economy and politics of communities dependent upon selling their products abroad, attracting foreign investment, or protecting local manufacturing from cheaper foreign products.

Transnational actors and multinational corporations have become significant features of the international system and can permeate domestic politics and the economy in various ways. For example, a transnational movement like Green Peace can catalyze forces in opposition to national and international projects in ways impossible for national groups or international organizations. Multinational corporations introduce yet another dimension into international politics. For example, the American subsidiary member of a multinational corporation with offices in Western Europe may have interests within the new European market that diverge from the interests of an American company looking to export goods to that same market.

All these influences, domestic and foreign, are played out within an international system characterized not only by its permeability but also by its fluidity. Today, the United States is searching for a viable position of world leadership in a world of profound political change. In a world such as this, what *are* the interests of the United States? What should we seek to accomplish, with whom should we join, and on what basis?

When George Washington in his Farewell Address spoke of "our true policy to steer clear of permanent alliances," he hoped for a day "when we may choose peace or war, *as our interest, guided by justice*, shall counsel" [emphasis added]. What a marvelous counsel to our foreign policy: "interest, guided by justice." Is it possible? According to George F. Kennan, a diplomatic historian and pragmatic diplomat, it may not be desirable. Writing in 1951, he observed:

> *Whoever says there is a law must of course be indignant against a lawbreaker and feel a moral superiority to him. And when such indignation spills over into military contests, it knows no bounds short of the reduction of the law-breaker to the point of complete submissiveness—namely, unconditional surrender. It is a curious thing, but it is true, that the legalistic approach to world affairs, rooted as it unquestionably is in a desire to do away with war and violence, makes violence more enduring, more terrible, and more destructive to political stability than did the older motives of national interest. A war fought in the name of high moral principle finds no early end short of some form of total domination. (Kennan 1951, 101)*

Although Kennan's view may seem cynical, power politics may be the most realistic policy:

> *In the absence of a world government that could govern and safeguard it, each state knows that it can depend on no one but itself for its own preservation and safety. Self-protection is the only protection in an essentially anarchical system. In short, the very nature of the state system breeds feelings of insecurity, distrust, suspicion, and fear. . . . (Spanier 1985, 1–2)*

The realists may push their case too far. First, a balance-of-power system can be a perfectly acceptable floor for just action as well as power politics. Second, various acts of intervention to right imbalances have shown that international behavior based on right plus might are needed to maintain (and may possibly raise) the floor of acceptable international behavior. Third, we live in a democratic age in which the strategy of "power politics" is politically unacceptable and impractical. Publics crave the belief that their leaders are pursuing just actions. The most one can realistically expect is that the rhetoric of justice will be cast in moderate tones. Finally, we live in an international system that has witnessed the accumulation of international law and international organization in a variety of peaceful arenas (from courts of justice to the management of competing economic claims); this, too, is part of the reality of international politics.

International politics is no longer the special preserve of diplomats and warriors. The politics of foreign policy or of internationalized domestic policy can be played out on different levels and involve a variety of actors. Its politics can be primarily multilateral, bilateral, or domestic. It can involve relations with foreign allies, competitors, antagonists, or neutral parties. The politics of foreign policy is also played out at home, where it can involve presidential–congressional relations, interagency relations, national–state–local relations, and a variety of interest groups, ranging from trade unions lobbying for a textile tariff act to Chinese Americans lobbying for refugee status for dissident Chinese students.

American foreign policy also involves a wide range of instruments. Even a basic list would include legal measures within international, federal, and state law; diplomatic measures within multilateral and bilateral situations ranging from crisis management to the maintenance of normal diplomatic relations; defense policy, including strategic planning, procurement, deployment, training, organization, and weapons development; economic policies, such as trade, aid, investment, and boycotts; technology policy for peaceful and military purposes; immigration and refugee policy; and cultural and educational policies, including cultural exchange, educational exchange, tourism, and travel.

Some of these policies involve the allocation of scarce resources at home or abroad. These include funding for military installations, defense contracts, foreign aid, embassies and consulates, research grants, and study fellowships. They may involve distributive outcomes through "iron triangles" in rather routine and noncontroversial ways; or these resources may require redistributive policies, sharp cutbacks, or new initiatives that may engender sharp ideological differences and filter politics up to the highest levels.

Foreign policy may also involve the regulation of human behavior at home or abroad. Examples of foreign policy regulation include tariffs and quotas for specific goods and nations; banning the importation of defective or otherwise undesirable goods; restrictions on the sale of weapons to foreign nations; and providing refugee status to a particular opposition group in a foreign nation.

Finally, foreign policy may involve crisis responses to problems of a serious nature that come as a surprise and demand immediate action (Ripley and Franklin 1987, 28). Examples of such crises include the Japanese attack on Pearl Harbor in 1941; the discovery of Soviet missiles in Cuba in 1962; the Iranian kidnapping of American hostages in late 1979; and the Iraqi invasion of Kuwait in 1990.

Several basic conclusions can be drawn about the politics of foreign policy-making in the American system. The first is the permeability of the American system itself. Domestic issues penetrate the making of foreign policy, and domestic issues can, in turn, become internationalized. The second is the fluidity of the international system and the reemergence of a balance-of-power system in which the United States must search for a viable position of world leadership. A third conclusion has to do with the variety of foreign policies and policy instruments. Finally, it is important to note the importance in both foreign and domestic politics of the enduring issues of resource allocation and government regulation.

| ACTIVITY |

Rethinking Foreign Aid*

The last decade of the twentieth century has brought the United States and the world to a new global situation that few envisaged and for which no nation has prepared. The United States and much of the rest of the world have been preoccupied since the end of World War II with the cold war, the product of a basic conflict of interests between the Soviet Union and its Communist allies on the one hand, and the United States and its allies on the other. The American analysis of this struggle led to a number of corollaries: Countries needed to be prosperous to withstand the lure of communism, since poverty might drive people to trade freedom for the promise of bread. Economic development and industrialization in other countries were advantageous for the United States and the West, since their trade would then increase and benefit all parties. Though political liberty might not be necessary for economic development, prosperity would enhance the prospects for democracy in other nations, thus promoting a world in which the United States would be more at ease. Free nations had to be militarily strong enough to defend themselves against Communist incursions in their area and to take part in the overall American-led containment of communism and the Soviet Union.

Out of this analysis came the American willingness to institute a program of foreign aid, that is, the provision of economic assistance that combines an American tradition of generosity with the active promotion of what are perceived to be U.S. national interests. Seemingly simple, the term "foreign aid" has come to cover an exceedingly complex set of policies. These include alleviating famine and the effects

---

*Adapted from "Rethinking Foreign Aid," in *Great Decisions 1991* (New York: Foreign Policy Association, 1991), pp. 43–50. Used by permission.

of disasters; promoting agricultural production and industrialization in nations that are deficient in one or both; providing U.S. know-how and technology to meet basic health, education, and housing needs; supplying weapons, training, and funds to support the armed forces of friendly countries; compensating nations for supporting American military forces; rewarding governments in a material way for embracing American ideas or interests; and other purposes too numerous to list.

Although the cold war is over, the United States still has many other national interests to pursue and a leadership role to fulfill. How can foreign aid help it carry out its goals?

For each of the policy options below, develop a list of advantages and disadvantages. Which policies are most likely to be supported by the "realist" school, which sees international politics as the pursuit of power in the name of the national interest? Which would be most likely to gain support from those who argue for a foreign policy based on the principle of justice? Which policy do you think the United States should adopt?

- Give economic aid for development only, and separate the economic and security assistance programs. Specifically, cut economic support for Israel, Egypt, Greece, Turkey, and Portugal, and increase development assistance, especially for sub-Saharan Africa and the Caribbean.

- Tie economic aid to criteria such as political pluralism, free enterprise, observance of human rights, and environmentally sound development.

- Assign aid on the basis of need rather than on the basis of a government's ability to use it.

- Internationalize U.S. development aid.

ACTIVITY

Designing a Political Science Lesson

Choose one of the application areas discussed in the previous section: allocation of scarce resources, regulation of behavior, or preservation of the national interest. Look through the newspaper or newsmagazines to find an issue that falls in one of these areas. Design a lesson plan on that issue that will help students understand how the concepts of choice, justice, and power are embedded in the issue.

Reflecting on the Chapter

A game metaphor is often used in describing politics. Indeed, politicians themselves often use sports metaphors in their public speeches. Do you think such metaphors are an appropriate way of thinking about politics? Why or why not? Try to think of a metaphor that captures your views of politics.

References

Aristotle. *Politics*. Trans. E. Barker. New York: Oxford University Press, 1962.

Association for Supervision and Curriculum Development. *Public Schools of Choice*. ASCD Issues Analysis. Alexandria, Va.: ASCD, 1990.

Augustine, Saint. *City of God against the Pagans*. Trans. W. M. Green. Cambridge, Mass.: Harvard University Press, 1964.

Buehrig, E. H., ed. *Essays in Political Science*. Bloomington, Ind.: Indiana University Press, 1966.

Corwin, E. S. *The President: Office and Powers*. New York: New York University Press, 1940.

Crick, B. *The American Science of Politics: Its Origins and Conditions*. Berkeley and Los Angeles: University of California Press, 1959.

Deutsch, K. W. *Politics and Government: How People Decide Their Fate*. 3rd ed. Boston: Houghton Mifflin, 1980.

Easton, D. *The Political System: An Inquiry into the State of Political Science*. New York: Knopf, 1953.

———. "The New Revolution in Political Science." *American Political Science Review* 63, no. 4 (December 1969): 1051–61.

Elazar, D. J. *American Federalism: A View from the States*. 3rd ed. New York: Harper & Row, 1984a.

———. "The American System as a Federal Democracy." In *Teaching about American Federal Democracy*, ed. S.L. Schechter. Philadelphia: Center for the Study of Federalism, 1984b.

Finifter, A. W., ed. *Political Science: The State of the Discipline*. Washington, D.C.: American Political Science Association, 1983.

Graham, G. J., and G. W. Carey. *The Post-Behavioral Era: Perspectives on Political Science*. New York: David McKay, 1972.

Great Decisions 1991. New York: Foreign Policy Association, 1991.

Gunnell, J. G. "Political Science: Promise and Practice." In *Social Studies and Social Sciences: A Fifty-Year Perspective*, ed. S. P. Wronski and D. H. Bragaw, 59-70. Washington, D.C.: National Council for the Social Studies, 1986.

Kennan, G. F. *American Diplomacy 1900–1950*. Chicago: University of Chicago Press, 1951.

Kissinger, H. A. *American Foreign Policy*, 3rd ed. New York: W. W. Norton, & Co., Inc., 1977.

Levy, L. W. *Original Intent and the Framers' Constitution*. New York: Macmillan, 1988.

Lipson, L. *The Great Issues of Politics: An Introduction to Political Science*, 6th ed. Englewood Cliffs, N.J.: Prentice Hall, 1981.

Louri, T. *The End of Liberalism: The Second Republic of the United States*, 2nd ed. New York: W. W. Norton, & Co., Inc., 1979.

Neustadt, R. *Presidential Power*. New York: John Wiley, 1976.

Patrick, J. J., and C. W. Keller. *Lessons on the Federalist Papers*. Bloomington, Ind.: Social Studies Development Center and Organization of American Historians, 1987.

Rawls, J. *A Theory of Justice*. Cambridge, Mass.: Harvard University Press, 1971.

Ricci, D. *The Tragedy of Political Science: Politics, Scholarship, and Democracy*. New Haven, Conn.: Yale University Press, 1984.

Ripley, R. B., and G. A. Franklin. *Congress, the Bureaucracy, and Public Policy*, 4th ed. Chicago: The Dorsey Press, 1987.

Schechter, S. L. *Foundations of Freedom: Citizenship Education*. Albany: New York State Bar Association, 1989.

Siedelman, R., and E. J. Harpman. *Disenchanted Realists: Political Science and the American Crisis, 1884–1984*. Albany: State University of New York Press, 1985.

Smith, H. *The Capital Power Game: How Washington Works*. New York: Ballantine Books, 1988.

Sorensen, T. C. *Decision-Making in the White House: The Olive Branch or the Arrows*. New York: Columbia University Press, 1963.

Spanier, J. *American Foreign Policy Since World War II*, 10th ed. New York: Holt, Rinehart, and Winston, 1985.

Storing, H. J., ed. *Essays on the Scientific Study of Politics*. New York: Holt, Rinehart, and Winston, 1962.

Tocqueville, A., de. *Democracy in America*. Trans. Henry Reeve. New York: Schocken Books, 1962.

Voeglin, E. *The New Science of Politics*. Chicago: University of Chicago Press, 1952.

Teaching Resources

American Government Simulations. Garden City, N.Y.: Focus Media, 1992. Computer simulations.

American Political Science Association, 1527 New Hampshire Avenue, NW, Washington, DC 20036.

Authority and *Justice*. Calabasas, Calif.: Center for Civic Education, 1990. CCE (5146 Douglas Fir Road, Calabasas, CA 91302) also sponsors a Constitution competition.

Council for the Advancement of Citizenship, One Dupont Circle, Suite 520, Washington, DC 20036.

Decisions, Decisions. Watertown, Mass.: Tom Snyder Productions. Computer simulations.

Education for Freedom. Denver: First Amendment Congress, 1991. The First Amendment Congress (1445 Market Street, Suite 320, Denver, CO 80202) also publishes a free newsletter.

Engle, S., and A. Ochoa. *Education for Democratic Citizenship*. New York: Teachers College Press, 1988.

Great Decisions. New York: Foreign Policy Association. Published annually. The Foreign Policy Association (729 Seventh Avenue, New York, NY 10019) also publishes other resources.

Ketcham, R., et al. *Participation in Government: Making a Difference*. Littleton, Mass.: Copley Publishing Group, 1988.

McKenna, G., and S. Feingold. *Taking Sides: Clashing Views on Controversial Political Issues*. Guilford, Conn.: Dushkin, 1992.

National Issues Forum. Dubuque, Iowa: Kendall-Hunt. Published annually.

Patrick, J. J., and C. W. Keller. *Lessons on the Federalist Papers*. Bloomington, Ind.: Social Studies Development Center and Organization of American Historians, 1987.

Patrick, J. J., and R. C. Remy. *Lessons on the Constitution*. Boulder, Colo.: Social Science Education Consortium; Washington, D.C.: Project '87, 1985.

Perspectives. Arlington, Va.: Close Up Foundation, 1990.

Powers of the Government. Warren, N.J.: Optical Data, 1992. Videodiscs.

Public Issues Series. Boulder, Colo.: Social Science Education Consortium, 1988–1993.

Starr, I. *Justice: Due Process of Law*. Minneapolis: West Publishing, 1981.

Turner, M. J., and S. Lake. *U.S. Government: Resource Book for Secondary Schools*. Santa Barbara, Calif.: ABC-Clio, 1989.

Update on Law-Related Education. Chicago: American Bar Association. Published 3 times yearly.

Zola, J. R., and J. P. Zola. *Teaching about Democracy*. Boulder, Colo.: Hal Clarke Press, 1989.

8

STUDYING AND TEACHING ECONOMICS

Suzanne Wiggins Helburn and H. Michael Hartoonian

ACTIVITY LIST

• • •

Constructing a graphic representation, p. 171
Consensus building, p. 174
Analyzing a case study, pp. 177 and 199
Analyzing textbooks, p. 182
Developing a retrieval chart/discussion, p. 184
Discussion, p. 188 and 191
Designing a case study, p. 200
Journal writing, p. 200

ACTIVITY | **What Is Economics?**

Draw a circle in the middle of an 8½-by-11-inch sheet of paper. Write the word *economics* inside the circle. Now make a diagram (a conceptual map) of your view of what the field of economics involves. Take ten minutes to draw your diagram. Then, in small groups, compare diagrams and construct one for your group as a whole on a piece of newsprint or on the chalkboard. Create a list of questions about economics you would like to have answered.

INTRODUCTION

Economics and politics have always been intertwined. Increasingly, economic decisions and political issues are becoming global in scope. U.S. domestic economic problems, which loom large indeed, are dwarfed by the momentous changes in the world economy: the collapse of Eastern European and Soviet-style command economies, the development of major world competitors to the United States, vast free trade zones such as the European Union, the worldwide disruption of oil, the dizzying movements of the worldwide stock exchanges, the long-term environmental crisis, the increasing polarization of rich and poor nations.

The relative decline in U.S. economic power and performance is reflected in many of our domestic problems: a lagging rate of economic growth, stagnating real wages, the dislocation of industries and workers, increasing international trade deficits, and a soaring federal government budget deficit. Other trends in our domestic economy are also worrisome. The Savings and Loan crisis and the Wall Street scams of the 1980s raise questions about the moral functioning of business. The century-long movement of women into the labor force has created new markets for goods and services but has also been accompanied by profound changes in family structure and child rearing.

The importance of these issues demands that economics have a central role in the social studies curriculum. The problem is deciding what economics to teach and how to relate it to the crucial problems facing our nation and the world today. The choice of content is further complicated by the different and conflicting approaches to studying economics.

Most K–12 economics curricula and textbooks introduce students to the basic market features of the U.S. economy and teach pupils how to make personal economic decisions based on rational trade-offs. These curricula and materials are widely available from publishers and through the programs offered by such organizations as the National Council on Economic Education and Junior Achievement. (See the Teaching Resources section at the end of this chapter for references to those organizations.)

Although the "free market" approach to teaching economics is useful in explaining the virtues of decentralized market decision making, it does not, in our opinion, provide an adequate foundation for understanding the economic side of history. Nor does it provide a neutral framework for studying the economic dimensions of public policy. In fact, a principal point of this chapter is that there *is* no neutral framework. All approaches to studying economics embody underlying beliefs and values. This chapter does not lay out a framework for designing a course in economics. Rather, it suggests ways to expand traditional economics courses to include viewpoints presented in this chapter, to engage students in important economic public policy debates, and to incorporate economics in other social studies courses.

This chapter seeks to expand your understanding of economics by focusing on the following objectives:

- *Economics as perspective.* You will study how perspectives on capitalism have changed over time and differ according to political and ideological beliefs, and how these diverse perspectives provide different insights about economic performance and problems.

- *Economics as choice influenced by ethics and ideology.* You will be introduced to the principal schools of economic thought and will explore how ideology and ethics influence economic choices, including personal economic decisions.

- *Economics as policymaking.* You will apply policymaking strategies to economic problems, all of which raise questions as to the need for government intervention in market decisions. You will learn how to combine the study of public policy and economics.

- *Economics as a scientific community.* Learning about the history and sociology of the discipline of economics will help you understand it as a community of economists, who have developed the neoclassical paradigm (way of studying economics). You will also learn how other traditions provide useful insights about economic history and contemporary economic problems.

We hope to encourage you to explore the different traditions in economics and to apply them in your teaching.

DEFINING ECONOMICS

The economics discipline can be described along at least three dimensions: the subject of study, the method of study, and the social organization of economists into a profession.

One way to define economics is to describe what it is about—the subject matter. Economics is the social science discipline that deals with human problems related to material well-being. It is about the economy, the economic system. Economics is mainly about capitalist economies organized through decentralized systems of markets. These are capitalist because most production is organized through businesses run for profit. Later in the chapter, we give a brief history of the development of economics, illustrating that (1) the economic problems studied have shifted over time, reflecting the stage of economic development and the economic problems of the time; and (2) underlying beliefs about the effectiveness of capitalism affect the subject matter and method of studying economics.

Another way to define economics is to describe the way economists think—the method. From this perspective, economics is the study of the logic of rational economic choice, of *economizing*. Economists try to devise methods for determining optimal resource allocation. By optimal, they mean the best (lowest cost) use of resources to meet the demand for goods and services, when demand is determined by the existing distribution of purchasing power in the society. These methods can be used to determine how to maximize output, profits, and satisfaction. They can also be used to measure the trade-offs or the costs and benefits of alternative actions. One important application of the logic of optimization is in public policy analysis. Much of the practical work economists do involves giving advice about how to, when to, and why or why not to intervene in the market system to improve its performance.

Still another way to define economics is with respect to the people involved—the community of professional economists whose members have common training and similar jobs. That is, most economists practice a common *discipline,* or way of thinking, and a common *paradigm,* or way of doing research and studying practical problems. The economics profession is dominated by the neoclassical school, so those views prevail with respect to underlying assumptions about how capitalist economies work, what economic problems are most important, how to solve them, how to do research, and how to teach economics.

Other traditions in economics, although they have a lesser influence in the profession, do persist. All scientific paradigms depend on a fundamental set of beliefs. In economics, those beliefs relate to how well capitalist economies operate and how they change. Those presuppositions or beliefs are, fundamentally, political in nature. Part of the explanation for the success of neoclassical economics is that it conforms more closely to commonly held beliefs about the effectiveness of the capitalist market system, which, of course, it helps to perpetuate.

ACTIVITY

Distinguishing between Economics and the Economy

One source of confusion to beginners studying economics is distinguishing between *economics* as a field of study and the *economy* as a system within which people function. This relationship between an economy and economics is like the relationship between practice and principles, between what we do and what we believe. Whereas practice is constrained by patterns of behavior, demographic trends, and environmental factors, principles are based on cultural assumptions and intellectual constructs that give meaning to our everyday practice.

Listed below are several statements about economics and the economy. In small groups (three to five people), discuss each statement to reach a consensus (agree or disagree). Assign a recorder to keep track of the words or ideas about which there is the most disagreement. At the end of the exercise, and again at the end of the chapter, your group should write definitions of *economics* and the *economy*. Share definitions in a general class discussion, using a flip chart, a chalkboard, or an overhead projector. Compare for general agreement and identify areas of disagreement.

Agree-Disagree

_____ 1. An *economy* always operates within some framework of *economic* principles and ethics.

_____ 2. *Economics* is the study of how people make rational choices and, as such, is unaffected by ideological influences.

_____ 3. Any *economic* issue or problem will have more than one best solution, because the *economy* is more complex than an economic theory.

_____ 4. Public *economic* policy is simply a reflection of private decisions made within the *economy*.

_____ 5. *Economic* policymaking is always a political act.

_____ 6. The *economy* is to *economics* as behavior is to conscience.

ECONOMICS OR POLITICAL ECONOMY?

Differences in thinking about economics can be understood by contrasting contemporary and older views of the nature of the subject. Today, economists consider themselves scientists trying to discover the facts and laws that describe the operation of the economy. They model their work after nineteenth-century physics and place great emphasis on developing economic theories or models of the operation of market economies.

Mainstream neoclassical economists today define economics as the study of the social allocation of scarce resources among competing ends. They emphasize the exchange aspect of an economy: People trade goods and services and, thereby, allocate scarce resources so as to satisfy human material wants. Neoclassical economics pictures society as a system of exchanges between individuals who have freedom of choice and who always act rationally; that is, they act to promote their own economic or material interests by maximizing their economic gain. The subject matter is divided into two areas: *microeconomics* and *macroeconomics*.

Microeconomic theories predict the operation of individual markets in determining prices, wages, profits; allocating resources between markets; and determining the distribution of income among individuals. Neoclassical economists view the market system as a self-correcting system of competitive markets that adjusts supply of scarce commodities to demand for goods and services. It is a decentralized system (no one is in charge), which is nevertheless coordinated through competition between buyers and sellers. Changes in supply-and-demand conditions are signaled through changes in prices; in turn, these price changes induce changes in amounts bought and sold. Because of the competitive process, individual market participants, seeking to maximize their own gain, also promote the welfare of society as a whole.

Macroeconomics considers the economy as a whole, as a circular flow system between individuals, who own factors of production and demand final consumer goods, and businesses, which produce the output and make investment decisions that determine economic growth (see Figure 8.1). Macro theory explains the reasons for total growth of the economy and the causes of periodic business cycles that create inflation, too much unemployment, or both.

This view of economics as a science, and in isolation from other aspects of society, particularly politics, is relatively recent. The first economists called themselves political economists because they were interested mainly in recommending appropriate policies for regulating the emerging capitalist market economy; they understood that such policies always involved political—that is, power—relations. They also considered political economy as part of moral science because the decisions affect human well-being and require just solutions. They recognized that major public policy questions affected the distribution of wealth and power among the different classes of landowners, merchants, factory owners, and laborers. They distinguished between policies that promoted the good of society as a whole and those put forward to promote vested interests of a particular powerful group. Thus, the eighteenth- and nineteenth-century political economists, whom we will briefly discuss later, took for granted the moral dimension of public economic policies.

As political economy gradually became transformed into the science of economics, its practitioners distanced themselves from both politics and ethical considerations. Most economists today argue that, as scientists, they are interested only in the facts (what is), not in values (what ought to be). Nevertheless, we will argue that ethical considerations and values cannot be eliminated from economic issues; they can only be ignored or hidden. Economic decisions always are based on the person's view of what should be done. Therefore, how society operates, what actually

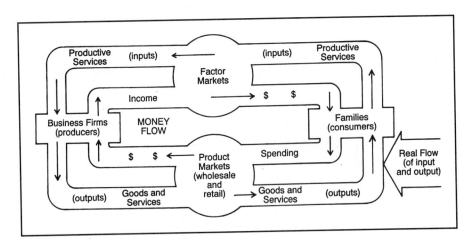

Figure 8.1   Circular flow of a money-exchange economic system

happens, is a function of the moral attitudes of its participants. One of the big issues confronted in this chapter is whether, in fact, people are basically egoists, seeking to maximize their own ends. If self-interested, are they narrowly focused on economic gain? If so, is some government intervention necessary to promote the public interest?

Mainstream, neoclassical economics is based on a particular view of capitalism and of morality. Implicitly, in arguing that the free market works well because people act in their own self-interest, it assumes that people are naturally egoistic and do not act out of higher principles. Neoclassical economists believe that market competition succeeds quite well in coordinating these individual decisions to maximize production, wealth, and satisfaction for individual participants. Thus, they accept the view that "the good" for society is the sum of what individuals consider their individual good. Nevertheless, neoclassical economists recognize that the system is not perfect and that limited government intervention is sometimes called for.

ACTIVITY

The Feminization of Poverty

Part 1

Students coming out of an economics class are in heated debate over the feminization of poverty. After you read the following, in small groups discuss what assumptions about people, the economic system, and public policy are implied in each viewpoint. For each individual's statement, identify an idea out of which policy could be constructed. For example, Milton proposes the use of negative income taxes—the receipt of a tax credit for low-income people similar to the system now in operation. What policies can you find in the other statements?

Teddy: Well, what should we do about these women and their kids who are on welfare? I didn't realize how little of basic expenses are paid by welfare. The prof said that a woman with two small kids can just barely get by in this town on $1,000/month just to feed herself and kids mainly bread and beans, live in a run-down furnished two-bedroom apartment, wear hand-me-downs, get around town by bus, and have minimum telephone service, with nothing left over! And her welfare check and food stamps only cover two-thirds of the $1,000.

Phyllis: Don't be taken in by that liberal drivel. That's what these women choose. If they have babies, they need to be responsible for them. Stay with their husbands, *have* husbands, learn how to be good mothers. These women should go out and find a job now that they've gotten themselves in the mess. And, anyway, he padded the costs. I bet poor people find something cheaper to live in than an apartment that costs $400/month. The welfare system just invites these people to have kids, leave their husbands, and live off us. What keeps the system going? All the bureaucrats who run the system! And to think I'm paying for their telephones!

Huey: Phyllis, in addition to being mean-spirited, you're unwilling to put the problem in social and historical context. The plight of these women and their children is the result of so-called progress in this century. Your progress has been gained at the expense of blacks and Hispanics. These people didn't ask to be on welfare, and most of them want to get off and get a good job. Capitalism breeds both rich and poor. The poor didn't lobby for welfare programs. Politicians created welfare and all the rest of the social safety net programs to keep poor people from revolting. The problem is that these so-called welfare programs are now costing too much because the percentage of poor people has been growing. In addition, businesses are beginning to worry about where they're going to get cheap labor. The power elites are worried that these women are not raising kids to be future workers.

Milton: Phyllis is right about the facts, but we need a social net to protect the worthy poor. Instead of maintaining this monstrosity of welfare bureaucracy and dependency, the government needs to let the market system work. Use the income-tax system to subsidize these people minimally. Give them enough to get by temporarily, but not enough to encourage them to stay on welfare.

Pat: These women need more than a negative income tax. The Family Support Act of 1988 has started welfare reform in the right direction—encouraging women to get job training and find a job. But it is only a halfway effort. These women need real training, good-paying jobs, and good, subsidized child care to help their children succeed in school. The child support enforcement in the 1988 act is good, too; fathers should pay to raise their children even if they are not living with them. There is a lot of pressure on family life today. The only way to bring stability back is to provide the support necessary to help parents and children. And we need to be doing this for *all* families.

Part 2:

The term *feminization of poverty* was introduced by Diana Pearce several years ago to highlight the fact that women and their children make up a larger and larger percentage of those living below the poverty line. To illustrate the diversity of thinking among economists, three sets of explanations of this problem are summarized below, each representing a different school of thought.

Neoclassical economists explain feminization of poverty as a result of changing preferences based on new labor market supply-and-demand conditions that affect women. First, women are participating in the labor force at an accelerating rate, because the cost of staying home is too high. As real wages increase, women prefer to work for wages and buy services they used to provide for the family. Second, increased divorce rates mean a higher percentage of single mothers heading households who must work. Third, these women take low-paying jobs because they have less training and prefer female occupations, working part-time. Also, they are not as committed as men to paid work (they are more interested in their private lives), so they are not willing to change jobs, move, or accept promotions. Fourth, government welfare programs that provide public assistance for childbearing and childrearing reduce incentives for single mothers to work for pay. Neoclassical economists recognize some need for a social safety net for poor women, but they would design policies to induce both parents to pay for their own children's childrearing.

Institutional economists explain the feminization of poverty as an evolutionary, historical phenomenon based on changing technology and societal values: On the one hand women want to participate in the world of paid work and middle-class material standards of living; on the other hand, they want a family life and female rights. These societal pressures affect individual women and their children in different ways. In addition, the United States is made up of subcultures of people of color, and subculture values conflict with those of the mass culture. Poverty is socially caused, not the fault of the poor, and social welfare programs are totally inadequate, so that they commit poor families to poverty. Because of labor market discrimination, uneducated women and minorities can get only low-paying jobs. The large number of women flooding into women's jobs make wages even lower in these occupations. Institutionalists favor higher social welfare payments to the poor, a complex of government programs to improve education and work opportunities for low-income women, and health and education programs for these families.

Marxist economists also explain the feminization of poverty as a historical process. However, emphasizing class analysis, they link the movement of women into the labor force in this century with the needs of capitalist development, and

Figure 8.2   Women's pay continues to lag behind men's, in part because of segregation in the workforce.

they explain existing conditions in labor markets, such as segmented markets, as capitalist reaction to class conflict. Marxists argue that the capitalist system depends on continual capital accumulation controlled by the capitalist class. In turn, capital accumulation is based on profits and, therefore, on a cheap labor supply. In seeking new ways to invest their profits, capitalists continually introduce new goods and services, undermining home production. In turn, this "frees" women, a cheap source of labor (since they still value their family responsibilities), to enter the labor market and induces them to do so to pay for the new products. Furthermore, because of previous class conflicts, the labor market is segmented. Their analysis of the operation of labor markets is similar to that of the institutionalists. Marxists would join women's groups and labor unions and try to organize more effectively to increase their power and successfully achieve their goals.

Questions

Given these typical responses from the neoclassical, institutionalist, and Marxist perspectives, try to place each student reaction from Part 1 within one of the three schools of thought in economics.

In small groups, compare the different positions by identifying differences in their views of facts, definitions, interpretations of facts, and values. Discuss the merits of these different positions. Decide which parts of the explanations from each position sound most reasonable to you.

Write a statement of your position and defend it in 100 words or less.

THE EVOLUTION OF CAPITALISM AND ECONOMICS

Economics, or more accurately, political economy, was one of the inventions of capitalist development; before the seventeenth century, there was no pressing need to understand the economic system. Until the late Middle Ages, economic activity in Europe was predominantly agricultural and organized locally through feudal fiefdoms. However, the Crusades in the twelfth and thirteenth centuries vastly increased trade and commerce. The flow of commodities into Venice and Genoa from the East moved throughout Europe, encouraging municipal development and more trade. That induced some discussion of economics by churchmen, the most famous of whom was Saint Thomas Aquinas, who developed the doctrine of just price, a value system designed to maintain everyone in his or her station in life. The just price covers only labor and other production costs.

As trade continued to expand, the center of power moved from the church to civil authorities. By the sixteenth and seventeenth centuries, an economic system organized around market towns had grown up and become complicated enough to create some controversy. Merchant capitalist enterprise and increasingly strong central governments benefited from monopolies in foreign trade. They also encouraged domestic production through local producer monopolies, guilds of independent master craftsmen protected from outside competition; these guilds controlled both the secrets of the trades and local markets. Public discussion of economic issues became common, as pamphleteers argued various special-interest positions but generally advocated mercantilist policies to promote a favorable balance of trade (exports that exceeded imports) by protecting home production from foreign competition and encouraging exports.

Thus, slowly at first and then with accelerating speed, the agricultural, self-subsistent local economies of feudal society gave way to bourgeois, town society dominated by commercial interests. By 1750 in Great Britain, the first capitalist country, conditions were ripe for transition from commercial to industrial capitalism. Britain had a well-developed network of prosperous trading centers, including London, a center for international commerce. It profited from a brisk foreign trade and a colonial empire, a large domestic market, and a labor force of workers who had been turned off the land by the enclosure movement and were flocking to the cities seeking wagework.

By 1776, when Adam Smith wrote his famous book, *The Wealth of Nations*, he could foresee a new era. He described the beginnings of industrial capitalism and the enormous potential for growth and wealth made possible by the new system. During the mercantilist era, merchants made profits and accumulated wealth by taking advantage of trading opportunities—by buying cheap and selling dear. But Adam Smith emphasized *industrial capitalism*, a new and growing phenomenon—capitalist control of manufacturing to make profits by controlling the organization of work. Smith described the increased productivity of the pin factory created by a new kind of division of labor involving dividing the tasks in pin manufacture into simpler tasks performed by different people, illustrating how the same number of workers could vastly multiply their daily output.

The Classical Economists

Adam Smith was the first of the classical political economists, an approach that dominated economic thinking for more than a century. Seeking to understand the dynamics of the capitalist market economy, classical economists focused on the causes of economic growth and the impact on growth of the distribution of income among the principal social classes of the time: landlord, capitalist, and wageworker. They explained growth in terms of changing class relations and, in particular, the increasing importance of the capitalist or "middle class." By focusing on the importance of capitalists' profits in promoting growth, classical economists emphasized class conflict. They viewed the economy as a system of reproduction in which goods produced in the previous period became "capital," stocks of goods necessary to provide for production in the current period. Economic growth depended on increasing the capital stock of products available for production and consumption from period to period by investing the surplus (the excess output over basic needs) from the previous period to expand production in the current period. Capitalist control of the surplus production over and above that necessary to maintain the population was the source of further expansion. Therefore, the key to economic growth lay in high profits received by capitalists.

In *The Wealth of Nations*, Smith argued that the clue to economic growth lay in giving a free hand to capitalists who were revolutionizing the process of production. Smith recognized in the chaotic hubbub of commercial activity a social system at work. Through the operation of competitive markets, these capitalists were lowering prices and destroying the older, costlier methods of production. Instead of using their profits as revenue to finance consumption, capitalists saved and invested in stock (means of production and of subsistence for workers) to expand production. The appropriate government policy, therefore, was a laissez-faire policy of noninterference in the operation of markets except to protect property. Such a policy would promote natural liberty and the competitive process, through the operation of the "invisible hand" of the decentralized, competitive market system (assuming, of course, that people are moral actors).

David Ricardo, a successful stock broker and member of Parliament, wrote the *Principles of Political Economy and Taxation* in 1817. He defended free trade policies that would keep grain prices low through competition from cheaper imported grain. Low agricultural prices meant lower wages which, in turn, would mean higher profits and, thus, more investment and development of industrial production. Ricardo also explained the source of growth in the amount of labor power the economy was able to bring into productive use to produce capital stock. Thus, he developed the labor theory of value, a theory of price determination based on the cost of production of commodities. According to this theory, prices tend to reflect the amount of labor time and the quality of labor used to produce a product.

By midcentury, industrial capitalism had spread to iron and steel; great strides in mechanized production had created demand for both machinery and improved transportation. The free trade battle had been won, Britain was exporting both goods and capitalism around the world, and the United States was becoming a formidable competitor. Despite the tremendous economic progress created by the twin revolutions in technology and business, factory and mine workers were a miserable lot. Fifteen-hour workdays were not uncommon; children of six and seven worked the mines and in the factories. Conditions at work and in workers' living quarters were lethal, as indicated by the fact that the average life span in industrial northern England was only thirty-seven years, a full twenty years less than in unindustrialized southern England.

| ACTIVITY | **Analyzing High School History Texts' Treatment of Capitalism and Adam Smith's Theory** |

In small groups, study four or five high school texts in either U.S. or world history. Is the term *capitalism* used? If so, is it used accurately? How is economic growth of the nineteenth and twentieth centuries explained? How might these explanations be improved through insights from Smith and Ricardo?

Our experience is that growth is explained in these texts as resulting from the industrial revolution, which, in turn, is described purely in terms of technological advances. There is no mention of the development of industrial capitalists.

Karl Marx

By the time Marx began writing *Das Capital: A Critique of Political Economy* in the 1850s, class distinctions between landlords and capitalists were fading away. Class conflict had shifted to battles between capitalists and their workers. To analyze capitalism, Marx focused on the effect of conflicts between workers and capitalists on class income, economic development, and the long-term viability of capitalism. He took for granted the transitory nature of capitalism, which produced great riches but dehumanized workers and capitalists alike. He considered capitalism the penultimate stage of historical development. Like the feudal society it superseded, through the working out of its own internal contradictions, it would create the conditions for its own destruction. It would be replaced by a socialist society characterized by the free association of workers and an environment in which people could develop their human potential.

Marx objected to the classical economists' preoccupation with the study of exchange, which, he argued, masked the exploitative nature of the system by ignoring relations of production. He developed Ricardo's labor theory of value into a theory of exploitation of labor, the source of class conflict in capitalism. According to Marx, profits represent a surplus based on the unpaid labor of workers—a kind of rip-off of workers that is hidden from view through the process of market exchange. According to Marx, this can happen because capitalists hire workers at the going wage; once workers are hired, however, the capitalists control the actual labor process and can exact as much labor time and energy as they can get away with. Thus, workers produce enough value (commodities) to pay for their own wages plus surplus value that becomes the property of the capitalist and is the source of profits and capital accumulation. In turn, these exploitative working conditions drive workers to organize to improve their lot, creating continual class conflict.

Marx emphasized that capitalism requires continual capital accumulation and expansion. Capitalists are in business not merely to make profits but also to expand (accumulate) their capital. That means that they must constantly expand their business and look for new outlets for investing their capital. This never-ending process involves a continuing tendency for capitalist producers to take over the production of goods and services previously produced at home or in small workshops. This is the process of "commodification." Commodification occurs as more and more products are produced by business instead of at home. One by one, things formerly made at home—cloth, clothing, food, meals, tools—have become commodities, products produced for exchange and profit.

Thus, Marx saw as inherent in the capitalist mode of production continuing expansion driven by an anarchic market system. He considered the market system utterly chaotic, as evidenced by recurrent business cycles that damage workers and many capitalists. He developed a theory of capitalist crisis that explains business cycles; the theory is based on the tendency of firms to overinvest and drive down profits because of inadequate demand for the final goods. Business cycles, in turn, create ever more monopoly power through the centralization of capital in fewer and fewer hands as big firms gobble up collapsing ones.

Because of competition, capitalists are always under pressure to introduce new techniques of production and to speed up economic activity. The result, Marx predicted, would be capitalism's annihilation of "space with time": Distances become insignificant through faster modes of communication and transportation.

There is also, according to Marx, continual pressure to integrate noncapitalist countries and ways of living into the market system. He described this as a process of *uneven development*. Capitalism started in a specific place—Great Britain—and in specific industries—textiles, iron, and steel; then it spread to other locations and industries. Eventually, it would create a world market system. At any one time, however, different countries display different degrees of capitalist organization.

By the end of the nineteenth century, western Europe was capitalist, and the United States and Germany were rivaling Britain's economic power. Capitalist countries were also imperialist, stretching their dominion over noncapitalist countries and regions worldwide. This was an era of tremendous capitalist self-confidence. Real incomes of workers in capitalist countries were increasing. Workers were organizing unions and political parties, but their agendas were for reform, not revolution. Classical and Marxian economics gave way to an approach to economics that would help solve the problems of an established capitalist system.

ACTIVITY

Smith, Marx, and Economic History

Part 1

In many ways, Marx's theory of political economy was heavily influenced by the classical economists. He was interested in the same general problem as they were: the causes of capitalist economic growth and the sustainability of the system. In small groups, discuss the similarities and differences between Smith, Ricardo, and Marx. Construct a retrieval chart (or matrix) like the one below to record similarities and differences. Then make comparisons.

Subject	*Smith & Ricardo*	*Marx*
Role of Competition		
Meaning of Capital Accumulation		
Importance of Capital Accumulation		
Source of Profits		
Nature of the Market System		

Part 2

Marx is best known as the father of modern communism. Most Americans are so opposed to communism that there is a great emotional negative reaction to Marx based on too little knowledge of the man's scientific work.

In fact, Marx wrote next to nothing about socialism or communism. He predicted an eventual historical movement to communism, but he considered it unscientific to guess what form such a society would take. Instead, his main contribution to economics and to revolutionary movements was his analysis of capitalist society. In that endeavor, Marx offered important insights about capitalist development and made remarkable contributions to the study of economic history. He also predicted many of the characteristics and dynamics of the modern capitalist world. Discussing the following questions will help you discover the power of Marx's views in interpreting economic history and today's world economy.

1. How does Marx explain worker exploitation in capitalist society? Give some examples of this exploitation from what you know of working conditions in the nineteenth century and today, of how employers control the work process to get more work out of workers. How, historically, have workers responded to those strategies?

2. How, in Marx's theory, does exploitation explain the source of capitalist profits and capital accumulation? Why do you think Marx called workers "wage slaves"?

3. What does Marx mean by the tendency in capitalist society toward commodification? How is it related to capital accumulation? Give some examples of commodification that are going on today in the United States. How does the process of commodification explain some aspects of the increasing participation by women in paid work and the feminization of poverty?

4. Marx identified a tendency toward speeding up production and the circulation of capital in capitalist society. Why? What does he mean when he says that in capitalism, space is annihilated by time? Give recent examples and discuss how this tendency affects everyday life in the United States today.

5. Marx predicted a tendency for all countries to become part of a world capitalist market system. According to Marx, what factors create this tendency? How are poor nations affected by and integrated into the world market system?

Neoclassical Economics

By the 1870s, there was no longer any question about the growth or survival of capitalism. Everyone took the system for granted, and economists shifted their attention to microeconomic questions related to the efficiency and equity of the market system.

Neoclassical economists ignored class conflict and questions about historical development. They considered profits as legitimate earnings to the owners of real capital. Land, labor, and capital were no longer perceived as belonging to different classes. Basically, any economic agent's behavior could be predicted using the theory describing how to maximize gain in a given situation; the classical economists' emphasis on different classes in capitalist society disappeared. Earnings are determined by the productivity of factors of production. All owners of productive factors earn the value of their contribution to production. There is no surplus, the price of a product equals the cost of production, and normal profits are considered part of economic cost.

Alfred Marshall, professor of economics at Cambridge University, developed the English version of neoclassical economics, which is still taught today in college microeconomics classes. Marshall demonstrated how equilibrium, the balance of supply and demand, was achieved in one market. He showed that both supply conditions *and* demand conditions determine price. He also distinguished between short- and long-term effects on price determination, showing that the classical economists' emphasis on cost as the determinant of prices was a long-term view.

Marshall devoted his energies to establishing economics as a legitimate scientific discipline. He discarded the name *political economy* in favor of *economics*. He helped found the Royal Economics Society and the *Economic Journal*, the society's professional journal. At Cambridge, he succeeded in separating economics from the moral sciences. Finally, his textbook, *Principles of Economics*, published in 1890, codified the teaching of economics, and became the standard text for forty years.

Nevertheless, Marshallian economics began to break down in the 1920s. One of the weaknesses of neoclassical theory was that it almost ignored macroeconomic questions. Although Britain suffered high rates of unemployment throughout the 1920s, neoclassical theory ignored the problem, regarding it as a short-term phenomenon reflecting temporary disequilibrium.

Although Marshall ignored the effects of money on the economy, he did use the quantity theory of money to explain inflation, arguing that changes in the price level were explained by changes in the money supply. The quantity theory of money is based on the equation of exchange: $MV = PQ$. This states that the quantity of money in circulation times the velocity of money (the number of times money changes hands) equals the money value of all goods produced for sale (price times quantity). If we assume that the economy always operates at full employment, the Q, or total quantity produced, is constant. We can also assume that the velocity of money is a constant. Then the equation of exchange can be reorganized to show that $P = V/Q \times M$. That is, the general price level is proportionate to the money supply. If the money supply increases, so does the price level. Marshall and other economists insisted that the fact that modern market economies use money has no other effect on economic activity except on the general price level.

The Keynesian Revolution

By 1935, the worldwide depression had been going for five years, and Britain had experienced unemployment for fifteen years. In *The General Theory of Employment, Interest and Money*, published in 1936, John Maynard Keynes, a student of Marshall's, developed a theory to try to explain unemployment. His analysis created the Keynesian Revolution and shifted the focus from microeconomics to short-run macroeconomic problems of unemployment and inflation.

Keynes objected to the neoclassical assumption that changes in the money supply have no effect on the real economy—on output and employment. He considered monetary and financial manipulation a primary reality of modern market economies; his macroeconomic theory of a monetary economy could explain persistent unemployment in terms of these manipulations.

Emphasizing the function of money as a store of value, Keynes argued that holding money is a hedge against an uncertain future. In fact, monetary and financial transactions link the present with the future. He considered it essential to model the economy over time and to understand the role money plays in such a world. He also accepted the existence and legitimacy of labor unions and other worker attitudes that disinclined them to accept lower money wages just because the price level falls.

Keynes developed a theory that explained why the economy can operate for extended periods of time at less than full employment. Basically, he argued that this happens whenever aggregate demand for goods and services is inadequate to maintain the level of output and employment. That is, he rejected the long-accepted reasoning that whatever income is not spent on consumption would be saved and spent on investment in new plant and equipment. Neoclassical economists thought that changes in savings would automatically be channeled into investment in capital expansion. If savings were large compared with investment, then the interest rate would drop; at these lower interest rates, business would borrow money to increase investment. Keynes rejected this view, arguing that when people save income, they *don't* spend. This decline in aggregate demand will *not* necessarily be offset by investment spending, in which case aggregate demand declines, so that income and output drop.

Keynes argued that individual attempts to save actually result in reduced saving for the whole economy. He called this tendency the *paradox of thrift*. In bad times, individuals try to increase their savings. However, if everyone follows suit, aggregate demand declines; therefore, income declines and people end up actually saving less. Keynes argued that because there are these *fallacies of composition* operating at the macro level, it is inappropriate to assume, as neoclassical economists do, that the macro result represents a simple summing up of individual decisions. Thus, it is not true that what is good for the individual, when added up for the whole economy, results in the public good.

He argued that in times of uncertain business climate, businesspeople lose their nerve and tend to use their capital to speculate in short-term financial assets instead of investing in new plant and equipment. Keynes argued that, in fact, in Britain capitalists were becoming less and less willing to take big risks, preferring to play the various money and stock markets. To eliminate unemployment and promote a business climate conducive to investment, Keynes advocated monetary and fiscal policies to manage aggregate demand, maintain full employment, and encourage low interest rates. Thus, his theory justified government and central bank intervention to stabilize the economy. His views are the basis of twentieth-century liberalism.

ACTIVITY

Keynes and Macroeconomics

In small groups or as a class, discuss the following questions. Students should take turns facilitating the discussion.

1. Why is it true that when all individuals try to save, aggregate saving for the economy as a whole declines?
2. In Keynes's view, why is macroeconomics different from microeconomics?
3. Why does Keynes's reasoning justify government intervention in the economy?
4. President Nixon stated that we are all Keynesians, yet many conservatives consider Keynes dangerous; sometimes they call him a socialist. Why do you think they say that, and do you agree?
5. Using Keynes's theory of justified government intervention in the economy, what policy or policies would you recommend to the federal government to address current economic problems?

• • •

Analyze your discussion. Did most students participate, or did a few students dominate the discussion? What might the facilitators have done to draw more students into the discussion? Did most interaction occur through the facilitators, or was there student-to-student interaction? Did you have enough information to participate fully in the discussion? As a teacher, how would you handle a discussion in which students need additional information?

The American Institutionalists

Early in the twentieth century, John R. Commons, Wesley Mitchell, and Thorstein Veblen developed institutional economics as an alternative to the neoclassical orthodoxy. Institutionalists are interested in effecting progressive social change that leads to human betterment. Therefore, they think of economics as problems-oriented inquiry, as a process of understanding the operation and evolution of the economy and its economic institutions to solve its problems. This orientation draws heavily on John Dewey's philosophy of pragmatism.

Institutionalists object to the neoclassical approach, which starts with the assumption that individuals act entirely out of their own narrow economic self-interest. Institutionalists, combining inductive and deductive methods, develop theories of institutional evolution based on empirical study of the actual economy.

Institutionalists also reject the attempts of neoclassical economists to create a value-neutral science. They consider life a problem-solving process and argue that progress can be promoted by choosing the right values—democratic, egalitarian, communitarian values. In particular, they believe that government should be used to curb excessive power and to provide goods and services that are not adequately provided through market incentives.

Institutionalists, who see all economies as evolving cultural systems, focus on how change comes about and how to promote positive change. They take a holistic approach, focusing on the interrelation of economic, cultural, and political aspects of social behavior. To explain institutional change, they consider social structure and power relations much more important than the behavior of the individual.

Contemporary Debates

Neoclassical economists have successfully fended off their adversaries, sometimes incorporating certain aspects of their theory or methodology. Thus, Keynes's macroeconomic "revolution" was tamed and incorporated into the neoclassical/Keynesian synthesis in the post–World War II period. However, the synthesis excluded many of Keynes's more profound insights. It is based on a mathematical model, which predicts how the economy will adjust to changes in aggregate demand for goods and services and changes in the money supply based on how responsive markets are to changes in interest rates and how quickly prices adjust. Keynesians recognize that the economy can experience sustained unemployment and inflation, and they advocate discretionary action by government or the central bank to promote stability and growth.

The most recent refinement of neoclassical macroeconomics is rational expectations theory. It argues that because people are rational, they use whatever information is available to form their expectations about the future. In particular, they use the correct models of how the economy operates. For instance, they know that increases in the money supply cause inflation. So, if the Federal Reserve announces it will decrease the money supply enough to eliminate inflationary pressures, workers will assume that inflation will subside and will decrease their demands for higher wages, which will further reduce inflationary pressures. This theory suggests that expectations can change abruptly and predictably with changes in information available to the public. If this theory is true, it lends more credence to pre-Keynesian views that government intervention to increase employment is unnecessary and even destabilizing.

Another contemporary debate relates to public choice theory. Traditionally, neo-classical economists have recognized that not all markets function efficiently. In particular, external diseconomies may occur because of the failure of the price of the good or service to reflect the true cost of production. For instance, paper mills and nuclear power plants produce pollution, which is not accounted for in their cost of production because the plant does not have to clean up the polluted stream, ground, or air. Therefore, the prices of paper products and electricity are lower than they should be.

Markets also fail to provide enough of a given good or service if it is a *merit good*—products that need to be supplied to individuals in larger quantities than would be supported by private demand, because community wants exceed individual desires. For instance, today we want low-income children to receive the benefits of good preschools even though their parents cannot afford such care. Parents with adequate income might not demand enough child care from society's viewpoint. They want safe, inexpensive conveniently located care for their children, but they might not understand the importance of high-quality care to their child's development. In such cases, consumers will not purchase the optimal amount of the good from society's point of view.

Traditionally, economists have argued that government should design policies to eliminate these market failures and to increase the efficiency of market allocation of resources. This view of public economics has been challenged since the mid-1960s by public choice theorists, the most well-known of whom is James Buchanan. Public choice theorists apply the assumption that people are rational maximizers of their own interests to analyze how government works. They assume that no one in politics is really interested in efficient outcomes. Rather, they are interested in maximizing their own advantage. Therefore, political decisions are based on special-interest politics. The purpose of public choice theory is to understand the special interests operating in a given situation and explain why the policies that exist were chosen.

Public choice theory assumes that people, including politicians, bureaucrats, and regulators, act only in their own interest. People seeking special advantages from the government form special-interest groups to strengthen their influence. The way public institutions develop is based on the interaction of interest groups with different degrees of power. Public choice theorists consider it folly to intervene to increase market efficiency because the introduction of the policy and its enforcement will depend on the advantages it creates for powerful interest groups.

Thus, public choice advocates deny that anyone acts in the public interest. In fact, they deny the existence of a "public interest," because there is no "public," only a conglomeration of private interests. Public policy is decided through the interaction of interest-group politics, and intervention by well-intentioned economists will work only if the recommendations suit some powerful private interests.

Public choice theorists do, however, recognize a legitimate basis for intervention in the operation of government. They argue that any particular system can be improved by changing the rules under which it operates. Such changes must not be coercively imposed but should be based on popular demand. This opens the door for fundamental change in social institutions if people want it. In general, public choice theorists advocate a state of affairs in which competition among political interest groups determines public policy. They take for granted that the most powerful groups have the most influence. This, of course, is true for market competition as well. Implicit in this view is that there is nothing wrong with monopoly power.

Given the diversity of approaches to studying economics, it is important for social studies professionals to recognize the possibilities available in heterodox traditions. We hope this introduction encourages readers to explore some of the alternative traditions. As the following case study will indicate, each of the modern heterodox schools gives perspectives useful in understanding public policy debates.

ACTIVITY

The Neoclassical Paradigm's Uses in the School Curriculum

By now it should be clear that one function of neoclassical economics is ideological. It describes the market system in such a way as to justify it, to create allegiance to it, and to maintain it. In this sense, economics has always served an important educational function. In addition, the tools of rational economic choice created by economists are useful in training people to do a better job of looking after their own interests in a capitalist society. These two aspects of neoclassical economics form the basis of economic literacy campaigns in public school curricula. The basic lessons to be learned include the following:

- The self-correcting nature of market economies in responding to changes in supply and demand, promoting efficient resource allocation to satisfy consumer wants
- The importance and ethical value of the profit motive and pursuit of individual pecuniary interest
- The basic equity of unequal income distribution
- The importance of trade-off thinking to individuals and to society
- The importance of capitalists in promoting growth and prosperity
- The importance of economic growth and the process that brings it about
- The existence of market imperfections that may justify government intervention to improve market efficiency and economic stability, but the need to limit government intervention in the economy

In small groups, discuss the following questions:

1. With which of the seven objectives stated above do you agree? With which do you disagree? Explain your reasons.
2. Discuss the extent to which the final point above is consistent with or contradictory to each of the other six points.

3. James Madison declared that "if men were angels, we wouldn't need governments." As stated previously, most neoclassical economists consider some government intervention in the economy to be necessary. Why? Because men are not angels? Or is the nature of the economy such that even with the most ethical behavior, we would still need government intervention? Or are the public choice economists correct? Defend your position.

4. Based on what you have learned about the other schools of thought, what other economics learning objectives should be included in the curriculum?

TOWARD A PUBLIC POLICY–ORIENTED ECONOMICS CURRICULUM

Although we have no objection to many of the goals of economics education today, we believe that there should be more emphasis on public policy discussion. Not only is citizen education a primary goal of social studies, but, in addition, learning economic principles is most interesting when they are applied to real-life situations. We think it is vital that teachers help students engage in more effective economic decision making, both in their personal and in their public lives. A corollary concern is to encourage more public participation by future citizens. The remainder of this chapter introduces some issues directly related to economic public policymaking; then it provides a case study that illustrates the alternative approaches to economics presented in the previous section. (You can apply the decision-making strategy in Chapter 13 to the case study.)

The Role of Government in the Economy

The principal issue dividing adherents of different schools of economic thought is the role of government in advanced capitalist economies. Public choice economists argue that because people are fundamentally self-interested, government intervention in the market is really just an extension of market power into the public sector. Implied in this view is a bias against government intervention and in favor of free markets, because government programs and regulation are just another arena for economic competition.

Neoclassical economists believe government intervention is needed to correct market imperfections. They tend to favor policies that work on individual self-interest to provide economic inducements to change individual behavior. With respect to macroeconomic questions, they are most concerned about inflation.

Post-Keynesians think government must stabilize the economy and promote economic growth. They are particularly concerned with the high degree of financial instability in the economy and with the need for industrial planning to promote economic growth.

Institutionalists consider public policy formation a primary function of economists, and they believe government plays an important role in the economy. The role of government is not just to mediate between private interests but also to promote the public interest through the democratic process.

Marxists take for granted that government functions to maintain the capitalist system. Some Marxists consider the state the instrument of the ruling capitalist class, a coercive force to bring about changes in the interest of the capitalist class. Other Marxists see the state as another arena where class conflict is played out, arguing that the working class, environmental groups, the elderly, women, and minorities can gain some benefits through government intervention. Their strategy for change is to participate in organizing more effectively at the grassroots level.

The notions of public good and public interest are central to this debate. Keynesians of various shades and institutionalists are political liberals. Although they might highly value individual liberty, they also believe that there is something called the "public good," distinct from the private good as seen by each individual. To the extent that such public goals exist, the public interest must be defended by someone.

The Private and Public Life of the Citizen

In economics, we teach students to act in their own best interest. In civics classes, we teach them loyalty to country and the importance of participation in public life. Is there a discrepancy in goals between these two parts of the curriculum? Possibly not, if in economics students learn to think in terms of their long-run self-interest, which usually involves acting for the good of the larger society. Personal decisions usually have wider consequences.

We should not think of our public and private lives as competing. Caring about private life more than public life, or vice versa, is part of either/or thinking that places society in jeopardy. Thomas Jefferson focused on the relationship between public and private life when he introduced the concept of "public" happiness in his phrase "life, liberty, and the pursuit of happiness." Happiness here is not just a private pursuit but also a way to enhance private well-being and happiness through public consciousness, service, and support. True happiness is almost always a function of giving, of service, and of inclusive consciousness—that is, living beyond the confines of self. Both our political and our economic roots are firmly planted in the soil of inclusion— our private economic and political well-being depend upon the well-being of the community. This is the meaning of Adam Smith's statement, "self interest, properly understood" (Smith 1937, p. 57).

The most important understanding that we should develop within this inclusive notion is simply that any decision we make in one dimension will affect the other. Personal decisions we make about jobs, lifestyle, and family also affect the public sphere. A decision to follow a particular lifestyle, for example, will carry consequences that are political, legal, economic, social, aesthetic, ethical, and ecological. All those consequences have larger public policy ramifications. Obviously, public policy decisions, from raising interest rates to establishing Head Start early-education programs, affect individuals personally.

Policy Making: A Learning Strategy

Studying economics requires the use of policymaking strategies. One such strategy is briefly described here for your use with the case study that follows (see Chapter 13 for more details). This general strategy for policymaking is based on an exploration of the dynamics that exist between the ideal and the real: between social/personal principles and the "facts" of life. It encourages public dialogue about what we believe compared with what we do. How do we develop policies that bring principles and practice closer together?

Using this model requires that learning activities be designed to help students develop the abilities and dispositions necessary for policy construction and implementation. These include

- *Envisioning.* The identification, development, and evaluation of social ideals and theories that describe the preferred states of being toward which individuals in the society want to move.

- *Assessing the actual situation.* Use of scientific and other ways of gaining knowledge about aspects of social or personal life you wish to change, including the use of statistical data and qualitative information and impressions; the development of explanations (theories).

- *Constructing, evaluating, and implementing policies.* Continual comparison of the real and the ideal to make midcourse changes.

Keep these abilities or dispositions in mind as you read the following case study.

CASE STUDY: THE FEDERAL DEBT

Traditionally, balancing the federal budget has been a rallying cry in election years. Before the advent of Keynesian economics after World War II, politicians and citizens alike believed that a balanced budget for government and households was part of prudent financial management. Even President Roosevelt campaigned for a balanced budget in 1932. So did President Reagan in 1980. Today, many state and local governments are legally required to maintain a balanced budget. Keynes, however, argued that during a serious downturn, government should increase aggregate demand through increased spending or reduced taxes. In the postwar (World War II) era, most economists advocated balancing the budget over the course of the business cycle—incurring deficits during recessions and surpluses during expansions.

The recent ballooning of the federal debt can be attributed to several factors: (1) an increasing unwillingness of taxpayers to pay for government services or obligations; (2) the 1981–1983 deep recession and lower rate of economic growth; and (3) the Reagan administration tax cuts accompanied by the defense buildup. To reduce the federal deficit, Congress passed the Gramm-Rudmann-Hollings Act in 1985, which mandated reducing the deficit over time to achieve a balanced budget by 1991. The act requires the president to make across-the-board cuts in any year that the budget deficit is higher than allowed for. However, the 1985 act had only minor impact in reducing deficits, leading some lawmakers to back a constitutional amendment requiring that the budget be balanced every year.

The *federal deficit* is the difference between government revenues and spending in any one year. If the government runs a deficit, it must borrow money to pay the difference. The *debt* is the total stock of outstanding federal government obligations resulting from past deficits. One cost of government borrowing is the interest taxpayers pay to owners of government bonds and Treasury bills.

Citizens and politicians have been debating what to do about the current budget deficit. Some people think that the deficit is a major economic and social problem and must be cured at once, even if it takes tax increases. Other people claim that the deficit is not a problem and we should continue funding both defense and social programs—if necessary, by borrowing. Some believe that the deficit is a problem that can be cured only by cutting spending, because taxes are already too high. Others recognize the deficit as a problem but view spending cuts as a greater evil than a deficit.

Is a federal budget deficit something to worry about? If it is, can we cut the deficit without causing economic harm? What are our options? This debate is particularly interesting because it is as much about values and national priorities as it is about economics.

Table 8.1 compares the total debt, deficit, and interest payments with the Gross National Product (GNP) over time. If the ratios of these numbers to GNP are stable over time, then the growth in the debt (or the deficit) is merely keeping up with growth in the economy.

A related issue is the dispute over the size and proper function of government. Who will be hurt in the process of cutting the federal deficit? Table 8.2 describes changes in the composition of federal spending and tax revenues in the post–World War II era. The two largest categories of spending are defense and transfer payments (social security and medical needs). A relatively small percent of outlays are spent on nondefense purchases and grants to local governments, including federal spending on education, drug enforcement, roads and airports, pollution cleanup, antipoverty programs, foreign aid, health and scientific research and development, and the actual running of the government.

The public debt can be compared with changes in other borrowing. Some people argue that federal borrowing has not increased as fast as these other kinds of debt and that borrowing is beneficial if it pays for economic growth. They point out that debt—bonds, Treasury bills, commercial paper, real estate mortgages—are assets or wealth to the lender, usually a U.S. citizen or corporation. Table 8.3 describes the composition of debt for selected years.

Table 8.1 Changes in the U.S. Federal Debt and Deficit: 1929–1992

Date	Federal Debt % of GNP	Interest % of GNP	Deficit (bil. of current $)[1]	Deficit % of GNP	Govt. Spending % of GNP
1929	16%	0.7%	0.7		
1940	51	1.1	−2.9	3.0%	6.8%
1946	124	2.0	−15.9	7.5	18.5
1960	57	1.2	0.3	balance	18.3
1972	36	1.2	−23.4	2.0	18.0
1976	36	1.7	−73.7	4.3	17.6
1980	35	2.4	−73.8	2.8	19.4
1982	36	2.7	−128.0	4.0	23.5
1986	51	3.2	−221.2	5.3	18.4
1990	58	3.3	−221.4	4.0	22.5
1992	66	3.3	−290.4	4.8	22.8

[1]The deficit *includes* deposit insurance outlays.
Source: Economic Report of the President, *1990, 1992, 1994.*

Table 8.2 The Fiscal Year Budget of the U.S. Government, Excluding Deficit Insurance Outlays: Selected Years (In billions of current dollars)

	1946	1960	1966	1972	1980	1986	1991	1993
RECEIPTS	40	78	134	218	538	814	1122	1249
Individual income taxes	16	41	58	100	249	353	476	512
Corporate income taxes	12	22	31	34	70	80	105	135
Social Security taxes	5[1]	6[1]	30	63	182	327	461	516
Other	7	9	15	20	36	54	77	86
OUTLAYS	60	77	134	237	587	1018	1309	1484
Purchases								
national defense	48	51	56	76	137	274	326	307
other purchases			18	28	64	100	120	138
Transfer payments			34	79	241	393	509	646
Grants to local govt			13	33	87	108	147	182
Interest on the debt	5	9	9	14	50	131	183	181
Subsidies			5	6	10	22	23	30
All other	8	16						
DEFICIT	−21	+1	−.3	−19.2	−49.0	−203.9	−187.8	−235.2

[1]Not just social security.
Source: Economic Report of the President, *1962, 1987, 1992, 1994.*

Table 8.3	Composition of U.S. Debt: Selected Years, 1960–1990 (In billions of current dollars)

Year	Consumer Debt	Mortgage Debt	Corporate Debt	Government Debt		GNP
				State/Local	Fed.	
1960	60	207	939	70	284	515
1970	132	474	2,084	144	371	1,016
1975	205	792	3,444	220	533	1,598
1980	350	1,460	5,471	336	909	2,732
1985	592	2,303	9,400	569	1,817	4,015
1990	794	3,912	n.a.	n.a.	3,206	5,524

Source: Economic Report of the President, *1990, 1992.*

ALTERNATIVE PERSPECTIVES AND RECOMMENDATIONS FOR REFORM

Public Choice Recommendations

James Buchanan argues that deficits are a natural outcome of the Keynesian revolution. The permissiveness introduced by Keynesianism encouraged an ever present tendency—the expansion of the power of the state through special-interest pleading. The state becomes a leviathan, whose expansion of taxes and spending becomes difficult to contain.

Given public choice advocacy of market allocation and free enterprise, contracting the size of the federal government is a primary goal; reducing the deficit is a side issue. Nevertheless, these economists are unalterably opposed to public deficits. They believe that deficits contradict basic tenets of democratic society because they involve taxing future generations to pay interest and possibly to pay off the debt. Future taxpayers are financing our current consumption without their consent, a clear case of taxation without representation, which they consider both unconstitutional and immoral.

Public choice economists advocate a constitutional amendment to prohibit public deficits. Some argue that the budget should be balanced every year; others would agree to balancing it over the cycle if a strong, enforceable rule could be constructed.

Neoclassical Approaches

Mainstream economists also tend to object to large deficits and a growing public debt, and for the same reasons. They favor private over public spending. They think public deficits have a corrosive effect on the economy over the long term, eating away at the foundations of privately organized economic growth. They argue that large federal deficits reduce private investment because the increased government demand for loanable funds raises interest rates, "crowding out" private borrowers who are not willing to pay the higher interest rates created by increased government borrowing. Because private firms would be financing investment in real plant and equipment, increased government borrowing retards growth in the nation's capital stock. Government borrowing, which is not responsive to the level of interest rates, preempts private spending, which is. Thus, public spending pulls real resources away from private investment and the private economy.

Large federal deficits also interfere with the use of monetary policy to fight inflation. As noted above, increased federal borrowing creates pressures on interest rates, which can be offset only if the Federal Reserve increases the money supply. However, that creates more inflationary pressures.

Neoclassical economists are also concerned about dependence on foreign lenders. We cannot count on foreign investment to continue in amounts adequate to satisfy our needs. Furthermore, foreign lending and investing in the United States means that interest payments and profits earned by foreigners will flow out of the country.

Despite their concern about the size of the federal deficit, neoclassical economists do not favor a balanced budget amendment, which would further politicize economic policy making, making it harder to maintain stable economic growth. Furthermore, they do not think the deficit is as serious as it seems. For instance, it includes borrowing to make public investments, which will more than pay back their initial cost.

The Keynesian, Post-Keynesian, and Institutionalist Analysis

In contrast to neoclassical and public choice economists, these economists think holistically about the public welfare, and they believe that public services are a crucial part of a healthy economy. They believe that government deficits are important during recessions as a way to stimulate lagging aggregate demand. They argue that it is foolish to try to balance the budget during a recession. Keynesians are, however, concerned if deficits get out of line as a percentage of GNP. They recognize that financing the federal deficit through lending from foreigners could mean a loss of autonomy.

Like Keynes, some post-Keynesians consider advanced capitalist economies to be prone to stagnation, so that government policies to stimulate aggregate demand are necessary to maintain a healthy climate for business expansion. This implies that government deficits are necessary most of the time.

Institutionalists are not usually concerned about the size of the public debt. In line with their advocacy of an important role for government in the economy, they consider government public investment important. They argue that debt is a necessary institution in the modern world because it finances growth. Furthermore, it is paid off not by reducing consumption but through the growth that it promotes. Thus, if current government spending increases economic growth, through financing better airports, road construction, public education, health care, and the like, this stimulus more than compensates for the increased interest payments. However, institutionalists emphasize the importance of equal access to credit and low interest rates, and the responsibility of lenders to be responsive to production needs.

Both Keynesians and institutionalists downplay the crowding-out hypothesis. They argue that financial markets today are worldwide. That means that the credit demands of the U.S. Treasury are not as great as they would be if we had to depend only on domestic sources of credit. They are quick to point out that the Federal Reserve can affect the availability of credit and that inflation is created as much by excess private demand as by excess public spending.

Marxist Views

Marxists don't try to solve the federal deficit problem, but they do offer explanations of it. They see large public deficits as symptomatic of more profound contradictions in advanced capitalist economies.

James O'Connor has argued that advanced capitalist countries suffer from a continual "fiscal crisis of the state," owing to the contradictory tendencies toward a taxpayer revolt and an increasing demand for public investment and public expenditures. On the one hand, government is pressured to carry out *public investment* to respond to business needs for certain investments capitalists cannot provide or do not want to pay for. For instance, to compete in the world economy, we must maintain a healthy and educated labor force, a modern infrastructure, active, large, risky investments in research and development, and so on. On the other hand, to head off divisive class conflict, the state must incur ever increasing *social expenses,* such as unemployment compensation, social security, environmental cleanup, public health services, and welfare programs for the poor. This expansion of demands on government to spend, coupled with increasing unwillingness by taxpayers to pay for these programs, creates the "fiscal crisis of the state." This battle over the public budget is, in effect, one of the forms that class conflict takes in the present era.

ACTIVITY   ## Analyzing the Case Study

Poll the class to identify which of you prefer the public choice, the neoclassical, or the post-Keynesian/institutionalist position. Then form groups of three or four who have similar viewpoints. Use the following outline as a framework for developing an economic policy on the federal debt issue. When your policy is complete, be prepared to share it with the class.

A. Define the Problem

- What were the goals of the old public policy?
- What went wrong and why? Who is responsible for what went wrong? What is the evidence?

- What is the nature of the dispute? Include factual issues, definitional is-
    sues, legal claims (if any), and value conflicts.

B. Envision a More Ideal Condition

- In your group, develop a statement of your views on an "ideal" or im-
    proved condition. Construct your statement around a goal. What conse-
    quences do you foresee with regard to your position?

C. Relate Private Decisions to Public Policy

- How do private decisions and public policies complement or interfere
    with each other?

- How might private decisions help resolve this problem? How likely are
    they to be accepted by the individuals involved?

D. Construct Policy

Prepare a policy statement (an action plan) that includes the following:

- A goal statement of a more ideal situation

- Problems that interfere with achieving the goal

- Activities you believe will bring about the desired changes, along with a
    time line

Organize your work around the big questions involved in this case; for instance:

- What is the proper role of government in the economy?

- How should we pay for government services?

- Should government be responsible for stimulating the economy?

- Is there a public interest that is different from people's individual interests?

Designing an Economic Case Study

Using the preceding case study as a model, plan an instructional unit on an economic issue. Where would you gather information for students to use? How much
information would they need? How would you present the various perspectives on
the issue? What sort of policymaking model would you use with the students? Outline the unit in as much detail as possible.

Reflecting on the Chapter

Return to your concept map of economics drawn at the beginning of the chapter.
How would you now revise the map? Which economic tradition or school of
thought do your own views most closely parallel? Write some thoughts in your journal about these issues.

References

Albeda, R., C. Gunn, and W. Waller. *Alternatives to Economic Orthodoxy*. Armonk, N.Y.: M. E. Sharpe, 1987.

Ayres, C. *Theory of Economic Progress*. New York: Schocken Books, 1962.

Baran, P., and P. Sweezy. *Monopoly Capital: An Essay on the American Economic and Social Order*. New York: Socialist Review Press, 1966.

Barber, W. J., *The History of Economic Thought*. New York: Penguin, 1967.

Bottomore, T., et al. *A Dictionary of Marxist Thought*. Cambridge: Harvard University Press, 1983.

Buchanan, J., and R. D. Tollison, eds. *The Theory of Public Choice II*. Ann Arbor: University of Michigan Press, 1984.

Buchanan, J., and G. Tullock. *The Calculus of Consent*. Ann Arbor: University of Michigan Press, 1962.

Commons, J. R. *Institutional Economics*. New York: Macmillan, 1934.

Dewey, J. *Logic: The Theory of Inquiry*. New York: Henry Holt, 1938.

Eatwell, J., M. Milgate, and P. Newman, eds. *The New Palgraves: A Dictionary of Economics*. New York: Stockton Press, 1987.

Fusfield, D. *The Age of the Economist*, 2nd ed. Glenview, Ill.: Scott, Foresman, 1990.

Galbraith, J. K. *The New Industrial State*, 4th ed. Boston: Houghton Mifflin, 1985.

Gruchy, A. *Modern Economic Thought: The American Contribution*. Englewood Cliffs, N.J.: Prentice Hall, 1947.

Gwartney, J. B., and R. E. Wagner. "The Public Choice Revolution." *Intercollegiate Review* 23, no. 2 (Spring 1988): 17–26.

Heilbroner, R. L., *Marxism For and Against*. New York: W. W. Norton, & Co., Inc., 1980.

———. *The Nature and Logic of Capitalism*. New York: W. W. Norton, & Co., Inc., 1985.

———. *The Worldly Philosophers*, 6th ed. New York: Simon & Schuster, Touchstone, 1986.

———, ed. *The Essential Adam Smith*. New York: W. W. Norton, & Co., Inc., 1986.

Helburn, S., and D. Bramhall, eds. *Marx, Schumpeter, Keynes: A Centenary Celebration of Dissent*. Armonk, N.Y.: M. E. Sharpe, 1986.

Kane, E. J. *The S & L Insurance Mess: How Did It Happen?*. Washington, D.C.: Urban Institute Press, 1989.

Landreth, H., and D. Colander. *History of Economic Theory*, 2nd ed. Boston: Houghton Mifflin, 1989.

Mayer, M., *The Greatest-ever Bank Robbery: The Collapse of the Savings and Loan Industry*. New York: Charles Scribner's, 1990.

Minsky, H. P. *John Maynard Keynes*. New York: Columbia University Press, 1975.

O'Connor, J. *Fiscal Crisis of the State*. New York: St. Martin's Press, 1973.

———. *The Corporation and the State: Essays in the Theory of Capitalism and Imperialism*. New York: Harper & Row, 1974.

Olson, M. *The Logic of Collective Action: Public Goods and the Theory of Groups*. Ann Arbor: University of Michigan Press, 1965.

Pheby, J, *Methodology and Economics: A Critical Introduction*. New York: Macmillan, 1988.

Smith, A. *The Wealth of Nations*. New York: Modern Library, 1939.

Tollison, R. D. "Chicago Political Economy." *Public Choice* 63, no. 3 (December 1989): 293–97.

Veblen, T. *The Place of Science in Modern Civilization*. New York: B. W. Huebsch, 1919.

Teaching Resources

Applied Economics. Colorado Springs, Colo.: Junior Achievement, Inc.

Armento, B. J. "Promoting Economic Literacy." In *Social Studies and Social Sciences: A Fifty-Year Perspective,* ed. S. P. Wronski and D. H. Bragaw, 97–110. Washington, D.C.: National Council for the Social Studies, 1986.

Banaszak, R. A., and E. Clawson. *Strategies for Teaching Economics: Junior High School Level. Grades 7–9.* New York: National Council on Economic Education, 1981.

Brimmer, A. F. "Nature and Content of Contemporary Economics." In *Citizenship for the 21st Century,* ed. W. T. Callahans, Jr., and R. A. Banaszak, 103–115. Bloomington, Ind.: Social Studies Development Center and ERIC Clearinghouse for Social Studies/Social Science Education, 1991.

Clow, J. E., et al. *Teaching Strategies: Consumer Economics (Secondary).* New York: National Council on Economic Education, 1985.

Decisions, Decisions: Balancing the Budget. Watertown, Mass.: Tom Snyder Productions, n.d. Computer simulation.

Economics: Global Perspective Series. Boca Raton, Fla.: SIRS, annual.

Economics: What and When? New York: National Council on Economic Education, 1990.

Economics 94/95: Annual Editions Series. Guilford, Conn.: Dushkin, 1994.

Galbraith, J. K. "On Teaching a Fractured Economics." *Journal of Economic Education* 18, no. 2 (1987): 213–26.

Global Recall. Philadelphia: World Game Institute.

Miller, S. L. *Economic Education for Citizenship.* Bloomington, Ind.: ERIC Clearinghouse for Social Studies/Social Science Education, 1988.

National Council on Economic Education, Two Park Avenue, New York, NY 10016.

Pacific Century, The. South Burlington, Vt.: Corporation for Public Broadcasting, 1993. Video series.

Rural Communities: Legacy and Change. South Burlington, Vt.: Corporation for Public Broadcasting, 1993. Video series.

Schug, M. C. "Solving the Economic Mysteries of American History." *Social Education* 58, no. 1 (1994): special issue.

Schur, L. "What Economics is Worth Teaching?" In *Economics in the School Curriculum, K–12,* ed. Mark C. Schug, 21–32. Washington, D.C.: Joint Council on Economics Education and the National Education Association, 1985.

Simplicon. Culver City, Calif.: Social Studies School Service, n.d. Computer simulation.

STUDYING AND TEACHING
ANTHROPOLOGY

Roger C. Owen and Jack Zevin

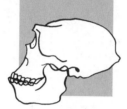

ACTIVITY LIST

• • •

ACTIVITY

Defining Ethnocentrism

Rudyard Kipling, a British author of the late 19th century who spent much of his life in India, once wrote:

> All good people agree,
> And all good people say,
> All nice people like Us is We
> And everyone else is They:

> But if you cross over the sea,
> Instead of over the way,
> You may end by (think of it!)
> looking on We
> As only a sort of They!

With a partner, analyze this poem, particularly the concepts of "we," "us," and "they." Discuss Kipling's reasons for noting that "good" and "nice" people think of themselves as different from everyone else. Consider why things change once good and nice people "cross over the sea."

Conduct your own field research by choosing several friends and talking with them about other peoples and places (e.g., the economic success of Japan, problems in Eastern Europe or Africa, or immigration of Asians or Latin Americans into your area). Try to arrange conversations between two friends and acquaintances while you listen. As the conversation proceeds, keep count of how many times non-white or non-Western peoples or specific persons are referred to as "them" or "other" and how often differences, rather than similarities, are mentioned. Note the amount of time involved by glancing at your watch as the conversation proceeds. Sample at least three conversations before you draw any conclusions about your peers' level of ethnocentrism.

• • •

Ethnocentrism is defined as a belief that one's own ethnic group, people, language, and customs are natural, special, and better than those of anyone else. If your students believe that, how can you teach them respect for other cultures and belief systems? Consider at least three ways in which you can heighten students' awareness of their biases and their fears or rejections of "others." Plan a lesson that uses materials that will open up the issue of ethnocentrism for discussion.

INTRODUCTION

The lifeway of the peaceful Hopi and the fierce Yanomamo; the physical contours of *Homo erectus*; the significance of puberty rites; the impact of caste and class on national societies; the vital importance of physical and cultural evolution to the understanding of our species; the universality of the belief in supernatural beings—all this and much more make up the subject matter of anthropology. Anthropology is a humane science: Its goal is to understand human development without reference to preconceived moral, ethical, aesthetic, or ideological convictions so as to provide means and methods to enable humankind to reach its full potential, whatever that may be.

Scientific anthropology began in the United States at Columbia University under Franz Boas around 1900, but for the first half of the twentieth century, anthropology was taught at only a few dozen elite schools to perhaps a few hundred students a year. After World War II, returning soldiers by the tens of thousands matriculated on soon-crammed campuses, increasing enrollments in virtually every department. Many of today's prominent departments of anthropology were established in that period. Although relatively few students majored in anthropology, increasing numbers enrolled in the courses and thus permitted departments to enlarge.

Although contemporary anthropology often dedicates itself to the study of modern societies, rural and urban, our subject matter is richly spiced with accounts of fascinating people in exotic times or places. Indeed, anthropology cut its teeth on the study of conquered and oppressed band and tribal societies. Because participant observation requires living closely with the people studied, as well as the adoption of a lifestyle consistent with the expectations of one's hosts, anthropologists have often come to know better than any other outsiders the problems experienced by the people they have studied. Intimate association with oppressed and exploited populations has led to a profession-wide concern for the fate not only of tribal and former tribal people but of all humankind.

Imbued with the conviction that all cultures can represent valuable solutions to human problems, anthropologists cherish cultural variation and tend to fear the homogenization brought about when developed states engulf less complex societies. This attitude of esteem for cultural diversity is a key ingredient of *cultural relativism*, an intellectual position that suggests that all cultural variations are understandable and valid within their own pattern of development. Cultural relativists view most specific cultural evolutionary developments with interest. For example, one may learn from and even esteem the long-enduring, if ended, band adaptation of the !Kung Bushmen of the Kalahari. The adaptations fostered by Hitler and Stalin, however brutal and abhorrent, are of no less intrinsic interest. It is important to note, however, that both Hitlerism and Stalinism were eradicated or modified by the concerted efforts of people who opposed the inhumane character of those despots. Thus, the general response to those specific developments was to change them.

Could not precollegiate students benefit from a social science/social studies program that treats such important social and cultural realities in an objective and nonjudgmental manner? Does not anthropology offer insights that would help young people understand problems facing the United States and the world? We believe the answer to these questions is yes.

What would anthropologists want high school graduates to know about anthropology if the subject were well taught at the precollegiate level? In this chapter, we will look at several subdivisions of anthropology. The basic division in the field is between physical and cultural anthropology, with the latter including linguistics, archaeology, and ethnology and ethnography. For each specialty, we will present one or more basic "propositions" pertinent to the specialty and shared by most or all anthropologists. Accompanying these propositions, we present several "case studies" and activities in which the propositions are illustrated and some of the methods of anthropological inquiry are explored.

PHYSICAL ANTHROPOLOGY

Proposition 1 Anthropologists believe that material evidence proves that the human species has evolved during the past several million years from earlier, simpler forms of life in response to natural processes that still operate.

Paleoanthropologists, of whom the Leakeys—Louis, Mary, and Richard—are the most famous, study the course of human evolution. These scholars seek and analyze fossil bones and other remains of our ancient ancestors. When successful, they attempt to reconstruct the world in which the creatures lived. Their research often requires them to work in concert with paleontologists, climatologists, geologists, geochronologists, and other specialists. Despite being scarcely more than 100 years old, paleoanthropology has achieved remarkable scientific maturity; it has outlined the major steps in human evolution for the past 60 million years.

Experts in the field believe that our species, *Homo sapiens sapiens*, has evolved during the past four million years from earlier primate forms: *Homo sapiens neandertalensis*, other early *Homo sapiens*, *Homo erectus*, and *Homo habilis (Australopithecus)*. They point out that, intertwined and simultaneous with physical evolution, shared human sociocultural behavioral characteristics began and grew: speech and language; use of tools; food-getting skills; social forms (probably including an incest taboo, kinship behaviors, and specialized terms for relatives); belief in spirits and other supernatural forces; storytelling, song, and dance; and, gradually, all the other cultural attributes that make us human. Prominent among these attributes are capacities for ambition, compassion, creativity, desire, hatred, love, tolerance, and violence.

These earliest cultural forms were developed in socially simple foraging communities of fifty or so people who obtained their livelihood by collecting plant and animal foods from their environment in ever more skillful ways. Scholars now refer to these kinds of societies as "hunters and gatherers," "bands," or simply "local groups." Band people, after a million years or more of existence, came to fill the habitable world about 12,000 years ago, when North and South America were first occupied by them.

The road to understanding the processes underlying human biological evolution has been a rocky, contentious one. Even today there are those who, for one reason or another, reject the pattern of development we have outlined. Some critics of evolutionary theory point to "Piltdown Man" as evidence that shabby scholarship and even fakery have been involved. We now know that, indeed, the Piltdown bones were forgeries. Its discovery and later "uncovery" as a fake provide the basis for our first investigative case study.

Case Study for Proposition 1: The Search for "Truth" Regarding the Human Past*

This case study is designed to illustrate the ways in which scientists attempt to verify and validate their conclusions and to indicate the intensity of scientific concern with validating hypotheses and eliminating those that are proven false.

Physical anthropologists have developed a widely accepted body of data that permits them to outline the course of human physical evolution and thus to answer the question "Where did we come from?" at least on the empirical or scientific level. Before Darwin, most Christian intellectuals believed that all species had been created at one time and were fixed and unchanging in their biological nature. Darwinism not only raised questions regarding the fixity of species but also encouraged researchers to seek nonbiblical, secular origins for human beings. Evidence for any new answer would have to measure up to the scientific standard then being established: Precise, controlled observations would have to be presented to the enlightened community of scholars, who would have the right and the duty to question, challenge, reject, or accept new proposals.

The first entries into the antiquity of man sweepstakes, a race that would roar into and through the twentieth century, were not ancient bones but rather oddly shaped and seemingly modified stones (see Figure 9.1). Nature, in its infinite capacity to wreak change upon the earth and its contents, cannot really successfully imitate the products of skilled human hands guided by tradition-bound technological goals. Although we now know that human intelligence has been directing the production of chipped stone tools for over two million years, only in the 1830s were simple tools first tentatively identified as of ancient origin. Ancient stone tools, along with bones of extinct animals, had then been found in Germany, France, and Java. Uncovered in caves and deep in gravel beds that seemed ancient, these products of human intellect were very different from the polished stone tools known from pre-Classic Roman and Greek times.

If very ancient people made these flints, where were their fossilized skeletal remains? Ancient toolmakers would certainly have left their bones somewhere in the vicinity. The search began. Actually, even before Darwin, unrecognized and ignored,

---

*Most of the data in this case study, unless otherwise attributed, were derived from Frank Spencer, 1990.

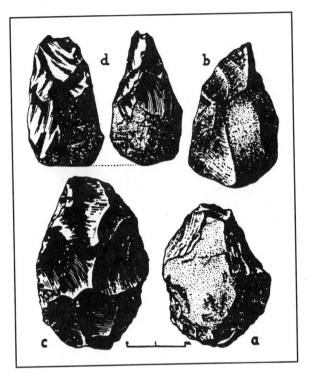

Figure 9.1 Ancient human stone tools from Europe and Africa. Tool 'a' may be two or more millions of years old. *From M. F. A. Montague,* An Introduction to Physical Anthropology, *1945. Courtesy of Charles C. Thomas, Publisher, Springfield, Illinois.*

one ancient skull had already been found on the island of Gibraltar in 1848 but had been unrecognized for what it was. The *Gibraltar skull* created little stir until after a more dramatic and important find occurred in Germany in 1856: the discovery of *Neanderthal Man*, named after the river valley in which the skull was found (see Figure 9.2). Accompanied by many other bones, including arms, legs, pelvis, and ribs, the skull cap and other bones were clearly evidence of a human form physically different in evident ways from nineteenth-century people. Although then pictured as bestial and probably fierce, we now know that Neanderthal was merely one in the long line of human forms and was, in most respects, much more like modern humans than nineteenth-century interpreters were willing to grant. Today, in fact, Neanderthals are generally regarded as a subspecies or race of *Homo sapiens*.

On the basis of these and other finds of ancient human fossil bones, paleontologists began to put together understandings of the evolution of modern humans. Two dominant points of view existed: the "dualist" view and the "monist" view. The first held that the Neanderthals and Homo erectus were ancestral to modern humans; the other held that these and other fossils were evolutionary "dead ends" and that modern humans came from some as-yet-undiscovered ancient creature not unlike modern humans. Because of the lack of agreement among experts as to the phylogeny (developmental pattern) of modern humans, room remained for varied

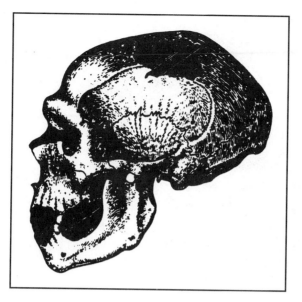

Figure 9.2   A Neanderthal skull. *From M. F. A. Montague,* An Introduction to Physical Anthropology, *1945. Courtesy of Charles C. Thomas, Publisher, Springfield, Illinois.*

explanations of the origin of the big brain of modern humans and the loss of ape-like features, such as protruding canine teeth and receding jaw.

Around 1908, in southeast England at a place called Piltdown in the Thames River valley, a part of a human skull was found by workers in a gravel bed. Later, other fragments of the skull were found by a Charles Dawson, a country lawyer, amateur geologist, and seeker of fossil bones. The gravel bed was believed to date from the beginning of the Ice Age, now known to have begun over two million years ago. Because of the great age of the gravel, if the bones were interred at the time the gravel was laid down, the skull (which came to be known as the Piltdown Man) would be the oldest known ancestor of modern humans and would strongly suggest that the earliest humans had not evolved in Africa or in Asia but had been early big-brained Englishmen! The bone fragments did appear old; all were very dark in color and matched the basic color of the rock and soil in which they were found. Dawson recruited to his dig Arthur Smith Woodward (later to be knighted for this and other work), a noted geologist who became "hooked" on the work. Also accompanying them on a first visit to the site was Teilhard de Chardin, a young French Jesuit and neophyte paleontologist who since 1908 had been a friend of Dawson's. Other fragments of the skull were uncovered. Fossil teeth and nonhuman bones were found as well, and so, too, did stone tools turn up, all dark in color and seemingly ancient. Then the bombshell exploded: An apelike jawbone appeared, found in the dirt by Dawson, evidently witnessed by Smith Woodward. This thick jawbone, very apelike in appearance, was not at all like that of the well-known Neanderthal and even less like those of modern humans. Next to appear, found by Teilhard (who would dig at the site only a few times), was a tooth that fit the jaw:

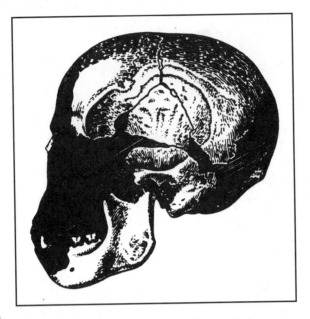

Figure 9.3   A reconstruction of the Piltdown skull. The skull was reconstructed using only the bones found—shown in white. *From M. F. A. Montague,* An Introduction to Physical Anthropology, *1945. Courtesy of Charles C. Thomas, Publisher, Springfield, Illinois.*

a lower right canine tooth that could never fit in a modern human head or in the head of any other then-known human ancestor (see Figure 9.3).

Did the jawbone and the tooth, so unlike modern or ancient human ones, belong with the skull? If the bones belonged together, this dawn-aged big-brained, ape-jawed early Englishman would strongly support those who believed that modern humans had not descended through a line from Homo erectus to Neanderthal but, instead, came from some as-yet-unknown European ancestor. Were these bones the then-long-sought "missing link" between modern humans and other, earlier primates?

Dawson, Smith Woodward, and others continued to work diligently for months and years at the site, but no more ancient human remains were ever found there.

How to know? What to accept? The Piltdown battle was engaged. Most scientists who had a public identity had to take a stand. Were the bones and the tools legitimate?

A number of scientists immediately denied the possibility that the jaw and the tooth belonged to the skull; others insisted that Piltdown represented a new and important form of "Dawn" man, a form that would enlighten understanding of human evolution. Arguing that the skull and the jaw belonged to a single individual were all the principals of the discovery: Dawson, Smith Woodward, Teilhard de Chardin, Arthur Keith, and others. A private critic of Piltdown, Martin Hinton, a zoologist and museum curator who had worked for but intensely disliked Arthur Smith Woodward, went on record dismissing any association between the cranium and the jaw.

In 1953, after decades of debate pro and con, extensive research demonstrated that all the Piltdown bones and tools represented an elaborate and professionally prepared hoax. The bogus bones, all carefully stained to appear to be of great age, as were some of the flint tools found with the bones, consisted of a deliberately altered modern human skull and the carefully filed-down jawbone of a young female orangutan. The jawbone, deliberately modified so that it lacked features that would have immediately identified it as belonging to a nonhuman primate, had to have been skillfully selected by an expert to fool other experts.

The Piltdown case study illustrates clearly the continuing efforts of scientists to establish a reliable, agreed-upon interpretation of the reality that surrounds us.

ACTIVITY ## Thinking about Scientific Evidence

When experts are "fooled" by evidence into drawing incorrect conclusions, the public enjoys the bad publicity that follows. Hoaxes make good copy and sell books and papers. However, interpreting evidence in anthropology and especially archaeology is often a tricky business.

Form small groups. In your group, list artifacts an archaeologist would likely find in a dig or in a cave where prehistoric peoples lived. Rank each item 1, 2, or 3, with 1 indicating that an object would provide a great deal of information about the people who lived there and a 3 indicating that an object would reveal very little.

Select the object your group believes would reveal the most information. Prepare a presentation explaining why you selected the object and describing the kinds or categories of information that would be deduced from the object.

After each presentation, discuss the possibilities for forgery or for reaching unwarranted conclusions. As you discuss your ideas, consider the following questions:

- Would forgeries be easy to tell apart from the "real" artifacts?
- How much intelligent guesswork or "extrapolation" is necessary to create a theory that explains a discovery and identifies its purpose and place in time?
- What rules of evidence might an anthropologist or an archaeologist use to decide whether to take a theory seriously?

• • •

When you evaluate a student's work, how will you distinguish between original and plagiarized writing, between someone's own thinking and ideas borrowed from other sources that might not have been credited?

Proposition 2 The range of human cultural potential appears to be shared equally by all normal human populations.

The scientific study of human physical ("racial") variation is older than paleo-anthropology, having interested the Greeks and the Romans. The most influential classification of human varieties was that done by Carolus Linnaeus, a Swedish botanist who, in 1735, classified humanity into four great "racial" categories: red, yellow, black, and white. Research has dismissed this simplistic scheme of color categories, although it remains a part of our popular culture. In fact, there are no clear boundaries between Linnaeus's "races"; most humans are shades of light brown, some darker and some lighter, and the variations in skin color are gradual.

In the contemporary study of human variation, researchers focus on its genetic basis as well as on the influence of evolution and culture, and study a variety of features—for example, the shape and form of our bodies, our skin texture and color, or blood groups and their distributions. Dark-skinned people, for example, are topics of current research. Until several hundred years ago, they were all concentrated near the equator, where their ancient ancestors had to deal with the intense solar radiation that makes dark skin adaptive. In fact, since the human species originated in the tropics, it might be assumed that all humans were dark skinned until some migrated to the northern regions of Europe and Asia, where excess melanin made them prone to rickets.

As the twentieth century closes, anthropologists can point to few variations of social importance from one human population to another. We are a remarkably homogeneous species beneath our skins; witness the fact that organs can be transplanted easily from a person of any origin to another so long as the donor and the recipient are of the same blood type. Today, anthropologists teach that all humans are of a single race, a race that has many geographically variant types possessed of many essentially trivial differences: skin and hair color, body shape, eye form and color, and so on. Tragically, in many parts of the world, "race" remains a four-letter word that can kill!

Exhaustive research by anthropologists seeking to find significant variations in cultural capacity between human populations has disclosed no major differences. In all important ways (linguistic, intellectual, sensory, artistic, mechanical, etc.), all human populations appear to share the same range of variation in ability. The conclusion of physical anthropologists, as of the early 1990s, is that there is no biological basis for the categorization of some world populations as superior in important ways, and others as inferior. Such perceptions are based upon social, not genetic, criteria.

More recent research has investigated the question of male/female similarities and differences. Some of the earliest gender-behavioral research was done by Margaret Mead in the early 1930s, when she began to challenge the notion that "biology is destiny." Her work among Pacific islanders indicated that gender roles varied sharply from culture to culture, thereby calling into question the common acceptance of inherent male/female gender roles. Cumulative research results are similar to those achieved with respect to race: In most or all capacities that are culturally important, men and women are remarkably alike—with the exception of reproduction proper.

Contributions to the World Food System

Some people measure human accomplishment in military terms, and others point to developments that enhance sustenance as a key measure of innovation and growth. The foods we eat originated in different parts of the globe and were developed by the peoples that first recognized their potential.

Form a "sharing circle" to create a list of common foods, including favorites from each food group: grains, meats and dairy, vegetables, fruits, and spices or flavorings. Ask each person in the circle to tell the group about one of his or her favorites or about a food he or she eats on a regular basis (e.g., tomatoes); then write this on a sheet of paper being passed around the circle. No one may repeat any other person's choice, but each person handed the paper should add a place of origin to the previous person's food choice. By the time the circle is completed, each participant should have had the opportunity to name a food and speculate on the area from which his or her neighbor's choice probably came. If you are not sure of a country of origin for, say, tomatoes, then give the name of a continent (e.g., Africa).

Save your list for use after you have read Case Study 2.

Case Study for Proposition 2: Who Is Capable of Building Civilization?

We don't know how long humans have attributed various negative qualities to people who didn't look like themselves, but it probably has not been very long as evolutionary time goes. For the millions of years that our species has been evolving, local groups of people would, in their lifetimes, not only not meet people who looked very different from themselves but would also rarely, if ever, meet someone they did not already know! Throughout those eons, people lived in small groups we now call bands or tribes, in which all or most members were more or less equal in the estimation of everyone, including themselves.

Some 10,000 years ago, growing populations in many parts of the world encouraged people to develop means of getting more calories from restricted land areas. This they did by beginning to grow crops while continuing to harvest wild foods. When advances in horticultural and animal husbandry, such as irrigation, fertilization, or use of the plow pulled by draft animals, permitted individuals to produce sufficient food for several or dozens of people, specialization of labor increased. With increased specialization and differentiation of economic function came variations in wealth, status, and power. For every hundred farmers, there might be one shopkeeper, blacksmith, moneylender, produce buyer, worship leader, director of public activities, judge, general, tax collector, or even ruling clique or individual. These specialists, usually resident in a central place such as a port, a castle, or a town, came to accumulate wealth, knowledge, connections, and power such that they were able to manipulate or control the lives of farmers, who thus came to have lesser power and prestige.

Early centralized societies often found their self-interests overlapping with similar, neighbor societies, and conflict and wars often resulted. Warfare led to conquest of one polity by another, with the result that if all the "enemy" were not simply killed (a common enough tactic), some or all of the surviving losers were made into slaves—that is, communal residents deprived of all civil and economic rights except as defined by the dominant members of the society, usually the conquerors.

Cretians, Egyptians, Persians, Chinese, Greeks, Romans, Cambodians, Japanese, and many other ethnic groups have provided chapters in this phase of human history, most of which have already been written in detail by historians. Now being written are the similar developments of complex, stratified societies in sub-Saharan Africa and in the Americas. It is this latter context—North, Central, and South America—to which this case study is dedicated.

More than 500 years ago, Europeans began to spread out from their small but productive continent, taking their cultural patterns with them. Several attributes gave them an advantage over those they would encounter in Africa, Asia, and the Americas. Important among them was the belief that they possessed the "true" religion, Christianity, which they were sworn to uphold and disseminate to "heathens" wherever encountered. Coupled with Christian belief came a strong sense of hierarchy; that is, those on top gave orders, those below obeyed. This intellectual discipline, when combined with tools of iron and other metals, with weapons such as swords, muskets, and cannons accompanied by the fearsome four-legged demons upon which they could ride, served to intimidate or eliminate the capacity of most societies to stand against even small numbers of well-equipped Portuguese, Spaniards, English, French, or Dutch explorers or missionaries who, nearly always, were accompanied by soldiers.

In 1519, a Spaniard, Hernán Cortéz, attacked the Aztec at Tenochtitlan, their capital city located in central Mexico upon the ruins of which Mexico City has been constructed. By 1521, European diseases, which were previously unknown to the Americas and to which the native people consequently lacked any immunity (smallpox, measles, mumps, chicken pox, gonorrhea, and many others), and the collaboration of many native societies had destroyed the power of the Aztec city-state which at that time dominated central and southern Mexico. Francisco Pizarro, another Spanish conqueror, achieved much the same in what is now Peru when, in 1532, he seized the Inca capital, Cuzco, and executed thousands, including the ruler and most of the nobles of that widespread and powerful empire.

In what is now the United States, populated by less complicated, noncentralized local societies (mainly bands and tribes), conquest was not so abrupt. Disease and colonization generally brought about the rapid weakening and dissolution of native societies before large-scale military action was necessary.

Conquest cast Native North and South Americans into a lowly ranked, racially defined category within which they were denied education and access to good nutrition and were relegated to serf or slave status. Yet, neither being conquered nor losing a war proves that the people of a society are inferior in other, less evident ways, such as in intellectual ability, emotional capacity, or the capacity to judge right from wrong.

In several domains, native America was well ahead of Europe and other world regions by 1492. Achievements of pre-Columbian Americans fell into a number of important cultural fields: agronomy; astronomy; curing of illness; and others. Perhaps the greatest achievement of pre-Columbian Americans was in plant domestication and plant-growing technology. Of the thirteen most used food plants in the world today, several are of Native American origin: corn (Indian maize); common beans (navy, pinto, black, kidney, lima, etc.); "Irish" and all other potatoes, including sweet potatoes; manioc or cassava; and peanuts. Today, one-third of the world's major plant foods are of Native American origin (see Table 9.1).

Other Native American plants, of lesser quantitative importance perhaps, have shaped the contemporary world's cuisine. Imagine ice cream without vanilla or chocolate; Italian food without tomatoes; or Indian curries without chili peppers. Although not a food plant, tobacco, now unfortunately used worldwide, was domesticated by ancient Americans, as were Pima cotton, chicle, and a host of other useful but less well known plants.

Table 9.1   Some Commonly Used Food Plants and Plant Products First Used by Native Americans

---

achiote	coca	maple syrup (sugar)	rubber
achira	cochineal cactus	marigolds	sapodilla
allspice	coconut	mate	sapote
amaranth (several)	copaiba	nuts (Brazil, butter,	sarsaparilla
anil (indigo)	copal	cashew, hickory,	sassafras
anona	cotton (Pima)	pecans, pine, etc.)	sisal
apazote	cranberry		soursop
(chenopodium)	cypress	oca	squash
arrowroot	dahlia	panic grass	star apple
artichoke (Jerusalem)		papaya	strawberry
barbados cherry	elderberry	passionflower fruit	sunflower
barbasco	guava	pawpaw	surinam cherry
beans (common,	guayabilla	peanut	sweet potato (yam)
haricot, lima,	guayule	peppers (chile,	sweet sop
kidney, navy, etc.)	henequen	cayenne, chiltepin,	tapioca (manioc)
cacao (chocolate)	hog plum	paprika, pimento,	tejocote
cascara	ipecac	sweet, etc.)	tobacco
chaya	jocote	persimmon	tomatillo (husk
chayote	lupine	pineapple	tomato)
cherimoya		pitahaya	tomato
chia	maguey	potato (50+ varieties)	tuberose
chicle	maize (corn)	prickly pear ("tuna")	vanilla
chinchona	marmey apple	pumpkins	
	manioc (cassava)	quinoa	

While most of the world was malnourished owing to inadequate amounts of food as well as its deficient nutritional quality, Native American farmers relying upon corn, beans, and squashes had an exceptionally well balanced diet, especially when supplemented with game and fish. The quality of the Native American diet was matched by the reliability of harvests, ensured by a widespread irrigation technology accompanied by the occasional use of fertilizers, especially among the Inca.

Because Native Americans lacked draft animals (no native herbivores were suitable for such domestication), the plow, and tools of iron, the conquerors judged American food-growing efforts to be inferior and usually replaced the native agricultural effort with cattle ranches or commercial plantations. The majority of Native Americans, of course, unwittingly accommodated their conquerors' disdain: They died by the millions of disease, malnutrition, starvation, and conflict.

But pre-Columbian people in the Americas were able to domesticate virtually all plants that were useful to them or to us! Since 1492, no significant native American plants have been added to the list of domesticates.

ACTIVITY

Testing Your Hypothesis about the Origins of Plants, Crops, and Foods

Compare Table 10.1 with the list your sharing circle created in the previous activity. Discuss the following questions in reviewing both lists.

- Which commonly used food plants were not on your list?
- Which of those on the new list are unfamiliar to you?
- What percentage of origins were correctly identified?
- According to the new list, a large proportion of food plants are from the Americas, developed by Native Americans. Is that surprising to you? Why or why not?

• • •

Would you like to add a few questions of your own to this activity?

How might you adapt this lesson for use in a world studies, U.S. history, or economics class?

CULTURAL ANTHROPOLOGY: LINGUISTICS

Proposition 3   Language has been essential to human cultural development in all societies, past and present.

Most anthropologists believe that the creation and use of language are the primary foundations upon which human adaptation rests. The study of language, begun by the ancient Greeks, Romans, and Hindus, began to flower in eighteenth- and nineteenth-century Europe quite apart from those intellectual developments that would lead to anthropology. During the late nineteenth century, anthropologists joined the investigation and began to study and classify tribal languages. Linguistics received a great boost when, during the twentieth century, following the work of Boas and the British ethnographer Malinowski, the use of native languages in the field became mandatory for ethnographers. Hundreds of previously unwritten languages were recorded in notebooks, thus making available to linguistic scholars a great wealth of data. The collecting of additional linguistic material continues.

Descriptive linguists record speech by using the International Phonetic Alphabet, which permits any spoken sound to be given a written symbol. These recordings are then analyzed for three structural elements common to all languages: significant signaling units (phonemes), meaning units (morphemes), and rules of arrangement (grammar). Descriptions of specific languages, when published, permit comparison with other described languages to establish similarities and possible relationships.

Historical linguistics examines the genetic relationships of described languages to study the history of and change in language clusters. Languages that can be shown to be related to each other—English and German, for example—are grouped into families, and related families are then placed into *phyla*. The Germanic family, to which English belongs, is a member of the Indo-European phylum, one of about forty phyla into which linguists have been able to group the world's thousands of languages. It is possible that all languages stem from one source, but we may never possess the means to know whether that is true.

Some linguistic specialists investigate how language is acquired. Despite the great differences among languages, all possess certain structural features, such as actors, actions, and descriptive terms. This has led Noam Chomsky, a leading linguistic theorist, to propose that basic language rules are inborn and part of our evolutionary, biologically based heritage.

Other linguists devote themselves to the study of the social functions served by language. Regional, class, gender, and other dialects exist in all societies. Once learned, one's dialect becomes a mark of social membership. For example, in British society if you learn and speak the Cockney dialect, you can be marked for life as a member of the working class. If in the United States you speak one of a number of dialects other than that which the social style-setters speak, such as Black English, Spanglish, or Nuyorqueno, easy access to jobs within the middle class may be blocked.

Proxemics, the study of communication through space utilization and body movement, is yet another research interest of linguists. Hall (1959) suggested that each culture teaches its members nonverbal means of communication. The gestures one can make, whom one can touch and where, as well as the kind of regular body movements permitted, vary not only from one culture to another but also by social categories within each culture. In the United States, anyone who fails to learn our proxemic "grammar" and persistently touches the wrong people the wrong way—pinching, for example—might not only get a slap in the face but could even go to jail.

Case Study for Proposition 3: Human Language and Social Meaning

This case study is designed to encourage you to think about the way in which human language is used to create and maintain culture. A song from a recent study of Quechua language and culture illustrates the use of words to convey rhythm, meaning, and social commentary.

According to the anthropologist who collected the song that follows (Harrison 1989), this "harvest song from Ecuador addresses the problem of maintaining cultural identity for Quechua speakers, especially after they have entered into the processes of the school systems in the Andes. Although admission of indigenous persons to the educational system serves, on the one hand, to facilitate greater access to the Spanish-speaking enclaves of society, schooling can also serve to encourage separation from one's ethnic group."

Dimensions of Quechua Language and Culture*

Uyarilla		Listen,
doña Maria		lady Maria.
maytagarilla		Where in the world
kambak wawaka?		is your child?
*iscuila*llamun	5	In grade school.
yaykukun ninka		He is enrolling, they say,
*colegio*llamun		in high school.
yaykukun ninka		He is enrolling, they say.
mana *valilla*		He's not worth anything
walindanguka	10	[his penis hanging down].
uksha chumbiwan		With a belt of straw
chumbillishkaka		he has kept his pants up.
*buena litra*ta		Good handwriting
japishpa ninka		he's got, they say.
*buena firma*ta	15	An impressive signature
japishpa ninka		he's got, they say.
*amu*kunawan		With all the big bosses

*From *Signs, Songs and Memory in the Andes: Translating Quechua Language and Culture* by Regina Harrison, Copyright © 1989. By permission of the author and the University of Texas Press.

rimakun ninka		he is talking, they say.
doctor kunawan		With all the doctors
*parla*kun ninka	20	he is talking, they say.
*saludak*pipish		When one says hello to him
manashi *parlan*		he doesn't speak.
*saludak*pipish		When one says hello to him
manashi riman		he doesn't say anything.
*saludak*pipish	25	When one says hello to him
mana chaskinka		he doesn't receive our hello.
*saludak*pipish		When one says hello to him
mana rimanka		he doesn't speak.
alli *suertita*		A lot of good luck
charikushkaka	30	he has already held for himself.
*gobernadur*ta		From the governor
ña *gana*grinka		he begins to earn money.
chasna purina		Acting like that
layachu karka		he became a "white."
chasna kawsana	35	Living like that
layachu karka		he became a "white."
amukunata		From the *hacendados*
ña *gaga*grinka		he begins to earn money.
jatunkunata		From the big bosses
ña *gana*grinka	40	he begins to earn money.
kunanka jatun		Now a great man
tiyarigrinka		he's getting to be.
kunanka jatun		Now a great man
tiyarigrinka		he's getting to be.
*deputadur*ka	45	As a political representative
*gana*gripanka		he begins to earn money.
alli *sueldota*		A good salary
*gana*gripanka		he begins to earn.

ACTIVITY

Deconstructing a Song

Form small groups and read aloud both the Quechua and the English versions of the song. Invent a melody for the piece, or beat out a rhythm on a box or a drum. Ask two people in your group to take notes on each version of the song, paying particular attention to the following:

- Which patterns of sound are repeated (e.g., *wa, ka, na,* or *mun, tun, wan*)?
- Which ideas and phrases are reinforced?
- Which words are from Spanish?

- Which version is more poetic, rhymes better?
- What emotions predominate?

Next, ask the note takers to share their observations with the group. Identify the main messages of the song: social, economic, ethnic, and political. Discuss the song's point of view. Was it written by someone who seeks to preserve or break down a tradition? Why is school mentioned? Why is the protagonist of the song, a young man, accused of working to become a "white"? Who and what is the songwriter—male or female, rich or poor, pleased or displeased? How is language used to convey these ideas?

Contemplate the overall tone and meaning of the Quechua song for a few moments. Then read the remainder of Harrison's analysis of the song:

> *In this harvest song, the protagonist, a young boy, learns how to write and signs his name with a flourish. His education enables him to work for* hacendados *and politicians; he begins to earn a lot of money and he is successful, according to the commentary revealed in song. Yet this success causes him later to reject his own people so he can hang around with the* buena gente *(mestizo middle-class folks) in his Andean town.*
>
> *The song criticizes one Indian boy's success when that success is accompanied by a denial of his ethnic heritage. He no longer bothers to say hello to the people of his ethnic group; he is busy cultivating friendships with the non-Indians of the middle class. The degree of separation from his ethnic group is indicated clearly in his refusing to speak Quechua on the streets in a greeting of familiarity. There is also critical mention of his ultimate transformation:* layachu karka *[he turned into] a white man. While there is a small measure of ethnic pride that this young boy could attain wealth and status, the song also conveys a plea for maintaining strong ties with the community and indigenous cultural patterns.*
>
> *This song, a lesson about the virtues of cultural continuity, at the same time provides a text which attests to the vitality of Quechua as a language of communication. A number of loan words from Spanish (italicized in the song text) are easily incorporated into the phrasing of the harvest song. To halt extinction of the language, efforts must be made to infuse Quechua with a new vitality which allows for scientific and intellectual expression, allowing it to compete with a power structure fashioned by a legacy of colonialism. (Harrison 1989)*

Do you agree or disagree with the author's analysis? For example, is "success accompanied by a denial of ethnic heritage"? Is the piece a "lesson on the virtues of cultural continuity"? How does it "attest to the vitality of Quechua as a language"? How is your analysis different from that of the anthropologist?

• • •

Take a few minutes to choose a song you think would make an excellent vehicle for discussing human language and meaning. Write a brief classroom activity using the song. You may use the Quechua song if you wish.

CULTURAL ANTHROPOLOGY: ARCHAEOLOGY

Proposition 4   Through application of the scientific method to interpretation of material remains, it is possible to know the outlines and some of the content of past cultures.

Today it is widely known that archaeologists excavate in the ground to uncover remains of past cultures. By this means, they attempt to obtain a record of the past several million years of the world's nonliterate cultures, that is, those that lacked writing. Archaeologists, thus, are responsible for telling the human story for over 99 percent of its duration and also for most of its tangled global pathways. Archaeologists who study the more recent past also supplement and provide a check on the written records left by populations living in the historical era.

In their research, archaeologists commonly excavate on locations (sites) believed to harbor cultural remains. Sites are usually located either by regional surveys or in consultation with local experts. Artifacts (tools) and features (complex remains, including architecture and burials) are carefully identified, mapped, and preserved for laboratory analysis. For every day spent excavating, a week or more of work in the laboratory may ensue. To maximize recovery of information, archaeologists collaborate with many other scientists, including geologists, chemists, geochronologists, botanists, and, for ethnographic comparisons, ethnologists.

As local site reports have increased in number, regional descriptions have become possible and, today, an outline of the prehistory of earth has been written. This feat is even more remarkable when one considers that only a few thousand underfinanced archaeologists have written this "prehistoric" history, covering nearly 4 million years and 99.9 percent of human time, in a little over 100 years. That they must work only with "material" remains, many of which at their time of deposition would have been called "garbage" or worse, makes their achievement yet more remarkable.

CULTURAL ANTHROPOLOGY: ETHNOLOGY AND ETHNOGRAPHY

Proposition 5   Behavior patterns and cultural assumptions of humans can be studied scientifically and objectively.

Ethnographers study living people by residing with them and participating in their lives, usually for a year or more. Ethnographers generally learn the language of the people they study, take a census, and collect copious notes on most aspects of everyday life. Their formal concerns include kinship and genealogical characteristics; socioeconomic activities; the material world; political structure and conflict resolution; religious beliefs and organization; the thought and dream world; ecological relationships; and more. Margaret Mead was ethnography's most famous practitioner during the middle of the twentieth century.

A primary task of ethnographers is to come to see the world as their hosts do and thus understand their vision of the universe. By this means, ethnographers hope not only to discover the cultural directives to which their informants customarily respond, but also to lower or eliminate their own cultural biases.

In ethnography, this search for the hosts' own understandings of their activities is referred to as the *emic* approach. If successful, an emic investigation may provide a figurative cultural map that could be used to understand and even anticipate the behavior of the society's members in dealing with everyday life. Simultaneously, the ethnographer, as foreigner and scientist, makes his or her own informed judgments as to what actually occurs. This level of analysis is referred to as the *etic*. For example, if community members explain to the ethnographer that a comatose man is possessed of a demon (a rather common belief worldwide), that would provide an emic explanation; an etic explanation could come from a blood sugar test that indicated diabetes as the cause of the condition. Good ethnography consists of a careful weaving together of the two levels of analysis to understand the culture's adaptive system.

Case Study for Proposition 5: An Etic Analysis of Nacirema Body Ritual

Etic analysis has the possibility of distortion, misinterpretation, or misunderstanding, owing to either incomplete or inadequate data upon which to build a valid description of a culture. The following account, a compelling effort at an etic description of one body magic practiced by an exotic people, the *Nacirema* (pronounced *nock e rema*), tries to escape those pitfalls. When you have finished the essay, go back over it and try to create an emic commentary on Miner's etic presentation.

*Body Ritual among the Nacirema**

Nacirema culture is characterized by a highly developed market economy which has evolved in a rich natural habitat. While much of the people's time is devoted to economic pursuits, a large part of the fruits of these labors and a considerable portion of the day are spent in ritual activity. The focus of this activity is the human body, the appearance and health of which loom as a dominant concern in the ethos of the people. While such a concern is certainly not unusual, its ceremonial aspects and associated philosophy are unique.

The fundamental belief underlying the whole system appears to be that the human body is ugly and that its natural tendency is to debility and disease. Incarcerated in such a body, man's only hope is to avert these characteristics through the use of the powerful influences of ritual and ceremony. Every household has one or more shrines devoted to this purpose. The more powerful individuals in the society

---

*Excerpted by permission of the American Anthropological Association from H. Miner, "Body Ritual among the Nacirema," *American Anthropologist* 58, no. 3 (1956): 503–7. Not for further reproduction.

have several shrines in their houses and, in fact, the opulence of a house is often referred to in terms of the number of such ritual centers it possesses. Most houses are of wattle and daub construction, but the shrine rooms of the more wealthy are walled with stone. Poorer families imitate the rich by applying pottery plaques to their shrine walls.

While each family has at least one such shrine, the rituals associated with it are not family ceremonies but are private and secret. The rites are normally only discussed with children, and then only during the period when they are being initiated into these mysteries. I was able, however, to establish sufficient rapport with the natives to examine these shrines and to have the rituals described to me.

The focal point of the shrine is a box or chest which is built into the wall. In this chest are kept the many charms and magical potions without which no native believes he could live. These preparations are secured from a variety of specialized practitioners. The most powerful of these are the medicine men, whose assistance must be rewarded with substantial gifts. However, the medicine men do not provide the curative potions for their clients, but decide what the ingredients should be and then write them down in an ancient and secret language. This writing is understood only by the medicine men and by the herbalists who, for another gift, provide the required charm.

The charm is not disposed of after it has served its purpose, but is placed in the charm-box of the household shrine. As these magical materials are specific for certain ills, and the real or imagined maladies of the people are many, the charm-box is usually full to overflowing. The magical packets are so numerous that people forget what their purposes were and fear to use them again. While the natives are very vague on this point, we can only assume that the idea in retaining all the old magical materials is that their presence in the charm-box, before which the body rituals are conducted, will in some way protect the worshiper.

Beneath the charm-box is a small font. Each day every member of the family, in succession, enters the shrine room, bows his head before the charm-box, mingles different sorts of holy water in the font, and proceeds with a brief rite of ablution. The holy waters are secured from the Water Temple of the community, where the priests conduct elaborate ceremonies to make the liquid ritually pure. . . .

The daily body ritual performed by everyone includes a mouth-rite. Despite the fact that these people are so punctilious about care of the mouth, this rite involves a practice which strikes the uninitiated stranger as revolting. It was reported to me that the ritual consists of inserting a small bundle of hog hairs into the mouth, along with certain magical powders, and then moving the bundle in a highly formalized series of gestures.

In addition to the private mouth-rite, the people seek out a holy-mouth-man once or twice a year. These practitioners have an impressive set of paraphernalia, consisting of a variety of augers, awls, probes, and prods. The use of these objects in the exorcism of the evils of the mouth involves almost unbelievable ritual torture of the client. . . .

It is to be hoped that, when a thorough study of the Nacirema is made, there will be careful inquiry into the personality structure of these people. One has but to watch the gleam in the eye of a holy-mouth-man, as he jabs an awl into an exposed nerve, to suspect that a certain amount of sadism is involved. If this can be established, a very interesting pattern emerges, for most of the population shows definite masochistic tendencies. It was to these that Professor Linton, of Yale University, referred in discussing a distinctive part of the daily body ritual which is performed only by men. This part of the rite involves scraping and lacerating the surface of the face with a sharp instrument. Special women's rites are performed only four times during each lunar month, but what they lack in frequency is made up in barbarity. As part of this ceremony, women bake their heads in small ovens for about an hour. . . .

Our review of the ritual life of the Nacirema has certainly shown them to be a magic-ridden people. It is hard to understand how they have managed to exist so long under the burdens which they have imposed upon themselves.

Playing the Anthropologist Observer's Role

Did you think the analysis of the "Nacirema" was funny, trenchant, keenly insightful? Carry out an observation of your own using a school or a classroom as the focus. Call it the "learning rituals of the Loohcs," pronounced "looks."

Pretend you are on a field trip to a nearby school. Write an observation about life in the school building or in one classroom in the style and manner of Professor Miner, author of the Nacirema. Be dubious and critical about what you observe, taking extensive notes.

Create categories for observation that take into account common Loohcs rituals, such as the lesson, the "behave yourself" lecture, the recess or physical activity time, the gustatory period also known as lunch, and the test-taking ceremony. Also look at special-occasion rituals, such as assembly, class trips, contests, and school fairs. Be sure not to miss significant rituals such as the class welcome, the pledge of allegiance, and the homework collection and criticism times.

Interview all participants in the Loohcs society, including the principal, the teachers, students, and staff—even the lunchroom workers and maintenance crew. How does each view Loohcs life? Who is positive, negative, or neutral about his or her experience and for what reasons? Which rituals are widely shared and enjoyed and which are specialized and/or abhorred?

While accumulating data for your monograph on Loohcs society and culture, think about these questions:

- Can your observations be objective? Why or why not?
- Should observations be objective? Why or why not?
- Do observations agree or disagree with participants' views?

- In what way do your school observations and conclusions seem similar to or different from Professor Miner's treatment of Nacirema body rituals?

Proposition 6   Most human behavior is not mandated simply by inborn biological imperatives; cultural learning is the primary factor in determining human action.

Too often our actions are explained away popularly as being due simply to the operation of "human nature" or instincts comparable to those possessed by homing pigeons or by the territorially combative Siamese fighting fish. Were our human species possessed of such inborn behavioral directives, some human actions would have to be exhibited by all appropriate normal members of our species.

Commonly proposed as human instincts are ones with such labels as "maternal," "survival," "acquisitive," "territorial," "reproductive" or "aggressive." But many women choose not to have children and many societal members seek their own deaths. Rather than instincts, cultural directives tell individuals what to do in nearly every circumstance likely to arise. These directives vary from one culture to another and thus defy simplistic biological explanations.

Eye contact, body language, speech patterns, and touch all play a part in daily communications between peoples in every culture. For most of us, these actions are performed virtually without forethought; we often regard such manners as inborn, completely accepted, and "natural." So effortlessly do most of us born into a particular culture understand subtle body and speech cues that we overlook their importance and the way in which those behaviors evolved.

Anthropologists have identified what they call "distances" in public relations; these distances vary from society to society and within societies. Anthropologists Edward and Mildred Hall (1971) described four main distances that white middle-class Americans employ in public interactions:*

- Intimate, ranging from direct contact with another person to a distance of approximately 18 inches. Used for private activities such as making love.
- Personal, ranging from 1½ to 4 feet. Used by intimates when in public or, at the farthest distance, for one-on-one conversation.
- Social, 4 to 12 feet. Used in business transactions or conversations at social events.
- Public, ranging from 12 to 25 feet. Used by speakers with groups, including teachers and students (the closer ranges), or a public figure, such as the president (the farther ranges).

According to the Halls, people learn these distances just as they learn spoken language, "by observing and imitating poeple around them as they grow up." By

---

*Reprinted by permission of Edward T. Hall and Mildred Reed Hall. Oroginally appeared in *Playboy* Magazine.

imitating adults of the same sex, they learn gender signals. Other differences, such as regional or ethnic patterns, are also learned in childhood. The Halls emphasize the importance of this body language: "As long as each of us realizes the power of these signals, this society's diversity can be a source of great strength rather than a further—and subtly powerful—source of division."

ACTIVITY

Applying the Halls' "Four Distances" to Your Own Setting

Use the Halls' concept of the "four social distances" to research gender relations (i.e., the way boys relate to girls' and girls to boys' body language). Set up a notebook for several situations, taking systematic notes on the body language and distances displayed by boys and girls in the following situations.

	Intimate Distance	Personal Distance	Social Distance	Public Distance
• Out on a date in a movie or local restaurant or cafe				
• Talking about homework or reading assignments with each other in class				
• Ordering food or buying clothing in a local fast food chain or boutique				
• Presenting a report in class or making a speech in an assembly				

Think about these questions while you are recognizing body language stances and social distances:

- Which body movements seem to indicate attraction and which repulsion?
- What types of body language are accompanied by direct eye contact and what types are not?
- Are body movements and social distances different among boys and girls who have just met from what they are among those who already know one another?

Bring your records back with you to share with the group as a whole. Take fifteen or twenty minutes to formulate conclusions about the entire sample of behavior that has been collected. Does your research confirm or refute the Halls' concept of "social distances"? Are their specific predictions of distance and body language proved correct? Were there any outstanding differences in your findings? Have you and your classmates uncovered any subcultural variations?

• • •

You are likely, as a teacher, to encounter many students from subcultures different from your own. How does the preceding activity shed light on teacher interactions with such students? How might you find out more about conventions of body language among subcultures in the United States?

Proposition 7 All cultures studied by ethnographers have contained the same major features arranged in similar ways.

In the early part of the twentieth century, Clark Wissler proposed that all cultures possessed a set of core features. He believed that this universal pattern, which tended to give common form to all cultures, included speech, material traits, art, knowledge, society, property, government, and war. We now know, however, that most bands tend not to practice war or to permit private ownership of territory or of scarce resources.

Later, a British anthropologist, Alfred Radcliffe-Brown, put forward a simpler, yet more inclusive, set of universal principles underlying sociocultural adaptation. They are (1) the ecological, or the ways in which the system interacts with the physical environment; (2) the social-structural, or the means developed to maintain an orderly and predictable social life; and (3) the mental, or ideological characteristics that provide a rationale for their ecological and social relationships.

Families, often consisting of enduring collectives of several generations, socialize new members to meet traditional expectations, teaching children at least some aspects of "making a living," getting along with others, and sharing a belief system. As societies become more complex, other institutions, such as clubs, schools, churches, industries, and the military, take over many of the functions of the family. The needs of these institutions come to override those of individuals and families and to give differential shape to the actions within their society's boundaries.

Ethnographic research has shown that all cultures, from simple, local band societies of foraging people (now nearly extinct) to huge urban industrial states, possess highly symbolic, historically derived, ecologically relevant, ideological charters, often religious in nature, which define for the members a moral and ethical universe: good and evil, desirable and undesirable, possible or impossible. A good example of portions of a symbolic charter may be heard in the national hymns of the United States: "The Star-Spangled Banner," "God Bless America," and "America, the Beautiful." One need never read history, or travel to Kansas, or study the Bill of Rights to know what the United States, ideally, is devoted to.

Case Study for Proposition 7: Growing Up Human

To illustrate the similarity of basic cultural features and the processes involved in learning them, we have taken brief sections from two autobiographies of non-Western people. Our first vignette is that of a young African girl, Nisa, born among the !Kung people of the Kalahari Desert. The second vignette comes from the Apache Indians, a native people of the American Southwest; it is from the life of Geronimo. When this account was written, he was a prisoner of war held by the U.S. army.

One might expect a young Apache Indian of the nineteenth century and a small !Kung girl of the mid-twentieth to have undergone very different childhood experiences. As you shall read, they (and many of us) have gone through very similar contexts.

Nisa: Life in the Bush*

We lived in the bush and my father set traps and killed steenbok and duiker and gemsbok and we lived, eating the animals and foods of the bush. We collected food, ground it in a mortar, and ate it. We also ate sweet nin berries and tsin beans. When I was growing up, there were no cows or goats and I didn't know who the Hereros were. I had never seen other peoples and didn't know anything other than life in the bush. That's where we lived and where we grew up.

Whenever my father killed an animal and I saw him coming home with meat draped over a stick, balanced on one shoulder—that's what made me happy. I'd cry out, "Mommy! Daddy's coming and he's bringing meat." My heart would be happy when I greeted him, "Ho, ho, Daddy! We're going to eat meat!"

Or honey. Sometimes he'd go out and come home with honey. I'd be sitting around with my mother and then see something coming from way out in the bush. I'd look hard. Then, "Oooh, Daddy found a beehive! Oh, I'm going to eat honey! Daddy's come back with honey for us to eat!" And I'd thank him and call him wonderful names.

Sometimes my mother would be the one to see the honey. The two of us would be walking around gathering food and she'd find a beehive deep inside a termite mound or in a tree. I remember one time when she found it. I jumped and ran all around and was so excited I couldn't stop moving. We went to the village to get some containers, then went back again to the termite mound. I watched as she took the honey out. Then, we went home.

Long ago, when we were living in the bush, our fathers brought us plenty of food! And, animals full of fat—that was especially prized. Whenever my father brought back meat, I'd greet him, "Ho, ho, Daddy's coming home with meat!" And felt thankful for everything and there was nothing that made my heart unhappy.

---

*For permission to photocopy this selection, please contact Harvard University Press. Reprinted by permission of the publishers from *Nisa: The Life and Words of a !Kung Woman* by Marjorie Shostak (Cambridge: Harvard University Press), pp. 87–93. Copyright © 1981 by Marjorie Shostak.

Except if it was someone else in the village who killed something and came back carrying it. Then I'd look and think, "Uhn, uhn . . . that one, the people in his hut aren't giving people. If they have something, they never give it to us. Even when they do, they don't give enough so all of us can eat. They are stingy people." My heart would not be happy at all, because that would mean we would have to ask. So, the next morning we would sit around their hut. If they gave us a large portion, my heart would be happy and I would think, "Yes, these people, their hearts are close to ours. They gave mother and father some of what they had." Then everyone would eat.

But there is always one hut in the village where the people kill you when it comes to food. I remember when we were living with a group of Zhun/twasi and they were eating meat from an animal they had killed. My father asked for some, and they refused. I sat there, thinking, "I'll just sit here and wait. When Daddy kills an animal, then I'll eat meat." Because my father was a good hunter. . . .

When I was growing up, receiving food made my heart happy. There really wasn't anything, other than stingy people, that made me unhappy. I didn't like people who wouldn't give a little of what they had. Then my heart would feel bad and I'd think, "This one, I don't like." . . .

My older brother, Dau, was much older than I was. Even when I was born, he already had his own hut and no longer lived with us. Later, he married. But when I was still little, he would go hunting and come home with meat. And just as my father knew how to track and kill animals, my older brother also learned. The memories I have about him aren't unhappy ones—they are the times when my heart felt wonderful.

I used to follow him around wherever he went; I just loved him! Sometimes, when he wanted to go hunting, he'd say, "Why don't you just sit in the village? Why are you always following me?" I'd stay home and when he came back with meat, I'd greet him, "Ho, ho . . . my big brother's home!" . . .

I also remember the time I got burned. My mother had just come back from digging klaru bulbs, and had put them into a pot to cook into soft porridge. I kept asking, "Mommy, give me some. Why don't you give some to me? Mommy, give me some klaru." Finally, to quiet me, she took some she thought was cool enough from the top of the pot and put it in my hand, but it was still too hot. I dropped it and it landed on my leg. Before I could push it off, it burned me, leaving a large wound. I cried and cried and even after it got dark, I kept on crying. My father said, "Chuko, I've told you again and again, you shouldn't do things that cause Nisa to cry and be full of tears. Why don't you understand? Are you without ears? You keep doing things that make her cry. You, the mother of these little children, can't you understand things?"

People say that salt heals burns, so after they washed it out thoroughly, they crushed some salt into very small pieces and put it on. I wasn't afraid and just let them put it on. Then, I cried and watched as the salt made little bubbles on the wound, "Oh, this salt is terrible . . . eeeee . . . eeeee . . . !" The salt almost killed me. Really, it felt as though it was killing my leg. I almost died from the pain.

The burn lasted a long time and made walking difficult. I couldn't get up easily. When I had to go to the bush I would crawl on my hands. My father blamed my mother, "If you ever do something like that to Nisa again, I, an adult, and her father, will do the same thing to you! I'll take you and throw you into the fire. How could you have almost killed a child? Now, she can't even walk! I'd like to throw you into the fire right now. I won't, people say I shouldn't. But if you ever burn her like that again, I will!" My mother said, "You're right. If you were to throw me into the fire, there wouldn't be any wrong done because I was responsible for your child's getting burned. But she really has no sense. There's nothing worth anything in her head yet. She has no sense at all, not even about asking for food to be given to her."

We lived and lived and after a while the burn healed.

Geronimo*

I was born in No-doyohn Cañon, Arizona, June, 1829.

In that country which lies around the headwaters of the Gila River I was reared. This range was our fatherland; among these mountains our wigwams were hidden; the scattered valleys contained our fields; the boundless prairies, stretching away on every side, were our pastures; the rocky caverns were our burying places.

I was fourth in a family of eight children—four boys and four girls. Of that family, only myself, my brother, Porico (White Horse), and my sister, Nah-da-ste, are yet alive. We are held as prisoners of war in this Military Reservation (Fort Sill).

As a babe I rolled on the dirt floor of my father's tepee, hung in my tsoch (Apache name for cradle) at my mother's back, or suspended from the bough of a tree, I was warmed by the sun, rocked by the winds, and sheltered by the trees as other Indian babes.

When a child my mother taught me the legends of our people; taught me of the sun and sky, the moon and stars, the clouds and storms. She also taught me to kneel and pray to Usen for strength, health, wisdom, and protection. We never prayed against any person, but if we had aught against any individual we ourselves took vengeance. We were taught that Usen does not care for the petty quarrels of men.

My father had often told me of the brave deeds of our warriors, of the pleasures of the chase, and the glories of the warpath.

With my brothers and sisters I played about my father's home. Sometimes we played at hide-and-seek among the rocks and pines; sometimes we loitered in the shade of the cottonwood trees or sought the shudock (a kind of wild cherry) while our parents worked in the field. Sometimes we played that we were warriors. We would practice stealing upon some object that represented an enemy, and in our childish imitation often perform the fears of war. Sometimes we would hide away

---

*From S. M. Barrett, *Geronimo: His Own Story* (New York: Ballantine Books, 1970).

from our mother to see if she could find us, and often when thus concealed go to sleep and perhaps remain hidden for many hours.

When we were old enough to be of real service we went to the field with our parents: not to play, but to toil. When the crops were to be planted we broke the ground with wooden hoes. We planted the corn in straight rows, the beans among the corn, and the melons and pumpkins in irregular order over the field. We cultivated these crops as there was need.

Our field usually contained about two acres of ground. The fields were never fenced. It was common for many families to cultivate land in the same valley and share the burden of protecting the growing crops from destruction by the ponies of the tribe, or by deer and other wild animals.

Melons were gathered as they were consumed. In the autumn pumpkins and beans were gathered and placed in bags or baskets; ears of corn were tied together by the husks, and then the harvest was carried on the backs of ponies up to our homes. Here the corn was shelled, and all the harvest stored away in caves or other secluded places to be used in winter.

We never fed corn to our ponies, but if we kept them up in the winter time we gave them fodder to eat. We had no cattle or other domestic animals except our dogs and ponies.

We did not cultivate tobacco, but found it growing wild. This we cut and cured in autumn, but if the supply ran out the leaves from the stalks left standing served our purpose. All Indians smoked—men and women. No boy was allowed to smoke until he had hunted alone and killed large game—wolves and bears. Unmarried women were not prohibited from smoking, but were considered immodest if they did so. Nearly all matrons smoked.

Besides grinding the corn (by hand with stone mortars and pestles) for bread, we sometimes crushed it and soaked it, and after it had fermented made from this juice a "tis-win," which had the power of intoxication, and was very highly prized by the Indians. This work was done by the squaws and children. When berries or nuts were to be gathered the small children and the squaws would go in parties to hunt them, and sometimes stay all day. When they went any great distance from camp they took ponies to carry the baskets.

I frequently went with these parties, and upon one of these excursions a woman named Cho-ko-le got lost from the party and was riding her pony through a thicket in search of her friends. Her little dog was following as she slowly made her way through the thick underbrush and pine trees. All at once a grizzly bear rose in her path and attacked her pony. She jumped off and her pony escaped, but the bear attacked her, so she fought him the best she could with her knife. Her little dog, by snapping at the bear's heels and distracting his attention from the woman, enabled her for some time to keep pretty well out of his reach. Finally the grizzly struck her over the head, tearing off almost her whole scalp. She fell, but did not lose consciousness, and while prostrate struck him four good licks with her knife, and he retreated. After he had gone she replaced her torn scalp and bound it up as best she could, then she turned deathly sick and had to lie down. That night her pony came into camp with his load of nuts and berries, but no rider. The Indians hunted for her, but did not find her until the second day. They carried her home, and under the treatment of their medicine men all her wounds were healed.

The Indians knew what herbs to use for medicine, how to prepare them, and how to give the medicine. This they had been taught by Usen in the beginning, and each succeeding generation had men who were skilled in the art of healing.

In gathering the herbs, in preparing them, and in administering the medicine, as much faith was held in prayer as in the actual effect of the medicine. Usually about eight persons worked together in making medicine, and there were forms of prayer and incantations to attend each stage of the process. Four attended to the incantations and four to the preparation of the herbs.

Some of the Indians were skilled in cutting out bullets, arrow heads, and other missiles with which warriors were wounded. I myself have done much of this, using a common dirk or butcher knife.

ACTIVITY

Recording Your Own Family Saga

Like Nisa, the !Kung woman, and Geronimo, the Apache man, write your own story about how you grew up with your family and moved through several stages of life from infant to child to young adult. Tell how your family went about making a living, preparing food, contributing to the household chores, having fun, and meeting challenges. Be sure to include at least a couple of incidents that presented difficult problems for you; tell about your relationship to your mother and father or to other siblings or friends; and describe an event that made you feel proud of yourself. Limit your story to early and mid-childhood, and keep the length of your story under 1,000 words.

Once you have finished your tale, hand it to a friend or a classmate for editing and review while you look his or her account over. Note those events that resemble portions of the Nisa and Geronimo accounts, as well as events that seem quite different. Make a list of differences and similarities between your classmate's story and those of Nisa and Geronimo. What conclusions would you and your classmate draw about growing up: Do people generally report similar experiences with similar institutions such as the family, the group, and the business of making a living in an economy? Trade your story with several others to further test your hypotheses and conclusions about growing up.

• • •

Design a "tell your story" activity for use with secondary students.

PERSISTENT QUESTIONS

Anthropology has a substantial core of shared premises that all who study the field should be familiar with, but a number of controversial issues are still to be resolved.

Question 1: Is Anthropology a Science, a Humanity, or Both?

Most anthropologists insist upon the empirical, inductive methods of the "harder" sciences that search for causes and natural laws. Some insist, however, that deduction and even intuition are legitimate tools in an interpretive, humanistic, holistic anthropology. Scientists seek major hypotheses that will explain both general and specific events, past and present. Humanists utilize personalized interpretations that may prove to be highly individualized and nonreplicable, to be derived from the context of analysis rather than from general comparative theory. In our opinion, there is need for both points of view. No science—physical, natural, or social—is a closed system where only one dogma is to be tolerated.

Question 2: Is Anthropology a Product of Colonialism and Capitalism, Fairly Characterized as the Science of "White" People Studying Oppressed "Colored" People?

That hurts, but the question is a justifiable one. In the establishment of anthropology, the earliest field studies conducted were of conquered or colonial people. The British focused on Africa, Australia, and other of their then-colonial areas; anthropologists from the United States emphasized the study of Native Americans and Filipinos; the French studied Moroccans, Algerians, and populations of Central Africa, all areas under their colonial control. Only later did anthropologists turn to their own cultures as appropriate fields for study, and even then they concentrated on the less powerful segments of society. It is also true that some of the findings of anthropologists have been used by governments to justify and facilitate their control over conquered and suppressed peoples.

As more and more formerly subjected people entered the world of their conquerors, some took up a cudgel against anthropologists. They believe that anthropologists, who spent many years studying them and, admittedly, personally profited by so doing, should now be of help in alleviating their current social problems (see Deloria 1988). It is to be hoped that as anthropology enters its second hundred years, the vast database it has established will come to be applied to solve social and cultural problems.

Anthropology is no longer the province solely of Europeans and Euro-Americans. Today hundreds of anthropologists are of Third World backgrounds, often dedicating themselves to the study of their own people. Perhaps best known of these was

Jomo Kenyatta, Kenya's first president. Other Third World anthropologists have turned their anthropological gaze on Western culture, thus adding an invaluable perspective to our understanding of culture.

Question 3: As the Tribal People of the World Disappear, Will Anthropology Wither Up and Die?

Not very likely. As any sociologist will tell you, bureaucracies of any kind are loath to fold up their tents and steal away. Anthropology is no different. Furthermore, anthropology has a significant contribution to make in the study of contemporary societies. After the Second World War, as it became more difficult to encounter unstudied band and tribal people, anthropologists turned to the study of settled people, sometimes of recent tribal origin. "Peasant" communities, villages of people in rural contexts around the world, became a focus. As those investigations were being undertaken, the flow of rural people to urban areas, which began thousands of years ago, turned into a stream and then into a torrent: By the middle of the twenty-first century, it is likely that few, if any, small villages will remain in most of the world. In tune with these demographic shifts, anthropologists began to undertake studies of city people, often city people who recently had lived in peasant villages.

If world leaders are to establish peace and harmony, internal and external, upon which political stability and cultural growth rest, then they must come to grips with the problems associated with multiethnic societies, and with a world filled with billions of people who respond to different symbol systems. Anthropologists are uniquely positioned to work dispassionately to understand and to attempt to alleviate the conflict that so often results when different worlds meet.

If the leading citizens of modern states were familiar with the forces underlying sociocultural evolution perhaps they could appreciate that other ways of ordering human relationships and solving political problems than despotism, oppression, and violence must exist. As Franz Boas noted at the turn of the twentieth century: If only we will become cognizant of the ways in which societies operate, then "we may hope to govern our actions so that the greatest benefit to mankind will accrue from them."

ACTIVITY

Planning an Anthropology Unit

Proposition 8 The changing of cultures over time has been from the technologically simple to complex, from the noncentral to centralized, from bands to tribes to chiefdoms to states. Throughout human cultural evolution, the processes of change have favored the materially more complex cultures over the less complex.

Do some reading to develop your understanding of this proposition; Johnson and Earle (1987) is an excellent source. Then develop an outline for a two-week unit for a tenth-grade world history class; the unit should be designed to help students understand the proposition. Use at least one case study in the unit.

Reflecting on the Chapter

We believe social studies in our nation's schools is ready for an anthropological revolution. Can you imagine what that might mean? If all Americans came to understand from the anthropological perspective the sources of social conflict, poverty, persistent disease, infant mortality, war, Third World-ism, and other problems that afflict us, might we not begin to look to eliminating some of their causes?

References

Barrett, S. M. *Geronimo: His Own Story*. New York: Ballantine Books, 1970.

Deloria, V. *Custer Died for Your Sins: An Indian Manifesto*. Norman: University of Oklahoma Press, 1988.

Edley, M. A., and D. C. Johnson. *Blueprint: Solving the Mystery of Evolution*. New York: Dutton, 1989.

Ember, M., and C. Ember. *Science in Anthropology*. New Orleans: American Anthropological Association, 1990.

Geertz, C. *The Interpretation of Cultures*. New York: Basic Books, 1973.

Johnson, A. W., and T. Earle. *The Evolution of Human Societies: From Foraging Group to Agrarian State*. Palo Alto, Calif.: Stanford University Press, 1987.

Hall, E. T. *The Silent Language*. New York: Doubleday, 1959.

Hall, E. T. and M. R. Hall. "The Sounds of Silence." *Playboy Magazine* (June 1971).

Harrison, R. *Signs, Songs, and Memory in the Andes: Translating Quechua Language and Culture*. Austin: University of Texas Press, 1989.

Haviland, W. *Introduction to Anthropology*. New York: Holt, Rinehart & Winston, 1990.

Human Relations Area File, Yale Station, P.O. Box 2015, New Haven, CT 06520.

Lewis, O. *The Children of Sanchez*. New York: Random House, 1966.

Miner, H. "Body Ritual Among the Nacirema." *American Anthropologist* 58, no. 3 (1956): 503–7.

Montague, M. F. A. *An Introduction to Physical Anthropology*. Springfield, Ill.: C C Thomas, 1945.

Plog, F. *Central Themes in Archeology*. New Orleans: American Anthropological Association, 1990.

Podolefsky, A., and P. J. Brown, *Applying Anthropology: An Introductory Reader*. 3rd ed. Mountain View, Calif.: Mayfield, 1994.

Robinson, G. L. *Crosscultural Understanding*. Englewood Cliffs, N.J.: Prentice-Hall, 1985.

Seager, J., and A. Olson. *Women in the World: An International Atlas*. New York: Simon & Schuster, 1986.

Shostak, M. *Nisa: The Life and Words of a !Kung Woman*. New York: Vintage Books/Random House, 1983.

Spencer, F. *Piltdown: A Scientific Forgery*. New York: Oxford University Press, 1990.

Takaki, R., ed. *Strangers from Other Shores*. Boston: Little, Brown, 1989.

Turnbull, C. *The Human Cycle*. New York: Simon & Schuster, Touchstone, 1984.

Teaching Resources

Anthro-Notes: National Museum of Natural History Newsletter for Teachers, Smithsonian Institution, Department of Anthropology, Stop 112, Washington, DC 20560.

Anthropology 94/95: Annual Editions Series. Guilford, Conn.: Dushkin, 1994.

Appleton, N. *Cultural Pluralism in Education: Theoretical Foundations*. New York: Longman, 1983.

Atlas of Early Man, The. New York: St. Martin's Press, 1993.

Axtell, R. E., ed. *Do's and Taboos around the World: A Guide to International Behavior*. New York: John Wiley, 1990.

Bafa Bafa: A Cross Culture Simulation Game (or *Rafa Rafa* for lower grades). Del Mar, Calif.: Simile II.

Burger, J. *The Gaia Atlas of First Peoples: A Future for the Indigenous World*. New York: Anchor Books, 1990.

Childhood. New York: WNET, 1991. 7 videocassettes.

Crapo. R. H. *Cultural Anthropology: Understanding Ourselves and Others*. Guilford, Conn.: Dushkin, 1993.

Dig 2: A Simulation in Archaeology. Lakeside, Calif.: Interact, 1982.

Dynneson, T. L. "The Status of Pre-Collegiate Anthropology: Progress or Peril?" *Anthropology and Education Quarterly* 12, no. 4 (Winter 1981): 304–9.

———. "Trends in Precollegiate Anthropology." In *Social Studies and Social Science: A Fifty-Year Perspective,* ed. S. P. Wronski and D. H. Bragaw, 153–65. Washington, D.C.: National Council for the Social Studies, 1986.

Faces: The Magazine about People. Peterborough, N.H.: Cobblestone Publishing Co.

Fersh, S., ed. *Learning about Peoples and Cultures*. 2nd ed. Evanston, Ill.: McDougal, Littell, 1990.

Games, Activities, and Simulations for Teaching Anthropology. Culver City: Calif.: Social Studies School Service, 1981.

Higgins, P., and M. Selig, eds. "Anthropology and Precollege Education." *Practicing Anthropology* 8, no. 3/4 (1986): 186–97.

Johnson, M.S., ed. *Simulation Sourcebook*. Boulder: University of Colorado, Department of Anthropology, 1992.

Seeyle, H. N. *Teaching Culture: Strategies for Intercultural Communication*. Evanston, Ill.: National Textbook, 1993.

Smithsonian Institution, Office of Elementary and Secondary Education, Arts and Industries Building 1163, MRC 402, Washington, DC 20560. Newsletters, fact sheets, curriculum materials.

World Music Institute, 49 W. 27th Street, New York, NY 10001. Records/cassettes/CDs of the world's ethnic and folk music.

ACTIVITY LIST

• • •

---

*Steven Wanner contributed to an early version of this chapter.

ACTIVITY   **A Personal Geographic Perspective**

Geographer David Harvey has described "geographical imagination" as the individual's ability "to recognize the role of space and place in his own biography, to relate to the spaces he sees around him, and to recognize how transactions between individuals and between organizations are affected by the space that separates them" (Harvey 1973, 24). All of us have been exposed to important spaces during our lives. One of the first areas we become familiar with is the neighborhood in which we grow up. In this activity, we shall take a geographic view of that "place."

Using a piece of paper no smaller than 8½ by 11 inches, draw a map of the neighborhood you lived in as a child. Make sure your map has a title, a compass rose, an approximate scale, a legend, and a grid system for locating specific places. Give your map as much detail as possible. When you have finished your map, answer the following questions:

- How did you determine the boundaries of your neighborhood?
- Do any buildings not seem to fit in your neighborhood?
- What is the proportion of built objects to the area of natural objects?
- What features affected your interactions with others?

Now exchange maps with a classmate, and answer these questions about your classmate's map:

- List three things that seem to be important. Why did you select those three?
- Do any buildings not seem to fit in the neighborhood?
- Do natural objects play an important role in the neighborhood?
- What relationships can you see between the various objects shown?
- How is this map different from and similar to your own?

After you answer these questions, discuss your findings with the class. What can you conclude about the places where your class members grew up? What can you conclude about the geographic perspectives of your classmates?

• • •

How might you use an activity like the one just completed with middle or high school students? How would you adapt it? What objectives would it help you achieve?

INTRODUCTION

Complete understanding cannot come from single disciplines; each plays its special role. Geography, the study of earth as the home of humankind, reminds us that everything happens somewhere—all phenomena have a spatial dimension, and a spatial analysis is a rejection of the real world. From the geographer's point of view, all elements of the world can be properly understood only in their spatial context. For example, Brazil's gross national product per capita is about U.S.$2,800, but that national average masks a great deal of spatial variability within the nation: The population of Northeast Brazil, one of the poorest regions in the Western Hemisphere, has a per capita income comparable to that of Haiti, less than $500, whereas the South, centered on São Paulo state, has a per capita income of more than $8,000, making it one of the wealthiest parts of the hemisphere.

In addressing such spatial realities, geography focuses on fundamental human concerns:

- Space—both in the form of extent and separation of things and in the form of differential environmental quality and content—conditions physical and social activities and processes.
- Human activities both alter and define or "create" the character of place and the structure of space.

Geography's concerns clearly relate to vital issues at the local, national, and global levels. As policymakers and citizens have come to understand that what happens in other parts of the world—whether economic productivity in the Pacific Rim, political developments in Eastern Europe, or war in the Middle East—can have a direct impact on their well-being, they have rediscovered the importance of knowing about other areas and our relationships with them. As public policy, business activity, and ordinary life have been increasingly barraged by issues related to environmental health, quality, and change—issues ranging from waste disposal to global warming—people have been convinced of the importance of understanding society's relationships with the physical environment. As more of our flow of information arrives on the screens of television sets and microcomputers, people have been struck by the power of visual images, including the creative use of maps and spatial diagrams. In all of these cases, society has looked to geography for basic teaching and learning.

The discipline of geography developed its unique perspective over time, and this chapter examines that history as well as geography's role in the American school curriculum. We then present a process for teaching geography that engages students in examination of real-world issues. Together, these discussions are designed to give the reader a geographical perspective, a perspective that allows one to appreciate and understand the world in a unique way.

HISTORY AND NATURE OF GEOGRAPHY

Geography, as a formal academic discipline, is only a little over 100 years old; as a subject of human interest, however, it can be traced to ancient times. Like most disciplines, geography has fuzzy boundaries. Thus, geography is best understood by looking at its core, its central purpose: Geography examines one of the two fundamental material dimensions, space; the other dimension, time, is the focus of history. Since all phenomena and events occur in space and time, geography and history provide the foundation upon which other social and natural sciences base their interests in specific categories of phenomena—for example, rocks (geology), plants (botany), economic behavior (economics), and social relations (sociology). Geography does study physical phenomena (rocks and plants) and human phenomena (economic behavior and social relations), but it is not fundamentally interested in them per se. Rather, geography examines where things are and why, the spatial relations between phenomena, and the distinctiveness of place. Although those inquiries are important to both social and natural sciences, geography cannot be easily classified as either one.

Having said that geography is interested in the spatial relations of phenomena rather than in any particular category of phenomena, we must nonetheless affirm that geography does discriminate. It is most interested in those phenomena that help to characterize the earth's surface and the similarities and differences from place to place on that surface. For example, geographers would not study the responses of laboratory animals to HIV infection, but the place of origin and spatial diffusion of HIV among the human population is an important research subject in medical geography.

Geography's Four Traditions

Pattison (1964) pointed to the pluralistic history of the field by identifying "four traditions of geography." He referred to them as the "earth science, spatial, man–land [human–environment interaction], and area studies traditions." We shall use these "traditions" to take a brief look at the recent history of geography.*

Although studies that can be identified as geographical were conducted earlier, it was not until the nineteenth-century development of the university model that scholars identified themselves as professional geographers. Within the discipline, physical geography became the dominant field of interest and innovation in the latter part of the nineteenth century. Charles Darwin's work sparked enthusiasm for the natural sciences, and geographers increasingly associated themselves with that side of the field.

An American physical geographer, William Morris Davis, who began teaching at Harvard University in 1878, became the most influential figure of his time in American geography. Davis applied the concept of change over time (Darwin's notion of evolution) to landform evolution; that is, erosion produces landform changes in

---

*Much of this discussion is condensed from A. David Hill and Regina McCormick, *Geography: A Resource Book for Secondary Schools* (Santa Barbara, Calif.: ABC-Clio, 1989). Used with permission of the publisher.

stages from youth to maturity to old age. His attempt to study landforms scientifically and the terminology he developed were highly significant. Davis's cycle of erosion was widely taught for many decades, but it has fallen into disrepute among contemporary geomorphologists.

Geographers, working in the "earth science tradition," made solid contributions to the physical sciences. At the same time, some geographers gave such importance to the physical world that they diminished the role of human culture. That attitude led to a highly significant development in geographical thought in the latter part of the nineteenth century and the early part of the twentieth, the idea that nature determines culture.

That idea was by no means new in the nineteenth century; indeed, the Greeks believed that culture was linked to climate. But developments conjoined in the nineteenth century to rekindle the idea, not just in geography but in all the human sciences. Darwin's influence focused primary attention on discovering natural laws (statements explaining processes in causal terms), such as natural selection. Nature became paramount, and the social sciences began using the methods developed by the physical sciences. Animal organisms became analogies for human societies in the *social Darwinism* of Herbert Spencer, a British philosopher who first used the phrase "survival of the fittest."

In the United States, the books of one of Davis's students, Ellsworth Huntington, promoted environmental determinism. His textbooks, used in schools and colleges into the middle of the twentieth century, were replete with environmental explanations of all manner of human characteristics. For example, his climatic determinism held that mental activity was highest in the midlatitude cyclonic belts; in contrast, the tropics produced little mental activity.

Fortunately, the human–environment tradition in geography is much broader than environmental determinism. Indeed, determinism has produced strong reactions from such geographers as Carl Sauer, who founded the geography department at the University of California at Berkeley. Attacking environmental determinism, he reminded his students that similar environments have contained quite dissimilar cultures. For example, the Arctic, a harsh environment toward which one might expect a narrow range of cultural response, contains a surprisingly large number of cultural variations across North America, Scandinavia, and Siberia. In addition, a particular environment has quite different meanings and uses over time as peoples occupying it change or as technology changes. Furthermore, Sauer argued that environmental determinism was unscientific. Science, he said, may discover relationships but it cannot be based on the assumption of a particular relationship, which is exactly the position of environmentalism.

Finally, Sauer brought to the attention of geographers the earlier but overlooked work of the American conservationist George Perkins Marsh. His book *Man and Nature, or Physical Geography as Modified by Human Action* (1864) treated the other side of the nature-culture issue: how humans had changed environments.

Reaction to environmental determinism brought about a shift in emphasis in geography. Determinism was guilty of overgeneralization. In reaction, the pendulum swung in the opposite direction, and regionalism—Pattison's area studies tradition—flourished. Area studies or regionalism received particular attention in the United States between World Wars I and II.

The French school of regional geography, led by Vidal de la Blache, made no attempt to generalize, since it emphasized the uniqueness of each region with its distinctive *genre de vie*. The contrast between this perspective and one that seeks to formulate general theories could not be greater. The former, *idiographic*, is descriptive of particular things; the latter, *nomothetic*, is law-seeking. Debate over which perspective should be emphasized is one of the constants in the history of geographic thought.

Regional geography should not, however, be description without explanation. It is the study of defined areas of earth space. Geographers define a *uniform region* based upon the areal (spatial) distribution of a single physical or human characteristic (e.g., a plant species or a language dialect) or upon the distribution of several things (e.g., particular associations of climate, soil, crops, animals, and agricultural technology define a distinctive region formerly called the American Corn Belt).

Geographers also take a functional approach to regional geography. One of the most well developed functional relationships is the interaction of a node of settlement (such as a town) with its tributary territory. This relationship is often defined economically, such as the trade or service area of a town. It can just as well be based on other sorts of linkages across geographic space (e.g., the area of jurisdiction of a political capital, or the district served by a particular religious office).

When Pattison's article on the "four traditions" appeared in 1964, geography was in the midst of a major paradigm shift; the spatial paradigm was ascendant, challenging the earlier regional paradigm. The spatial tradition focuses on the measurement of earth and the spatial patterns upon it; more than the other traditions, it is the science of the significance of location.

Dissatisfied with descriptive regional studies that offered little of general scientific interest, human geographers, beginning in the United States in the 1950s, set out in search of theory and methods to make their field scientific and to improve connections with other sciences. The period would come to be called geography's "quantitative revolution," although it was as much, if not more, a conceptual revolution.

The first geographer to make a major contribution to location theory was Walter Christaller, who in 1933 had written his Ph.D. thesis on the size and spacing of towns in southern Germany, which he called *central places*. Christaller's central-place theory, which explains the distribution of cities in space by the concept of spatial hierarchy, has generated an enormous amount of research and alternative hypotheses on human settlement patterns.

In the 1950s, the geography department at the University of Washington became the principal center of innovation for geography's quantitative revolution. William

Garrison introduced location theory and associated mathematical and statistical methods to his graduate students at Washington, many of whom became the next generation of geography's theoretical leaders. They worked on transportation and industrial location problems, interregional trade, urban spatial patterns, movements of customers to central places, residential patterns, location of services, planned shopping centers, and urban growth processes. Their work supported planning, for example, on the effects of the interstate highways on land use and other spatial patterns.

ACTIVITY

Asking Geographic Questions

The most basic geographic question is *where*. Suppose that four geographers, each working in one of the "four traditions," were studying the map in Figure 10.1. Try to pose a "where" question that you think each one might ask.

Geographers also want to know *why* and *how*. In other words, they want to know about processes that make things happen or explain things. Try to pose "how" and "why" questions about the map from the four traditions as you now understand them. This will be difficult now but will become easier as you work your way through this chapter. In a later section, we discuss geographic questions in considerable detail.

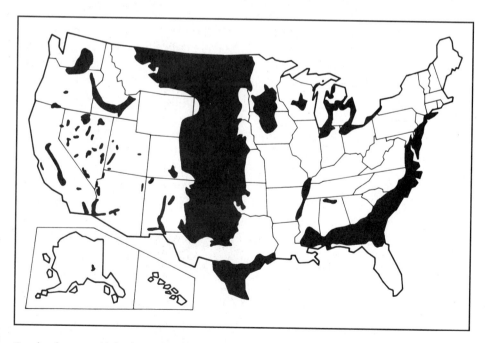

Figure 10.1   Cropland areas with highest potential for wind erosion. *Source: U.S. Department of Agriculture, Soil Conservation Service. Agriculture Information Bulletin Number SSS.*

Contemporary Geography's Pluralism

Since the 1960s, which were dominated by the "spatial tradition," geographers have developed a host of new approaches. *Behavioral geography*, which tries to identify the mental processes through which individuals respond to and act upon their environments, grew rapidly in the late 1960s and the 1970s. Behavioral geographers studied the movement of ideas across earth space, or *spatial diffusion*, and the movement of people, or *migration*. Behavioral approaches to location decision making revealed that previously expected least-cost solutions, as would be predicted by economic location theory, are rare. Instead, locational decisions are frequently best understood as results of policy compromise among powerful interest groups.

Geographers also applied the behavioral approach to problems of the human response to natural hazards. Those studies revealed that the *environmental perception* of the individual decision maker (e.g., a floodplain manager or resident) is more important in understanding the human adjustment to the hazard than are the actual physical and economic conditions of the environment. For example, a farmer might build a house on a river's floodplain because he believes the river will not flood again during his lifetime, even though another large flood could occur in any year.

Also encompassing this tradition but with a different perspective are cultural and historical geography. For example, cultural geographers who identified with the work of Carl Sauer disregarded the quantitative revolution and maintained the tradition of detailed fieldwork in the non-Western, nonindustrialized world, especially to understand the historical evolution of cultural landscapes. Harold Brookfield, an Australian geographer, was highly critical of geographers who stress the form and content of the landscape while ignoring underlying explanations that derive from social organization, human behavior, attitudes and beliefs, and the characteristics and interrelationships of human groups.

Since the 1970s, geographers have increasingly criticized the "logical positivist" approach of some of the work in the spatial and human–environment traditions. Logical positivism promotes the view that knowledge can be neutral, value-free, and objective and that it can be discovered through the empirical procedures of the natural sciences. As early as 1947, John K. Wright introduced the term *geosophy* to refer to the study of geographical knowledge. He noted the extremely eclectic nature of this knowledge, deriving as it does from all peoples. Much of it is subjective and conditioned by the complex interplay of cultural and psychological factors.

Following Wright, David Lowenthal (1961) stressed that our individual experience constrains each of us to live in a parochial, personal world that is different from those even of other individuals in our own culture. Furthermore, each culture has its own experience, which separates it from other cultures. Arguments such as these stimulated numerous cultural geographers to study the expressions in the landscape of personal taste and cultural norms, thus creating a *humanistic geography* that stood in sharp contrast to positivism.

Figure 10.2   How might a geographer who takes a logical positivist approach interpret this landscape differently from a humanistic geographer?

The geographer Yi-Fu Tuan (e.g., 1974) used the term *humanistic geography* to refer to an approach that removes geography from the physical and social sciences and places it within the humanities. For him, geography is a mirror; to know geography is to know ourselves. The study of landscapes is the study of the essence of the societies that produced them, just as the study of literature and art reveals much of human life. Tuan argued that science tends to minimize the role of human awareness and knowledge, whereas a humanistic approach tries to understand how geographical phenomena reveal the quality of human awareness.

Also within the humanistic mode, Ann Buttimer (1983) urged geographers to study the values that infuse all of our lives and thoughts; personal and cultural style, she argued, contribute to geographical knowledge. She believes that abstract theories of social science separate us from the values and meanings of everyday "lifeworld." Also, she asserts that preconceived analytical models make us more interested in establishing control over people than in attempting to understand the dynamics of their lives and thus helping to advance the process of human development.

Since the 1970s, geography's many stripes have included reformist (*welfare geography*) and revolutionary (*radical* or *Marxist geography*) approaches. Welfare geography, addressing serious environmental and social problems, has emphasized questions of inequality: Who gets what, where, and how? Radical geographers call for both revolutionary theory and revolutionary practice. For instance, David Harvey (1973) argued that the only way to eliminate ghettos was to eliminate the market economy that has produced them. Experimenting with numerous approaches, such as probing for greater understanding of the structures that underpin society, geographers today, like those in the past, argue for a fundamental reevaluation of the discipline.

Summary of General Characteristics

Today, geography is more pluralistic than it has ever been in its long history. So, you might ask, given this variety of approaches and interests, what is geography and what are its fundamental characteristics? As stated earlier, geography is the study of the earth as the home of humankind; it examines the earth's surface as the space within which the human population lives.

A fundamental characteristic of the discipline is an emphasis on location, the concern with the locational or spatial variation in both physical and human phenomena on the earth's surface. Geography tries to establish locations accurately, to represent them effectively (usually but not necessarily with maps), and to disentangle the factors that lead to particular spatial patterns.

A second characteristic is geography's emphasis on human–environmental relations. Here the stress is on the systems of interrelations of phenomena, the links between aspects of the natural environment of a particular area and the human population occupying or modifying it.

A third characteristic of geography, regional analysis, fuses the spatial and ecological approaches described earlier. Appropriate spatial segments of the earth's surface, termed regions, are identified, their internal (intraregional) form and human–environmental linkages traced, and their external (extraregional) relations established.

For some geographers, the process of region building, sometimes called the *areal differentiation* of the earth's surface, represents the field's highest purpose. Others argue that the most significant advances have come from systematic studies, often in association with neighboring disciplines. The relative importance of these two approaches—regional and systematic—forms an area of methodological debate. Although the subject matter of geography is logically indivisible, the study of the earth's surface as the home of humankind is so complex that it must be divided to be manageable. The two traditional ways of doing this are (1) regional geography, in which we consider each part of the earth's surface in turn, region by region, and (2) systematic geography, in which we study a significant theme or element (e.g., economic activity or political organization) and trace it systematically over the whole earth.

Finally, as geography has evolved in the United States during the twentieth century, it has developed a number of skills and perspectives that are attracting special attention in the 1990s. Reduced to simple terms, they focus on the importance of linkages between places, the importance of linkages between diverse kinds of phenomena in place, and the value of viewing data in spatial context as a basis for reasoning and learning. In the past generation, encyclopedic compendia of information about places have gradually given way to theory-based understandings about spatial relationships. The degree of sophistication in appreciating nature–society relationships has advanced dramatically, and traditional uses of print maps are shifting rapidly toward uses of computer-based digital geographical databases, spatial displays on microcomputer screens, and decentralized printouts of patterns of specialized interest.

| ACTIVITY | **Identifying Issues of Concern to Diverse Geographic Specialities** |

With your classmates, organize the class into small groups and assign each group a different geographic specialty—for example, political geography, cultural geography, urban geography, population geography, and economic geography. In these groups, look through several newspapers and newsmagazines, identifying current issues that would be of interest to your geographic specialty.

For each issue you identify, develop several questions you might ask about the issue. Be sure your questions show geography's emphasis on location and on human–environmental relations. Discuss whether the group thinks a regional or a systematic study would be more appropriate.

• • •

After the groups have shared their issues and questions, reflect on how trying to think like a geographer in this activity and the previous one was helpful and/or frustrating for you. How might you be able to use an exercise like this with secondary students? What are the possible pitfalls? benefits?

GEOGRAPHY IN AMERICAN EDUCATION

In discussing the history and nature of geography as a discipline and as a body of knowledge, we have naturally emphasized the content of geography—the evolution of its concepts, theories, and methods. However, geography is also a subject matter in the institutional context of education, which itself has a history.

Geography's Shifting Role in the Curriculum

Throughout the history of high school geography, the subject emphasis has continually shifted, as has the subject's status in the curriculum. The publication of Guyot's *Physical Geography* in 1873 helped to shift the focus of high school geography from locational to physical geography (Rumble 1946; Rosen 1957). This trend, which began in the 1850s, was reinforced in 1892 by the NEA's Committee of Ten, which provided for the first time a definition of the nation's secondary school curriculum (Robinson and Kirman 1986). This influential committee's report (National Education Association

1894) led to the establishment of physical geography as the basis for general science teaching and for the teaching of all geography (James and Martin 1981).

After 1908, both the NEA and the Association of American Geographers (AAG) recommended that physical geography be replaced by economic and commercial geography designed to meet the needs of terminal students in vocational high schools (Mayo 1965). The percentage of high school students electing physical geography fell drastically, and geography courses began disappearing from the high schools. Commercial geography was the only survivor, with only 4 percent of the students in 1934. Geography lost its position as an admission subject in most liberal arts colleges during that period, no doubt because of its new vocational reputation.

While geography experienced this precipitous decline in the curriculum, it was being subsumed within a major new curriculum category, the social studies. The biggest impact of the social studies movement came in the years following World War I (Vuicich and Stoltman 1974). Geography's place in the social studies might have been strengthened at that time, but geographers held that geography was not a social study alone and refused to participate in the NEA social studies curriculum development process of 1916 (James 1969; Stoltman 1987). That left nongeographers to create the geography that was to be included in social studies. Physical geography was left out, partly to be incorporated into "earth science," an element of the science curriculum.

World War II reawakened interest in geography, especially world and regional geography; studies of European countries, cartography, meteorology, and conservation also gained in popularity. Those changes prompted the NCSS to reassess geography's role and to recommend that it have a stronger position in the social studies curriculum (Vuicich and Stoltman 1974). During the late 1950s and the 1960s, the AAG's High School Geography Project (HSGP) brought together schoolteachers and university professors "to prepare an improved course in high school geography" (White 1970). Unfortunately, like nearly all social science projects of the time, its acceptance and use were minimal (Weiss 1978). Although the HSGP course was not widely adopted, its influence can still be seen today in some instructional materials.

Textbooks are an important indicator of educational practice and of the status of geography (Manson 1981; Winston 1984). Recent work by Hoffman (1990) shows that most geography texts do not encourage an inquiry-oriented geography education. They emphasize selected facts rather than the explanation of facts and the description of patterns rather than the explanation of patterns. Rarely do they offer alternative theories, and even more rarely do they examine theories in the light of facts.

ACTIVITY

Analyzing Geography Textbooks

Hoffman (1990) developed an instrument for measuring the degree to which a textbook stressed processes (how things happen) rather than merely describing facts. He chose several significant "process concepts" in human geography (e.g., urbanization, cultural diffusion, economic development, migration) and developed a series of questions about the way those process concepts were treated. For example, for the concept migration, to what extent does this textbook use the following?

		No Use		Some Use		Much Use
1.	A variety of migration facts	1	2	3	4	5
2.	A comprehensive definition of migration	1	2	3	4	5
3.	A comprehensive generalization/theory of migration	1	2	3	4	5
4.	More than one generalization/theory of migration	1	2	3	4	5
5.	Migration generalization/theory to analyze migration facts	1	2	3	4	5

The points for the five questions are totaled; the higher the score, the higher the process orientation. One can compare textbooks by analyzing how each treats the same concepts. If two texts are compared for their treatment of the process of migration, the text having the higher score on the scale would rate higher. It is best to compare on several concepts before generalizing about the process orientation of texts.

Using Hoffman's idea, compare secondary geography textbooks for the degree to which they are process-oriented. Work in four small groups, with each group analyzing one of the concepts listed above. Do any of the texts have a strong process orientation? What reasons might you suggest for the general lack of process orientation in secondary geography textbooks?

Renaissance in Geography Education

After more than a half century of neglect in U.S. schools, geography was rediscovered in the late 1980s (Hill 1989). On April 18, 1991, then-President Bush announced *America 2000: An Education Strategy* (U.S. Department of Education 1991), which defined geography as a core subject to be promoted and assessed in a broad program of educational reform (National Education Goals Panel 1991, 14). The core subjects have continued to receive emphasis under the Clinton administration (see Chapter 2).

From 1984 to 1994, the *Guidelines for Geographic Education: Elementary and Secondary Schools* (Joint Committee1984) was the most influential document in geography's recent resurgence, countering the perennial complaint that the discipline had no generally agreed-upon statement clarifying the essentials of geography for school people (Manson 1981; Kohn 1982). Its five "fundamental themes in geography" (see following section) and its clear learning outcomes for each theme gave needed direction, which was used for curriculum and materials development and for teacher training (Natoli 1988). This document's wide acceptance encouraged the development of separate elaborations for the elementary (Geographic Education National Implementation Project 1987) and secondary levels (Geographic Education National Implementation Project 1989).

The Geographic Education National Implementation Project (GENIP), formed in 1985, was the first joint venture of all four national geographic organizations—National Council for Geographic Education, Association of American Geographers, National Geographic Society, and American Geographical Society. The National Geographic Society (NGS) emerged as the most potent change agent because of its ability to make a large financial commitment and to quickly develop and conduct new programs. The society's Geography Education Program (1988) began spending $4 to $5 million a year in 1987. Its centerpiece is a network of state-based geographic alliances. Coordinated by academic geographers, the alliances work with classroom teachers, academic geographers, administrators, and other citizens to promote geographic education in their respective states.The most recent achievement in geography's renaissance is the publication *Geography for Life: National Geography Standards 1994* (Geography Education Standards Project 1994), which is described in a later section.

GEOGRAPHY'S FIVE FUNDAMENTAL THEMES*

Location

Location is the most basic of geographical themes. Our ability to locate ourselves in geographic space satisfies a deep human need. Without this spatial ability, we would be literally lost. Location derives from three characteristics: direction or orientation, distance, and connection or relative position. Our ability to coordinate these characteristics allows us to locate, to behave as if we had maps in our heads.

All things happen somewhere. Knowing where things happen is essential to understanding them. Imagine the following stories broadcast on television network news:

- A powerful volcano erupted today.
- Fighting broke out today between government troops and dissident forces.
- Toyota announced today the location of its new assembly plant.

Now, none of those facts is a *geographic fact,* because each lacks locational information. Without information about location, events are meaningless. The first geographic question asked about any phenomenon is, Where is it?

---

*Condensed from A. David Hill and Regina McCormick, *Geography: A Resource Book for Secondary Schools* (Santa Barbara, Calif.: ABC-Clio, 1989), Chapter 1. Used with permission of the publisher.

Position on the earth's surface is either mathematically specified or described in relative terms. We call the former *absolute location* and the latter *relative location*. Absolute location is based on a mathematical reference system. The most commonly used is the Cartesian reference system, which specifies the location of a point by its distance from two lines that intersect at right angles. The geographic grid of latitude and longitude is a Cartesian reference system, with the equator serving as the horizontal axis and the prime meridian serving as the vertical axis.

A more expansive concept is relative location, which is specified by the relationship of one place to some other place or places. For example, in the first news story, the volcano's location might have been described as "near the Gulf Coast in southern Mexico" or "a few miles south of the city of Villahermosa."

Without absolute location, we would be unable to navigate, travel, transport, or communicate efficiently beyond our immediate locales. Without relative location, we could not "place" anything in our "mind's eye." More important, we could not understand geographic space as dynamic and changeable.

Knowing where something is raises the question, Why is it there? If we are told that Toyota is building a huge assembly plant in Columbus, Ohio, we might well ask, "Why there?" Why are there active volcanos in Mexico, Chile, and Hawaii but not in Illinois, Siberia, or Brazil? Fundamental to the "why" question is the assumption that reasons for the location of phenomena can and should be identified. Thus, geography seeks to understand *spatial processes*—that is, the methods or systems that affect the content of earth space and that help us explain why things are located where they are.

Place

Having asked, Where? and Why there? we now ask, What's it like there? When we begin to answer this question, a location takes on character, it becomes a place. In that sense, humans create places. Place is obviously not a narrow concept. We are so familiar with the term that the theme of place is deceptively simple. Geographic questions about place suggest how profound the concept really is: What is a place? How are places described? What makes places distinctive? What makes places similar to other places? How do places change?

Three things give identity to a place: (1) the physical environment, which is the product of natural processes; (2) the *built* or *artificial environment*, which is produced by human action; and (3) the meanings invested in the place, which are the human intellectual and emotional responses to the place. The first two things are tangible, material, and "objective," and the third is intangible, nonmaterial, and "subjective."

The earth's surface is by no means uniform in either physical or human characteristics. Physical differences derive from the natural processes that produce landforms, bodies of water, climate, soils, natural vegetation, and animal life. Physical geography addresses those processes. Human geography focuses on the ideas and human actions that shape the character of places. Places vary in their population, as well as in their settlement patterns, architecture, kinds of economic and recreational activities, communication networks, ideologies, languages, and their forms of economic, social, and political organization.

An important principle of human geography is that over the long run, individual and social survival and development occur because of successful, or adaptive, decisions. By that we mean that people learn in place about how to live in place. People are forever manipulating their environments, changing them for many reasons. Places thus become the expressions of the human individuals and groups that control them. People having manifested themselves in places, the places thus become extensions of the selves; people create "ownership" of place. This bond, this love of place is a principal element of human awareness. Humans develop strong associations with places. This *sense of place* is the intangible but fully authentic meaning that we invest in an environment, and it is a principal criterion for distinguishing places.

Human–Environment Interaction

Relationships between humans and the physical environment are among the most distinguishing features of place. They are so important and attention to them is so much a part of geography that they constitute a separate theme. Three key ideas underlie this theme: (1) humans adapt to the environment; (2) humans modify the environment; and (3) humans depend on the environment.

Each physical environment poses its own set of difficulties for human settlement. Despite wide environmental variation, humans have settled in virtually every corner of the world. We refer to this kind of environmental problem-solving as *adaptation*.

Changing environmental conditions prompt new cultural adaptations. Normally, the physical environment does not change rapidly, but contact with other cultures and technologies can quickly create, in effect, a new environment—that is, a new set of conditions requiring a response. For example, the Inuit culture began to change with the first contact with whaling ships in the nineteenth century. Whaling increased as a way of life while hunting declined. Subsistence could be secured at a faster rate with the introduction of rifles.

The Inuit adopted the snowmobile quickly. It replaced dog sledding within a few years after its introduction in the 1960s. Inuit dogs were neglected and slowly disappeared. Increased costs of operating snowmobiles caused further adjustments. Some Alaskan Inuit became increasingly dependent on outside assistance and wages because they lacked the capital to replace snowmobiles and the expertise to repair them. As a result of the intrusion of Western goods and a money economy, Inuit now work for wages, but many are unemployed.

This example illustrates not only adaptation but also a second key idea of human–environmental relationships, namely, that humans modify the environment.

The snowmobile scars the Arctic; plant recovery is slow and damage is evident many years after the snowmobile tracks have been first cut. Such disturbances to long-standing human–environment relationships usually create complex effects because of the principle of *environmental unity*. Geographers think of the human and natural elements and relationships among them as systems in which one change brings about other changes. Adaptation and modification are interrelated processes.

Human capacity to change environment increases with technological ability, and modern tools and techniques are being introduced to change landscapes nearly everywhere. Many of the changes are inadvertent, the unplanned secondary effects of other changes. For example, coal burning adds sulfur dioxide to the atmosphere, which creates "acid rain," which destroys forests, pollutes lakes and streams, and kills wildlife. One secondary effect of burning is that the carbon dioxide and other gases accumulate in the atmosphere, where, some scientists think, they may contribute to global warming.

A solid knowledge of the systemic nature of the three key ideas of human adaptation to, modification of, and dependence upon environment is absolutely necessary for the survival of humankind. In that sense, human–environment interaction is the most important theme of geographic inquiry. Yet the themes are closely interrelated. Human-environment interactions *within* places are increasingly dependent upon interactions *between* places, which is the fourth fundamental theme of geography.

Movement

It is impossible to conceive of human existence without movement; all things needed for an individual's survival are not in a single place. Relationships across earth space, which geographers call *spatial interactions*, constitute a fourth theme, the central question of which is, How and why are places related to other places?

Disequilibrium causes spatial interaction. Earth space, as separation, leads to the differentiation of places. At the same time, differentiation leads to disequilibrium and spatial interaction to resolve it. For example, all places do not have water. If I am thirsty, I must go across the room to the water fountain to quench my thirst—that is, to resolve this spatial disequilibrium.

We often wish to move to places that we *perceive* as offering more desirable opportunities. For movement to actually occur, the incentives must be strong enough to overcome the barriers to spatial interaction. Rural-to-urban migrants in the Third World today have decided it is worth paying the price to move from what they perceive to be a poor territory to a richer one.

Migration, diffusion of ideas, and trade are examples of spatial interaction. These homogenizing processes reduce differentiation. They make places (and peoples) similar to other places (and peoples). The diffusion of today's consumerism—the use of mass-produced industrial products—is creating a kind of cultural uniformity over a vast part of the earth.

Complementarity of places creates movement. Places that produce coal, iron ore, and limestone are complementary because those products are part of the steel-making process. Places where a newspaper is read and the place where it is printed are complementary because they are parts of an information flow process. If places are not complementary in some way, there is no basis for spatial interaction between them.

Spatial interaction is the purpose of what we call *spatial systems*. These systems consist of nodes, pathways, and areas. To envision a spatial system, think of an airline's route map. The nodes are the cities served; pathways are the routes linking the cities; and areas are the territories or hinterlands from which passengers and cargo are drawn to the nodes. Spatial interaction in that system creates an ever changing set of conditions for all the places it affects.

Spatial interaction creates places. Think for a moment about the nature of cities. Cities exist because they perform different functions for the population of some larger tributary area. Cities are nodes in spatial systems.

Changes in patterns of spatial interaction change places. Manaus, on the Amazon, became a metropolis in the nineteenth century when it supplied the world with natural rubber; its population declined sharply when Malaysia captured the rubber market. Manaus is on the rebound today as a transportation and service center in the rapid exploitation of the Brazilian Amazon.

Spatial interaction creates a demand for even more spatial interaction. People in a place that is spatially isolated must be self-sufficient. As the world economy penetrates to such places, the people become more and more dependent upon goods and services produced in other places. As knowledge of new products and services spreads to them, new demands are created and new needs are felt, which only more spatial interaction can satisfy.

When spatial interaction is threatened, serious consequences can ensue. For example, world trade depends upon unimpeded passage for ships on the high seas and through certain strategic lanes and narrow corridors, called "choke points." The Panama and Suez canals, the Bab el Mandeb, and the Strait of Hormuz are some of the world's most crucial choke points. Powerful states exercise their military might to maintain open access through these places because of their economic, political, and military significance.

Region

The characteristics of the earth's surface are so numerous and complex that some way of meaningfully simplifying earth space for purposes of geographic study is needed. The region fulfills that purpose. A region is an uninterrupted area of the earth's surface that displays unity according to selected criteria. A region is a geographic tool. We use it in trying to answer the question, How and why is this place similar to and different from other places?

Regions exist in our minds. We invent them. Some regions become so popular through constant portrayals on maps and references in books and other media that we think of them as real objects, as part of the natural scheme of things, such as mountains or oceans. Indeed, in popular parlance the word *region* has about the same meaning as the words *area, place,* and *territory.*

We regularly use the regional concept in human affairs. The world is divided into many political regions, or countries (called states by political geographers), which themselves are divided into smaller and smaller units (e.g., provinces, counties, and municipalities). States cooperate in regional pacts for economic or military purposes (e.g., the European Union or the North Atlantic Treaty Organization). At the local or urban scale, special-purpose regions are formed for everything from education to transportation to fire protection.

Conflict also creates regions, some temporary and some that become virtually indelible. For example, East and West Germany represented the partitioning of territory based on political ideology, a scheme that lasted for over forty years. To promote its policy of apartheid, the government of South Africa established, at the national scale, the black regions, called homelands, and, at the urban scale, black townships.

An axiom of geography is that regions change. For example, "the South" has meant different things at different times. Before the Civil War, its economy was based on local subsistence agriculture and a wealthy plantation-slave-cotton export economy. The war destroyed that structure, and for many years afterward the South was a region of great poverty and economic stagnation. Gradually, manufacturing developed, at first by the transfer of textile industries from the North to locations in the Carolina Piedmont; later, a broader industrial base developed. Today, the South is experiencing rapid population growth as people migrate in from old northern industrial cities in what has come to be called the "Rust Belt."

Regions today are interconnected in a world economy despite great political and economic differences. As regionalization in economic development shows, this interdependence does not mean equality. The regional structuring of the world after World War II had both political and economic dimensions. Politically, the East and West split into regions of socialism and capitalism, a split that began disappearing with the momentous changes in Eastern Europe in the fall of 1989. The economic dimension produced a North–South cleavage, rich and poor regions, respectively. Despite powerful attempts to draw them in, much of the South did not polarize into either East or West but, rather, remained nonaligned in the "Third World." As the South, they aligned against the North—both East and West—and demanded a dialogue to build a "New International Economic Order." Its purpose is to create *interdependence with equality.* Geography examines the regional restructuring emerging as the world adjusts to these demands and to other changes.

Summary

Each of these five "fundamental themes in geography" covers its own set of concepts and ideas that are interrelated to concepts and ideas found under the other themes. Geographic investigation, no matter what the problem, is likely to draw upon more than a single theme.

As the preceding discussion has tried to demonstrate, the themes offer an approach to the multifaceted subject of geography. When used together as a guide to asking questions, these themes help one understand how geography examines the world. The themes should not, however, be used simplistically and mechanically as ends in themselves. In fact, teachers are cautioned *not* to teach the themes per se but, rather, use the themes as a teaching tool. Although the themes provide a useful framework, they do not represent the content of geography, which is taken up in *Geography for Life*.

ACTIVITY

Identifying the Five Themes

Read the following vignette. Find evidence of the relevance of each of the five themes of geography in the story.

> *"You're listening to Y108 in the Mile High City, Denver, Colorado." Kevin rolled out of bed as his clock radio came on. As he stumbled to the bathroom, he heard his mother yell, "Remember to take a short shower. We're supposed to be conserving water."*
>
> *"Is it my fault there wasn't enough snow in the mountains to fill the reservoirs?" he thought, but he knew better than to say it out loud. He didn't need a lecture this early in the morning. His mother was a social studies teacher at North High School, and she loved to lecture about the environment.*
>
> *After he had dressed, Kevin ate breakfast—bananas and corn flakes, with a cup of hot chocolate. By the time he had finished, his mother was already in the Toyota. He grabbed his book bag and dashed out the door to get a ride to school. By the time he got to the car, his eyes were stinging. Pollution was bad today.*
>
> *Today might be a pretty good day. A Latin American dance group was performing at a special assembly; that meant no math and no spelling! And besides, he enjoyed mariachi music, although it was frustrating not to be able to understand the Spanish lyrics to some of the songs.*

● ● ●

How might you use a vignette of this kind in developing a geography lesson for secondary students? Outline a lesson in which students might use or write a vignette like the one presented above.

GEOGRAPHY FOR LIFE

Geography for Life: National Geography Standards 1994 (Geography Education Standards Project 1994) was written over a period of 27 months and went through six drafts. Public hearings and written comments of hundreds of geographers, teachers, and interested citizens made it a consensus document on the content of geography: what all students should know and be able to do. Educational policy required that the standards should:

- Be world-class and challenging
- Focus upon a limited set of the most important and enduring knowledge and skills of the discipline
- Be useful in real-world contexts
- Reflect sound scholarship within the discipline
- Be developmentally appropriate (i.e., regardless of students' perceived ability, the standards should be achievable with proper supports and sustained effort)

The intended outcome of *Geography for Life* is a geographically informed person who (1) sees meaning in the arrangement of things in space; (2) see relations between people, places, and environments; (3) uses geographic skills; and (4) applies spatial and ecological perspectives to life situations. In *Geography for Life,* eighteen geography standards are grouped into six essential elements; each standard is written so it completes the sentence: The geographically informed person knows and understands . . .

The World in Spatial Terms

1. How to use maps and other geographic representations, tools, and technologies to acquire, process and report information from a spatial perspective.
2. How to use mental maps to organize information about people, places, and environments in a spatial context.
3. How to analyze the spatial organizations of people, places, and environments on Earth's surface.

Places and Regions

4. The physical and human characteristics of places.
5. That people create regions to interpret Earth's complexity.
6. How culture and experience influence people's perceptions of places and regions.

Physical Systems

7. The physical processes that shape the patterns of Earth's surface.
8. The characteristics and spatial distribution of ecosystems on Earth's surface.

Human Systems

9. The characteristics, distribution, and migration of human populations on Earth's surface.
10. The characteristics, distribution, and complexity of Earth's cultural mosaics.
11. The patterns and networks of economic interdependence on Earth's surface.

12. The processes, patterns, and functions of human settlement.

13. How the forces of cooperation and conflict among people influence the division and control of Earth's surface.

Environment and Society

14. How human actions modify the physical environment.

15. How physical systems affect human systems.

16. The changes that occur in the meaning, use, distribution, and importance of resources.

The Uses of Geography

17. How to apply geography to interpret the past.

18. How to apply geography to interpret the present and plan for the future.

Space does not permit a full discussion of all eighteen standards; instead, we shall comment briefly on each of the six essential elements.

The World in Spatial Terms

Geography studies the relationships between people, places, and environments by mapping information about them into a spatial context. Where these things are, how and why they are distributed across earth space, and how they relate to each other are all parts of seeing the world in spatial terms.

Seeing the world geographically requires an understanding of various tools to be able to interpret and make maps; recognize relationships in and between places; make generalizations; and understand the concepts of distance, direction, location, connection, and association. These abilities and concepts are basic to what makes geography unique: the spatial perspective.

Maps, globes, photographs, satellite images, and geographic information systems (GIS) are geographic tools. They are essential to portraying, analyzing, evaluating, and predicting human and physical patterns and processes on earth's surface. They play a crucial role in helping people make sense of a complex world, and they improve the human capacity to move about and plan activities.

Developing locational knowledge, for example, knowing where places are and why they are there, is also a part of being a geographically informed person. This knowledge, developed through factual learning, serves as a personal framework for geographic knowledge. Geographic images and the impressions students have of places are organized by these personal frameworks, which are sometimes called *mental maps*.

Geographic literacy also demands an understanding of how space on earth is organized. Such understanding requires observation and analysis as well as an awareness that the patterns observed on earth's surface reflect geographic processes.

Places and Regions

The identities and lives of individuals and peoples are rooted in particular places and in those human constructs called regions. Geography is concerned with the nature of places and regions. What physical and human characteristics identify them? Why do they matter to us? How do they change?

Knowledge of place helps people make informed decisions about where to live, work, travel, and seek new opportunities. Places form and change as a result of physical and human processes. The physical characteristics of a place are caused by the long-term interaction among physical processes. These processes produce the landforms, bodies of water, climate, soils, vegetation, and animal life on which human life depends. The human characteristics of a place result from the interaction of human processes. These processes produce particular settlement patterns, political systems, architecture, commerce, and other activities and enterprises.

As described earlier, regions are areas that display similarity in terms of selected criteria. Regions are created to clarify the complexity of human and physical features on earth's surface. Regions are geographic generalizations that portray broader patterns from great and oftentimes confusing detail. Studying how and why regions change helps people understand and interpret the past, participate responsibly in the present, and plan effectively for the future.

The way people think about places and regions varies according to how they organize, interpret, and use information. Personal attitudes, experiences, and values are important in shaping these variations. Differences in cultural background, age, gender, and experiences contribute to the perceptions people have about places and regions. Understanding places and regions helps one appreciate different perspectives and develop the cooperation needed to resolve conflict.

Physical Systems

Geography is primarily concerned with physical systems because they influence earth as the home of humankind. Physical processes shape earth's surface and interact with plant and animal life to create, sustain, and modify ecosystems.

Processes of nature create the physical environments upon which human life depends. Understanding earth's physical features and the processes that produce them is essential to geography. Therefore, students must know the characteristics of landforms, weather and climates, soils, bodies of water, vegetation, and animal life and how these characteristics are distributed over earth's surface.

A variety of physical processes, such as weathering, erosion, and vegetation change, shape the environment over time and space. These processes and their associated patterns can be explained by concepts such as system, boundary, force, threshold, and equilibrium.

Climates, landforms, and soils are physical systems. An ecosystem—a complex physical system—is an interdependent association of plants, animals, air, water, and land. Ecosystems form distinct regions with the biosphere that vary in size, shape, and complexity. Understanding the nature and distribution of ecosystems and the influences of physical processes throughout the environment is crucial to understanding the role of humans within the physical world.

Human Systems

Humans create many kinds of systems to live on earth as they see fit. People are central to geography in that human activities help shape earth's surface, human settlements and structures are part of earth's surface, and humans compete for control of earth's surface.

The geographic study of human populations focuses on location, movement, and the dynamics of population size. Populations tend to locate in clusters rather than spread out evenly over the land; these patterns depend on both physical and human environments. People make long-term, permanent migrations and short-term, temporary journeys, often on a daily basis. Migration is often the result of the way people perceive a place. Population growth, decline, and equilibrium patterns are influenced by medical, cultural, and economic issues.

Culture defines every human society because it encompasses identity, purpose, place, and vision. Culture has meaning beyond a single group in a specific place. The study of locations, spatial patterns, and processes of cultures provides a means to analyze how people interact with each other and their environments. Culture is a force that can both unify and impede connections and communication among peoples.

Although economic development is highly uneven across the globe, economic interdependence links the developed and developing countries.

Settlements, whether rural or urban, have many identifiable patterns, such as architecture, sacred space, and economic activities. Settlement patterns reflect changing cultural attitudes toward place as well as shifts in technology, population, and resource use.

Earth space is divided into political, economic, social, and cultural spaces, ranging in scale from local to global. Political spaces, which are created by both cooperation and conflict, may be as small as the school attendance area or as large as an alliance among nations. Economic space includes a firm's marketing regions and international trading blocs. Social and cultural spaces range from households to the administrative regions of world religions. The partitioning of space into social, economic, and political spheres of influence is dynamic and ongoing.

Environment and Society

Humans depend upon the physical environment for its resources, but human systems also modify the physical environment. Such change is largely a consequence of both technology and the ways in which human societies value and use earth's natural resources.

Increasingly, people are called upon to solve complex problems resulting from the interaction of human and physical systems. Physical systems offer opportunities and constraints for human activity. Humans control and use the output of physical systems—natural resources—to survive and prosper. Humans sometimes face the consequences of exceeding the environment's capacity and resource base. Changes to the environment created by humans play a significant role in shaping local, regional, and global economic, social, and political conditions.

The concept of resources has changed over time. Initially, when populations were smaller, resources were assumed to exist in abundance and were available for almost limitless use. The concept of nonrenewable resources did not evolve until some resources appeared to be in short supply. Unwise resource use can negatively affect the environment and quality of life.

Humans interact with the environment through technology. Technology has enabled us to use some natural resources at ever-increasing, possibly unsustainable rates, but new technologies also change our perception of resources. For example, nuclear reactors now generate a substantial portion of the world's electricity, and once-discarded materials are now recycled.

The Uses of Geography

Knowledge of geography enables people to develop an understanding of earth as it was, is, and might be. The geographically informed person should be able to make better use of the world at present and improve the capacity for planning for the future.

Everything happens in time and space. A thorough interpretation of the past must, therefore, include the geographic context: Where did the event occur? In what kind of human and physical environment did it happen? How was the event related to events in other places? What resources and technologies did people have? How did they move from place to place? What environmental constraints did they face? Any interpretation of human events and conditions that ignores the geographic context is incomplete and unrealistic.

In the next century, humans will face many complex and controversial issues concerning the development needs of an immense and growing human population and the Earth's ability to sustain that population. To cope with these fundamental issues effectively, tomorrow's citizens must be geographically informed.

ACTIVITY   ## Using the Standards

For the standards to be meaningful for teachers, they must be made concrete through concepts and examples that exemplify the very broad understandings in the standards. *Geography for Life* provides such examples, but teachers may find other examples more relevant to their curriculum or students. Consider, for instance, standard 9, which focuses on the characteristics, distribution, and migration of human populations. At grades 5–8 for this standard, *Geography for Life* states that the student should know and understand:

1. The demographic structure of a population
2. The reasons for spatial variations in population distribution
3. The types and historical patterns of human migration
4. The effects of migration on the characteristics of places

Imagine that you are teaching a seventh-grade geography course in your home town. What concepts about migration would you want to develop in helping students achieve this standard? (If you are not sure what concepts would be most important, you may want to do some reading on migration.) What examples related to migration would you use to develop these concepts? How would those examples be both relevant to your students and useful in developing understanding of the concepts you have listed?

ISSUES-BASED GEOGRAPHIC INQUIRY

We now turn our attention to the process of teaching and learning in school geography. In this section, we address the pedagogy of issues-based geographic inquiry. We stress this approach because it serves the broad goals of the social studies—to teach citizenship, disciplined knowledge, and critical and reflective thinking. Inquiry is essentially the method of science. It poses questions and proposes answers about the real world, and it tests its answers with real data. This is exactly what geographers do. What better pedagogy to teach geography?

Geography in the social studies curriculum should serve the general goals of social studies education; indeed, geography provides an essential means to responsible citizenship and civic action through the information, concepts, and fundamental themes included within geography education (Stoltman 1990). However, the specific objectives of geography education must come from the discipline of geography, which contains the body of facts, concepts, generalizations, and theories that constitute geographic knowledge and understanding.

We place a high value on active learning and higher-level thinking, taking the position that these characteristics are best achieved when learners are engaged in geographic inquiry. In issues-based geographic inquiry, the data are related to real-world issues. The learner pursues answers to geographic questions by working with data using geographic methods. This process should lead to outcomes that represent significant cognitive, affective, and skill learning. These outcomes can be elaborated as the (multiple) instructional objectives. Summative evaluation, which assesses the effectiveness of the instruction (or the materials) in achieving the objectives, is the final phase of a model we propose for issues-based geographic inquiry (Figure 10-3).

Let us now examine each part of the model in some detail.

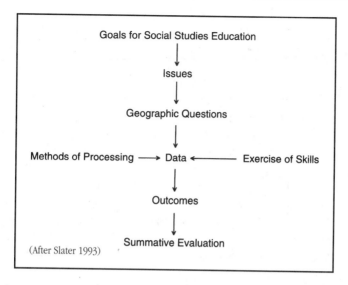

Figure 10.3   A model for issues-based geographic inquiry

Goals for Social Studies Education

Goals for social studies education are found in many sources (e.g., National Council for the Social Studies 1984, 1989). The district or the state in which you teach is likely to have a curriculum document setting forth broad program goals for social studies. A relevant goal might be "The Social Studies Curriculum should enable students to develop (5) critical attitudes and analytical perspectives appropriate to analysis of the human condition" (National Commission on Social Studies in the Schools 1989, 6).

Issues in Geography

Several criteria should be used to identify issues. Issues should

- Occur in the real world
- Be developed with real data
- Have both personal and global implications
- Have long-term or perennial status

Issues-based geography education responds to two significant, interrelated educational concerns: motivation and reality. The investigation of issues can motivate learners; humans are often intrigued by conflict and diverse interpretations and points of view. When subject matter is framed by real-world issues and real data, the student may see its relevance and be less inclined to ask: Why are we studying this?

Outcomes may be quite unpredictable with the use of real-world issues, but that very unpredictability is an exceedingly important lesson. It is important to analyze "what went wrong?" or "how did change occur?" What specific factors led to the unpredicted outcome? Geography is dynamic; if students are conditioned to think otherwise, they are getting inferior geography educations.

General issues are often manifested at various scales—personal, local, regional, national, or global. Geographic study should include inquiry at several scales. At the local level, almost daily one can find examples of conflicts over land use and the siting of public and private facilities. For example, facilities such as sewage-treatment plants and airports are called "noxious" because they create undesirable environmental effects such as odor and noise. (Examples are popularly called NIMBYs, the acronym for the "Not-In-My-Backyard" syndrome.) In these locational conflicts, the issue is often one of balancing equity (spatial justice) with efficiency (cost to the public). Because these cases typically cause great local controversy, they usually offer good issues-based examples for geographic inquiry.

One cannot assume that an issue will necessarily be of interest to students simply because it is local. Rather, the quality of personal engagement is at the heart of successful instruction. Personal relevance can be achieved by identification with real people, especially at the students' own or slightly older age levels, and by connecting to everyday human life in other ways.

In instruction, we should focus on issues that are long-term in nature—the perennial problems of the human condition; examples include spatial justice, quality of life, territorial conflict, interdependency, and environmental change. We need to look for "issue durability" not only because it is a mark of the significance of the issue but also because it is a hedge against the obsolescence of instruction. Specific examples of these issues will change over time. For example, just as the political geography of Europe has recently changed, so, too, is the geography of South Africa changing following the end of apartheid. Yet the geographic manifestations of an East and a West Germany and of a policy of apartheid will not be quickly eradicated, and the general issues of political democracy and spatial justice will likely become manifest in other places.

Geographic Questions

Slater (1993) contributed the core of the issues-based geographic inquiry model we have developed here. She argued for the "practical utility of identifying questions and sub-sets of questions as the initial task in organising and planning learning activities" (p. 1). In the model we have presented, the questions that guide student inquiry ensure that issues are examined from a geographic perspective.

The significance of questions in learning should not be underestimated. Slater draws on Collingwood (1939) in arguing that questions and answers must be directly linked to achieve an "intellectually satisfying understanding of an issue, topic or problem" (Slater 1982, 2), but she also cites Gagne (1970), Ausubel (1960), and Bruner (1960, 1966) in support of the importance of questions. The role of questions in her learning theory is to guide inquiry to avoid separating the process of investigation from the drawing of conclusions. When students are asked to learn conclusions without learning how they are arrived at, we perpetuate the tradition of a product-centered education bereft of higher-level thinking.

There is no necessary sequence to geographic questioning. It may begin with a host of possible interests. For example, one might ask where the phenomenon of interest is located and then proceed to further questions (Hill and McCormick 1989). Why is it in that place? What is the character of the place and why does it have that character? What consequences follow from having this phenomenon in this place? How do people live there and why do they live that way? How do these living arrangements affect the people and the place? What is changing about these arrangements? How is this place related to other places and why? What is changing about these relationships and at what rate is change occurring? How and why are these relationships changing or not changing? How and why is this place similar to and different from other places? What are the consequences of those similarities and differences?

Each question deals with the nature of space on earth. Furthermore, these questions are not mutually exclusive; they are interrelated. They constitute a structure of questions about earth space. They are guided by the "five fundamental themes" discussed earlier.

To encourage higher-level thinking, guiding questions need to be quite general. Because they are broad, these larger questions are typically capable of division into subquestions, some of which will be "closed" or "convergent" (asking for specific facts or the recall of conclusions) and some of which should be "open" or "divergent" (subject to interpretation and to several possible responses). It is important to reach a balance between the two: Too much convergent questioning may discourage critical thinking and lead to little beyond rote memorization, and too much divergent questioning may discourage learning grounded in fact and substance.

Slater (1982, 8), drawing on Blyth et al. (1976), gave a range of five types of questions, from closed to open, that *taken together* encourage higher-level thinking:

1. Demanding recall

2. Encouraging classification and ordering

3. Encouraging the use of data to draw conclusions

4. Encouraging awareness of the limitations of data or evaluation of data

5. Encouraging awareness of the processes of reasoning used

ACTIVITY **Forming Geographic Questions**

Review the five types of questions just discussed. Write at least two examples for each type of question, using one issue as your topic for all the questions.

Data and Skills

Central to Slater's question-driven model is the exercise of skills in the processing of data to answer questions and derive generalizations. Geographer Philip Wagner (1960, 3) wrote:

> Among all the branches of human knowledge, that which is called Geography contains the largest single body of factual information. Moreover, the further supply of such information potentially available, but "not yet catalogued," is limitless. No single person can ever hope to know more than a small portion of what it is possible to know about even the mere location of places on the earth's surface.

This statement should be a caution to teachers that it is possible to achieve as a course objective comprehension of only a relatively small number of geographic facts. Other implications also stem from this statement. Geographic education must (1) teach ways of organizing facts into meaningful patterns that promote effective inquiry; (2) help students discriminate, sorting out useful from trivial facts, and develop an awareness of the limitations of facts; and (3) find ways of insinuating the learning of useful facts into activities that stress conceptual learning, problem solving, and decision making.

Geographic facts may reflect either primary or secondary sources of information. Primary data are drawn from direct observation and other human sensory input, including measurement, photography, sketching, interview, and survey. Secondary data are found in newspapers, periodicals, books, atlases, maps, charts, graphs, tables, black-and-white and color ground and aerial photographs, satellite imagery, and computer data banks, to name only a few possible sources.

Students need several geography skills, specified in *Geography for Life* (Geography Education Standards Project 1994), as follows:

- Asking geographic questions
- Acquiring geographic information
- Organizing geographic information
- Analyzing geographic information
- Answering geographic questions

It is exciting to work with maps, peeling away layers and layers of misinformation and ignorance to reveal vital spatial information, ideas, and generalizations. Computers are increasingly being used to do this kind of work and much more. Just imagine many maps of the same area at the same scale, each containing a different kind of information. Now imagine being able to call up with a computer all the information about a place so that it can be analyzed to solve a practical problem. That is just one of many new capabilities for data gathering and analysis that have come to be associated with Geographic Information Systems (GIS), which is revolutionizing how research and problem solving are done in a variety of fields.

As students work through the process of geographic inquiry, they will develop intellectual, social, and practical skills (Slater 1982). Intellectual skills include such things as perceiving and observing, understanding instructions and information, questioning and hypothesizing, and communicating facts, ideas, and feelings. Social skills may include participating in group decisions, adopting a role, leading a group, and behaving responsibly and courteously. Practical skills include such things as reading, writing, using a map, interviewing a town planner, taking photographs, plotting data on a graph, and sketching a building.

Outcomes

Slater (1982) used the term *generalizations* to incorporate higher-order thinking into her model, subsuming cognitive, affective, and skill development under this rubric. Since the term is usually associated with the cognitive domain, however, we use the broader term *outcomes* in our model.

According to Slater (1982, 47), "Generalizations complete an enquiry by codifying understanding"; that is, they bring separate facts and ideas together, linking them in some concluding (although not necessarily permanent) form. They give meaning to the work students have been doing. Generalizations can be answers to questions, hypotheses or theories, resolutions or decisions reached in a conflict, or statements of understanding and meaning of problems.

Outcomes appear at the end of our issues-based geographic inquiry model. According to the model, it is at this point, following data processing, that students arrive at generalizations, reexamine preconceived ideas, attitudes and values, or otherwise have cognitive, affective, and skill dimensions reinforced, modified, or enhanced.

Learning does not necessarily occur in the simple, linear fashion implied by this model. Furthermore, teachers planning inquiry activities must think of outcomes much earlier; indeed, the outcomes are the objectives, the understandings, attitudes and values, and skill development that students are working toward (Slater 1982). (That is not to suggest that all learning can be planned; indeed, serendipity may and often does enrich inquiry-oriented learning.)

Geography for Life (Geography Education Standards Project 1994) provides the most definitive guide to outcomes in geography. It offers hundreds of examples of "learning opportunities" that address the eighteen content standards as well as geographic perspectives and skills.

Although evaluation is the last phase of our issues-based inquiry model for geography, we shall not deal with it here, since evaluation is discussed more generally in Chapter 15. However, geography teachers should use *Geography for Life* to help evaluate student outcomes.

ACTIVITY

Analyzing an Issues-Based Inquiry Lesson

In your college's curriculum library, locate an issues-based geography lesson. One excellent source is *Geographic Inquiry into Global Issues* (Hill, Dunn, and Klein 1995). Use the following questions to analyze the lesson.

1. List and explain ways the student must become an active learner as part of the lesson.
2. Why is this a good geographic issue? Explain and cite as many reasons as possible.
3. Your principal has asked you how this lesson helps achieve the general goals of social studies. Write a one-page answer to that question for your principal.
4. How does this lesson encourage students to examine values and attitudes? Give two examples.
5. Cite three skills needed by students to complete this activity.
6. Write three or four geographic questions guiding student inquiry through the lesson.
7. What geography standards do you think students will address by doing the lesson? What understandings from other disciplines does the lesson develop?
8. How might you "localize" this issue for your students?
9. Suggest at least one way that additional data concerning this activity might be presented to students.
10. Identify how specific parts of the "Model for Issues-Based Geographic Inquiry in Secondary Schools" relate to specific parts of the lesson.

ACTIVITY

Developing an Inquiry-Based Geography Unit

Using the model for issues-based geographic inquiry presented in the preceding section, develop a plan for a geography unit you believe will engage students. Be sure that your unit addresses each component of the model, as well as the instructional strategies you will use in presenting the unit to students. How will you engage student interest and connect the issue to everyday life? How will you organize the presentation and use of data? What evaluation procedures will you use? When you have finished your unit plan, describe how the unit addresses one or more of the eighteen geography standards.

Reflecting on the Chapter

Has this chapter affected your geographic perspective? Review Harvey's description of the geographical imagination (page 238) and reflect on your ability to "recognize the role of space and place in your own biography." Devote some space in your journal to the relevance of geographic perspective and imagination to you as a person and as a prospective geography teacher.

References

Ausubel, D. P. "The Use of Advance Organizers in the Learning and Retention of Meaningful Verbal Material." *Journal of Educational Psychology* 51, no. 5 (1960): 267–72.

Blyth, W. A. L., et al. *Curriculum Planning in History, Geography and Social Science*. London: Schools Council/Collins, 1976.

Bruner, J. S. *The Process of Education*. Cambridge: Harvard University Press, 1960.

———. *Toward a Theory of Instruction*. Cambridge: Harvard University Press, 1966.

Buttimer, A. *The Practice of Geography*. New York: Longman, 1983.

Collingwood, R. G. *An Autobiography*. New York: Oxford University Press, 1939.

Gagne, R. M. *The Conditions of Learning*. New York: Holt, Rinehart & Winston, 1970.

Geographic Education National Implementation Project. GENIP. *K–6 Geography: Themes, Key Ideas, and Learning Opportunities*. Washington, D.C.: GENIP, 1987.

———. *7–12 Geography: Themes, Key Ideas, and Learning Opportunities*. Washington, D.C.: GENIP, 1989.

Geography Education Program. *UPDATE*. Washington, D.C.: National Geographic Society, Spring 1988.

Geography Education Standards Project. *Geography for Life: National Geography Standards 1994*. Washington, D.C.: National Geographic Research and Exploration, 1994.

Harvey, D. *Social Justice and the City*. Baltimore: Johns Hopkins University Press, 1973.

Hill, A. D. "Rediscovering Geography: Its Five Fundamental Themes." *National Association of Secondary School Principals Bulletin* 73, no. 521 (1989): 1–7.

———, ed. *Placing Geography in the Curriculum*. Boulder, Colo.: Colorado Geographic Alliance and Center for Geographic Education, 1988.

Hill, A. D., J. M. Dunn, and F. Klein. *Geographic Inquiry into Global Issues*. Chicago: Encyclopaedia Britannica Educational Corporation, 1995.

Hill, A. D., and R. McCormick. *Geography: A Resource Book for Secondary Schools*. Santa Barbara, Calif.: ABC-Clio, Inc., 1989.

Hoffman, G. "A Study to Design and Test a Content Analysis Tool to Measure the Geographic Process-Orientation of High School Geography Textbooks." Master's thesis, University of Colorado at Boulder. 1990.

James, P. E. "The Significance of Geography in American Education." *Journal of Geography* 68, no. 8 (1969): 473-86.

James, P. E., and G. J. Martin. *All Possible Worlds: A History of Geographical Ideas*, 2nd ed. New York: John Wiley, 1981.

Joint Committee on Geographic Education. *Guidelines for Geographic Education: Elementary and Secondary Schools*. Washington, D.C.: Association of American Geographers; Macomb, Ill.: National Council for Geographic Education, 1984.

Kohn, C. F. "Looking Back: Working Ahead." *Journal of Geography* 81, no. 2 (1982): 44–46.

LaPrairie, L. A. "Certification Requirements and Enrollment as a Measure of the Status of High School Geography among the Social Studies in the United States." Master's thesis, University of Colorado at Boulder. 1989.

Lowenthal, D. "Geography, Experience, and Imagination: Towards a Geographical Epistemology." *Annals of the Association of American Geographers* 51 (1961): 241–60.

Manson, G. "Notes on the Status of Geography in American Schools." *Journal of Geography* 80, no. 7 (1981): 244–48.

Mayo, W. W. *The Development and Status of Secondary School Geography in the United States and Canada.* Ann Arbor, Mich.: University Publishers, 1965.

National Commission on Social Studies in the Schools. *Charting a Course: Social Studies for the 21st Century.* Washington, D.C.: National Council for the Social Studies, 1989.

National Council for the Social Studies. "In Search of a Scope and Sequence for Social Studies." *Social Education* 48, no. 4 (1984): 249–62.

———. "In Search of a Scope and Sequence for Social Studies." *Social Education* 53, no. 6 (1989): 376–87.

National Education Association, *Report of the Committee of Ten on Secondary School Social Studies.* New York: American Book Company, 1894.

National Education Goals Panel. *Measuring Progress Toward the National Education Goals: Potential Indicators and Measurement Strategies.* Discussion document. March 25, 1991.

Natoli, S. J., ed. *Strengthening Geography in the Social Studies.* Washington, D.C.: National Council for the Social Studies, 1988.

Pattison, W. D. "The Four Traditions of Geography." *Journal of Geography* 63, no. 5 (1964): 211–16.

———. "The Educational Purposes of Geography." In *Evaluation in Geographic Education, National Council for Geographic Education 1971 Yearbook,* ed. D. G. Kurfman. Belmont, Calif.: Fearon, 1970.

Robinson, P., and J. M. Kirman. "From Monopoly to Dominance." In *Social Studies and Social Sciences: A Fifty-Year Perspective,* ed. S. P. Wronski and D. H. Bragaw. Washington, D.C.: National Council for the Social Studies, 1986.

Rosen, S. "A Short History of High School Geography (to 1936)." *Journal of Geography* 56, no. 9 (1957): 405–13.

Rumble, H. E. "Early Geography Instruction in America." *The Social Studies* 37, no. 6 (1946): 266–68.

Slater, F. *Learning through Geography,* rev. ed. Indiana, Penn.: National Council for Geographic Education, 1993.

Stoltman, J. P. *Geography Education for Citizenship.* Bloomington, Ind.: Educational Resources Information Center; Boulder, Colo.: Social Science Education Consortium, 1990.

———. *The "Where" and "Why There" of Geography in the K–12 Curriculum.* Paper presented at the Western PLACE Conference of the Colorado Geographic Alliance, Boulder, Colo., 1987.

Tuan, Y. *Topophilia: A Study of Environmental Perception, Attitudes, and Values.* Englewood Cliffs, N.J.: Prentice-Hall, 1974.

U.S. Department of Education. *America 2000: An Education Strategy.* Washington, D.C.: U.S. Department of Education, 1991.

Vuicich, G., and J. Stoltman. *Geography in Elementary and Secondary Education*. Boulder, Colo.: ERIC Clearinghouse for the Social Studies and Social Science Education Consortium, 1974.

Wagner, Philip L. *The Human Use of the Earth*. Glencoe, Ill.: The Free Press, 1960.

Weiss, I. R. *National Survey of Science, Mathematics, and Social Studies Education*. Research Triangle Park, N.C.: Center for Educational Research and Evaluation, 1978.

White, G. F. "Assessment in Midstream." In *From Geographic Discipline to Inquiring Student*, ed. D. J. Patton. Washington, D.C.: Association of American Geographers, 1970.

Winston, B. J. "Teacher Education in Geography in the United States." In *Teacher Education Models in Geography: An International Comparison*, ed. W. Marsden, 133–49. Paris: Papers for the 25th Congress, International Geographical Union, 1984.

Teaching Resources

Backler, A., and J. Stoltman, eds. *Geography Education*. Bloomington, Ind: Phi Delta Kappa, 1988.

Crews, K. A., and P. Cancellier, eds. *Connections: Linking Population and the Environment* [Teacher's Guide and Student Resource Book]. Washington, D.C.: Population Reference Bureau, Inc., 1991.

Culturgrams. Salt Lake City: Data Technology Resources, 1993. Database software.

Decisions, Decisions: The Environment. Watertown, Mass.: Tom Snyder Productions, n.d. Computer simulation.

Focus. New York: The American Geographical Society, published quarterly.

Geographical Review. New York: The American Geographical Society, published quarterly.

Geographic Education National Implementation Project (GENIP). *7–12 Geography: Themes, Key Ideas, and Learning Opportunities*. Washington, D.C.: GENIP, 1989.

Geography Search. Watertown, Mass: Tom Snyder Productions, n.d. Computer simulations.

Geo-Safari. Dominguez Hills, Calif.: Educational Insights, 1989. Computer game.

Hardwick, S. W., and D. G. Holtgrieve. *Patterns on Our Planet: Concepts and Themes in Geography*. New York: Macmillan, 1990.

Harris, C. D., ed. *A Geographical Bibliography for American Libraries*. Washington, D.C.: Association of American Geographers.

Helburn, N. "The Geographical Perspective: Geography's Role in Citizenship Education." In *Social Science Perspectives on Citizenship Education*, ed. R. E. Gross and T. L. Dynneson, 116–40. New York: Teachers College Press, 1991.

Hill, A. D., ed. *Placing Geography in the Curriculum*. Boulder, Colo.: Colorado Geographic Alliance and Center for Geographic Education, 1988.

Hill, A. D., J. M. Dunn, and F. Klein. *Geographic Inquiry into Global Issues*. Chicago: Encyclopaedia Britannica Educational Corporation, 1995.

Hill. A. D., and L. A. LaPrairie. "Geography in American Education." In *Geography in America*, ed. G. L. Gaile, and C. J. Willmott, 1–26. Columbus, Ohio: Charles E. Merrill, 1989.

Joint Committee on Geographic Education. *Guidelines for Geographic Education: Elementary and Secondary Schools*. Washington, D.C.: Association and National Council for Geographic Education, 1984.

Journal of Geography. Indiana, Pa.: National Council for Geographic Education, Indiana University of Pennsylvania. Published 7 times per year.

Ludwig, G. S., et al., *Directions in Geography: A Guide for Teachers.* Washington, D.C.: National Geographic Society, 1991.

Mac Globe. Tempe, Ariz.: DC Globe, n.d. Mapping software.

Massachusetts Geographic Alliance. *Global Geography: Activities for Teaching the Five Themes of Geography.* Boulder, Colo.: Social Science Education Consortium, 1990.

National Council for Geographic Education. *NCGE Outline Map Blackline Masters.* Indiana, Pa.: National Council for Geographic Education, 1990.

National Geographic. Washington, D.C.: National Geographic Society. Published monthly.

National Inspirer and *International Inspirer.* Watertown, Mass.: Tom Snyder Productions, n.d. Computer simulations.

Natoli, S. J. *Careers in Geography.* Washington, D.C.: Association of American Geographers, 1988.

Petersen, J. F., ed. *Discovering Geography: Teacher-Created Activities for High School and Middle School.* San Marcos: Texas Alliance for Geographic Education and Southwest Texas State University, 1988.

Posey-Pacak, M. A. *Earth at Risk: Instructional Materials on the Sustainable Development and Management of the Environment, A Resource Guide for K–12 Teachers.* Washington, D.C.: Geographic Education National Implementation Project, 1991.

Save the Planet. Pitkin, Colo.: Save the Planet Software, 1991. Database software.

SimEarth. Novato, Calif.: Broderbund, n.d. Computer simulation.

Slater, F. *Learning Through Geography,* rev. ed. Indiana, Penn.: National Council for Geographic Education, 1993.

Stoltman, J. P. "Research on Geography Teaching." In *Handbook of Research on Social Studies Teaching and Learning,* ed. J. P. Shaver, 437–47. New York: Macmillan, 1991.

USA Profile. Midland, Mich.: Active Learning Systems, 1985. Database program.

Where in the World, USA, Europe, Is Carmen Sandiego. Novato, Calif.: Broderbund, n.d. Computer games.

World Name Game. Merritt Island, Fla.: Robert L. Lloyd, n.d. Computer game.

World Resources Institute. *Teacher's Guide to World Resources 1994–95.* Washington, D.C.: World Resources Institute, 1994.

11

STUDYING AND TEACHING HISTORY

James R. Giese

ACTIVITY LIST

• • •

ACTIVITY

An Exercise in Autobiography

Historian L. S. Stavrianos (1989) has said that all global history begins with auto-biography. History is not something that stands outside us; we all make history and are at the same time intimately influenced by it. For Stavrianos, excursions into autobiography help us place ourselves in time and in the context of other human stories. Accordingly, we begin this chapter with an exercise based on your autobiographies.

Think back to your junior and senior high school years. Focus on the best history teacher you had. Jot down all the characteristics of that teacher you can recollect. What were his or her habits and methods? What did that teacher ask students to do? What did he or she do that facilitated your learning? Why was this teacher effective? (You may need to define *effective* before answering.) How do you account for the fact that you remember this teacher so vividly?

If you had no history teachers who call up fond images, list characteristics that were ineffective.

In small groups or in the whole group, make a master list of positive and negative characteristics. What generalizations or hypotheses can you develop concerning effective or ineffective history teaching? What would your profile of the exemplary history teacher be? What are some of the practices or characteristics you would hope to avoid, to emulate, or to improve upon in your own teaching?

INTRODUCTION

Your reflections in the preceding activity should have highlighted how successful teachers face the challenges of teaching history. Their wisdom, as well as that of historians and other educators, can point us in fruitful directions. These challenges, and the need for decisions about them, have framed the discourse of this chapter. The following issues are central:

- What is history? How do historians construct history? What aspects of those procedures should be included in history instruction?
- What purposes does history serve?
- How can we engage our students with history?
- What (or whose) history do we teach? How do we select among the vast array of potential historical subjects, topics, varieties?
- How can we plan effective instruction in history?

THE PAST, MEMORY, AND HISTORY

If you could ask the question "What is history?" of a typical high school student or the average person in the street, how do you suppose he or she would answer? Responses would probably be along the following lines: "History is the facts about the past"; "History is *the* story of the past as agreed upon by most historians"; "History is chronology" (i.e., one darned thing after another); "History *is* the past." Although each of those responses might contain a grain of truth, each represents an impoverished view of the nature of history.

History is not the past, although the past is its focus. History is not *the* story as agreed to by most historians, but a multiplicity of stories. History is not just facts, although truth claims and warranted judgments are fundamental to its stories. And history is not simply chronology, although it is fundamentally about change over time.

| ACTIVITY | **Defining History** |

Your current views about the nature of history are extremely important. In your journal, write a paragraph, make a list, construct an outline, prepare a cognitive map, or develop an idea web that describes or illustrates your sense of history as a subject or a discipline. Think about what history is and can do.

You may also want to think about what history contributes to your life. What is its potential contribution to your students? Next, recast your ideas in the form of a succinct rationale statement for the teaching of history.

The Past

"The past is everywhere," David Lowenthal (1985, xv) reminds us.

> *All present awareness is grounded on past perceptions and acts; we recognize a person, a tree, a breakfast, an errand because we have seen or done it before. And pastness is integral to our own being: "We are at any moment the sum of all our moments, the product of all our experiences," as A. A. Mendilow put it. Centuries of tradition underlie every instant of perception and creation, pervading not only artifacts and culture but the very cells of our bodies. (Lowenthal 1985, 185).*

The past is ever present in our lives. Few waking hours are devoid of recall or recollection. Despite the omnipresence of the past in our lives, knowing or understanding the past is an elusive matter. The most important thing about the past is that it cannot be directly observed. We may have memories or evidence of the past. We may check the relative validity of both memory and evidence, but only against other memories and documents, not against the past itself.

Just as it cannot be directly observed, neither can the past be replicated in any meaningful sense. Every historical situation or episode is in most respects unique. To be sure, specific events may display common patterns of behavior, of decision making, of geopolitics, of invention, or any number of other general characteristics. Yet because of the nature of historical time and of human beings and their interactions, no historical episode is ever exactly like any other. The stuff of history, then, is discrete and particular: There was only one Pearl Harbor, one Glorious Revolution, one Seneca Falls Convention, and one Nat Turner Rebellion.

Memory

Our transactions with the past are based on memory. Of the several types of memory, the most important for our purposes are instrumental and affective memory. Instrumental memory is usually used for some immediate practical purpose—recalling whether we paid the rent, the date and time of an important meeting, the name of a person whose face is familiar. Affective memory usually relates to more intense and personally meaningful episodes or situations we have experienced:

- Smelling a bar of soap in the shower, which brings back memories of your grandfather's old shaving mug, the sights, sounds, and textures of the old farmhouse.
- Finding a picture of you, your brother, and your mother at a Cinco de Mayo picnic and remembering the games played all day, the tables heaped with food, catching your hand in a slamming car door, and going to bed dog-tired.

What we remember is intimately related to who we are, to who we think we are, and to our present concerns. Being highly subjective and intensely personal, memory often produces incredibly vivid recollections, but these are just as often erroneous—that is, they don't match up with the past others may recall or recollect. The validity of our own memories cannot be measured against the past, only against the possible validity of other memories, and only if we choose to do so.

Although memory is highly personal, it has collective aspects. We are often in situations in which we compare our own memories of a particular episode, event, or situation with those of others who shared that experience. How often have you discovered that your own recall was quite different from that of others? In comparing memories, our own views are sometimes called into question and at other times corroborated.

Some of our memories are actually the residue of shared recall. Think of your memories about your early childhood. Some may, in fact, be your own—but some are likely the product of family folklore, the stories you heard about episodes in which you participated but about which you probably have little personal recall. Over time, these stories have become part of your own personal recollections.

People seem to want to link their own personal memories with collective memory and public history. For example, your grandparents can probably describe in great detail where they were and what they were doing when they heard the news in late 1941 of the Japanese attack on Pearl Harbor. Your parents can likely recall the setting in which they heard the news of John F. Kennedy's assassination in 1963.

Memory expands and changes over time. As we age and have new experiences, the total stock of our memories expands. Yet it also shrinks because we forget some of the things we once knew. Memory thus sifts again what has already been sifted by perception.

Our memories are also revised; we constantly reorder or rewrite them in light of subsequent experience. At the time a specific event occurs, we can seldom predict what or how much that event will later signify. For example, a person going through a divorce may think it is the worst thing that could have happened, only to find out retrospectively that the divorce was actually liberating.

Memory, then, does not simply preserve the past in some immutable storehouse. Memory helps us to understand the past and adapt it to enrich our understanding of the present.

History

What, you might ask, does all this have to do with history? History and memory are distinguishable less as types of knowledge than in attitudes toward that knowledge. Memory is normally taken to be given and true. History and the sources upon which it is based are scrutinized for accuracy and empirical validity. Memory is most often private. History is collectively produced and shared. Memory is crucial for individual identity and sense of self. History is crucial for social preservation and collective self-awareness. Because it is individual, memory is often fleeting, ephemeral. Because it is collective, history is characterized by its endurance. Memory and history are both avenues of interaction between the past and the present. Both rely on subsequent experience to give meaning to prior episodes. They both tell us things about the past not known at the time (Lowenthal 1985).

Just as perception sifts an individual's experience, which is again sifted by memory, history sifts through human experience to sort out the relevant and the meaningful. The past is simply too vast a canvas to be captured in its entirety. Just as current preoccupations influence the individual's recall of the past, so do current frames of reference—intellectual and cultural preoccupations—of historians influence the questions they ask and the stories they tell about the past. Finally, just as hindsight influences the revision of memory, so, too, does it influence the historian. Subsequent events profoundly influence our interpretation of any specific historical situation or episode. We see the effects of U.S. involvement in Vietnam differently in the 1990s from the way we could in 1968 or 1975, not merely because new masses of evidence have accumulated, but also because further events have unfolded, including the end of the cold war, better relations with the People's Republic of China, the emergence of new areas of global concern, and the apparent effectiveness of conventional U.S. military forces in such places as the Middle East.

As historians tell their stories, they must use what they know of the outcome. The tempo, contradictions, and time scale of the story reflect (or should reflect) that retrospective knowledge; the very process of telling the story, of giving it coherence, demands creative change of the events, episodes, and situations experienced by contemporaries seriatim, in more or less isolated and incoherent bits. Indeed, many of the concepts or generalizations historians use—concepts such as "the Renaissance," "the Reformation," "the New Deal," "the Progressive Era," "the Holocaust"— could be fully recognized and articulated only after they were virtually complete. Partly because of hindsight, and partly because of our attempt to tell meaningful stories about the past, the past we reconstruct is more coherent than it was when it happened. At the same time, we know about the episode less intimately.

The High School Reunion

Think back to your senior year of high school. What is the first memory that comes to your mind? What feelings, smells, sights, and sounds does that single memory evoke? What connections does that memory conjure up?

Next, think about how you would respond to or answer each of these questions:

- What music did you listen to?
- Who were your heroes?
- What three adjectives best describe your school experience?
- What were the moral messages you heard from parents, teachers, others?
- What did you do for fun?
- What values separated you from adults?

Form small groups to debrief what you have done. Organize these groups by the decade or year of graduation from high school or, if most of your class graduated in the same decade, by such other elements as geographical region, size of school, or urban, suburban, and rural settings.

After you have organized your groups, share the individual work completed above. Were group members' memories similar or different? Were there common types of memories, feelings, connections? Make a graphic display of your collective responses to the six questions. Is there little, some, or much consensus about these matters?

Up to this point, you have been exercising your memories of high school. Now we turn to a bit of educational history to help you put those experiences in historical context. Read the following description of the recent history of high schools in the United States and reflect upon your high school experiences through that frame of reference.

The drive for order within the high school setting has become so pervasive, so overwhelming that success is measured almost exclusively in those terms. It, rather than "the use of the mind" . . . , has become the pervading ethos in high schools. Reading serially from a textbook, filling the blanks on a dittoed sheet, showing a film or videotape are all classroom activities that are at least tolerated if not encouraged because they reduce the dreaded loss of control. Engaging students in a way that will make them use their minds is a risky business, and only the brave or the unusually fortunate teacher will venture into activities that may encourage that. . . .

Toleration is almost universally regarded as a laudable quality. . . . Adolescents are given license to make a mockery of their education if that is their inclination, and, if their high school education amounts to nothing, it is they, not the institution, who are at fault. . . . "The teacher is there to babysit. You're on your own. If you get it fine. If not, that's okay too." The problem is that . . . there are winners and losers in this academic marketplace. And the losers are more likely to be America's underclass, the poor and the racial and linguistic minorities. (Kliebard 1987, 92–94)

• • •

Explore with your classmates ways you might be able to use exercises in the past, memory, and history with the students you will have in secondary history courses.

THE HISTORIAN'S SOURCES

Types of Sources

The sources historians use are many and varied. It is conventional for historians to distinguish between primary sources and secondary sources. A primary source is some direct record of the past left behind by the people who are the subject of the historian's study. Primary sources are the actual records that have survived from the past. Secondary sources are accounts about the past produced by people writing at some remove from the event, episode, or situation under study. Whereas a primary source usually dates from the time of the events being studied, a secondary source usually dates from a later time.

A couple of examples should suffice to clarify the difference. In 1904, Lincoln Steffens published *The Shame of the Cities*, a collection of articles he had written for *McClure's Magazine* between 1902 and 1904. Exposés of pervasive corruption in American municipal government, these articles have been important primary sources for historians interested in progressive political reform at the turn of the twentieth century. Richard Hofstadter's *The Age of Reform* (1955) is a secondary account of the progressive era that uses Steffens's work as one of its primary sources.

Although the past is not directly observable, it does provide an abundance of clues to what may have occurred—artifacts, books, papers, government documents, letters, oral accounts, diaries, maps, photographs, reports, fiction, coins, stamps, and many other things. These clues constitute what historians call the historical record. Here we meet one of the paradoxes historians continually confront. On the one hand, the sheer volume of the historical record is staggering. At the same time, the record comprises only scanty traces of all the activity in which billions of humans have engaged in the past (see Commager and Muessig 1980).

Evaluation of Sources

The historical record is highly selective, often biased, and always incomplete. Most of what happened in the past is undocumented, and not every document produced

Figure 11.1   Photographs have been a primary source available since the mid-ninteenth century. What might you need to keep in mind in evaluating a historical photo like this one?

is preserved for future use. Much of what is available has been accumulated by accident. Furthermore, much historical evidence is actually incidental to the situations described. On the other hand, some of the available records are left because of the self-conscious action of historical actors. Many people keep journals and write diaries, autobiographies, and business and personal letters, some of which are written explicitly for posterity and the historical record.

Some primary sources are more useful than others, depending, of course, on what question the historian seeks to answer. In making preliminary judgments about the usefulness of primary historical sources, historians usually adopt the principle of immediacy—that is, the closer the source is in time and place to an episode under investigation, the better the source.

Every source is biased in one way or another and must therefore be scrutinized skeptically and critically. Every individual piece of evidence (source) must also be carefully scrutinized and cross-checked with other evidence. The historian must think about who is producing any given source and what his or her purpose was in producing it. The relevance of this stricture is probably most obvious with respect to sources that try to persuade the reader or attempt to justify an individual's actions: political speeches, party platforms, newspaper editorials, autobiographies of famous persons. Yet it applies equally well to other types of sources.

As an example, consider the U.S. federal census of population, virtually without peer among national government censuses as a long-term time series of statistical information. However, the census is not as comprehensive as its compilers, funders, or users would wish. Some people do not voluntarily participate in the census—believing, for example, that their privacy will be violated or that they should not participate because they are foreign nationals. Others simply forget to fill out or return the forms. Some make errors when completing the forms, although many of these are now caught by the Census Bureau. When census enumerators go out into the field, some people are difficult to find, their neighbors cannot supply accurate information, or in our highly mobile society, people have recently moved. Sometimes enumerators fear going into certain neighborhoods because they are reputed to be dangerous.

Historically, these problems were arguably even greater because the census was conducted by amateurs who may have been political appointees or have had little training. Census canvassers were sometimes paid by the entry (the more people they found, the more money they earned), which encouraged overcounting. The point is that all sources, even one of such generally high quality as the U.S. federal census, have their limitations as well as their virtues (see Dailey, Englehardt, and Giese 1989).

| ACTIVITY | **Analyzing Primary Sources** |

Kyvig and Marty (1982) suggest the following questions for interrogating primary sources. Use these questions to analyze the document that follows.

- Was it created through a hasty spur-of-the-moment act, a routine transaction, or a thoughtful, deliberate process?
- Did the recorder possess firsthand knowledge or simply report what he or she was told?
- Was the recorder a neutral party, or did he or she have interests or biases that might have influenced what was recorded?
- Did the recorder produce the document for his or her own use, for one or more selected individuals, or for a larger audience? Was the document meant to be public or private?
- Was the recorder's intent to inform or to persuade?
- Was the information recorded immediately or after some lapse of time? How large a lapse?

In the document reprinted below, slave owner David Shriver advertised a reward for a slave—Peter—who had run away from his master's plantation in Maryland in June 1800.

> *Ran away last night, from the subscriber, living on the waters of Little Pipe Creek near Westminster Town, Maryland, a tall, well-made and active country born Negro Man, named PETER, about 30 years of age, 5 feet 8 or 10 inches high, wears the wool on the top of his head commonly platted, and when loose is very long and bushy, but will likely have it cut short: there remains the mark of a burn near the wrist, on the back part of one of his hands, believed to be the right, which he received when young; has a down look when spoken to, but is a handsome erect figure, with smaller features than is common for a Negro of his size and speaks German nearly as well as English; he was brought up by me to plantation work chiefly, of which he is very capable; but can do a little at blacksmith, shoemaking and carpenter's work, and has some knowledge of making gun barrels—He had on and took with him a fur hat about half worn; a homemade full'd lincy doublet of a yellowish color, a swansdown jacket, with yellow flannel backs and lining, a pair of tow-linnen trowsers, which he wears very high and a pair of common half worn shoes, but as he is an artful fellow, and has money, it is expected he will soon exchange them. He also plays on the fiddle and fife tolerably well. Whoever takes up said Negro, and brings him home, shall receive if 15 miles from home 5 dollars; if 30 miles, 10 dollars, if 60 miles 20 dollars, and if 100 miles or upwards the above reward, of 10 dollars if lodged in any gaol, and notice given me thereof by a letter. (June 20, 1800) (Shriver papers, Maryland Historical Society)*

In small groups, discuss your analysis of this primary source. How credible is this eyewitness?

• • •

History textbooks often include primary sources. The number of sources and the manner in which they are used varies widely from textbook to textbook. Select a textbook and analyze it with respect to how primary sources are used. What are students expected to do with those sources? What kinds of instructional strategies are suggested? How effective are those strategies? Can you think of ways to improve upon them?

THE HISTORIAN'S WORK

Historical Questions

"A moment's reflection," historian David Hackett Fischer (1970) has said, "should suffice to establish the simple proposition that every historian, willy-nilly, must begin his research with a question." Continuing, Fischer asserts that

> *questions are the engines of intellect, the cerebral machines which convert energy to motion, and curiosity to controlled inquiry. There can be no thinking without questioning. . . . Moreover, there can be no questioning in a sophisticated sense without hypothesizing, and no systematic testing of hypotheses without the construction of*

hypothetical models which can be put to the test. . . . Without questions of some sort, a historian is condemned to wander aimlessly through dark corridors of learning. Specific forms of question-framing depend in a considerable degree upon the kinds of answers which are sought. These elemental aspects of questioning are common to all historical inquiry, and indeed to empirical investigation in every field. (pp. 3–4)

If questions are so fundamental, where do they come from? The sources of historians' questions are many and varied. Historians, like other people, are remarkably different with respect to their interests, values, and experiences. Each historian exists in his or her own subjective past—the personal meaning that attaches to nationality, social group, ethnicity, class, family, schooling, and so on—as well as an ongoing present. These and other factors make up the historian's frame of reference. These aspects of frame of reference may be seen most readily by comparing the work of historians of different countries about a similar topic—for example, the work of British and U.S. historians about the American Revolution.

Historian Robert Allen Skotheim showed how time, place, and values affected historians in a collection of essays titled *The Historian and the Climate of Opinion* (1969). By climate of opinion, Skotheim meant "the fundamental assumptions and attitudes shared by significant elements of a population at a given time." Using the concept of climate of opinion, Skotheim demonstrated several radical shifts in American historical writing in the twentieth century. In the early 1900s, the "progressive historians" were much influenced by the thoroughgoing climate of reform, the conflict between "the interests" and "the people," and the optimism that things could be made progressively better. In the 1950s, the "consensus historians" were influenced by a conservative climate: the perceived threat of communism, the cold war, and concern about American character and values. And in the 1960s, the so-called new left or neo-progressive historians were concerned with the perceived oppressiveness of American social institutions, civil rights, and the war in Vietnam (also see Wise 1973; Kraus and Joyce 1985). Each successive climate of opinion decisively influenced the questions historians asked as well as the answers they found.

Influences within the profession and discipline also affect historians' questions. Historians feel pressure to secure tenure and promotion, to enhance their reputation, to publish in the best journals and with the best publishing houses. Their work is subject to private (refereed journals and academic presses) and public (book reviews, responses to papers given at association meetings) scrutiny and discourse. Those influences tend to keep historians attuned to the state of the collective body of historical wisdom and the kinds of questions deemed important at any given time. (For interesting discussions of historians' professional lives, see Kammen 1980a, and 1982.)

As historians search for questions, or topics to study and write about, they look at available secondary accounts—what is the state of our shared knowledge about the topic—as well as the available evidence relating to the topic. Only by gauging this interplay can the historian identify important problems with their attendant issues, hypotheses, sources, and eventually stories. An example may clarify these matters.

The historiography of slavery in the United States has changed considerably since the early twentieth century when the first scholarly studies appeared. The history of slavery has been influenced by changing American values, as well as by a shifting problematic within the field of study itself.

The 1918 publication of U. B. Phillips' *American Negro Slavery* marks the beginning of modern scholarship on slavery. Phillips's questions were rather broad: How did the institution work? Was it profitable? If not, what other reasons supported its longevity? What influence did slavery have on the South? Resting as it did on meticulous research in plantation records, Phillips's book was long considered the definitive interpretation of slavery. However, it was also clearly influenced by the author's Southern background and racist assumptions.

Phillips portrayed slavery as a benign institution in which masters were kindly and concerned with the welfare of their bondsmen. Slaves did not work hard, were well cared for, and generally did not rebel against the slave system. On the whole, according to Phillips, slavery was unprofitable and was maintained by masters for racial and cultural reasons.

Over the years, historians chipped away at Phillips's interpretation. Herbert Aptheker (1943) and others emphasized the number and violence of slave rebellions. Richard Hofstadter (1944) questioned Phillips's almost exclusive use of records from large plantations which, he argued, were not representative of slavery as a whole. Economists Alfred H. Conrad and John R. Meyer (1958) demonstrated slavery's profitability. However, it was not until Kenneth Stampp's *The Peculiar Institution* appeared in 1956 that Phillips's interpretation was challenged systematically.

Stampp, a white liberal, declared at the outset: "I have assumed that the slaves were merely ordinary human beings, that innately Negroes *are*, after all, only white men with black skins, nothing more, nothing less." Based on vast scholarship, *The Peculiar Institution* demolished Phillips's interpretation. Above all, slavery was a labor system designed to control and exploit labor for the profit of the masters. The food, clothing, and medical care given slaves was inadequate by any decent standards. Slaves were forced to work long hours, often driven by the lash. Their family life and community life were practically destroyed by pervasive power of the masters who sought to "make them stand in fear." Finally, slaves resisted in all sorts of ways—malingering, breaking tools, running away, and occasionally through violent rebellion.

Soon after Stampp established slavery's malevolence, Stanley Elkins wrote an equally powerful book, *Slavery: A Problem in American Institutional and Intellectual Life* (1959), which changed the problematic—the basic questions historians ask about slavery. Elkins asked: What was slavery really like? What were its effects on the slaves themselves? Elkins drew upon the behavioral sciences, comparative history, and model building to understand slavery.

For Elkins, blacks could not be just like whites because of their experience in slavery. Contemporary observers' descriptions of slaves as "Sambo" characters who lied, stole, shirked work, played the fool, and generally acted like children before their masters were so pervasive, Elkins held, that they must have contained some truth. Elkins asked how such a personality was formed. He drew on then-recent comparative studies of slavery in the Americas, which judged slavery in the South to have been the harshest in the Western Hemisphere (a judgment significantly revised by subsequent research).

Elkins coupled that judgment with an analogy drawn from the experience of Jewish inmates in Nazi concentration camps: The camps created infantilized, docile Jews; the plantations created infantilized, docile blacks. Bound in closed circles in which masters exercised absolute power, slaves were stripped of their cultural heritage, their family life, and every other institution that might have served to mitigate the harsh impact of slavery on their lives.

Much of the ensuing literature on slavery was stimulated by Elkins's work. The focus on the slaves themselves and the increasing use of new, especially black, sources were the most important aspects of this shift in frame of reference. Interestingly, this shift was invigorated by the changing sociology of the historical profession; that is, as blacks and women began entering the profession in increasing numbers, many took up the history of slavery as their primary area of study. Not surprisingly, several of the books discussed below were written by blacks and women. Most of the research stimulated by Elkins disputed his interpretation in almost every particular.

The subsequent scholarship is voluminous, and only a small bit of it can be included here. John Blassingame's *Slave Community* (1972) and Herbert Gutman's *Black Family in Slavery and Freedom* (1975) showed that, despite the harshness of the slave regime, slaves were able to create communities beyond their masters' control and to fashion vital institutions quite functional to their needs. Eugene Genovese (*Roll, Jordan, Roll*, 1974) and Albert Raboteau (*Slave Religion*, 1978) have reinforced this view. Richard C. Wade's *Slavery in the Cities* (1964) and Robert Starobin's *Industrial Slavery in the Old South* (1970) demonstrated that slavery was not simply an agricultural and rural phenomenon—it was quite variable in location and uses.

Charles Joyner's *Down by the Riverside* (1984) shows how slaves fashioned a distinctive culture in the lowlands of South Carolina. Jacqueline Jones (*Labor of Love, Labor of Sorrow*, 1985) and others have begun to detail the life in the slave huts and plantation houses and the interaction of the two. Indeed, as Thomas C. Holt (1990) argues, "the consensus that slaves played a crucial role in making their own world is the beginning point for most recent scholarship in Afro-American history" (p. 218).

As Eric Foner (1990a) summarizes the secondary literature of slavery:

The cumulative impact of the recent literature has been enormous. For one thing, it leaves little doubt as to the centrality of slavery to the course of nineteenth-century American history. . . . It is no longer possible to view the peculiar institution as some kind of aberration, existing outside the mainstream of American development. Rather, slavery was intimately bound up with the settlement of the Western Hemisphere, the economic development of the antebellum nation, and the structure of national politics. (p. 78)

ACTIVITY **Analyzing Historiographical Essays**

Historiographical essays—that is, writings on the history of the history of specific topics, periods, or subject areas—are usually commentaries on the current state of research. Such essays appear in a variety of places, including the bibliographical essays at the end of scholarly books; historical journals such as *The Journal of American History, American Historical Review*, and *Reviews in American History*; and edited collections of such essays. Examples of the latter include *The Past Before Us* (Kammen 1980b), *The Promise of American History* (Kutler and Katz 1982), *The New American History* (Foner 1990b), and *The Reinterpretation of American History and Culture* (Cartwright and Watson 1973).

Individually or in small groups, select a topic, subject, or field and find a recent historiographical essay. How has the historiography of your selection changed over time? What are the critical turning points, and how may you account for them? Share your findings with the class.

• • •

In small groups, brainstorm ways of incorporating these ideas in secondary history classes.

Select a textbook used in secondary history courses. Does the textbook include information about the dynamic nature of historiography? If so, how? How effective are those approaches? How might you improve upon them?

Historical Facts

History does not exist apart from facts. They are the very lifeblood of historians' stories. However, as historian David Hackett Fischer (1970) argues, there are no facts that everyone needs to know.

Many historians have addressed this issue. For E. H. Carr (1961), the common-sense view of facts was that

history consists of a corpus of ascertained facts. The facts are available to the historian in documents, inscriptions, and so on, like fish on a fishmonger's slab. The historian collects them, takes them home, and cooks and serves them in whatever style appeals to him. . . . [The facts of history, rather] are like fish swimming about in a vast and sometimes inaccessible ocean; and what the historian catches will depend partly on chance, but mainly on what part of the ocean he chooses to fish in and what tackle he chooses to use . . . depending on the kind of fish he wants to catch. (p. 24)

Historical facts do not come to us ready-made, full of meaning and significance. Historians, as we have seen, ask questions about the past. Typically, they next develop hypotheses about the possible relationships among the facts. They then go to the sources to find the facts to prove or disprove their original hypothesis or explanation. In turn, historians modify the questions and the hypotheses as they go along. In the process, the historian selects facts, imbues them with certain tentative meanings, and weighs them in the context of other facts. Slowly the story or interpretation emerges.

Facts cannot be separated from values, as argued by Cleo Cherryholmes (1990):

> *Where facts and values become confused . . . or intertwined is the moment one is forced to acknowledge that factual statements are products of value judgments. A fact can be asserted only after a value judgment is made that one fact is worth stating and that it is more worth stating than are other facts. A fact* is a statement and making a statement is an action and taking an action results from making a decision and a decision cannot be made without reference to values. *Sometimes, of course, it is useful and important to separate statements like "On June 12, 1990, George Bush was President of the United States," from statements like "George Bush was the greatest President of the 20th century." But the valuative structure that leads one to pay attention to the presidency in the first place always precedes factual statements about the presidency. (pp. 439–40)*

ACTIVITY

The Historian's Work*

This activity is designed to illustrate the recursive nature of the historian's work. Below are several sources relating to this historical question: "What happened on Lexington Green on April 19, 1775?" Read each document and answer the questions that follow.

DOCUMENT 1

To the best of my recollection about 4 o'clock in the morning being the 19th of April, the 5 front companies was ordered to load which we did. . . . It was at Lexington when we saw one of their companies drawn up in regular order. Major Pitcairn of the Marines second in command called to them to disperse, but their not seeming willing he desired us to mind our space which we did when they gave us a fire then run off to get behind a wall. We had one man wounded of our Company in the leg, his name was Johnson, also Major Pitcairn's horse was shot in the flank; we returned their salute, and before we proceeded on our march from Lexington

---

*Adapted from Peter S. Bennett, *What Happened on Lexington Green? An Inquiry into the Nature and Methods of History* (Menlo Park, Calif.: Addison-Wesley, 1970). Used by permission of the author.

I believe we killed and wounded either 7 or 8 men. (Ensign Jeremy Lister, youngest of the British officers at Lexington, in a personal narrative written in 1782)

Questions

1. Who was Jeremy Lister? What happened according to his account?
2. What hypothesis might you begin with for explaining what happened on Lexington Green?

DOCUMENT 2

Lieutenant Nunn, of the Navy arrived this morning . . . and brought letters from General Gage, Lord Percy, and Lieutenant-Colonel Smith, containing the following particulars of what passed on the nineteenth of April last between a detachment of the King's Troops in the Province of Massachusetts-Bay and several parties of rebel provincials. . . . Lieutenant-Colonel Smith finding, after he had advanced some miles on his march, that the country had been alarmed by the firing of guns and ringing of bells, dispatched six companies of light-infantry, in order to secure two bridges on different roads beyond Concord, who, upon their arrival at Lexington, found a body of the country people under arms, on a green close to the road; and upon the King's Troops marching up to them, in order to inquire the reason of their being so assembled, they went off in great confusion, and several guns were fired upon the King's troops from behind a stone wall, and also from the meeting-house and other houses, by which one man was wounded, and Major Pitcairn's horse shot in two places. In consequence of this attack by the rebels, the troops returned the fire and killed several of them. After which the detachment marched on to Concord without any thing further happening. (*The London Gazette*, June 10, 1775)

Questions

1. How does this account square with Lister's?
2. Does this account force you to make any modifications of your hypothesis?

DOCUMENT 3

19th. At 2 o'clock we began our march by wading through a very long ford up to our middles; after going a few miles we took three or four people who were going off to give intelligence; about five miles on this side of a town called Lexington, which lay in our road, we heard there were some hundreds of people collected together intending to oppose us and stop our going on; at 5 o'clock we arrived there, and saw a number of people, I believe between 200 and 300, formed in a common in the middle of the town; we still continued advancing, keeping prepared against an attack though without intending to attack them; but on our coming near they fired one or two shots, upon which our men without any order rushed in upon them, fired and put them to flight; several of them were killed, we could not tell how many, because they would go behind walls and into the woods; We had a man of the 10th Light Infantry wounded, nobody else hurt. We then formed on the Common, but with some difficulty, the men were so wild they could hear no orders; we waited a considerable time there, and at length proceeded on our way to Concord. (April 19, 1775, diary entry of Lieutenant John Barker, British army officer)

Questions

1. What more have you learned of the events of April 19 from this source?
2. Does it corroborate or contradict any facts or your hypothesis?

DOCUMENT 4

Friends and fellow subjects: Hostilities are at length commenced in the Colony by the troops under command of General Gage; and it being of the greatest importance that an early, true, and authentic account of this inhuman proceeding should be known to you. . . . By the clearest depositions relative to this transaction, it will appear that on the night preceding the nineteenth of April instant, . . . the Town of Lexington . . . was alarmed, and a company of the inhabitants mustered on the occasion; that the Regular troops, on their way to Concord, marched into the said town of Lexington, and the said company, on their approach, began to disperse; that notwithstanding this, the regulars rushed on with great violence, and first began hostilities by firing on said Lexington Company, whereby they killed eight and wounded several others; that the Regulars continued their fire until those of said company, who were neither killed nor wounded, had made their escape. . . . These, brethren, are marks of ministerial vengeance against this colony, for refusing, with her sister colonies, a submission to slavery. . . . We profess to be his loyal and dutiful subjects. . . . Nevertheless, to the persecution and tyranny of his cruel ministry we will not tamely submit; appealing to Heaven for the justice of our cause, we determine to die or be free. (Letter, Joseph Warren, President pro tem of Provincial Congress, Watertown, Massachusetts, to Benjamin Franklin, April 29, 1775)

Questions

1. How does this account corroborate or contradict the testimony you have read before?
2. What influence does this document have on your hypothesis or interpretation of events at Lexington?

DOCUMENT 5

We NATHANIEL MULLIKEN, PHILIP RUSSELL [and 32 other names of men present at Lexington Green on April 19, 1775], . . . all of lawful age, and inhabitants of Lexington . . . do further testify and declare, that about five o'clock in the morning, hearing our drum beat [for assembly], we proceeded towards the parade, and soon found that a large body of troops were marching towards us, some of our company were coming up to the parade, and others had reached it, at which time the company began to disperse, whilst our backs were turned on the troops, we were fired on by them, and a number of our men were instantly killed and wounded, not a gun was fired by any person in our company on the regulars to our knowledge before they fired on us, and they continued firing until we had all made our escape. (Deposition sworn by 34 minutemen before three justices of the peace, on April 25, 1775)

Questions

1. Again, think about corroboration, contradiction, and how this additional evidence affects your understanding of the situation.

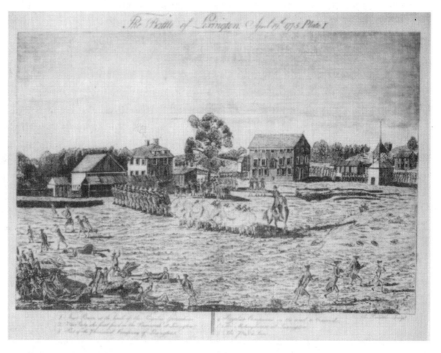

Figure 11.2   The action on Lexington Green as drawn by artist Ralph Earle. The engraving was made by Connecticut militiaman Amos Doolittle, who visited Lexington a few days after the fighting. What appears to be happening in the engraving? Does it seem to be in agreement with any of the documents? *Source: From* The American Revolution: A Picture Sourcebook *(New York: Dover Publications, Inc., 1975).*

All the evidence is now at hand. First, put the sources in rank order based on the credibility of the witnesses. Justify your decisions. Next, write a brief paragraph describing what happened at Lexington Green on April 19, 1775. In small groups, compare your ratings of the sources and your accounts of Lexington Green. What differences and similarities do you observe?

Finally, compare your work with the following accounts. Which more closely agrees with the facts of the case? Which more closely agrees with your own account?

ACCOUNT 1

Major Pitcairn screamed at us: "Lay down your arms, you lousy bastards! Disperse, you lousy peasant scum!" . . . At least those were the words that I seem to remember. Others remembered differently; but the way he screamed, in his strange London accent, with the motion and excitement, with his horse rearing and kicking. . . . with the drums beating again and the fixed bayonets glittering in the sunshine, it's a wonder that any of his words remain with us. We still stood in our two lines, our guns butt end on the ground or held loosely in our hands. Major Pitcairn spurred his horse and raced between the lines. Somewhere, away from us, a shot sounded. A redcoat soldier raised his musket, leveled it at Father, and fired. My father clutched at his breast, then crumpled to the ground like an empty sack. . . . Then the whole British front burst into a roar of sound and flame and smoke. (Excerpt from Howard Fast's novel, *April Morning*, published in 1961)

ACCOUNT 2

In April 1775, General Gage, the military governor of Massachusetts, sent out a body of troops to take possession of military stores at Concord, a short distance from Boston. At Lexington, a handful of "embattled farmers," who had been tipped off by Paul Revere, barred the way. The "rebels" were ordered to disperse. They stood their ground. The English fired a volley of shots that killed eight patriots. It was not long before the swift-riding Paul Revere spread the news of this new atrocity to the neighboring colonies. The patriots of all of New England, although still a handful, were now ready to fight the English. (From *The United States: Story of a Free People*, a high school textbook published in 1963)

THE USES OF HISTORY

Even historians disagree as to whether history has any practical value. Some agree with philosopher George Santayana, who said that "those who *cannot remember* the past are condemned to repeat it" (in Commager and Muessig 1980). Others take the opposite view, agreeing with historian Arthur M. Schlesinger, Jr. (1966), who said somewhat ironically that "those who *would remember* the past are bound to repeat it." Given this range of opinion, what may we say about the usefulness or purpose of studying history? This section discusses some of the claims made about the purposes of history and how those purposes might guide instruction.

Generalizations

Most working historians would probably say that historical inquiry is concerned above all with the unique and particular. Yet explaining an episode forces one to repudiate too stringent a notion of uniqueness. Although any two events are different in some respects, those differences can be known and explained only within the context of comparisons with other, potentially similar, phenomena.

Analogies are a special form of generalization. As P. J. Rogers (1972) has said:

> It is never the case that events are exactly repeated (how could they be?). It is that different events may be alike in respects which our judgments and experience suggest are particularly significant. This is how comparisons are made, and categories formed. It is also what analogy is. Things are not analogous if they are identical. (p. 99)

However, "any intelligent use of analogy must begin with a sense of its limits" (Fischer 1970). An analogical inference between A and B presumes that those two phenomena are similar in some respect but dissimilar in others. Analogy is only suggestive; analogy alone cannot prove the fact of the inference made.

Concepts

According to most observers, there are few autonomous historical concepts. The concepts historians use depend a good deal on what they study. In fact, the concepts of history are really the concepts of art, science, politics, economics, sociology, and so on, according to what one is studying the history of. From a conceptual point of view, then, history is less a discrete form of knowledge, marked by peculiar concepts, than a dimension of knowledge in every discipline or field of study.

Even though history has few concepts all its own, historians use an incredibly large number of concepts. For example, historians often refer to such sociological concepts as *community, society, stratification, social structure, status,* and *role.* They also use such political science concepts as *power, social control, interest group,* and *the state.* From economics they use *scarcity, production, interdependence, specialization and division of labor,* and *market,* among others. Concepts are indispensable to studying, writing, and teaching history (see Gustavson 1955).

The upshot is that historical data are largely meaningless without the structure, the intellectual framework, of concepts and generalizations. The implications of this line of thinking for instruction should be obvious.

Empathy

One of the justifications for the study of history is the notion of empathy. In his essay "Empathetic Reconstruction in History and History Teaching" (1983), David Stockley describes empathy as follows:

> *First, empathy is equated with the desire to enter into the minds, to step into the shoes, of another person in another time and place. Second, empathy is to be encouraged as a valuable form of gaining "vicarious experience of humanity." Third, empathy is all about understanding people's motives and actions so that they appear to the student or historian as both rational and justifiable. Finally, an empathetic reconstruction can only take place successfully when the student is able to construct a "frame of reference" within which to view the historical agent's actions. . . .*

Empathy may help to develop in students important habits of mind. By extending the range of students' knowledge of human agents in particular situations, facing particular human problems, and developing possibly reasonable solutions, history also appears to offer a potentially valuable source of vicarious experience across time, place, and even culture.

Finally, empathizing with historical agents serves as a reminder that we must sometimes suspend our knowledge of the outcomes of a situation to fully understand it. As Donald Pratt (1985) reminds us, "For most students of history, there is an inevitability about the past which obscures the role of human choice." It is precisely those choices that students must explore and understand.

Perspective or Hindsight

Another justification for the study of history is the notion of perspective or hindsight, which is, in many respects, the opposite of empathy. According to philosopher of history Louis O. Mink (1987), perspective or hindsight is "at least in part a claim that for historical understanding of an event one must know its consequences as well as its antecedents; that the historian must look before *and* after" (p. 72).

By virtue of hindsight, we can know more about a total historical situation than any contemporary historical actor could. In that way, what happened subsequently can be viewed as part of the context of the historical situation. This knowledge is fundamental to the ways we tell our stories and structure our narratives.

The Lessons of History

Some believe that history has more practical uses. However, no matter what one may urge as the purposes of history, it does not "guide us with the clarity of a tourist's road map or a mariner's chart," as historian Carl Gustavson (1955) has said.

> *The lessons of history are not as easy to discern as some people would have us believe. Any statement in which the prefatory "History teaches us that. . . ." is used as a*

springboard should be very carefully scrutinized; the accompanying assertion may be quite valid and acceptable, but the odds are against it. (p. 5)

Historian Lester Stephens (1974) adds, "The broader and more widely applicable the lesson reputes to be, the greater the danger that evidence will refute it."

Prediction

There is a good deal of debate about whether history can be used for predicting the future. Some flatly deny it. Others argue that historical knowledge may be put to such uses, at least in limited and conditional ways. For example, historian P. J. Rogers (1972) argues that "we have excellent grounds for supposing (from the state of present observed facts) that the short-run future (made up of events shaped by those facts) will resemble the present (and recent past), made up of events which are the effects of similar facts" (p. 89).

Unlike the natural scientist, no historian can predict the occurrence of specific events. It is quite impossible to predict that on X date, Y country will have a change of government or will attack country Z. Yet, "weak sense prediction—or better, rational inference, modest and circumspect, drawn with a degree of confidence proportionate to the strength of the supporting evidence—is of the very nature of the historian's work. . . . It is, in short, inherent in the nature of explanation" (Rogers 1972, 89–92)

ACTIVITY

Enhancing Historical Empathy and Perspective

Decision makers rarely have all the information they would like to have, nor do they have any assurance that their decided course of action will have the desired results. In this sense, all decisions are contingent and probabilistic. Being able to empathize with a historical actor's situation is an important part of historical understanding.

Part 1

Below are a number of excerpted primary sources concerning World War II in Asia. The focus is 1945. All these bits of information were available to Truman and his advisors in making the decision to drop atomic bombs on Hiroshima and Nagasaki. Use this information and the decision-making matrix in Figure 11.3 to explore Truman's decision to drop atomic bombs on Japan. You may want to make a copy of the matrix allowing room to fill in the information called for in each box.

Data Available to Truman and His Advisors

1. From April 1 to June 21, 1945, U.S. Army and Marine units fought to remove the Japanese from Okinawa, a 60-mile-long island less than 500 miles from Japan. The

---

Occasion for Decision
What is the situation requiring a decision?

Goals, Values, Constraints
- What are my goals? What do I hope to accomplish?
- What do I value?
- What do I least want to happen?
- Primary Goals:
- Secondary Goals:

Alternatives
- What are the possible choices?
- Can a decision be avoided?

| Alternative 1: | Alternative 2: | Alternative 3: |
| Conventional military action* | Negotiation and diplomacy* | Shock use of atomic weapons* |

Possible or Probable Outcomes
- What are the possible or probable consequences of each alternative course of action?
- What are the perceived costs and benefits of alternative courses of action?
- In view of my goals, which consequences are best and worst in this situation?

Alternative 1:	Alternative 2:	Alternative 3:
• Good:	• Good:	• Good:
• Bad:	• Bad:	• Bad:

The Decision
- What choices should I make?
- What piece of information would most likely lead me to change my mind?

*These are the alternatives suggested by historian Herbert Feis. In addition, there were alternatives within each major option. Naval blockade, continued strategic bombardment, and military invasion of Japan were three courses of conventional military action considered by American leaders. Atomic weapons might be used by unannounced dropping, explicit warning, or demonstration in some unpopulated place. Russian mediation and giving the Japanese assurances concerning the Emperor were diplomatic options.

Figure 11.3   Matrix for decision making

fighting was bitter: 12,000 U.S. servicemen were killed and several thousand wounded; 80,000 Okinawan civilians were killed; 70,000 Japanese defenders were killed. Fewer than 300 Japanese soldiers were taken prisoner; hundreds of kamikaze—suicide plane—attacks were made on U.S. naval forces.

2. In April 1945, the Joint Chiefs of Staff (JCS) directed Admiral Nimitz and General MacArthur to make plans and preparations for attacking Japan. The Navy favored seizing positions on the China coast from which to blockade and bomb the Japanese home islands. Their belief was that Japan could be defeated without invasion. Admiral King pointed out that the Japanese would have many advantages if the Allies invaded the home islands—room for maneuver, difficult mountainous and familiar terrain, and close sources of supply.

The Army believed that blockade and bombing would be less costly than invasion but that there was no guarantee of success. Army planners argued that Germany had been intensively bombed for years without crippling effect. Moreover, the invasion of the China coast would also be costly in the number of casualties.

Commanding General Arnold of the Army Air Corps estimated "that the military and economic capacity of the Japanese nation can be destroyed by an effective dropping, on Japan, of 1,600,000 tons of bombs."

3. The JCS's plans for invading Kyushu and Honshu (presented to Truman on June 18) called for 767,000 American troops; casualty rates were projected to be about 35 percent, or 268,000 killed and wounded.

4. An Army opinion poll showed that 66 percent of American soldiers in the southwest Pacific believed that eighteen months duty was enough—such men should be rotated home. They were experiencing a sense of hopelessness and despair over the prospect of apparently endless combat duty.

5. To mass sufficient manpower for the invasion, American troops would be transferred from Europe. General Marshall warned that "war weariness in the United States may demand the return home of those who have fought long and well in the European war regardless of the effect of such a return on the prosecution of the Japanese war."

6. The Allied policy of Unconditional Surrender, originally announced at Casablanca (1943) by FDR and Churchill to assuage Stalin's misgivings about his allies, stated that the Allies would not negotiate terms of surrender with their enemies. By 1945, many U.S. leaders viewed this policy to be a major obstacle to inducing the Japanese to call it quits. The primary issue was that the unconditional surrender policy offered the Japanese no guarantees concerning the fate of their emperor or the imperial system. The policy was also seen to have increased Japanese resistance. In addition, a number of Allied pronouncements during the war strongly implied that the emperor would be deposed at the end of the war.

7. In July 1945, U.S. intelligence intercepted coded message traffic between Tokyo and the Japanese ambassador to the Soviet Union. Analyses of those messages revealed that Japanese leaders were anxious for the Soviets to mediate diplomatic

negotiations for peace between them and the Allies. Secretary of the Navy James Forrestal concluded after reading the intercepts that the Japanese cabinet appeared to have decided "that the war must be fought with all the vigor and bitterness of which the nation is capable so long as the only alternative is unconditional surrender."

8. Early 1945 found the Manhattan Project (the top-secret, $600 million per year project to develop an atomic weapon) working at desperate speed to complete its work. A successful test of the bomb was achieved on July 16 in New Mexico. Truman, in Potsdam, was tremendously buoyed by the news.

9. Physicist Leo Szilard wrote the following account of a meeting he had had with Secretary of State Byrnes on the eve of the Potsdam Conference:

> *The question of whether the bomb should be used in the war against Japan came up for discussion. Byrnes did not argue that it was necessary to use the bomb against the cities of Japan in order to win the war. He knew at that time, as the rest of the Government knew, that Japan was essentially defeated, and that we could win the war in another six months. At that time Mr. Byrnes was much concerned about the spreading of Russian influence in Europe. . . . Mr. Byrnes' concern about Russia I fully shared, but his view that our possessing and demonstrating the bomb would make Russia more manageable in Europe I was not able to share.*

10. Before the A-bomb test, American military planners had clearly desired Soviet participation in the Asian war, particularly to keep Japanese forces in Manchuria occupied. After the test, Soviet participation appeared unnecessary, if not undesirable. The Soviets indicated they would declare war on Japan by mid-August.

11. After the defeat of Germany and the discovery that they had not been close to having an atomic weapon, some of the scientists working on the Manhattan Project had doubts about its use. Leo Szilard circulated a petition which said in part:

> *The military advantages and the saving of American lives achieved by the sudden use of atomic bombs against Japan may be out-weighed by the ensuing loss of confidence and by a wave of horror and repulsion sweeping over the rest of the world and perhaps even dividing public opinion at home. . . . a demonstration of the new weapon might best be made . . . on the desert or a barren island . . . after such a demonstration the weapon might perhaps be used against Japan if the sanction of the United Nations (and of public opinion at home) were obtained.*

12. Scientist Arthur Compton, member of a panel established to advise the Interim Committee formed by Truman in May 1945 to develop atomic policy, described discussions about alternative uses of the atomic bomb:

> *If a bomb were exploded in Japan with previous notice, the Japanese air power was still adequate to give serious interference. . . . It was now evident that when the time came for the bombs to be used we should have only one of them available, followed afterwards by others at all-too-long intervals. . . . Though the possibility of a demonstration that would not destroy human lives was attractive, no one could suggest a way in which it could be made so convincing that it would be likely to stop the war.*

Questions

1. Fill out the decision-making matrix based on the information Truman and his advisors had at their disposal. What would your decision have been? Do you think Truman's decision was justified?

2. Did the decision-making exercise help clarify the issues as contemporaries saw them? Did this exercise help you empathize with Truman and his contemporaries?

Part 2

Historians do not simply want to know what contemporaries thought of their situation. They want to know the whole story insofar as it can be ascertained. To gain perspective on the decision to use atomic weapons, we must widen our net and find evidence that contemporaries could not be aware of: information about the Japanese military situation as they saw it; the disposition of the Japanese government; what happened as a result of dropping the bomb.

As you read the items below, think about how each might affect the view you developed above.

1. Japanese Air Force General Noboru Tazoe described their plan for meeting the expected invasion to American officials after the war:

The air force plan was to attack the Allied fleet by Kamikaze planes. . . . We expected annihilation of our entire air force, but we felt that it was our duty. The army and navy each had 4,000–5,000 planes for this purpose. . . . We thought we could win the war by using Kamikaze planes on the ships offshore; the ground forces would handle those which got through. Based on the Leyte and Okinawa experiences, it was contemplated that one out of four planes would sink or damage an Allied ship.

2. Commander of the U.S. Army Air Corps summarized the effects of conventional bombing of Japan, which began in November 1944, as follows:

We had hit some 60 Japanese cities with our regular H.E. (High Explosive) and incendiary bombs, and as a result of our raids, about 241,000 people had been killed, 313,000 wounded, and about 2,333,000 homes destroyed. Our B-29's had destroyed most of the Japanese industries and, with the laying of mines, which prevented the arrival of incoming cargoes of critical items, had made it impossible to carry on a large-scale war. . . . Accordingly, it always appeared to us that, atomic bomb or no atomic bomb, the Japanese were already on the verge of collapse.

3. The U.S. Strategic Bombing Survey was established to evaluate the effects of strategic bombing on Germany and Japan. They concluded:

The Hiroshima and Nagasaki atomic bombs did not defeat Japan, nor by the testimony of the enemy leaders who ended the war did they persuade Japan to accept unconditional surrender. . . . The impact of the Hiroshima attack was to bring further urgency and lubrication to the machinery of achieving peace. . . . in all probability prior to 1 November 1945, Japan would have surrendered even if the atomic bombs had not been dropped, even if Russia had not entered the war, and even if no invasion had been planned or contemplated.

4. Atomic physicist Edward Teller regretted that he had not circulated Leo Szilard's petition among the scientists and engineers at Los Alamos. In his recollections, he remained convinced there were alternatives to direct military use of the bomb.

We could have exploded the bomb at a very high altitude over Tokyo in the evening. Triggered at a high altitude, the bomb would have created a sudden, frightening daylight over the city. But it would have killed no one. After the bomb had been demonstrated . . . we could have told the Japanese what it was and what would happen if another atomic bomb were detonated at low altitude.

5. Secretary of War Henry Stimson, writing in 1947, was without regret for his part in the decision to use the bomb.

My chief purpose was to end the war in victory with the least possible cost in the lives of the men in the armies which I had helped to raise. In light of the alternatives which, on a fair estimate, were open to use I believe that no man, in our position and subject to our responsibilities, holding in his hand a weapon of such possibilities for accomplishing this purpose and saving those lives, could have failed to use it and afterwards looked his countrymen in the face. . . . this deliberate, premeditated destruction was our least abhorrent choice. The destruction of Hiroshima and Nagasaki put an end to the Japanese war. It stopped the fire raids, and the strangling blockade; it ended the ghastly specter of a clash of great land armies.

6. A *Fortune* Magazine survey published in December 1945 asked Americans about their feelings concerning use of the atomic bomb. Only 4.5 percent believed that they should not have been used at all, 13.8 percent thought that a demonstration should have been made, 53.5 percent believed that the bombs should have been used as they in fact had been, and 22.7 percent thought even more bombs should have been dropped "before Japan had a chance to surrender."

7. In 1965, J. Robert Oppenheimer, director of the Los Alamos laboratory that produced the first bombs, was asked his feelings about the use of the bombs. He said in part:

I have a deep, continuing, haunting sense of the damage done to European culture by the two world wars. The existence of the bomb has reduced the chance of World War III and has given us valid hope. . . . I believe it was an error that Truman did not ask Stalin to carry on further talks with Japan, and also that the warning to Japan was completely inadequate. But I also think that it was a damn good thing that the bomb was developed. . . . I only regret that it was not done two years earlier. It would have saved a million or more lives.

8. In 1981, Paul Fussell wrote in the Washington Post:

I was a 21-year-old second lieutenant leading a rifle platoon . . . [and] although still officially in one piece, I had already been wounded in the leg and back severely enough to be adjudged, after the war, 40 percent disabled. But even if my legs buckled whenever I jumped out of the back of a truck, my condition was held to be satisfactory for whatever lay ahead. When the bombs dropped [and news circulated that the invasion would not take place] . . . we cried with relief and joy. We were going to live. We were going to grow up to adulthood after all.

9. Robert C. Batchelder argued that there were two ways of morally judging the decision to use atomic weapons. In his words:

Two fundamental ways of judging the morality of the use of the atomic bomb appeared during 1945 and 1946. The first was (in the broadest sense) utilitarian; the primary concern of those using this approach was the consequences of the act in question. Will the war be shortened? How many lives will be lost? Will long-term consequences be good or evil? The method is calculative: good and evil consequences are balanced one against the other, and the right act is that which produces the most good—or, at any rate, the least evil. America's leaders used this method in determining to drop the atomic bomb on Japan. It was the choice . . . of the lesser evil. . . .

The second basic ethical approach to the question of the atomic bombing of Japan was formalistic: it was concerned with the rightness or wrongness of the act in itself. What determines the rightness or wrongness of an act is not its consequences but its inherent quality. If the act conforms to an objective moral standard, it is permissible; if not, it is forbidden or condemned. The standard to be applied in the case of Hiroshima may be summed up in the commandment "Thou shalt not attack noncombatants directly." . . .

10. Approximately 350,000 people were believed to have been in Hiroshima on August 6. It is difficult to establish the number of deaths caused by the bomb, but authorities believe 140,000 people died by the end of 1945. One survivor described the moment the bomb fell as follows:

Was it the flash that came first, or the sound of the explosion, tearing up my insides? I don't remember. I was thrown to the ground, pinned to the earth, and immediately the world began to collapse around me, on my head, my shoulders. I couldn't see anything. It was completely dark. I thought of my three children, who had been evacuated to the country to be safe from the raids. I couldn't move; debris kept falling, beams and tiles piled up on top of me.

Finally I did manage to crawl free. There was a terrible smell in the air. . . . I rubbed my nose and mouth hard with a towel. To my horror, I found that the skin of my face had come off in the towel. (Guillain 1980)

11. Survivors, called *hibakusha*, suffered both physical and psychological damage. Many were treated as outcasts. The girl described in the following story was unusual, in that her fiance did not abandon her:

Many hibakusha *felt they had been set apart by the bomb. They felt alienated, too damaged to live whole lives. Among these was Fumiko Monshita. . . . Her sweetheart returned while she was in the hospital recovering from radiation illness. He visited her daily and still wanted to marry her. She felt she had to refuse him. All over the city women who had been pregnant and close to the hypocenter at the time of the bombing were giving birth to mentally retarded babies with abnormally small head circumferences. . . . Her sweetheart wanted to marry and became very angry at Fumiko's refusal. . . . She remained adamant. She "loved him too much to marry" and perhaps to perpetuate "A-bomb disease" into another generation. (Wyden 1984, 335)*

12. Shinzo Hamai served as Hiroshima's mayor for twenty years, working to rebuild the city. He said:

I think the atomic bomb was an inhuman weapon and should never have been used. But the bomb was dropped during wartime, and of course such things can happen in war, so I understand how America came to use it. But what I cannot understand— and what we in Hiroshima greatly resent—is Truman's claim that he did the right thing in dropping the bomb and that he has no regrets. (Lifton 1967)

Questions

1. Taking all the evidence together, how would you judge the decision to drop the atomic bombs on Japan? Write a position paper expressing your judgment concerning this situation.

2. Analyze this activity's use of primary source documents, how it distinguishes empathy and perspective, and the simulated decision making. What are the activity's strengths and weaknesses? With your classmates, explore ways to enhance the strengths and improve upon the weaknesses.

WHAT HISTORY DO WE TEACH?

Deciding what history to teach is a complicated issue. Factors affecting teachers' decisions include the scantiness of instructional time, the constraints imposed by school district or state mandates and standardized tests, the dearth of suitable instructional materials, and the lack of time for planning classroom activities, grading papers, guiding individual projects, and the like. In addition, selection is influenced by one's views concerning the purposes of history. Last but not least, *how* a teacher organizes instruction also has implications for *what* is taught. As a teacher facing numerous choices that will profoundly influence the instructional environment in your classroom, you will find that content and pedagogy intersect at every turn.

Among the considerations history teachers should think about when organizing instruction are how to engage students with history, how to ensure that students are active learners, how to provide for depth rather than simply coverage, and how to use such materials as textbooks and primary sources. Teachers must also think about ensuring that multiple perspectives are presented and that several varieties of history—especially social, local, and family history—are included in the course.

Engaging Students with History

One of the primary challenges you will face as a history teacher will be to engage your students in a meaningful dialogue with the past. For history to have personal value for students, the teacher must take into account students' current interests and concerns, making the connection between students and history as explicit as possible. That is, of course, not to say that student interest should be the only determinant of what history topics you teach or how you teach them. Students often cannot imagine what the relevance is of, say, the Reformation, the French Revolution, or any number of other possible subjects. Yet the topic may have immense power and relevance.

Given that you will have only a limited amount of time with any given class of students, and given that such time constraints preclude your teaching every topic or concept you might desire, engaging students with what they do study—to promote their desire to engage with the past beyond the confines of your course—may be the most important instructional outcome you can obtain.

Students as Active Learners

This principle of instruction addresses a number of perceived problems in history instruction, including engagement. Teaching that emphasizes facts and the textbook puts students in a passive role and conveys the impression that history is a settled story. The avoidance of controversy makes the story told rather unreal, if not downright suspect. Finally, the message often conveyed to students is that the textbook assignment or the worksheet will be easy—that little effort is necessary to accomplish the learning task. This belies the difficulty of authentic intellectual work (see, for example, Newmann 1988).

Myriad instructional strategies *do* actively engage students in authentic work, promoting active student learning without slighting content. Simulations, role plays, mock trials, case studies, small-group cooperative learning projects, and individual research projects can all actively engage students in their own learning and meaning construction.

Depth versus Coverage

As Fred Newmann (1988) has observed, a fundamental problem in the high school curriculum is that we try to teach too much. Students rarely get the opportunity to study any topic in depth. Indeed, Newmann argues, we are addicted to coverage.

The addiction to coverage is not lost on students. As John, a student interviewed about his social studies courses, observed:

> *The course in European history is a classic example. We covered 2,000 years. Every week we were assigned to cover a 30-page chapter. The teacher is a stickler for dates and facts. We had 50 dates a week to memorize. The pity of it all is that now we don't remember any of them. . . . I'd like to have worked where you dig in depth, but it's a double-sided sword, because if you're constantly going in-depth about each thing you come across, then you're not going to get very far. It's quantity versus quality. The only reasonable thing is you've got to find a balance. . . . (Newmann 1988, 346)*

The addiction to coverage affects students and teachers alike. As John implied, survey coverage is often a waste of time. Students memorize material for quizzes and tests but retain little of that information. Teachers feel guilty about leaving out so much despite their best efforts at coverage, and they are apologetic about their students' poor understanding of what they try to teach them. Perhaps most important, superficial coverage promotes habits of mindlessness, for classrooms become places where students learn unexplained nonsense, where students cannot explore important topics in depth, and where teachers' talents for exploring and elaborating important understandings are squelched.

For Newmann, depth must replace coverage as a primary principle for organizing instruction. Depth is more likely to facilitate lasting retention and transfer of knowledge, to foster thoughtfulness, and to help students cope with the knowledge explosion.

Obstacles to realizing depth over coverage include the legitimate need for coverage, in the sense that students must be exposed to new material; the mounting pressure on schools and teachers to prove their effectiveness through tests that tend to measure acquisition of superficial bits of information; teachers' socialization for coverage, in that few of us have had many in-depth experiences ourselves; students' expectation that a vast number of bits and pieces of information will be covered; and the lack of curriculum materials that promote in-depth study.

Problems with Textbooks

There is widespread agreement that textbooks are a problem, although less agreement about the nature of the problem (see Fitzgerald 1979; Graves and Slater 1986; and Sewall 1988). The critics castigate textbooks for poor or bland writing, an emphasis on coverage over depth of treatment, omissions of all sorts, absence of any discernible story line, and absence of point of view.

Many factors shape textbooks into the compendia of information they typically are. State and district curriculum guides are highly variable; publishers want to sell their books in every available market. Every teacher or textbook selection committee wants a topic of special interest included in the text.

Textbooks are the most readily available of curriculum materials, and many people—including parents and administrators—clearly like them. It also seems certain that a textbook will be assigned (or available) for use in your teaching job. The question is, What are you going to do with it?

Primary Sources

This chapter has emphasized using primary historical sources. As we grapple with original sources, we can hardly escape the conclusion that these documents tell us, in contemporaries' own words, about real people who face real problems and issues in real situations. We discover that they, like ourselves, make decisions and solve problems with less-than-perfect information at their disposal; they did not know, any more than we can know, what the outcomes of their actions or solutions might be. We also learn that these people, no matter how different they may be in some respects, are not totally unlike us either. We also discover that human history is not inevitable; it is ultimately about humans making choices.

Although primary sources help us empathize with people in the past, many students have difficulty dealing with them. Primary sources are often written in difficult language, but many edited and modernized primary sources are available. Teachers should feel free to edit and update language to make sources usable with the widest possible range of students.

Of course, instructionally useful primary sources do not just fall into the teacher's lap. Over time, you will collect many, through trial and error finding those most useful with students.

ACTIVITY

Analyzing a Lesson

Review the activity on pages 294–301, and analyze it from the following perspectives:

1. How could you engage students in this activity?
2. How might you tailor the lesson to assure that students have an active role?
3. The activity shows one approach to depth. What trade-offs with coverage must be made when conducting an activity of this sort? What would you omit to allow time to conduct this activity?
4. How might the activity be linked with a U.S. or world history textbook?
5. Do any of the primary sources need work to make them useful for students? What specifically could you do?

Multiple Perspectives

History must be approached from a multiplicity of perspectives. History is not simply a single story on which all (or even most) contemporary observers or historians agree. The multiplicity of perspectives necessitates debate, contention, weighing facts, perspectives, and truth claims of various kinds. The use of multiple perspectives will take from teachers some of the burden of being the "sole source of information" or "the font of wisdom." Their inclusion will also increase the likelihood that students will find people and perspectives with which they can identify. Multiple perspectives can be brought to bear no matter what textbook you use or what district mandates you must follow (e.g., see Holt 1989).

Social History as a Way to Personalize History

History has often been criticized for being essentially the story of how the victors won and how the elites ruled. This tendency has been called "enshrined history."

An outpouring of scholarship since the mid-1970s has been aimed at just this problem. Social history in particular is predicated on the idea of writing the history of all those formerly left out of the story of victors and elites. What social history has discovered is the story—the multiplicity of stories—of ordinary people and how they made their own history. We now know a good deal more than we used to about the history of women, of minority groups of all kinds, of work groups, of class and other social groups, among others. We understand as never before that people, no matter what their circumstances, are active creators of their own lives, worlds, and meanings—they are instrumental in making their own histories. And now we have a good deal of material to draw upon for telling those stories (see, for example, Stearns 1982; Gardner and Adams 1983; Rosenzwieg and Stearns 1985).

More Local and Family History

One of the ways history teachers have tried to personalize history instruction is to spend at least some time on local history (Downey and Metcalf 1982; Kyvig and Marty 1982). This approach has a number of virtues, including making history more concrete and easier for students to grasp.

As with all techniques and approaches, some dangers lurk here. Local history can be parochial when it is done "for its own sake" or is so narrowly focused that one loses sight of the larger context of which it was a part. Local history may be filiopietistic when it is an uncritical celebration of the locality, group, or persons under investigation. However, if local history is approached from some larger frame of reference and in the spirit of honest, critical investigation, it has many virtues. It is certainly a useful vehicle for building partnerships with the local community in which the school resides.

Family history has similar virtues and potential pitfalls. However, it has two additional virtues that may recommend its inclusion in history courses. First, family history is an excellent means by which students can come to grips with time and chronology. Tracing one's ancestors, say through birth dates and turning points in family history, lends itself to cross-comparison with events and processes of a more general significance. This approach is one way to make the time perspective more concrete for students.

Second, family history is a means of making more personal the processes of world history. This may be its primary advantage over local history as an instructional strategy for world history courses. It seems safe to say that many, if not most, of our classrooms have become demographic microcosms of the world's people and cultures. Family history projects of various kinds can tap that "living social studies text" to good effect (e.g., see Lichtman 1978; Berrier 1982).

Designing a Social or Local/Family History Unit

Working in small groups or individually, design a unit of instruction for use in U.S. history, world history, Western civilization, or another pertinent history course. The unit should consist of at least one week's work and should be complete, including objectives, procedures, and all necessary materials. The unit should provide for multiple perspectives and should cover a topic from social history or local/family history.

As you construct the unit, pay particular attention to such things as student engagement; how the unit will nurture depth of understanding; what strategies you will

Figure 11.4   Oral history projects can enhance local history units

use; what work students will do; what use, if any, you will make of the textbook; what primary sources you will use and whether they need editing or some explanation.

After completing the unit, exchange units with other students for their critique and feedback.

ACTIVITY ## Interviewing for a Job Teaching History

Clarifying your beliefs about the nature of history and how to teach it may be essential for your performance at your first job interview. In groups of five or fewer students, develop a set of questions you would anticipate a search committee might ask a prospective history teacher in a job interview. After you have developed these questions, refer to your journal and other notes you have made during your work in this chapter. Use them to help you prepare for the interview.

Next, conduct simulated job interviews. One way of structuring the activity is to have one group serve as the interview team for another group. Persons serving on the interview team should probe the responses made by the interviewees.

After everyone has been interviewed, discuss the activity with the whole class.

Reflecting on the Chapter

The preceding exercise was designed, in part, to bring closure to the chapter. It was also designed as an untraditional way to assess or evaluate your work on this chapter. How well do you think the activity achieved this second purpose?

References

Aptheker, H. *American Negro Slave Revolts*. New York: International Publishers, 1943, 1969.

Bennett, P. S. *What Happened on Lexington Green? An Inquiry into the Nature and Methods of History*. Menlo Park, Calif.: Addison Wesley, 1970.

Berrier, G. G. "Doing Family History Projects with High School Students." In *Teaching American History: New Directions,* ed. M. T. Downey, Bulletin 67, 40–41. Washington, D.C.: National Council for the Social Studies, 1982.

Blassingame, J. W. *The Slave Community: Plantation Life in the Ante-Bellum South*. New York: Oxford University Press, 1972, rev. 1979.

Carr, E. H. *What Is History?* New York: Random House Vintage, 1961.

Cartwright, W. H., and R. L. Watson, Jr., eds. *The Reinterpretation of American History and Culture*. Washington, D.C.: National Council for the Social Studies, 1973.

Cherryholmes, C. "Social Studies for Which Century?" *Social Education* 54, no. 7 (1990): 438–42.

Commager, H. S., and R. H. Muessig. *The Study and Teaching of History*. Columbus, Ohio: Charles E. Merrill, 1980.

Conrad, A. H., and J. R. Meyer. "The Economics of Slavery in the Antebellum South." *Journal of Political Economy* 66, no. 2 (April 1958): 95–130.

Dailey, G., L. Englehardt, and J.R. Giese, eds. "Bicentennial of the U.S. Census Special Edition." *Social Education* 53, no. 7 (1989).

Downey, M. T., and F. D. Metcalf. *Using Local History in the Classroom*. Nashville: American Association of State and Local History, 1982.

Elkins, S. M. *Slavery: A Problem in American Institutional and Intellectual Life*. Chicago: University of Chicago Press, 1959.

Feis, H. *The Atomic Bomb and the End of the War in the Pacific*. Princeton: Princeton University Press, 1961.

Fischer, D. H. *Historians' Fallacies: Toward a Logic of Historical Thought*. New York: Harper & Row, 1970.

Fitzgerald, F. *America Revised*. New York: Random Vintage, 1979.

Foner, E. "Slavery, the Civil War, and Reconstruction." In *The New American History,* ed. Foner, 73–92. Philadelphia: Temple University Press, 1990a.

———, ed. *The New American History*. Philadelphia: Temple University Press, 1990b, for the American Historical Association.

Gardner, J. B., and G. R. Adams, eds. *Ordinary People and Everyday Life*. Nashville: American Association for State and Local History, 1983.

Genovese, E. *Roll, Jordan, Roll: The World the Slaves Made*. New York: Pantheon, 1974.

Graves, M. F., and W. H. Slater. "Could Textbooks Be Better Written and Would It Make A Difference?" *American Educator* (Spring 1986): 35–41.

Guillain, R. *I Saw Tokyo Burning*. New York: Doubleday, 1980.

Gustavson, C. *A Preface to History*. New York: McGraw-Hill, 1955.

Gutman, H. G. *The Black Family in Slavery and Freedom, 1750-1925*. New York: Pantheon, 1975.

Hofstadter, R. "U.B. Phillips and the Plantation Legend." *Journal of Negro History* 24, no. 2 (1944): 109–24.

———. *The Age of Reform*. New York: Knopf, 1955.

———. *The Progressive Historians: Turner, Parrington, and Beard*. New York: Random Vintage, 1969.

Holt, T. C. "American History." In *Charting a Course,* 49–52. Washington, D.C.: National Commission on Social Studies in the Schools, 1989.

———. "African-American History." In *The New American History,* ed. E. Foner, 211–32. Philadelphia: Temple University Press, 1990.

Jones, J. *Labor of Love, Labor of Sorrow: Black Women, Work, and the Family from Slavery to the Present*. New York: Basic Books, 1985.

Joyner, C. *Down by the Riverside: A South Carolina Slave Community*. Urbana, Ill.: University of Illinois Press, 1984.

Kammen, M. "Introduction: The Historian's Vocation and the State of the Discipline in the United States." In *The Past Before Us,* ed. Kammen, 19–46. Ithaca, N.Y.: Cornell University Press, 1980.

———. "Vanitas and the Historian's Vocation." In *The Promise of American History: Progress and Prospects,* ed. S. I. Kutler and S. N. Katz, 1–27. Baltimore: Johns Hopkins University Press, 1982.

———, ed. *The Past Before Us: Contemporary Historical Writing in the United States*. Ithaca, N.Y.: Cornell University Press, 1980b.

Kliebard, H. "Compromise and Diversity in the American High School." *History of Education Quarterly* 27, no. 1 (Spring 1987): 89–100.

Kraus, M., and D. D. Joyce. *The Writing of American History*. Norman: University of Oklahoma Press, 1985.

Kutler, S. I., and S. N. Katz, eds. *The Promise of American History: Progress and Prospects*. Baltimore: Johns Hopkins University Press, 1982.

Kyvig, D. E., and M. A. Marty. *Nearby History: Exploring the Past around You*. Nashville: American Association for State and Local History, 1982.

Lichtman, A. J. *Your Family History*. New York: Random House Vintage, 1978.

Lifton, R. J. *Death in Life*. New York: Random House, 1967.

Lowenthal, D. *The Past Is a Foreign Country*. Cambridge: Cambridge University Press, 1985.

Mink, L. O. "The Autonomy of Historical Understanding." In *Louis O. Mink: Historical Understanding*, ed. B. Fay, E. O. Golob, and R. T. Vann. Ithaca, N.Y.: Cornell University Press, 1987.

Newmann, F. M. "Can Depth Replace Coverage in the High School Curriculum?" *Phi Delta Kappan* 69, no. 5 (1988): 345-48.

Phillips, U. B. *American Negro Slavery: A Survey of the Supply, Employment and Control of Negro Labor as Determined by the Plantation Regime*. New York: D. Appleton and Company, 1918.

Pratt, D. *The Vital Past: Writings on the Uses of History*. Stephen Vaughn, ed. Athens: University of Georgia Press, 1985.

Raboteau, A. J. *Slave Religion: The "Invisible Institution" in the Antebellum South*. New York: Oxford University Press, 1978.

Rogers, P. J. "History." In *Philosophy of Education and the Curriculum*, ed. K. Dixon, 75–134. Oxford, England: Pergamon Press, 1972.

Rosenzwieg, L. W., and P. N. Stearns. *Themes in Modern Social History*. Pittsburgh: Carnegie-Mellon University Press, 1985.

Schlesinger, A. M., Jr. *The Bitter Heritage*. New York: Fawcett, 1966.

Sewall, G. T. "American History Textbooks: Where Do We Go from Here?" *Phi Delta Kappan* 69, no. 8 (1988): 553–58.

Skotheim, R. A., ed. *The Historian and the Climate of Opinion*. Reading, Mass.: Addison-Wesley, 1969.

Stampp, K. M. *The Peculiar Institution: Slavery in the Ante-Bellum South*. New York: Knopf, 1956.

Starobin, R. S. *Industrial Slavery in the Old South*. New York: Oxford University Press, 1970.

Stavrianos, L. S. *Lifelines from Our Past: A New World History*. New York: Pantheon, 1989.

Stearns, P. N. "Social History and the Teaching of History." In *Teaching American History: New Directions*, ed. M. T. Downey, Bulletin No. 67, 51–63. Washington, D.C.: National Council for the Social Studies, 1982).

Steffens, L. *The Shame of the Cities*. Chicago: McClure, Phillips, 1904.

Stephens, L. D. *Probing the Past: A Guide to the Study and Teaching of History*. Boston: Allyn & Bacon, 1974.

Stockley, D. "Empathetic Reconstruction in History and History Teaching." In *History and Theory: Studies in the Philosophy of History*. Beiheft 22, 1983.

Wade, R. C. *Slavery in the Cities: The South, 1820–1860*. New York: Oxford University Press, 1964.

Wise, G. *American Historical Explanations: A Strategy for Grounded Inquiry*. Homewood, Ill.: The Dorsey Press, 1973.

Wyden, P. *Day One: Before Hiroshima and After*. New York: Simon & Schuster, 1984.

Teaching Resources

American Heritage Teacher's Guide. New York: American Heritage. Published monthly.

American History Re-creations. Lakeside, Calif.: Interact, 1984.

Building a History Curriculum: Guidelines for Teaching History in Schools. Westlake, Ohio: Bradley Commission, 1989.

Chronos. Watertown, Mass.: Tom Snyder Productions, n.d. Timeline software.

Communism and the Cold War. Warren, N.J.: Optical Data, n.d. Videodisc.

Davidson, J. W., and M. H. Lytle. *After the Fact: The Art of Historical Detection*. Atlanta: Random House, 1986.

Downey, M. T., ed. *Teaching American History: New Directions*. Washington, D.C.: National Council for the Social Studies, 1982.

————. *History in the Schools*. Washington, D.C.: National Council for the Social Studies, 1985.

Escalation: Decision Making in the Vietnam War. South Hamilton, Mass.: Critical Thinking Press, 1991. Computer simulation.

Family Tree Maker. Fremont, Calif.: Banner Blue, 1989. Software.

Giese, J. R., L. S. Parisi, and L. R. Singleton. *A Humanities Approach to U.S. History: Activities and Resources for Secondary Teachers*. Boulder, Colo.: Social Science Education Consortium, 1990.

Giese, J. R., and L. R. Singleton. *U.S. History: A Resource Book for Secondary Schools*, Vols. 1 and 2. Santa Barbara, Calif.: ABC-Clio, 1989.

GTV: A Geographic Perspective in American History. Warren, N.J.: Optical Data, 1991. Videodisc.

Hawke, S. D., and J. E. Davis. *Seeds of Change*. Menlo Park, Calif.: Addison-Wesley, 1992.

History Teacher, The. Long Beach, Calif.: Society for History Education. Published quarterly.

Journal of World History. Philadelphia: World History Association, Department of History, Drexel University. Published semiannually.

Kyvig, D. E., ed. *Nearby History Series*. Nashville: American Association for State and Local History, 1986–.

Ladenburg, T. *SSEC American History Series*. Boulder, Colo.: Social Science Education Consortium, 1989–1992.

Lockwood, A. L., and D. E. Harris. *Reasoning with Democratic Values: Ethical Problems in United States History*. New York: Teachers College Press, 1985.

Magazine of History. Bloomington, Ind.: Organization of American Historians. Published quarterly.

National Center for History in the Schools, University of California at Los Angeles, Moore Hall 231, 405 Hilgard Avenue, Los Angeles, CA 90024-1521.

National Council for History Education, 26915 Westwood Road, Suite A-2, Westlake, OH 44145-4656.

National Endowment for the Humanities, 1100 Pennsylvania Avenue, NW, Washington, DC 20506.

National History Day, University of Maryland, Caroline Hall, College Park, MD 20742.

Point of View. New York: Scholastic, 1990. Computer database.

Public Issues Series. Boulder, Colo.: Social Science Education Consortium, 1988–1993.

Resource Packets: Meeting the People of the Past. Sturbridge, Mass.: Old Sturbridge Village, n.d.

SIRS: National Archives Supplementary Teaching Units. Boca Raton, Fla.: Social Issues Resource Series, 1985–.

Smithsonian Institution, Office of Elementary and Secondary Education, Arts and Industries Building 1163, MRC 402, Washington, DC 20560. Newsletters, fact sheets, curriculum resources.

Teaching History: A Journal of Methods. Emporia, Kans.: Emporia State University. Published semiannually.

Teaching with Documents: Using Primary Sources from the National Archives. Washington, D.C.: National Archives and Records Administration and National Council for the Social Studies, 1989.

Western Civilization and World History. Annapolis, Md.: Instructional Resource Corporation, n.d. Videodiscs.

Women's History Curriculum Guide. Windsor, Calif.: National Women's History Project, n.d.

INTEGRATING THE CURRICULUM

James C. Schott

ACTIVITY LIST

• • •

ACTIVITY

Writing to the Future

As a class, select a recent newspaper headline. Imagine that your child was born on the day the headline appeared. Give this child a name and write her or him a letter to be read on her or his twenty-first birthday. In the letter, explain the meaning of the event referred to in the headline.

Pick a partner and trade letters. Now imagine that you are the child reading the letter twenty-one years from now. After reading the letter, list all the questions about the event you would want to have answered. Work with your partner to consolidate your lists.

Next, join with another pair and share your lists; make whatever revisions you think are necessary. In conjunction with the other members of your group, decide what specific sources you would use to answer the questions. Finally, for each question, decide if any of the academic disciplines would contribute useful information. List each of the disciplines you think would be helpful and the information you think it would provide.

In a class conversation, explore the following question: How do the academic disciplines hinder the social studies curriculum and how do they make a positive contribution to it?

In your journal, write a reaction page beginning "Based upon this activity, I believe the role the academic disciplines should play in the social studies curriculum is . . ."

INTRODUCTION

It is difficult to find an area of contemporary educational writing in which curricular integration is not at least mentioned as part of the prescription for fixing the ills of schooling. "The reform movement of the 1990s calls for an integration of school subjects: a conceptual convergence of the natural sciences, mathematics, and technology with social and behavioral sciences and the humanities into a coherent whole. A unity of knowledge will make it possible for students to take learning from different fields of study and use it to view human problems in their fullness from several perspectives" (Hurd 1991). Schooling that is less fragmented and more grounded in students' personal knowledge, integration advocates argue, will more effectively engage students in school and in their own learning. The reemergence of integration can be seen in creation of interdisciplinary teams at the middle school level and in development of core programs at the high school level.

Yet the rhetoric of integration has not been translated into practice in most American schools. One reason is the ongoing disagreement over what role the academic disciplines should play in the school curriculum, the question with which you grappled in the foregoing activity. Although the disciplines have had a persistent influence on the organization of curriculum and the education of teachers, scholars have often charged that the problems of fragmentation and disengagement stem not from the disciplines but from the poor quality of instruction in the classroom. The remedy proposed by scholars is not to eliminate or mix the disciplines but to better educate teachers in the disciplines so they will do justice to discipline-based knowledge. Many scholars believe that efforts to integrate the curriculum only dilute the potent discipline-based knowledge produced by scholars.

A second reason for the failure to implement integrated curricula is confusion about what *integration* means and how it can be achieved. This confusion makes it difficult for educators to develop an integrated curriculum and plan for its implementation, planning that must take into account such institutional barriers as scheduling and standardized testing.

Because many social studies educators see our field as inherently integrative, issues related to integration are particularly relevant, touching as they do on such fundamental questions as what to teach and how to teach it. The purposes of this chapter are to explore with you the relationship between the academic disciplines and the curriculum; to consider varying definitions of *integration*, or points along an integration continuum; and to present some models of integration that are currently being used in social studies.

THE ACADEMIC DISCIPLINES AND THE SCHOOL CURRICULUM

Philosophical Positions Regarding Knowledge and Integration

Academic disciplines create abstractions or models of some aspect of the real world. Within their limitations, the disciplines have generated useful methods of inquiry, standards of verification, and explanations of phenomena. It is no accident that these fields of study are called disciplines. The purpose of a discipline is to establish a set of rules, procedures, and standards by which scholars judge the validity and accuracy of propositions or findings generated by their colleagues. Disciplined study demands a rigor not usually found in everyday discourse or decision making.

Science and, by association, social science carry with them an aura of authority. The disciplines provide language and definitions of concepts that give an air of precision and objectivity to the way we communicate about the social world. Advocates of a curriculum that emphasizes discipline-based knowledge argue that "educators must recognize that the source of our understanding of the world, for better or worse, is rooted in the scholarly disciplines. Our knowledge of the world depends on the methodologies, questions and organization of knowledge implicit in the social sciences, history and the other humanities" (Woyach and Remy 1989, 9–10).

The characteristics of the social sciences, and the political clout of social scientists, have allowed the disciplines to dominate the school curriculum. Yet many educators see the disciplines as having a fragmenting and deadening effect on schools and students. Ernest Boyer (quoted in Brady 1989, 1) has lamented that "what students are asked to relate to in school [is] increasingly cut off from the human experiences subject matter is supposed to reflect." These observations have prompted the current widespread calls for curricular integration.

Yet the preeminent influence of the disciplines in shaping the school curriculum has also tended to frame the discourse about integration. Such terms as *interdisciplinary*, *multidisciplinary*, and *cross-disciplinary* imply that successfully combining the disciplines is the goal to be achieved. But there is an important distinction between saying that the object of integration is to "create learning experiences that demonstrate the relationship of the disciplines" (Jacobs 1989, 5) and saying that integration's purpose is to "address problems, issues, topics holistically to help students create meaning and order out of the world in which they find themselves" (Bellack 1978, 94).

Thus, we must look beyond the disciplines to beliefs about knowledge in order to define the purposes of integration and its relationship to the academic disciplines. Richard Pring (summarized in Court 1991, 4–5) outlined four distinct positions that will help you clarify the relationship between beliefs about the nature of knowledge and positions regarding curricular integration:

1. The essential unity of all knowledge: the belief that discipline distinctions are artificial and misrepresent the unity of all knowledge. A person of this persuasion is likely to support holistic curriculum proposals that begin with real-world concerns, perhaps resembling what Peter Elbow calls nondisciplinary courses. In such courses, students select a single particular and examine it from the widest possible range of conflicting models, metaphors, hypotheses, conceptual schemes, sets, and disciplines, seeking to develop powerful explanations of the particular instance (Elbow 1986, 9).

2. The problem-solving or inquiry method as the basis for integration: the belief that the school should not "prepackage" the connections a child is to make. Students must integrate their own experience through their inquiry. A person of this persuasion is likely to support a broad range of integration efforts, stressing use of the disciplines as resources in understanding the problem or issue, not as educational ends in themselves.

3. Broad fields of experience: the belief that there are three or four broad areas, such as humanities, mathematics, science, and the arts, which support each other and into which all subjects can be grouped. Someone of this persuasion would likely support interdisciplinary studies within each of the broad fields and between fields.

4. The interrelationships of the disciplines: the belief that distinct and autonomous forms of knowledge exist but are connected in complex conceptual ways. A person of this persuasion is not likely to be willing to combine disciplines, but would probably support programs in which a topic is studied from the perspectives of several disciplines, with each maintaining its separate integrity.

ACTIVITY

Reflecting on Instruction and the Nature of Knowledge

Divide a sheet of paper into fourths, designating each section for one of the views of knowledge just described. For each section, try to identify several courses you have taken in your university experience that reflected that view of knowledge.

Which section has the most courses listed? Which has the fewest? Were the courses in any particular section, as a group, more rewarding, engaging, or meaningful to you? Do you think your response to this group of courses can be linked to the professors' conception of knowledge? to your own conception of knowledge?

Return to the foregoing discussion of conceptions of knowledge. Which position best represents your beliefs about knowledge? Do you agree with how we indicate that that view of knowledge would affect positions regarding curricular integration? Write some thoughts on these questions in your journal and keep them in mind as you work through the rest of this chapter.

A Personal View of the Paradox

We face a paradox. On the one hand, we humans seem compelled to take things apart to figure out how they work. Children dismantle toys and can't get them together again. Biology students dissect frogs. Social scientists categorize human experience.

On the other hand, it seems, we have an equally strong desire to see things in their wholeness. The ecological movement strives to understand the interconnectedness of living things. The whole-language movement teaches that communicating is a complex process involving more than the discrete skills of translating words. Some social scientists have attempted to construct theories to explain all social interactions. And some educators, recognizing that the balkanization of knowledge in the curriculum leads to meaningless fragmentation, have attempted to find ways to put knowledge back together by integrating the curriculum.

Just as there is no way to reconstruct the frog on the dissecting table, however, there is no way to reconstruct reality from the bits and pieces of the individual disciplines. Social reality is more than the sum of the social sciences. The anthropologist Clyde Kluckholm (1985) succinctly described the limited ability of the disciplines, even en masse, to deal with reality:

> To some people with neat academic minds the fields of knowledge dealing with human behavior are laid out like a series of formal gardens with walls in between. . . . .Some scholars indeed visualized these high, tight walls as actually existing and defended their frontiers against all poachers. But in actual practice some walls were never built or were so low they were easily leaped over by the more intrepid students; others have crumbled in the past decade or two. . . . hence between and beyond the boundaries of the several social sciences, there is a vast no man's land.

In fact, what lies beyond the boundaries is the unity of experience—the perceptions, emotions, metaphors, and so on, that make up the wholeness of experience.

Social reality, as it is experienced, is not separable from the larger reality of weather, buildings, mountains, grass, and animals we face each day. The disciplines, whether the social sciences or the physical and biological sciences, create abstractions of reality that are useful analytical tools. Just as dissecting the frog will reveal information about the nature of the frog's internal organs in a way no other activity will, similarly the social sciences provide a means of categorizing experience and explaining relationships that contributes to our understanding. Nonetheless, when the scientist and the social scientist have finished their work, the object of their study is lifeless. There is little resemblance between the pieces of flesh and bone on the cutting table and the live swimming, jumping, basking animal in the pond.

Out of this paradox emerges an enduring controversy. The tension between the drive to dissect and the drive to understand reality in its entirety is an apt description of the way we humans experience the world and give meaning to what we experience. Brain-based learning research and constructivist psychology both support the view that searching for meaning in experience, developing patterns and relationships are natural human functions. Educators need to understand that school learning should both acknowledge and exploit these natural tendencies.

Borrowing from postmodern conceptions of the nature of reality and the writings of Alfred North Whitehead, Donald Oliver (1990) has drawn an important distinction between two ways of knowing—grounded knowing and technical knowing—that is helpful in thinking about the academic disciplines and their role in an integrated curriculum. According to Oliver, "grounded knowing apprehends (or metaphorically 'feels') the natural history in which events or occasions emerge and become. . . . So grounded knowing begins with and includes vague sensibilities, feelings, inarticulable thoughts and imagination, as well as the more precise and technical description of occasions as they come into being, as they exist, as they pass on."

Technical knowledge is distinct from grounded knowledge in that it begins with language describing sharply delineated qualities of events, with a defined set of events that can be precisely stated. "Technical knowledge comes out of our efforts to create highly controlled and managed settings, as in the case of human babies born in a hospital delivery room, although, of course, the fullness of the occasion is far more profound than the technical statement that ends up in a medical file." But the technical knowledge is utilitarian, predictable, efficient, adaptive, and comfortable. "Whatever its limitations, technical knowing is tremendously useful in the narrow utilitarian sense. It allows us to do business in the marketplace of people, products, and service" (Oliver 1990, 68).

Technical knowledge generated by the disciplines is the predominant and legitimate form of knowledge in schools. One of the consequences of dispensing only technical knowledge is that students do not consider school knowledge to be real knowledge. Integrative programs that simply attempt to weld the various disciplines together continue to miss the opportunity to provide students with meaningful "grounded" experiences.

ACTIVITY

Creating Visual Metaphors

Figure 12.1 shows the author's conception of the relationship between the disciplines and reality. Does this drawing represent your own beliefs? What visual metaphor would best represent your own views of this relationship? Display your sketch with those of your classmates. How many different conceptions were produced? How does creating and analyzing these metaphors contribute to your thinking about the role of the social science disciplines?

ACTIVITY

A Case Study of Curriculum Integration

Much of the confusion in defining integration arises because the term is used to describe diverse programs and approaches. The following account is based on a teacher's journal, kept while working on a committee to develop interdisciplinary curriculum. As you read these excerpts, try to create a map or continuum showing approaches to integration. Use Drake's ideas as a starting point, but also add ideas you developed in the previous section.

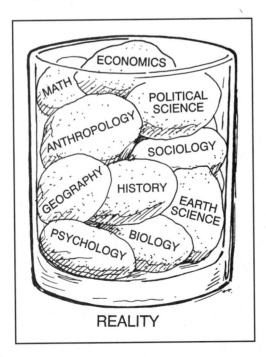

Figure 12.1   One conception of the relationship between the disciplines and reality.

INTEGRATING THE CURRICULUM:
HOW OUR TEAM DISSOLVED THE BOUNDARIES*
by Susan M. Drake

We were three men and three women, strangers to each other, selected from across the province to develop interdisciplinary curriculums funded by the Ontario Curriculum Superintendent's Cooperative. Each of us had expertise in a different subject area. We all had active contracts with different school boards. Our mandate was to extend the curriculum ideas in *Holistic Learning: A Teacher's Guide to Integrated Studies* (Miller, Cassie, and Drake 1990) at the middle school level by creating a curriculum that would focus on themes.

We spent nine days together over the course of a year developing integrated curriculums. When I reviewed the journal I kept as team leader, I found that the process we had undergone was clear.

Letting Go of Old Models

We had to let go of old models. We came to this realization again and again. Letting go can be a painful process, and when each of us came to a place where we couldn't find meaning, we would revert back to the way we knew best. . . .

If we had to characterize the curriculum process in one phrase, the best way to describe it would be "dissolving the boundaries." Each of us brought boundaries to this project; we saw in retrospect how artificial they were—they existed because of the ways in which we had each been taught to view the world. When we began to trust our own experience, we found that the boundaries dissolved in many different areas. . . .

The Multidisciplinary Experience

As we began building our curriculum, we tried to identify the subject areas involved in each teaching activity offered so that any teacher could pick up the document and see where he or she fit in. We ourselves represented English, history, geography, science, graphic arts, intermediate special education, physical and health education, and environmental studies. As we worked on a theme, we found we could easily see the place for "our" subject area, and that it was easy to develop teaching strategies.

We were able to include content from other disciplines also, but we found ourselves squeezing in such areas as mathematics that we weren't familiar with. When we involved a math teacher in the process, however, the natural place of math became obvious; we had been limited by our own narrow perspectives. So, while we began the project looking at curriculum building through the lens of our own areas of expertise, we eventually became able to see how some content from other areas could fit into the framework. Later, we realized this was our *multidisciplinary* approach (Figure 12.2).

The Interdisciplinary Experience

As we became more comfortable and actually got down to sharing strategies for a theme, we found there were fewer distinctions across subject areas than we had thought; indeed, content overlapped. These connections existed because of the theme being explored, not because the subject areas were formally related. This discovery led us to let go of the notion that we should teach certain facts in certain grades. We carefully labeled each activity, breaking it down into the subject areas that were involved. This seemed very important at the time; we wanted to make the document user-friendly and accessible to all. That we often had to struggle to break down an activity into different areas did not seem as important as the fact that we could do it. We later saw this as our *interdisciplinary* stage (Figure 12.3).

The Transdisciplinary Experience

After working with curriculum for several days, we began to see the futility of breaking things down into their smallest parts. The content and the theme were one and the same; there were no real diversions into subject areas unless we made them. This stage we labeled *transdisciplinary* (Figure 12.4). We abandoned the labeling of subject areas; that is, we erased the divisions we had created up until this point and let the activities stand by themselves. . . .

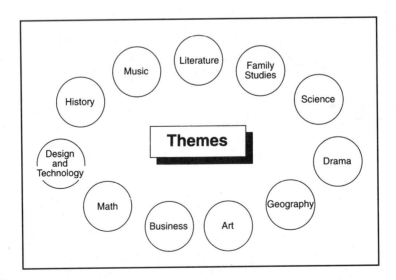

Figure 12.2   A multidisciplinary approach

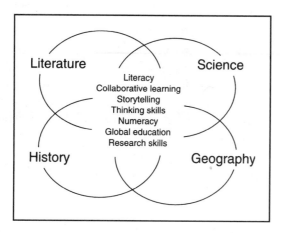

Figure 12.3   An interdisciplinary approach

Figure 12.4   A transdisciplinary approach

We believe that our experience is a natural progression that most people will have to go through when working on collaborative, interdisciplinary curriculum design. The more experience we had working with others of different expertise, the wider our focus became. As our lenses widened, we could see more and more of the natural connections across the curriculum. Eventually, we may become "connection experts" rather than subject experts. Each stage requires a shift in perspective, and each stage is valuable. The important objective of each stage, however, is making connections.

Questions

1. Describe the continuum or map you developed based on these excerpts and your previous reading and discussion. Compare your map or continuum with another student's. How are they alike?

2. Do you think curriculum designers must naturally progress through the stages described by Drake? Why or why not?

3. Note that Drake reached her conclusions after reviewing her journal. Review your own journal. What ideas or thoughts about the social science disciplines have you recorded that may influence your views on curriculum integration? Can you identify "personal boundaries" that would affect your participation in a curriculum integration effort? Does the idea of dissolving those boundaries appeal to you? intimidate you? Write some thoughts on these questions in your journal.

TYPES OF INTEGRATION AND THE BARRIERS TO IMPLEMENTATION

Types of Integration

Integration can occur in a variety of ways and at several levels (e.g., the school level, the departmental level, the grade level, the classroom level, and the lesson level). *What* is integrated can also vary, from content to skills or processes ("thinking across the curriculum") to all aspects of the school environment. Consequently, a map of the "integration territory," such as you began developing above, can be very helpful. In this section, we present one such map (see Figure 12.5) for your use in refining your thinking. This map is based on the work of Heidi Jacobs (1989) and Roland Case (1991b). Although this organizing scheme reflects increasing integration of the content at a particular grade level and increasing integration of the elements of the school environment, there are two other dimensions of integration that may exist independently. *Horizontal* integration and *vertical* integration refer to the distinction between integrating across subject areas at a grade level (horizontal) and integrating within a subject area from grade level to grade level (vertical).

At one end of the continuum that forms the central portion of this map is discipline-based instruction. Each discipline-based course is taught by a subject matter specialist in a separate time block in the day. This is the traditional secondary school configuration, in which separate subjects are taught with little or no deliberate attempt to show relationships among them. However, other aspects of integration can be present at this level. For example, the instruction in a particular subject can be well integrated from grade level to grade level (often called articulation). Instruction may also be integrated with students' experiences, or particular processes or skills (e.g., writing or critical thinking) may be integrated across subject areas.

If the social studies teacher and the literature teacher get together and agree to teach the history of World War I and *All Quiet on the Western Front* during the same three weeks, they have taken the next step on the continuum, to the parallel discipline design stage. At this stage, there is still no deliberate effort to work across disciplines, only an agreement to teach parallel material and "hope that students will find the implicit linkages" (Jacobs 1989).

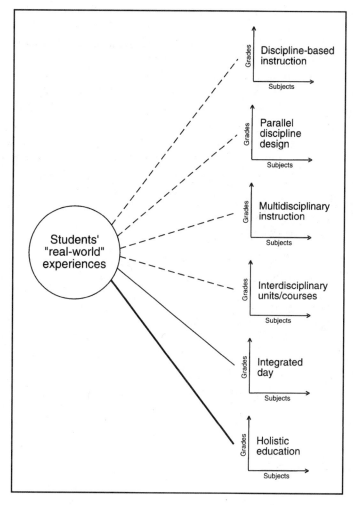

Figure 12.5   A map of types of curriculum integration

The next level of integration is called multidisciplinary; at this level, complementary disciplines are brought together to examine a theme or topic. For example, a history teacher presenting a unit on the 1920s might present several lessons based on economics, followed by several lessons on social history. Multidisciplinary integration can also occur across departments, as when a social studies teacher and a science teacher work together to present a unit on the "Ethics of Science."

Interdisciplinary units or courses, which are next on the continuum, involve greater blurring of the disciplinary boundaries. At this level, instruction may be focused on a particular theme, problem, or issue, with insights from the disciplines drawn upon as necessary to understand that theme, problem, or issue.

Approaching the end of the continuum is the integrated day program. As envisioned by Jacobs, in such programs the entire school day is "based primarily upon themes and problems which emerge from the child's world. The emphasis is on an organic approach to classroom life. The child's questions and interests rather than the school or state syllabus determine the content of the curriculum." Thus, the link between this form of integration and the students' real-world experiences is strong; however, vertical integration may be very difficult without documents to guide teachers at different grade levels. Many middle school reform proposals call for a curriculum that combines student concerns and interests and the society's requirements for students.

Holistic integration implies that everything in the school environment is integrated. "The elements implied in this form of integration include formal and informal practices, routines, methods, rules, and other school-based influences on students learning" (Case 1991a, 3). At this level, Jacobs suggests that programs may be residential, so that the informal living context is also part of the program; she cites A. S. Neil's Summerhill as an example of such a model.

| ACTIVITY | **Revising Your Map of Types of Integration** |

Revise your own map of the types of integration to reflect any changes in your thinking after reading the foregoing section. Are there additional dimensions that you want your model to reflect? If so, how will you show them graphically?

Imagine that you are a high school teacher assigned to teach eleventh-grade U.S. history. Think of an example of each level of your own continuum appropriate for this teaching assignment. What problems would you anticipate in trying to implement each example?

Barriers to Integration

At each level of the continuum shown in Figure 12.5, increased bureaucratic, organizational, and behavioral changes are necessary for successful implementation. For example, "parallel discipline design" requires very little change in the traditional school structure or in the teacher's lesson plans. In contrast, major changes in curriculum, school organization, teacher roles, and school district policy would be required to implement an integrated day model in most secondary schools.

Case points out that horizontal or vertical integration may well hinder integration in the other dimension. For example, a school that effectively integrates sixth-grade social studies, science, and language arts around themes may find it difficult to provide for a cohesive, articulated science program across the middle school grades. Similarly, a social studies department that has worked hard to establish a well-integrated secondary social studies program might resist the destructive effects a theme approach would have on their plan.

Lack of resources for integrated teaching represents another impediment to successful integration of the curriculum. The departmentalization of secondary schools has led textbook companies to create materials based upon the separate disciplines. Integrated study often requires that students and teachers have access to more specialized and varied materials than are available in standard textbooks. This problem will not be easily solved, since programs that grow out of students' interest may mean smaller markets for—and therefore smaller profits from—materials on any particular topic, issue, or theme.

Although teachers can develop their own materials, doing so is a time-consuming and intellectually demanding task. Since most teachers have been trained in discipline-based university programs, they may not be well prepared to undertake this task without assistance from others with training in other areas. Making time for teams of teachers to develop curriculum is probably even more difficult than finding time for an individual teacher to do so.

Testing programs represent yet another force hindering efforts to integrate the curriculum. Nationally normed and standardized tests place a premium upon acquiring specific bits of factual information generated by specific disciplines. An integrated program that allows students flexibility to pursue issues and ideas in their own way may not provide the data needed to score well on such tests.

The kind of "expert" discipline-based knowledge that is demanded by such tests is also susceptible to being used by teachers for purposes of control. When discipline-based knowledge is taught as a dictionary of facts, the teacher remains in control of the "right answers." Even though such an approach shortchanges both the students and the disciplines, many teachers are comfortable with it and therefore resistant to approaches they believe would lessen their control in the classroom.

Taken together, these factors and those discussed earlier provide a strong base for the traditional discipline-based curriculum. Advocates of the models of integration described in the next section must consider these factors in planning to implement integrated programs.

ACTIVITY   **Force-Field Analysis**

Pick the point on your map of integration where you would like to start your teaching career. Write a goal statement to reflect how you will pursue that integration goal. On the force-field analysis form that follows, note the supporting and restraining forces for your self, significant others, and the school as an institution. Choose one of the restraining forces related to yourself (e.g., your training may not have provided you with enough scientific information to allow you to integrate science and social studies successfully) and develop an action plan to address that force.

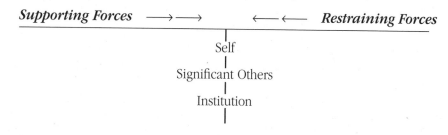

Supporting Forces $\longrightarrow \longrightarrow$ $\longleftarrow \longleftarrow$ *Restraining Forces*

Self

Significant Others

Institution

MODELS FOR INTEGRATION IN SOCIAL STUDIES

Following the "map" provided in Figure 12.5, this section provides strategies and models for integration at four levels: parallel discipline design, multidisciplinary, interdisciplinary, and integrated. Discipline-based instruction is adequately treated in previous chapters of this text, and holistic programs are beyond the scope of this chapter.

Parallel Discipline Design

As noted earlier, parallel discipline design does not require a great deal of change; it may simply require reordering of topics already treated. For example, if a U.S. history teacher and a literature teacher decide to try parallel discipline design, the literature teacher may simply reorder the literary works normally treated so that they fit the chronological organizer used by the history teacher. Similarly, a government teacher wishing to work with the mathematics teacher on a social statistics unit might reorganize his or her course so that students look at demographics first, when the math teacher normally presents a statistics and graphing unit. A geography teacher might reorder units so that students could deal with policy related to acid rain shortly after students have learned about the chemistry of the problem in physical science.

Parallel discipline design may work fairly well in middle schools, where the same groups of students tend to have the same teachers; however, more ambitious integration efforts are often under way at the middle school level, superseding the need for parallel design. In junior highs and high schools that offer primarily discipline-based instruction, teachers who agree to cooperate in this way may share only a few students. Thus, the benefits of the parallel discipline design are undercut by institutional factors. For young teachers, however, the process of talking with other teachers in support of parallel discipline design may be a useful way to begin expanding their thinking beyond the disciplines in which they were trained.

 ACTIVITY

Planning for Parallel Discipline Design

Choose one of the units listed below. Think of a way in which you might work with a teacher in another subject area so that your two classes were complementary. If possible, talk with an education student preparing to teach in another subject area about how the two classes could be coordinated.

> Environmental Problems in North America (6th-grade geography)
>
> Our State's Economy (8th-grade state studies)
>
> Special-Interest Groups in American Government (9th-grade civics)
>
> Colonialism and Independence: A Case Study of Nigeria (10th-grade world history)
>
> The Progressive Era: The Limits of Reform (11th-grade U.S. history)

Multidisciplinary Instruction

One current model being used to implement multidisciplinary programs at the high school level is called the core program. Although some core programs are interdisciplinary or integrated, a multidisciplinary approach is often most feasible to implement at the high school level, where teachers have strong ties to their discipline backgrounds.

Horizon High School in Adams County Five Star School District, a suburban area north of Denver, Colorado, has adopted an integrated multidisciplinary core for all tenth-grade students. The core program involves social studies, language arts, fine arts, science, and thinking skills organized around five themes: change, problem solving, perspective, diversity, and patterns.

The students are divided into six groups called "cores." Each core is under the direction of a three-person faculty team consisting of one teacher each from science, social studies, and language arts. The teachers have a common planning period each day to facilitate teamwork and communication. Block scheduling gives the teaching team access to its group of students for a three-hour time period each day. Each core has access to a double room with a movable wall, as well as a regular classroom.

Although Horizon's core is a multidisciplinary approach, social studies content tends to be the lead organizer. For example, when change is the theme of study, the Great Depression determines the literature read and the science topics studied. Similarly, the perspectives unit is driven by the Civil War period. For each unit, essential learnings are established for each subject area, as well as for a set of skills the teachers call *disciplines*. The following are examples from the perspectives unit.*

History

- Know the social, political, and economic causes of the Civil War from various perspectives.

- Examine the transitional nature of the Civil War regarding strategies, technology, and philosophy.

Literature

- Know the definitions and discuss examples of literary romanticism and realism.

- Cite examples from the readings that demonstrate how the authors' opinions reflect the era.

---

*Excerpted with permission from the Core Staff, Horizon High School, Thornton, Colorado.

Science and Technology

- After dissecting a heart, create a diagram of a heart and label parts and blood flow.
- Compare the decisions that Civil War victims made about their medical care with today's decisions related to organ/tissue transplant surgery.

Although much of the instruction and learning is discipline-based, some interdisciplinary experiences are provided through synthesizing activities. For example, within the problem-solving theme, students are assigned the task of doing a simulated broadcast from a Gatsby party as part of studying the 1920s. Students are engaged not in the individual disciplines but in the task of writing an authentic script, making the electronics work, and delivering a polished performance complete with commercial breaks.

Observations of the program provide little evidence that the students were asked to generalize about the organizing themes. In practice, the themes were not the goals of the study but tools for developing a multidisciplinary approach.

Although teachers maintain their departmental identities, in interviews they often referred to the need to become "generalists" in their work. Over the course of several years, teachers on a team report becoming more and more involved in the subject matter of their colleagues, to the extent that, in some cases, science matters are actually dealt with by the social studies teachers. Teachers are enthusiastic about the program, seeming to find a sense of adventure in the process of creating and teaching such a program.

Interdisciplinary Units/Courses

Interdisciplinary curricula, whether at the unit, course, or lesson level, can be organized in a number of ways. In this section, we will look at two principal organizers being used in social studies: themes and issues. For each, we will also look at related instructional approaches.

Themes and the Case Study Method   *Themes* is another term that has been used ambiguously in the educational discourse. The typology of themes and examples provided by Case might be helpful in determining what is meant by a theme and how themes can be used to organize instruction:

- Places (e.g., Egypt, our neighborhood, deserts, the moon)
- Events (e.g., making the pyramids, building the A-bomb)
- Eras (e.g., the Depression, pre-Copernican Europe)
- Concepts (e.g., friendship, harmony, time, creativity, beauty)
- Generalizations (e.g., humans are social animals, history repeats itself)

- Phenomena (e.g., biological change, war, growing up, acid rain)
- Entities (e.g., bears, atoms, multinational companies)

These themes are not unlike the organizers used for many traditional discipline-based courses and do not, in themselves, suggest how interdisciplinary instruction would be markedly different. Thus, it is informative to look at instructional approaches used in interdisciplinary instruction.

Many of the types of themes listed by Case can be treated through the case study approach, which involves intensive analysis and discussion of an individual person, a community, an event, or the like. The case study approach integrates not only content from various disciplines but also thinking and discussion skills and students' own experiences.

Many case study activities depend on primary source material collected by the teacher or on special readings created by the teacher. These readings provide the data on which students base their analysis of the case. Instruction proceeds in a play-debrief-replay pattern. The use of the term *play* is significant; students actively engage in "mind play," meaning that they are not pressured to arrive at a specific, predetermined answer. The unimpeded flow of ideas gradually grows more disciplined and more productive as students develop habits of thinking, but the spontaneity of "play" is never lost. (See Chapter 13 for more information on the case study method.)

Clearly, the case study method demands new roles for teachers, as well as new dynamics between teachers and students. These roles can be discerned in the following case study.

ACTIVITY

A Case Study on Injustice

The following reading describes a Canadian high school classroom focusing on a case study entitled "A Case of Injustice in Our Time." The teacher-developed case focused on the uprooting and internment of Japanese Canadians during World War II. The case was written around several "big ideas":

1. The internment of Japanese in Canada was the result of the federal government's discriminatory policies.
2. The government's actions reflected Canadian paranoia and racist attitudes toward Asian minorities.
3. The legislative power of the War Measures Act allowed Canadians to justify stripping Japanese Canadians of their civil rights.

The case contained many threads that could be followed, such as the role of propaganda in wartime, but the teacher chose to focus on racial prejudice. The case was supplemented by reading *Obasan* by Joy Kogawa and seeing the film *Come See the Paradise*.

As you read the report by a classroom observer, look for evidence that students are integrating knowledge from several disciplines. Also critique the teacher's handling of issues as they arose—What did he do well? What might have been improved?

A CASE FOR SOCIAL STUDIES*
by Selma Wasserman

Rich's directions are brief. The groups are to discuss the study questions appended to the case, observing two fundamental rules: (1) all students have the right to express their own ideas, and (2) all students' ideas are to be heard and treated respectfully. I ask the group forming near my chair if I may sit in with them. They shrug an indifferent assent. . . .

The four students in my group—Mark, Steve, Taryn, and Carla—lay the sheet with the five study questions out in front of them. These study questions are rich, provocative, and open-ended, calling for students to think about issues rather than to recall specific facts. Taryn assumes leadership, vocalizing the first question: What hypotheses can you suggest that might explain the treatment of the Japanese-Canadians during World War II? Mark shuffles through his notebook. Steve and Carla are quiet, uncertain. Taryn repeats the question and presses them: "Didn't you guys read the case? I'll bet you didn't read the case."

Mark (defensively): I read it. (Steve and Carla nod agreement.)

Taryn: So what do you think?

The discussion begins to come alive. Mark is an active participant and takes the position that the Japanese got what they deserved. "After all," he asserts with an air of one who has the truth and is disgusted by those who don't see it his way, "they bombed Pearl Harbor." Steve, although less vocal, is clearly Mark's ally.

Taryn argues vehemently in opposition. She cites data, for example, that Pearl Harbor is in the United States and *not* in Canada, and she asks, "What did that have to do with us?" But Mark shrugs this off. "Canada and the U.S.—it's the same," he says to Taryn's raised eyebrows. He adds that "the Japanese in Canada were spies, anyway, who would betray Canadian secrets to Japan, and that is why they had to be taken away."

I see Taryn growing more incensed with Mark's close-minded, made-in-Hollywood arguments. To her credit, she stays calm, presenting data to refute Mark's points. She points out that the Japanese were Canadian citizens, that they were being "convicted" without due process, and that their actual ties to Japan were, in many cases, remote. She also cites the fact that Germans in Canada, despite German aggression in Europe, were not subjected to similar treatment.

Mark and Steve are unyielding. They have made up their minds. "The Germans, after all, did *not* bomb Pearl Harbor," they say with authority, as if this explains

*Excerpted from Selma Wasserman, "A Case for Social Studies," *Phi Delta Kappan* 73, no. 10 (1992), 793–95. © 1992 Phi Delta Kappan, Inc.

everything. They are both locked, with dogmatic insistence, into a set of beliefs that they will not allow to be penetrated by the light of data.

The two boys and girls are similarly split on the rest of the study questions. The longer the discussion continues, the more the prejudicial attitudes of the boys are revealed and the more Taryn is astonished by their close-mindedness. Carla, siding with Taryn, may lack the personal power, the verbal skills, or the thinking capabilities to take on her share of the debate; in any event, her support is largely nonverbal. Forty minutes evaporate like a drop of water on a red hot griddle. . . .

Rich is going to spend the next 40 minutes debriefing the whole class on the study questions. He reminds the class of the first two discussion guidelines and invites responses to the first question. Arms wave as students vie for "air time," and immediately the discussion picks up steam. What I saw in my small group of four is now unleashed in the whole class. There is a clear split between those students who share Mark and Steve's views and those who agree with Taryn and Carla, but I am disturbed that the split is heavily weighted in support of Mark. Racist feelings, thinly veiled by the rationalization of "wartime necessity," are strong, ugly, and unacknowledged.

I watch Rich, who is new to case-study teaching, lead the discussion group. I know how tempting it is to admonish students when they are protesting ideas that are "wrong-headed"—to *tell* them that they are wrong or silly or should change their attitudes! I know too how futile such admonitions are. Students do not change their beliefs when we tell them to. Our hope is that experiences and reflection will make them more intelligent processors of information.

Rick avoids any telling. He listens to students' ideas thoughtfully and then respectfully paraphrases them in a way that zeroes in on the significant issues, so that the ideas are expressed in a richer, more focused way. This he does without rewarding an idea as "good" or condemning it as "without value." He makes it look as if he has been doing this kind of teaching all his life. The room begins to feel like a pressure cooker, yet the guidelines for discussion are consistently observed. I note that more and more students are asking for "air time" and that participation is close to 100 percent. I attribute this to the way Rich has orchestrated the interactive dialogue and made it clear that students can say anything they think without being judged on the value of their ideas. Later in the semester, one student confirmed this by writing on her course evaluation, "We feel safe to say what we think in this class."

One student who has been a key player in the whole-group discussion is deeply affected by what her classmates have revealed. When Yoshimi gets her turn to speak next, she ventures into dangerous waters. "I'm getting the terrible feeling"—she looks at her shoes—"that if this were happening today—if the police came to my house and took my parents and me away like that—none of you"—she looks up, eyes filling—"would stand up for me." Everybody talks at once, as Yoshimi, shoulders bent, tries to keep the tears back. My own eyes fill, and I am humbled by the courage of this small, slight girl.

No one has noticed that the class is over. (No bells ring in this school.) No one leaves. Rich shouts directions now about the next day—that the discussion will continue. A few students pack up and head for the door. Several cluster around Yoshimi. Rich works his way over to them. There is more they want to say, for they are angry, hurt. Yoshimi is also worried that she has gone too far. Will this mean she will lose some friends? Rich, who is as overwhelmed as the students by what has occurred in the class, continues to maintain his neutrality, while at the same time offering reassurance. He explicitly praises their participation and applauds them for standing up for what they believe. . . .

A week later, when we talk again, he reports that on the following day he spent the entire class period in further discussion, once again ensuring that all students' views were heard respectfully and affirming his position that social studies includes the examination of different points of view in relation to historical events. . . . By the time Rich had taught his second case, "Let's Have a War! That's a Good Idea," which was a narrative treatment of Canada's entry into World War I written by his colleague Joe Glsuka, he had become a case study convert. "I'm convinced," he said. "This is the way to teach social studies."

Questions

1. Into which of Case's categories of themes would you place this case study? Explain your selection.

2. What evidence did you find of content integration? of integration of thinking skills with content? of integration of students' own experiences with content?

3. How would you describe the teacher's role in this classroom? Is it a role you would be comfortable taking? Why or why not?

4. What did you like about this approach? What problems did you observe? How do you think the teacher could have dealt better with those problems?

Themes and the Inquiry Approach Themes can also be explored using an inquiry approach, if the subject of study is recast as a question for student exploration. Some examples derived from Case's list of themes provided earlier are

- The Depression—What were the major causes of the Depression?

- Acid rain—Is new national legislation needed to address the acid rain problem?

- Our neighborhood—Do any unusual patterns of birth defects or causes of death exist in our neighborhood? If so, what are the possible causes?

- Growing up—How has the experience of adolescence changed for young Americans since 1950?

Inquiry lessons, units, or courses are interdisciplinary because students draw from and use the methods of all relevant disciplines in attempting to answer the identified question. The products of the inquiry can be presented in a wide variety of forms, including models or replicas, plays or performances, dioramas or murals, written or oral reports, or audiovisual presentations; thus, information from other disciplines can be brought to bear on the creation of the product as well. Chapter 13 provides additional information on inquiry teaching.

Issues   An issue can be defined as a question involving a choice or decision over which there is disagreement about what should be (or should have been) done. Use of the word *should* in this definition indicates that investigation of issues involves exploration of values, as well as data and theories. Examples of issues include the following:

- Should further technological innovation involving production of radioactive waste be discouraged?
- To what extent should the government be responsible for protecting the health and safety of its citizens?
- When is it right to challenge legitimate governmental authority?
- Should the United States be a refuge for the oppressed?

In a recent issue of *The Social Studies* devoted to issues-centered education, several advocates of this approach were asked to list its defining characteristics. Five characteristics emerged as common to all the definitions:

- Use of reflective questions, questions that have no right answer and require thoughtfulness and depth
- Use of open-ended questions, which require consideration of relevant evidence and competing values, and weighing of consequences
- Emphasis on examination of social practices using the ideals of democracy as the criteria for clarifying and testing practices
- Use of issues reflecting both personal and public components
- Centering the curriculum on ethical concerns and diversity of opinions (Evans 1992, 93)

ACTIVITY   **Analyzing Issues-Based Lessons**

Previous chapters in this book have contained a number of issues-based lessons, usually drawing primarily from one discipline for data on which to base discourse or decisions. Select one of those issues-based lessons and analyze it. To what extent is it interdisciplinary as currently written? How might you make it even more interdisciplinary?

Integrated Day

The integrated day level on our continuum is reflected in at least one current trend in education—the middle school movement, which has as its heart block scheduling, an integrated, student-based curriculum, and interdisciplinary teaming. The philosophy of interdisciplinary teaming is reflected in this strong statement from the staff of Cross Keys Middle School in Florissant, Missouri:

> *Teachers agree upon a concept which connects the students' learning and has no content area barriers. Teachers relinquish their areas of content specialization and begin to draw objectives and activities from their wide range of human talents and experiences both in and outside their formal training and area of certification. Once again they become human beings, competent and experienced in life itself first, and in content areas incidentally. (George 1992, 95)*

The notion of the integrated curriculum is reflected in the National Council for the Social Studies guidelines for "Social Studies in the Middle School," which define social studies curriculum as "an integration of experience and knowledge about human endeavors and human relations designed to foster informed and ethical participation in society" (Task Force 1991, 287). Rather than recommending a single set of courses, NCSS has adopted four statements of concern shared by individuals and society that could serve as the foundation for a social studies program driven by student concerns:

1. Concern with self: developing of self-esteem and a strong sense of identity within the context of history, culture, the humanities, and parts of the social studies program

2. Concern for right and wrong: development of ethics that will guide decision making according to the highest ethical standards

3. Concern for others: development of group- and other-centeredness through social studies content and community service

4. Concern for the world: development of a global perspective, which includes the knowledge and attitudes that reflect an awareness of the pluralistic, interdependent, and changing nature of the world community

James Beane (1990) has proposed that out of the intersection of the personal and social concerns of early adolescents emerges a set of themes around which the entire middle school curriculum could be organized (see Figure 12.6).

ACTIVITY

A Case Study in Student-Centered Curriculum Planning

The following account is based upon the experience of three teachers who worked with students to develop a thematic middle school unit. As you read, compare this case with your own experiences with middle school students.

Early Adolescent Concerns	Curriculum Themes	Social Concerns
Understanding personal changes	TRANSITIONS	Living in a changing world
Developing a personal identity	IDENTITIES	Cultural diversity
Finding a place in the group	INTERDEPENDENCE	Global interdependence
Personal fitness	WELLNESS	Environmental protection
Social status	SOCIAL STRUCTURES	Class systems
Dealing with adults	INDEPENDENCE	Human rights
Peer conflict and gangs	CONFLICT RESOLUTION	Global conflict
Commercial pressures	COMMERCIALISM	Effects of media
Questioning authority	JUSTICE	Laws and social customs
Personal friendships	CARING	Social welfare
Living in the schools	INSTITUTIONS	Social institutions

Figure 12.6   Intersections of personal and social concerns. *Source: From James A. Beane,* A Middle School Curriculum: From Rhetoric to Reality *(Columbus, Ohio: National Middle School Association, 1990). Used by permission.*

A CASE IN POINT*
Reported by James Beane

The group began by developing a list of questions they shared about themselves and their world. Next they looked at possible connections between "self" and "world" questions and the possible themes those connections suggested. Then they reached consensus on a theme for our unit (we settled on "Living in the Future") and planned activities to seek answers to the self and social questions. Along the way, they also identified the knowledge and skills they would need and where they were encountered in their previous school experiences.

All of us wanted to know, of course, what it would be like to use this thematic approach and whether it would work. Several things became clear to us as we planned the unit. First, early adolescents have powerful and significant questions. Second, they are capable of seeing connections between personal and larger world concerns, of naming themes, and of selecting topics that deserve group consideration. Third, early adolescents take this work very seriously; we spent several intensive hours in planning—enough to exhaust us older people. Fourth, early adolescents are able to identify engaging, worthwhile, and creative activities, as well as the knowledge and skills

*From P. S. George, et al., *The Middle School and Beyond* (Alexandria, Va.: Association for Supervision and Curriculum Development, 1992), pp. 98–100. Reprinted with permission of the Association for Supervision and Curriculum Development. Copyright © 1992 by ASCD.

they need to carry them out. For example, they decided to research family health histories to identify personal, future risk factors; to design a "preferable" community of the future; to survey age-mates at other schools about their desire for and fears about the future; to research past predictions for this decade; and to learn about ways of making personal goals and decisions.

Finally, and perhaps most startlingly, the students easily named the subject areas in which such knowledge and skills might ordinarily be found and where they had previously encountered some of them in school. That is, they understood the curriculum theory behind this project.

Two points consolidate this observation. The first is to report that these young people identified the knowledge and skills they would need to carry out the unit. These included reading, writing, researching, interviewing, problem solving, computation of percentages and ratios, graphing, drawing, listening, estimating, scheduling, photographing, question posing (for surveys and interviews), resource finding, comparing and contrasting, note taking, and using computer skills. They indicated they would need to know more about history, cultures, current events, new technology, health, geography, demographics, anatomy, biology, communications, mathematics, and more. In other words, they demonstrated not only the possibility for engaging integrated content but the need to do so as well.

The second point involves what they had to say about this kind of curriculum organization during a spontaneous question-and-answer period with the school principal. Some quotes are especially illustrative:

Things in school are always separated out. They should be together.

When teachers just tell us what to learn, it doesn't mean anything. They should let us have something to say about it.

We know there are things you want us to do that are important. If only you would do them in a way that was interesting to us.

There might be a set curriculum, but there ought to be different ways of doing it.

[On gifted and talented programs] There are so many activities in this, they can do what they want and go to different levels.

[On coming to school] You know I don't like to come to school. For this I would.

[From a student who is labeled "emotionally disturbed"] They usually make me go to a separate room during this time because people think I am a nobody. Here I am happy. I feel like a somebody.

We were struck not only by the sense of how this curriculum approach might work, but also by the implications the young people saw for institutional aspects of the school.

Questions

1. Are you surprised by the level of competence and interest noted among middle school students? How do your own observations of students at this level support or negate the observations reported here?

2. Which of the students' comments has the most significance for you? Explain the reasons for your choice.

Brainstorming

With the class, brainstorm the characteristics you think a teacher would need to be successful and satisfied teaching in an integrated middle school program. Consider knowledge, skills, attitudes, personality characteristics, and so on.

When the group has listed as many items as possible, go back over the list and circle all the items you think are applicable only to an integrated setting; that is, they would not be needed in a traditional discipline-based junior high curriculum.

Consolidate the circled items into one list. With a small group of four or five students, discuss where in your university experience you have received or could receive assistance in developing these characteristics.

Following the discussion, imagine that you have been informed by your superintendent that you have been offered an assignment to a new middle school. You will be part of a team to develop and teach an integrated sixth-grade curriculum. Write a two-page letter in which you either accept the offer or request another assignment. Be sure to include the reasons for your decision.

CAUTIONS AND CONCLUSIONS

As with many educational innovations, reports of successes with integrated programs have led other educators to hop on the bandwagon. For integrated programs to be successful, however, time and resources for planning and preparation must be available. Teachers must have the time to plan together to create or find new materials and prepare to teach content with which they may not be familiar. Students and teachers must be scheduled together in workable blocks of time with appropriate space and facilities. Resources must be acquired for use throughout the year.

Hiring appropriate personnel or reeducating current staff members is a final practical and sensitive consideration. The staff of Horizon High School believes the following characteristics are critical for teachers in integrated programs:

- Flexibility. Teachers must be willing to work cooperatively and to accommodate unexpected circumstances that develop.

- Willing to take risks. Teachers must be willing to step out of their traditional and well-known roles and ways of teaching.

- Willing to deal with frustration. When numerous people are involved in a program, things will go wrong.

- Team-oriented. Teachers must be able to function as team players.
- Able to see that struggles lead to growth.
- Able to have fun.

Although curricular integration has the potential to bring greater coherence to school learning, none of the methods or approaches that exist is an educational panacea; all can be poorly executed. Heidi Jacobs has identified two problems to which many integration projects fall prey. The first, which she calls the "potpourri problem," is the result of abandoning the disciplines as the basis for learning. Because no well-defined structure for integrated programs exists, educators seem tempted to sample a little of each of the disciplines. To be effective, programs— whether individual lessons or schoolwide curricula—must have an intellectual structure and coherence.

Jacobs's second problem is the "polarity problem," which arises when educators take either/or positions regarding integration. Faculty members who find their territory threatened or their role as teacher undermined may become antagonistic. Jacobs proposes addressing this problem by recognizing that integration can take place at various levels and acknowledging that the individual disciplines have a role to play even in integrated programs.

To be effective, integration must have educational significance. To simply organize schooling around themes or topics does not guarantee that the resulting learning will be worthwhile. Case distinguishes between curriculum that is organized around a topic but has no intellectual coherence or significance and curriculum that is integrated around a topic and has significance. The following examples illustrate the distinction.

Unit "0"—Apples

Mathematics: counting using apples as manipulatives

Language arts: reading *William Tell* and other apple-related stories

Art: drawing apples and exploring use of the color red

Science: making apple cider

Unit "1"—Apples

Mathematics: calculating statistics on apple industry production, employment rates, and the like

Language arts: reading nonfiction about the apple industry

Art: drawing graphic representations of the apple production process

Science: studying soil and climate conditions in relation to apple production

ACTIVITY   ## Designing an Integrated Thematic Unit

Select a topic or theme and outline an integrated unit around the theme. Make sure that your unit is truly integrated and is not simply a group of unrelated activities organized around a topic.

Form groups of four in which you discuss, critique, and revise your units until there is consensus that all the units are integrated around their themes.

Reflecting on the Chapter

In 1898, Alexis Bertrand wrote, "True instruction must be integral and . . . we should not divide and hand out in small bits that which is naturally one and indivisible" (quoted in Knudsen 1937, 16). In your journal, explain why you agree or disagree with Bertrand. Whether you agree or disagree, reflect on why you think most schooling is not much more integrated today than it was when Bertrand made this statement. What are the implications of your reasoning for teachers and students?

References

Beane, J. A. *A Middle School Curriculum: From Rhetoric to Reality.* Columbus, Ohio: National Middle School Association, 1990.

Bellack, A. "What Knowledge Is Most Worth Knowing." In *Curriculum Development Issues and Insights,* ed. D. E. Orlosky and B. O. Smith, 92–103. Chicago: Rand McNally, 1978.

Brady, M. *What's Worth Teaching.* Albany: State University of New York Press, 1989.

Case, R. *The Anatomy of Curricular Integration.* Burnaby, B.C.: Tri-University Integration Project, Simon Fraser University, 1991a.

———. *Integrating around Themes: An Overemphasized Tool?* Burnaby, B.C.: Tri-University Integration Project, Simon Fraser University, 1991b.

Court, D. *Curricular Integration and Teachers' Personal Practical Knowledge.* Burnaby, B.C.: Tri-University Integration Project, Simon Fraser University, 1991.

Drake, S. "How Our Team Dissolved the Boundaries." *Educational Leadership* 49, no. 2 (1991): 20–22.

Elbow, P. *Embracing Contraries.* New York: Oxford University Press, 1986.

Evans, R. W. "Introduction: What Do We Mean by Issues-Centered Social Studies Education?" *The Social Studies* 83, no. 3 (1992): 93–94.

George, P. S., et al. *The Middle School and Beyond.* Alexandria, Va.: Association for Supervision and Curriculum Development, 1992.

Hurd, P. D. "Why We Must Transform Science Education." *Educational Leadership* 49, no. 2 (1991): 33–35.

Jacobs, H. H. *Interdisciplinary Curriculum Design and Implementation.* Alexandria, Va.: Association for Supervision and Curriculum Development, 1989.

Kluckholm, C. *Mirror for Man: The Relationship of Anthropology to Modern Life.* Tucson: University of Arizona Press, 1985.

Knudsen, C. W. "What Do Educators Mean By Integration?" *Harvard Educational Review* 7, no. 1 (1937): 15–26.

Miller, J., B. Cassie, and S. Drake. *Holistic Learning: A Teacher's Guide to Integrated Studies*. Toronto: OISE Press, 1990.

Oliver, D. W. "Grounded Knowing: A Postmodern Perspective on Teaching and Learning." *Educational Leadership* 48, no. 1 (1990): 64–69.

Task Force on Social Studies in the Middle School. "Social Studies in the Middle School." *Social Education* 55, no. 5 (1991): 287–93.

Wasserman, S. "A Case for Social Studies." *Phi Delta Kappan* 73, no. 10 (1992): 793–801.

Woyach, R. B. and R. C. Remy. *Approaches to World Studies: A Handbook for Curriculum Planners*. Needham Heights, Mass.: Allyn & Bacon, 1989.

PLANNING FOR INSTRUCTION

CHAPTER

13

TEACHING STRATEGIES

Laurel R. Singleton

ACTIVITY

The Teacher–Student Relationship

Educators have used several metaphors to characterize students and the relationship between students and teacher. For example, some have thought of students as blank slates on which teachers could write, or empty cups into which teachers could pour knowledge. Others have thought about students as computers, whom teachers could program to process input. Still others have thought of teachers as guides, directing student travelers on a journey.

Reflect on your own experiences as a learner, as well as your interactions with younger students. What metaphor captures for you the relationship between teachers and students? Describe this metaphor in a few words or in a simple drawing.

INTRODUCTION

As has been pointed out in previous chapters, selection of teaching/learning strategies is an important part of planning instruction. The way in which you teach, as much as what you teach, contributes to your effectiveness. Your own individual teaching style will be based not only on your personality but also on your understanding of how students learn. Thus, the ideas you have gained from your educational psychology courses will be important in deciding how you will organize instruction in your classroom.

In this chapter, we introduce you to a variety of teaching strategies. The organization of the chapter clearly indicates some of the characteristics we would hope to see in your classroom as you begin teaching. Three beliefs about learning are especially important to us in identifying those characteristics:

1. Learning is not a process of transmission but a process of construction. This view, based on research in cognitive psychology, holds that people, as learners, "construct our own understandings of the world in which we live . . . by synthesizing new experiences into what we have previously come to understand" (Brooks and Brooks 1993, 4).

2. Classroom learning is a "social process that the teacher works to facilitate by helping students make sense of their experiences and further their understanding of the world" (Powell 1994, 34).

3. Individuals learn most effectively in different ways. They have learning styles—"characteristic cognitive, affective, and physiological behaviors that serve as relatively stable indicators of how learners perceive, interact, and respond to the learning environment" (O'Neil 1990, 5).

Entire instructional models have been developed in response to research on constructivism and learning styles. Although we do not deal with those models, we believe that teachers should be cognizant of those aspects of learning as they determine what kinds of learning environments they will create.

The first several sections of this chapter present fairly detailed introductions to four teaching approaches we believe are keys to engaging and effective social studies. If you were to implement these approaches, students in your classroom would be involved in inquiry, developing and investigating their own questions about the ideas you are presenting. They would, in particular, be involved in investigation of public policy issues, both currently and historically. Discussions in your classroom would be wide-ranging, stimulating students' thinking skills at every level; the discussions, rather than simply being a chance for you to check whether students can repeat information you have provided, would be genuine conversations in which students attempt to clarify and deepen their understanding. The atmosphere in your classroom would be one of cooperation, both in specific small- and large-group tasks you have designed and in an environment of acceptance and nurturing of ideas.

The final section of this chapter provides briefer introductions to a range of teaching strategies, suggesting that we hope your class will be one in which students are engaged in a variety of activities. Students are individuals who learn differently. Thus, provision for a range of ways to present and interact with information will enhance learning.

INQUIRY

Inquiry as an approach to teaching and learning in social studies emphasizes the process of deriving knowledge. It is based on the ways in which social scientists generate knowledge; that is, students learn by asking questions, generating hypotheses, collecting and evaluating data, and testing the hypotheses against the data to derive generalizations and theories. Beyer has elaborated these steps into a detailed picture of the inquiry process (see Figure 13.1).

The differences between this approach, which was a principal feature of many "New Social Studies" projects of the 1960s and 1970s, and the expository approach used in many classrooms are obvious. Students are active rather than passive learners. The development of questions and hypotheses, the collection and analysis of data, and the derivation of generalizations and theories teach students *how* to learn and think.

Initiating Inquiry Lessons

Inquiry lessons can be highly structured by the teacher. That is, the teacher may select the question to be investigated, as well as the evidence to be considered. Chapter 11's activity on the atomic bomb is an example of this kind of inquiry exercise. Such teacher structuring of inquiry lessons ensures that adequate data are available and allows the teacher to model the inquiry process and the skills required by it for students. Highly structured inquiry lessons, however, are likely to be less engaging

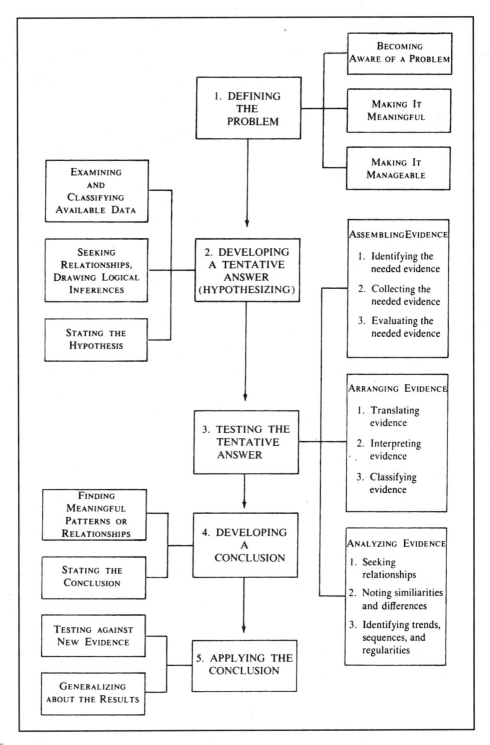

Figure 13.1   The process of inquiring. *Source: From B. K. Beyer,* Inquiry in the Social Studies Classroom *(Columbus, Ohio: Charles E. Merrill, 1971), p. 50. Used by permission of the author.*

and meaningful to students than those in which they have had a more active role in choosing the question for study and the means of investigating that question.

Teachers whose students have some experience with the inquiry process may be able to organize an entire course around student-initiated inquiries selected from within broad teacher-defined content parameters. Students having less experience with inquiry will require guidance throughout the process. That guidance may include using what Beyer calls indirect initiation of the problem by presenting students with a situation "that will create a question or perplexity in the minds of the students which they will want to resolve" (Beyer 1971, 57). Ways of creating such questions include providing students with opposing viewpoints on an issue, with a highly provocative quote, with information that challenges students' own beliefs, or with a mystery. Mysteries can be presented through pictures, artifacts, or stories. The following is an example of a statement that might be used to initiate an inquiry.

> *Veterans of the Persian Gulf War have complained of a variety of physical ailments, yet they are not known to have been exposed to any chemical or biological weapons.*

All these devices will stimulate student interest and allow them to frame their own questions while permitting the teacher to ensure that adequate research materials are available.

When students have framed a question for inquiry, they next develop hypotheses, or tentative answers to the question based on the evidence immediately available. Developing those tentative answers involves induction from bits of data, tapping students' existing knowledge of a topic, intuition, and creativity. As with the development of questions, development of hypotheses is most engaging and beneficial when students are generating the hypotheses themselves. For students unfamiliar with the process, teachers may have to provide prompts. Thinking aloud about how the teacher would develop hypotheses related to an inquiry question can effectively model for students how evidence, logic, and divergent thinking can be combined in the process.

ACTIVITY

Creating Questions in Students' Minds

Imagine that you are teaching a high school economics course. You want to conduct an inquiry unit on the national debt, using the case study from Chapter 8 as your starting point for planning. How might you present this topic to the students so they will readily frame questions for investigation and be motivated to seek answers to their questions? Also think about how you will encourage students to develop hypotheses about this topic. Think through the process of hypothesis formation for yourself so that you can provide a thinking model for students. How could you present this model effectively?

Testing Hypotheses and Reaching Conclusions

Once students have developed hypotheses, they test those hypotheses and reach conclusions about their validity. These steps in the inquiry process obviously involve many data-gathering and analysis skills as well as higher-order thinking skills. Students must determine what evidence is needed, decide how they will gather that evidence, gather and evaluate the evidence, analyze the evidence, identify trends or patterns in the evidence, and reach conclusions based on their analysis of the evidence. Throughout these phases, the teacher's job will be designing learning tasks that guide students through these steps and provide models of their successful completion. Clearly, your understanding of the methods of social scientists will be helpful to you in designing such experiences.

Applying the Conclusion

Once students have reached a conclusion, they should consider how it applies to other data, how it might be verified or disproved. This step in the process makes clear for students some of the assumptions about knowledge on which the inquiry process rests. These assumptions include the following:

- Knowledge is never complete; it is always tentative.
- Knowledge changes over time, as does the structure of knowledge.
- Seeking scientific explanations is a worthwhile human endeavor.

Inquiry has been differentiated from a problem-solving or issues-based approach because inquiry deals with questions that are testable (i.e., do not involve values), whereas problem-solving approaches require a synthesis of facts and values. This distinction has been questioned, however, and you may want to consider it in greater depth as you study issues-based approaches in the next section.

USING AN ISSUES-BASED APPROACH

A primary goal of the social studies curriculum has been and continues to be to develop in students the knowledge, skills, and dispositions needed to be informed and participating citizens in a democracy. As Shirley Engle (1990) has written, "Social education, particularly so in a democracy, is not a matter of just telling the story or of transmitting habitual ways of thinking to children. It is more importantly a matter of exciting children to think about their history, to explore the problems of history and society, and to engage in inventing new and better ways for human beings to relate to one another." One way of achieving this end is to adopt an issues-based approach to social studies instruction.

A problems-based approach does not negate the necessity for substantive learning on the part of students. To deal effectively with a broad range of issues, students need to understand concepts from all the disciplines. Nor must an issues-based approach necessarily be presentist. Key events or eras in history can also be approached as problems or issues requiring solutions (see, for example, the *Public Issues Series* or Lockwood and Harris 1985).

Several models for an issues-based approach to social studies have been developed (see, for example, Oliver and Shaver 1966; Newmann 1970; Engle and Ochoa 1988; Massialas and Evans forthcoming); we encourage you to explore all these approaches, as well as the approach to policymaking described below, which was developed by Michael Hartoonian.

Introduction to a Policymaking Learning Strategy

As a general strategy for thinking about policymaking, we need to explore the dynamics that exist between the real and the ideal: between social/personal principles and the "facts" of life. The approach to policymaking developed in this section encourages public dialogue about what we believe compared with what we do. What are our social theories or ideals? How do we measure up to those principles?

Documents such as the Declaration of Independence, the Preamble to the U.S. Constitution, and Martin Luther King, Jr.'s "I Have a Dream" speech provide statements of basic ideals. The policymaking model outlined here requires the evaluation of actual personal and social circumstances in the light of those ideals, and the devising of policies to bring the ideal and real circumstances closer together. It uses past experiences to help us focus on the future and to evaluate the ethical health of specific social groups and society at large.

This model requires that learning activities be designed to help students develop the abilities and dispositions necessary for policy construction and implementation. These include

- Envisioning—the identification, development, and evaluation of social ideals and theories that describe the preferred states of being toward which individuals and society want to move

- Assessing the actual situation—the use of scientific and other ways of gaining knowledge about whatever aspect of social or personal life you wish to change

- Constructing, evaluating, and implementing policies—continual comparison of the real and the ideal to make midcourse changes

Envisioning

Creating visions of preferred states of affairs or institutions is the first step in constructing any specific policy. In starting this process, we might ask the following questions:

- What do we believe in as a people?
- Under what conditions should we live?
- How should people be treated?
- What vision do we have of the ideal state, school, community, or family?
- How can this institution function better?

The process of conceiving of an ideal state, situation, or institution can be exciting as well as frustrating. Our images of what could be are often limited by our own history and our reluctance to take risks. Our theories may not reflect recent changes in demography, behavior patterns, and beliefs or assumptions about people and institutions. For example, the social welfare principles we hold for the United States include ideals and beliefs from the European Enlightenment as well as from American Indian cultures and the cultures of Africa and Asia. The assertion that we value individual freedom as well as group rights conflates old and new, as well as Western and non-Western ideals. Thus, in constructing visions of the future to guide policy formation, it is important to take into account the beliefs inherent in our views.

Constructing an image of a preferred state, community, or social institution requires a storehouse of ideas and imagination. We cannot build without "material." In this case, our materials are the social science concepts and intellectual constructs that incorporate the best of who we are and what we can become. These visions of a better state of affairs are also ethical statements that help us distinguish social from antisocial conduct and define limitations on freedom of actions in the struggle to create a society in which people can achieve their human potential.

A necessary ingredient for envisioning a preferred state of affairs is a setting where real conversation can take place. The qualities of real conversation and settings that encourage such conversation are discussed in greater detail in the section on "Discussions in the Social Studies Classroom."

ACTIVITY

Envisioning the Ideal in Education

In 1990, then-President Bush's administration and the National Governors Association joined forces to create the "National Goals for Education." Through these goals, the president and governors attempted to communicate their vision about the "ideal" in American education. The goals were revised by the Clinton administration in 1994. The goals are that by the year 2000,

1. All children in America will start school ready to learn.

2. The high school graduation rate will increase to at least 90 percent.

3. All students will leave grades 4, 8, and 12 having demonstrated competency in challenging subject matter, including English, mathematics, science, foreign language, civics and government, economics, arts, history, and geography; every school in America will ensure that all students learn to use their minds well, so they may be prepared for responsible citizenship, further learning, and productive employment in our modern economy.

4. U.S. students will be first in the world in mathematics and science achievement.

5. Every adult American will be literate and will possess the knowledge and skills necessary to compete in a global economy and exercise the rights and responsibilities of citizenship.

6. Every school in the United States will be free of drugs, violence, and the unauthorized presence of firearms and alcohol, and will offer a disciplined environment conducive to learning.

7. The nation's teaching force will have access to programs for the continued improvement of their professional skills and the opportunity to acquire the knowledge and skills needed to instruct and prepare all American students for the next century.

8. Every school will promote partnerships that will increase parental involvement and participation in promoting the social, emotional, and academic growth of children.

Working in small groups, identify the value premises or biases on which these goals are based. Do the goals reflect recent changes in demography or behavior patterns? As a prospective social studies teacher, do you agree that these goals describe a vision of the "ideal" in American education? If not, how would you modify or replace the goals to reflect your own values?

Assessing Present Conditions

The Declaration of Independence states that all men are created equal. Students look around and ask: "Are you crazy? Can't you see the real world? And what about women?"

Our visions of the world are just that—visions of what could and should be. But that's a far cry from what is. Trying to find out what is real is no simple matter, however. Our understanding of reality is always colored by our perceptions, values, history, methods of inquiry—in short, our worldview.

To collect impressions of the real world, we use words, numbers, pictures, even music. With these symbols, we create "logical" explanations that form the base of our reality. These explanations tend to be historical narratives; they are sequential and cumulative, and tell of the birth and growth of an event, a condition, or an idea. Since social reality is always changing, these narratives try to explain change. Three criteria must be met to offer an explanation:

- An explanation should accurately tell what happened over a period of time.
- An explanation should be communicated in a logical sequence.
- An explanation should include significant data about the subject to demonstrate the validity of the conclusions.

We must recognize, however, that these narratives illuminate in two directions. They shed light on the world our senses perceive and they reflect the value premises or biases we hold. Recognizing the subjectivity of the person who is trying to understand or explain events, people use many kinds of resources to describe reality. Some of us use more numbers or quantitative analysis; others are comfortable with words; still others prefer to use pictures or music. Together, these ways of explaining reality, or ways of knowing, can provide a fuller description of "what is" and a base for constructing a bridge between the real world and the envisioned one.

How does one find out about the world? What is the real story about pollution, population, unemployment, homelessness, literacy rates, standards of living, infant mortality, AIDS, military budgets, taxes, and so forth? What databases can we use? To whom should we talk? What should we observe?

Any description of reality will deal with change and continuity. It will establish some sense of causality. It will be placed within a temporal and spatial framework. The explanation will also be limited by the nature and quality of evidence (data) and the biases or frame of reference of the reporter.

| ACTIVITY | **Assessing the Present Condition of Education** |

Returning to the problem of American education, how would you go about determining the "real" with respect to the present condition of schools? What databases would be available? To whom would you talk? What would you observe? What forms of information—words, pictures, numbers, music—would best convey this reality for you?

Moving toward the Ideal

Building a bridge between visions of what could be and reality is the essence of policymaking. It is like constructing a bridge or a new road from "A" to "B," knowing all the time that the old bridge or road will continue to be used. The metaphor of building a new bridge while the old one is in use suggests that building is not enough; one must also be aware of the current traffic patterns and decide what to do with present needs of drivers.

Armed with knowledge of who we are and what we want to be, we can begin constructing policy. A basic plan or design for policymaking includes the construction of a time line; procedures for evaluating how effective the policy is in moving toward the planned idea of what could be; and strategies for midcourse corrections in the plan.

Figure 13.2 provides a framework you can use with students in developing policy. Note that an important inducement to encourage student participation in policymaking is their perception that they can make a difference. For that reason, it is important for students to make a *public statement* of some kind. That statement might take the form of letters to legislators, newspapers, or other citizens; publication of a newsletter or a series of articles; petitions; resolutions; models; booklets; presentations to other classes or the parent-teacher organization; and so on.

ACTIVITY | **Developing a National Education Policy**

Use the model in Figure 13.2 to develop a national education policy for the United States.

DISCUSSIONS IN THE SOCIAL STUDIES CLASSROOM

"At the heart of strong democracy is talk," says Benjamin Barber (1984), who identifies nine functions of strong democratic talk:

- The articulation of interests; bargaining and exchange
- Persuasion
- Agenda setting
- Exploring mutuality
- Affiliation and affection
- Maintaining autonomy
- Witness and self-expression
- Reformulation and reconceptualization
- Building community

In addition to being a foundation of democracy, discourse is also a means to improve learning. Thus, it is critical to social studies teachers and students. If interviewed, most social studies teachers would likely say they use discussions as a principal teaching strategy in their classrooms. Yet many classroom discussions lack the qualities that we are advocating in this section.

Classroom discussions are typically teacher-centered. Often they are used not to clarify or deepen understanding but to check whether students can repeat information

I. Defining the Issue and Envisioning a More Ideal Condition

    A. Define the Problem
        What is the problem?
        Is the problem widely accepted as a public problem?

    B. Envision a More Ideal Condition
        How would you describe an "ideal" or improved condition?
        What are your goals?
        What consequences do you foresee with regard to your position?

II. Assessing Present Conditions

    A. Present the Background of the Problem
        What are the facts of the current situation?
        What were the goals of the old public policy?
        What went wrong and why?
        Who is responsible for what went wrong?
        What is the evidence?
        How have other jurisdictions responded to similar problems?
        What is the nature of disputes about the problem? If there are conflicting views, include factual issues, definitional issues, legal claims (if any), and value conflicts.

    B. Identify the Participants in the Decision-Making Process
        Who are the participants?
        How did they become participants?
        What are their objectives?
        How might private decisions and public policies complement or interfere with each other?
        How might private decisions help resolve this problem? How likely are they to be accepted by the individuals involved?
        How do individual choices affect public consequences?

III. Constructing Policy

    A. Prepare a Policy Statement or Action Plan
        What is your goal?
        What problems interfere with your achieving the goal?
        What activities do you believe will bring about the desired changes?
        What is your time line for implementing these activities?

    B. Evaluate Your Recommendations
        Do you have enough evidence to clearly describe the situation?
        What alternative policies are possible?
        Why did you choose the alternative you chose?
        What are the possible economic, political, or social consequences of this action?

IV. Deciding What to Do

    A. Reevaluate your decision on the basis of Part IIIB.

    B. Develop your final policy recommendations.

Figure 13.2   A policymaking model

back to the teacher; that is, the strategy is actually recitation rather than discussion. In this section, we are talking about something different—purposeful discourse that helps individuals become loving critics of the group they are helping to develop—be it a group of two or a large community. This kind of discourse might more accurately be called *conversation*.

ACTIVITY	### Comparing Conversation and Discussion

Think of the last really good conversation you were involved in. Jot down some adjectives that describe the conversation, the people involved, the general setting and atmosphere.

Now think of a recent classroom discussion in which you participated. Jot down some adjectives that describe that discussion, the people involved, the general setting and atmosphere.

What were the key differences between your remembered conversation and the classroom discussion? What might be the significance of those differences for you as a student? for you as a teacher?

Developing an Environment Conducive to Conversation*

Conversation carries attributes of civility, discipline, clarity, personal and group interest, responsibility to listen and contribute to the dialogue, honor, and respect. In addition, there should be a logic and a vocabulary to which all parties in the conversation can relate. A lack of common vocabulary can be a stumbling block to good conversation but can be overcome with careful listening, use of reference materials, and attention to the context of the argument. In real conversations where one wants to understand and be understood, it is necessary to do the following:

- Consider and respect the linguistic backgrounds of the people involved.
- Pay attention to the ways the conversation relates to the lives of the participants.
- Ask for examples or restatements when misunderstanding or misinterpretation is possible.
- Recognize that conceptions people build through conversation are holistic, personal, and rooted in assumptions about society, people, events, and ideas gained over a lifetime.
- Take seriously what is said in the hope that the conversation will provide more understanding of the topic, as well as more self-awareness.

---

*This section was developed by Michael Hartoonian.

- Anticipate the direction of the conversation so that contributions can be complementary.

- Speak clearly; help others understand what you are saying by building logical sequences that others can follow.

The setting in which conversation occurs can be described metaphorically as an ecosystem. Ecosystems are defined by attributes such as balance, aesthetics, openness, functions, process, and renewal. We become concerned when pollutants throw the system out of balance, destroy its beauty, or close down processes necessary for renewal.

What pollutants make the school or classroom ecosystem unhealthy to the point of inhibiting real conversation? What are the aberrations that make the system dysfunctional? Although the research base for identifying the following as pollutants is unclear, be aware of (1) administrative/bureaucratic structures that emphasize form at the expense of substance and function and complicate matters through the use of rules, (2) language that is unclear, ambiguous, misleading, or contradictory, and (3) self-serving attitudes and behaviors.

The ecosystem metaphor suggests elimination, cutting away, or cleansing the system, not adding more things to it. Providing a healthy setting for conversation is fundamentally a conserving act, an act of simplification. Necessary conditions within the setting include an appreciation of beauty and of openness to and from all within the group. Intellectual and psychological comforts are important, with the warning not to make the setting too comfortable. Essentially, there should be a comfort level that allows mistakes and encourages experimentation, floating ideas, and full debate.

| ACTIVITY | **Observing Classroom Discussions** |

Observe several classroom discussions or conversations. Which one was most like the conversation described above? What was the teacher's role in the conversation? How did group members show respect for each other?

Using Questions in Social Studies Discussions

The authors of a recent review of the research on the questioning patterns of social studies teachers report that "teachers still ask a high frequency of low cognitive level questions and students still have little time to think before they are expected to respond" (Wilen and White 1991). This pattern persists in the face of evidence that (1) higher cognitive questions do stimulate higher-level thinking and increase student achievement (Gall 1984) and (2) when teachers wait longer for a student response before restating a question or asking another student, the length and quality of student answers increase, as do the number of students participating voluntarily, the confidence and motivation of students, the number of student-to-student exchanges, and student achievement on cognitively complex test items (Rowe 1986).

A number of models for using questions to develop higher-order thinking are available (see, for example, Bloom 1956; Guilford 1956; Woolever 1987). The following discussion is based on a model developed by Cornbleth (1977).*

Productive social studies discussions require the use of different types of questions. Questions differ in the kinds of thinking they prompt and in the functions they serve. Which questions (or questioning strategies) are most appropriate depends on several factors, including the goal and phase of the discussion. Some types of questions are more effective during the initiation phase, and others are better suited to the development and synthesis phases.

The initiation phase of discussion is intended to arouse interest and indicate the purpose of the discussion. When students know what is expected of them and are motivated to participate, discussion is more likely to be productive. Discussion can be effectively initiated by a single question or by a brief presentation followed by a question. In either case, it is important that the opening question be clearly phrased and open-ended.

The development phase is the body of the discussion and usually the longest segment. During this time, ideas generated in the initiation phase are elaborated, refined, compared, and evaluated. Alternatives are sought if initial ideas are found inadequate, and additional information is introduced as needed to test hypotheses.

The synthesis is the concluding phase of the discussion. During this phase, conclusions are reached, generalizations are formulated, decisions are made, or plans (for application or action) are designed.

Social studies questions can be divided into six types: personal belief/experience, memory, comprehension, creative expression, judgment, and follow-up. Some types of questions can be used more effectively in one phase of discussion than in another. Comprehension, creative expression, judgment, and follow-up questions are appropriate to all three phases. Personal belief/experience questions are more appropriate in the initiation and development than in the synthesis phase, while memory questions are usually suitable only in the development phase.

Personal Belief/Experience Questions   These questions request that individuals relate their own experiences, feelings, opinions, or preferences. No rationale or justification is expected or required, and there are no right or wrong answers. By eliciting students' beliefs and experiences, these questions provide data for concept development, as well as feedback regarding students' attitudes and interests. They

---

*The following discussion is excerpted from C. Cornbleth, *How-to-Do-It: Using Questions in Social Studies* (Washington, D.C.: National Council for Social Studies, 1977). © *National Council for the Social Studies. Reprinted by permission.*

also aid in increasing interest, attention, and participation by personalizing social studies, drawing on students' own experiences and relating them to the topic under consideration.

Examples

- How would you feel about moving to an unfamiliar neighborhood?
- In which of these ancient cultures would you have preferred to live?
- What are some ways in which government directly affects you?

Memory Questions   These questions ask for the recall of information previously presented by the teacher and textbook or acquired from other sources. Memory questions solicit simple repetition of information in its original form. They typically have only one right answer. The desired response may be a single word, a brief phrase, a listing of items, or an extended narrative.

Memory questions have relatively limited usefulness in discussion. Exclusive or even predominant use of memory questions would yield only superficial social studies knowledge and fail to promote skill development, decision making, or creativity. Memory questions also tend to block discussion when they suggest conclusions desired by the teacher or, in effect, ask students to "tell me what the textbook says." However, the judicious use of memory questions might assist the development phase of a discussion when actual information is needed to (1) form a base from which inferences can be drawn, (2) clarify a situation or a sequence of events, or (3) provide data for testing hypotheses. When the teacher asks memory questions in these instances, the questions serve what is essentially an assessment function; that is, the teacher uses memory questions to determine whether at least some students possess pertinent background information. If they do, their information would be shared with the other members of the group. If students do not have the information, the teacher would provide or otherwise help the students obtain it and then reopen the discussion.

Examples

- What are three different types of pollution?
- When were automobiles first used on a regular basis in the United States?
- In what sequence did these revolutions occur? (American, Chinese, French, Mexican, Russian)

Comprehension Questions   These questions ask for reasoning or information processing, such as comparing and contrasting, relating, identifying, classifying, inferring, hypothesizing, and generalizing. Comprehension questions can also involve interpreting data (by translating, paraphrasing, or explaining), distinguishing examples of a concept or phenomenon, applying ideas in new situations, analyzing data, organizing, reorganizing, and summarizing. Comprehension questions can have one best answer, but, unlike memory questions, there is rarely only one right answer.

Comprehension questions play a particularly important role in knowledge acquisition and concept formation, skill development, and decision making. They often are the key questions in the development phase of discussion. In using comprehension questions to encourage thinking, it is important to note that what is intended as a comprehension question might, in fact, be only a memory question if answers have been provided earlier and students are expected merely to repeat previously presented information. For example, asking students to identify differences between life in 18th-century English and Spanish America is a memory question if such differences have been reviewed earlier. However, if students have previously studied but not compared the two colonial societies, then it would qualify as a comprehension question. Thus, the context as well as the substance of a question affects the type of thinking likely to be generated.

Examples

- According to these maps, which areas have a climate suitable for growing citrus crops?
- What conclusions can be drawn from the data we have collected about voter participation in local, state, and national elections?
- What evidence of cultural lag is apparent in this case study?
- On the basis of what we have studied about attitude formation, what might be some ways of minimizing prejudice?

Creative Expression Questions   These questions ask for the construction or reconstruction of a new and different pattern—that is, the formulation of a novel proposal, product, or performance. Although the outcome is new for the individual, it need not be unique in a historical or global sense. Creative expression questions often pose hypothetical situations and ask students how they might respond, a sort of verbal role playing. Or they might request the production of oral, written, graphic, or dramatic communications, which can take any number of forms, including essays, collages, theories, and models.

Responding to a creative expression question involves thinking and feeling, combining ideas, experiences, and attitudes in some personally meaningful and satisfying way. It is this individualized or personalized aspect of creative expression that distinguishes it from comprehension. Although both involve information processing, creative expression also incorporates individuality and imagination.

Examples

- How would you account for the recurring reports of UFO sightings and contacts with nonhuman beings?
- Construct a plan for an ideal city. How would it look, sound, and smell?

- If you were president of the United States, what would be your energy policy?

- How might what is now the United States have developed differently if exploration and settlement had begun from the west instead of the east?

Judgment Questions   These questions ask for an evaluation of the worth, importance, merit, goodness, appropriateness, effectiveness, or efficiency of an idea, event, action, object, or individual. They go beyond personal belief/experience questions by asking for the criteria or standards used in making the judgment and the evidence that supports it. Criteria and evidence are sought either in the initial question or in follow-up questions. (Thus, a personal belief/experience question becomes a judgment question when it is followed by a request for justification. Also, judgment questions may be viewed as a special case of creative expression in which one is asked to reach and justify a personal value decision.)

Judgment questions encourage rational conflict resolution and decision making by involving students in examining alternatives and basing conclusions on relevant data. Although judgment questions have no one right answer, all judgments are not equal; a position is only as strong as the reasoning and evidence that supports it.

Examples

- Which of these proposals is most likely to be effective in solving our local housing problems? (What is the basis for your decision?)

- Agree or disagree with the following quotation from Carl Schurz's speech in the Senate, January 17, 1872, indicating the reasons and evidence that support your position: "Our country, right or wrong. When right, to be kept right; when wrong, to be put right."

- What is the best location for a new community recreation center? (How did you arrive at that conclusion?)

- Which twentieth-century invention has had the most impact on our way of life? (What criteria are you using to judge impact? What is the evidence supporting your decision?)

Follow-up Questions   These questions seek to develop responses, usually by requesting elaboration, clarification, or justification of the original statements. Although we occasionally follow up incomplete, partial, or inappropriate student responses (or no response) by rephrasing questions or providing clues, probing adequate responses is less common. We tend to move too quickly to another question or student, thus missing opportunities to develop ideas and to encourage thoughtful inquiry and reflection. Productive discussion depends in large part on the use of follow-up questions to increase the scope and quality of participation.

Follow-up questions can request further information or implications (elaboration), specification, explanation, examples (clarification), or criteria and evidence on which conclusions are based (justification). In addition, justification follow-up questions can suggest consequences, alternatives, or apparent contradictions for consideration. Some examples of justification follow-up questions were indicated in parentheses following the sample judgment questions presented earlier.

Additional examples

- What else happened?
- What would be an example of chauvinism?
- Why is that important to you?
- How would you summarize what you have just said?

Although the use of follow-up questions is strongly recommended, two qualifications should be noted. First, follow-up questions might be seen as threatening by some students. They might become reluctant to respond to any questions, fearing that all their responses would be challenged by the teacher. This possibility can be minimized, in part, by the manner in which follow-up questions are asked. For instance, depending on our tone of voice and facial expression, "What do you mean by that?" can communicate "How could you say something so stupid!"—a rhetorical nonquestion—or "I'm interested in what you're saying, but I don't quite understand."

A second possible misuse of follow-up questions occurs when the teacher becomes so involved in an extended dialogue with one student that others lose interest. It is often desirable to pursue a line of reasoning to explore an idea fully, but it is also desirable to maintain the attention and involvement of most, if not all, of the group. To accomplish both goals, one or two follow-up questions might be directed to one student, with additional follow-up questions directed to others.

All six types of questions can be useful in the development phase of a social studies discussion. Questions that call for creative expression and judgment are likely to be effective discussion openers because they provide focus and tend to stimulate interest and thought. Similarly, personal belief/experience questions and comprehension questions that call for inferences or hypothesizing are likely to be able to initiate discussion effectively. Comprehension, creative expression, and judgment questions are probably the most appropriate types of questions to use during the synthesis phase. Follow-up questions not only are useful in all phases but also seem to be crucial to the success of the discussion as a whole.

At the beginning of this section, we noted that it is important to provide time for students to think before responding to a question. Increasing so-called wait time from the average of less than one second to from three to five seconds has significant positive results. In addition, allowing time to think is a good model for participating in discussions as citizens. As Barber (1984) has said, "One measure of healthy political talk is the amount of *silence* it permits and encourages, for silence is the precious medium in which reflection is nurtured and empathy can grow."

Developing a Questioning Strategy

According to Cornbleth, "A questioning strategy is a purposeful sequence of inter-related questions intended to facilitate attainment of specific learning goals. While the key questions are preplanned and intended to be used in a specified order, effective strategies are flexible and open-ended. Varied types of questions are employed, pacing is variable, and outcomes are not predetermined. The combination of structure and openness contributes significantly to their effectiveness as discussion guides."

Review the unit and lesson plans you have developed in this course. Choose one and develop a questioning strategy for a key discussion in the lesson or unit.

COOPERATIVE LEARNING

In the past several years, cooperative learning has received more attention in the literature than virtually any other approach to teaching. The reasons for its high visibility are the benefits that its research base indicates cooperative learning holds. Among those benefits are improvements in self-esteem, liking of school and subjects, time on task, attendance, ability to work with others, student achievement (especially in grades 2–9), and interpersonal relations across ethnic and ability lines (Slavin 1990).

A number of models for using cooperative learning have been developed. For example, David and Roger Johnson (1987, 1989) have developed a cooperative learning model called Learning Together. Learning Together has five key elements: positive student interdependence; individual accountability for learning; face-to-face interaction among students; development of social skills; group assessment of their own effectiveness; and heterogeneous teaming. Robert Slavin's Student Teams–Achievement Divisions model (1978) also uses heterogeneous teams in which students help each other master material; although students take quizzes individually, team rewards are earned. Two characteristics of all the models are key: (1) positive interdependence, meaning that students rely on each other to meet group goals, and (2) individual accountability, meaning that students remain responsible for their own learning.

Clearly, development of a task for cooperative group work must be carefully done. According to Mary McCaslin and Thomas L. Good (1992), small-group instruction can allow students to become even more passive and dependent if the task is poorly designed. In such cases, students spend too much time on procedural problems, or small numbers of students dominate the groups, thereby defeating the purposes of cooperative learning groups.

An effective cooperative learning task should not be one that simply involves independent student work around a small-group table or group work that can be easily dominated by one or two students. Ensuring that the task is within students' capabilities is essential, as is allowing adequate time for task completion. It is also advisable to structure the task so that it can be easily explained in a minimum number of steps.

Indeed, structures are an important part of cooperative learning. Spencer Kagan (1990) defines *structures* as "content-free ways of organizing social interaction in the classroom. Structures usually involve a series of steps, with proscribed behavior at each step" (p. 12). Kagan points out that teachers use structures constantly in their work. For example, one of the common structures he identifies as "Whole-Class Question-Answer," in which the teacher asks a question, students who want to respond raise their hands, the teacher calls on one student, and that student answers, closing off the other students' chances to participate. If the student selected is wrong, the other students' chances are reopened, indicating that they profit from a classmate's mistake.

Kagan contrasts that structure with a cooperative structure he calls "Numbered Heads Together." In using this structure, the teacher numbers students within groups so that each student has a number from 1 to 4. When the teacher asks a question, he or she tells group members to put their heads together to make sure everyone knows the answer. The teacher then calls one of the numbers, and students with that number respond. This structure provides an example of positive interdependence; if one student in a group knows the answer, all students learn. However, students are still individually accountable, since individual students whose numbers are called must respond on their own.

One of the most widely known cooperative learning structures is the Jigsaw (Aronson et al. 1978; Slavin 1987). In the Jigsaw, each student in a cooperative learning group is assigned a topic on which to become an expert. Students assigned the same topic work together to master the material. They then return to their original groups and teach the material to group members.

Different structures are appropriate for different learning objectives. For example, Numbered Heads Together is useful in reviewing information and checking for comprehension, and the Jigsaw is appropriate for acquiring new material as well as reviewing previously covered material. A structure called the Three-step Interview is useful in sharing personal reactions, hypotheses, and other responses. Kagan recommends the structural approach because teachers do not have to master "cooperative learning" as such but can gain skill with one new structure at a time.

To be successful with a number of the cooperative learning structures or models, students need social skills, including communication skills, conflict resolution skills, and the ability to encourage and support others. To develop such skills, Johnson and Johnson (1990) recommend that teachers help students understand why the skill is important, define the skill and demonstrate when it should be used, and provide opportunities for frequent practice using the skill and reflecting on that use.

At times, it may be useful to assign one group member to act as an observer, noting strengths and areas for improvement in group skills. Teacher evaluation of group skills can also be helpful, especially if it is specific and includes positive observations, as well as suggestions for improvement. Assigning writing activities that require students to verbalize what they might do to improve their group skills can also be effective.

<table>
<tr>
<td>ACTIVITY</td>
<td>

A Jigsaw

In a group of four, number off from 1 to 4. Assign the following cooperative learning structures to group members:

Member 1: Roundtable

Member 2: Three-step interview

Member 3: Think-pair-share

Member 4: Team word-webbing

Now regroup, with all 1s together, all 2s together, and so on. In your new groups, find out more about the assigned strategy; then brainstorm social studies lessons using the strategy. Each member of the group should then pick one of the brainstormed ideas and develop a two-paragraph description of its use in the classroom.

Return to your original group and share the teaching ideas developed with the group.
</td>
</tr>
<tr>
<td>ACTIVITY</td>
<td>

Brainstorming Teaching Strategies

Brainstorm as many teaching strategies as you can think of. Stimulate your thinking by reviewing the strategies provided earlier in this book, as well as other strategies you have encountered in observing secondary classrooms. Post a class list of strategies on the chalkboard.

In groups of three, create a system for categorizing the strategies. Compare your system of categorization with that of another group. What criteria did the groups use to differentiate among the various strategies? How might the various criteria be useful in deciding when to use particular strategies?
</td>
</tr>
</table>

TIPS FOR USING A RANGE OF INSTRUCTIONAL STRATEGIES

The range of instructional strategies available to you is extremely varied. It is unlikely that we will, in this section, cover all the strategies you listed in the foregoing brainstorming activity. We hope, however, to provide you with some guidelines for using a number of strategies that can serve as a base for development of your own teaching style.

As you likely discovered, teaching strategies can be categorized in a variety of ways; for example, they can be classified according to whether they are teacher- or student-centered; individual, small-group, or whole-class; highly active or primarily passive; directed toward content, skill, or attitude objectives; and so on. We have organized this section by presenting activities as they might fall along a continuum from activities in which students are primarily gathering or generating information, to activities in which students are processing information and developing meaning, to activities in which students are applying what they have learned to a real-life setting.

Lecture

As a college student, you are likely very familiar with the lecture technique, since it is the predominant mode of instruction at the postsecondary level. Unfortunately, it also predominates in many secondary classrooms, even though research has shown that students retain little of what is presented through lectures. Furthermore, lectures generally address only knowledge-acquisition objectives and do not promote higher-order thinking or ethical decision making.

Even a teacher committed to active, student-centered learning may sometimes find a lecture necessary, however. For example, a lecture may be the most efficient way to present background information students will need to participate in a role play or analyze a primary source document. A lecture may also be a good way to begin a new unit or a long-term assignment for which the teacher wants to establish a common information base or point of view.

When you decide that a lecture is appropriate, plan the lecture very carefully. The cardinal rule for secondary teachers is *be brief*. Limit the number of points you will make, focusing on those that are most important. Outline your lecture—then shorten it. Combine the lecture with an active learning strategy.

Begin the lecture by engaging students' interest through a thought-provoking quotation or vignette, a puzzling or challenging question or problem, or a fact that contradicts what they believe to be true. Give the students a preview of the structure of the lecture (and follow the structure!). This technique will help them connect the information presented to their own knowledge structures. It will also be useful in note taking, which is a skill you can help students develop as you are lecturing.

Keep the presentation lively; move around the room, be animated, use humor when appropriate. Use concrete examples and make connections with what students have previously learned. Visuals—pictures, maps, artifacts, demonstrations—can be effective in retaining student interest and reinforcing the points you are making. Avoid digressions—even if you think the digression is a great story.

Build in time to check for understanding. Before each pause, summarize where you are in the overall outline for the presentation. During the checking time, both you and the students may want to ask questions that will help you ascertain whether they are attending and understanding and help them clarify points that were confusing.

At the end of the lecture, review the main points made, using the structure you presented in the preview.

Evaluating Lectures

Develop an instrument for evaluating lectures. Then use the instrument to evaluate lectures given by several of your professors. Which criteria do they most often meet? Which do they most often fail to meet?

Resource People in the Classroom

Because many social studies classes involve several specialized content areas, as well as public decision making, use of community resources in the classroom is particularly appropriate. Community resources can add information not available to teachers and lend authenticity to the issues being discussed. Indeed, research has shown that in the case of law-related education, use of such resource people can actually affect students' attitudes and behavior.

When considering how resource people could be used, do not limit yourself to guest lectures or question-and-answer periods with the students, although those may sometimes be appropriate. Resource people can also participate in such activities as simulated press conferences, panel discussions, role plays, and mock trials. They may also judge or mentor student projects.

Locating resource people requires time, but a few shortcuts are available. Consult other teachers who have used resource persons. Ask students what types of resource persons would be valuable and whether they know anyone who would fit the bill. Ask the officers of your parent organization to organize a list of parent-speakers. Contact such umbrella organizations as the Chamber of Commerce; they may provide referrals as a public service. Consult the education editor of the local newspaper or talk with staff of a regional service agency.

When a classroom visit is arranged, the teacher should explain the goals and objectives of the presentation, making clear how the presentation fits into the overall unit of study. The resource person should be given information about the class (age, grade level, size, knowledge of the topic, presence of any students having disabilities that might affect the manner in which a presentation is made), the room size, setup, availability of special equipment, and the time available. Teachers may find it helpful to provide resource persons with the list of do's and don'ts provided in Figure 13.3.

Don't:

- Lecture at students.
- Use jargon or unfamiliar words.
- Act condescending or omniscient.
- Become angry at unresponsiveness or comments and questions that are off track.
- React defensively to criticism.
- Read a prepared speech.
- Talk in a monotone.
- Assume that students either have or lack knowledge about a given point.

Do:

- Consider the age and experience of the audience.
- Maintain eye contact.
- Solicit response frequently.
- Encourage active participation early and throughout the presentation.
- Be yourself; let your personality show; be real; smile.
- Call on a variety of students and involve the teacher.
- Circulate around the room.
- Make sure that everyone hears all questions and answers.
- Know the objectives for your visit and how it relates to what students are studying.

Figure 13.3 Do's and don'ts for the resource person

Teachers should also prepare students for the resource person's visit. Students should understand the purpose of the visit and complete any preparatory work in advance (e.g., preparing questions to be asked in a simulated press conference). Special procedures, if any, should be explained before the visit.

Each presentation by a resource person should be assessed by the teacher, the students, and the resource person. The evaluation results should become a part of the teacher's permanent file on resource persons. Careful records of every presentation will allow teachers to make improvements, identify appropriate resources for future use, and avoid overuse or underuse of particular persons. Combining the records of several teachers can result in a directory of resources.

Brainstorming

Brainstorming is the process of generating as many alternative suggestions as possible to fit a given situation. The brainstorm is a useful classroom strategy because all students, regardless of level of academic achievement, can participate equally. It is nonthreatening because no evaluation is allowed, and it does not require prior preparation. In addition, a significant amount of information can be gathered quickly.

A critical concern, of course, has to do with what one chooses to have a class brainstorm about. The question should be clearly stated. It should be one for which there are multiple possible answers. Students should be able to generate ideas without extensive background knowledge. For example, displaying an artifact from another culture and asking students to brainstorm possible uses would be an appropriate brainstorming task, whereas asking them to brainstorm possible reasons for the Russian Revolution as an opening activity in a unit on Russian and Soviet history would not.

Specific rules for the brainstorming process (see Figure 13.4) should be shared and discussed with students before a brainstorming session begins. Allow students to call out their ideas without having to be recognized. All ideas should be posted without evaluative comments or editing. Critical comments can too often prevent creative but risky suggestions from being presented. The teacher can often stimulate a stagnant session by proposing truly outlandish ideas.

Another way to encourage creativity is to use the SCAMPER technique (see Figure 13.4). In this technique, students reexamine and apply each of the SCAMPER elements to the ideas already suggested.

The debriefing of a brainstorm should focus on the use of the ideas within the context of the teacher's purpose in conducting the brainstorm. For example, if the purpose of a brainstorm is to make students aware of how widespread the effects of air pollution are, the debriefing might focus on the sheer number of items generated

---

Rules of Brainstorming

1. Say anything that comes to mind.
2. Piggybacking on the ideas of others is good.
3. Don't evaluate or criticize what others say.
4. When you can't think of anything else, wait a minute and try again.

The SCAMPER Technique

S = substitute, subtract
C = combine
A = adapt, add
M = modify, minify, magnify
P = put to other uses, piggyback
E = eliminate
R = reverse

Figure 13.4   Tips for brainstorming

and their seriousness. On the other hand, if the purpose is to generate ideas for research projects, some evaluation of ideas using specific criteria related to suitability of research might be in order during the debriefing.

Analyzing a Lesson

Read the lesson provided as Figure 13.5. Expand on the lesson by

- Developing specific questions to debrief the brainstorming
- Outlining the brief lecture on music in twentieth-century protest movements
- Creating a way in which resource people could be used in the lesson

Also analyze the lesson from the standpoint of its overall effectiveness. Does it engage students by making connections with what they already know? Does it allow students to explore important concepts and then to develop explanations of those concepts and elaborate upon them? How might you improve the lesson?

Surveys

Social scientists in several disciplines use survey research techniques, which can also be adapted for classroom use. Surveys can be administered either to or by students. A survey of students' attitudes can be an effective way to begin a unit because it motivates student interest by stimulating thought and discussion on issues related to the unit topic.

When using a survey to stimulate thought and interest, ask each student to complete the survey independently in class. After students have completed the survey, form discussion pairs; this strategy will give all the students a chance to discuss their views.

Next, tabulate the responses for the class and conduct a discussion based on the results, focusing on the questions that generated the most variance in opinions. The teacher's role should be primarily that of a facilitator, encouraging students to support the opinions they express. Be sure at the end of the discussion to make a connection between the survey and the topic students will be studying. Returning to the survey at the completion of the unit may be useful in promoting student reflection.

Another use of the survey technique is having students develop and administer a survey, either within the school or in the community. The first step in developing such a survey is determining the study's purpose. A clear focus will keep the survey from becoming too lengthy; it will also help identify the kinds of people to be surveyed. Structuring the questions so they have a limited number of possible responses will make the data easier for students to analyze. However, they may want to include one open-ended question to experience the richness of the responses such questions can generate.

Music and Movements

Introduction: Music has been significant in many of the popular social and political movements of the 20th century. In fact, the post–World War II years saw what social historian and musicologist John Anthony Scott calls "an intense and widespread revival of interest in the traditional song heritage; new songs, some of them rivaling the finest creations of the past, have been born out of the agonies and struggles of our modern age." This activity will acquaint students with the work of several musicians of note and allow them to make inferences about the movements to which their work contributed.

Objectives: Students will be able to:

1. Describe the role music played in social movements.
2. Interpret the lyrics of songs written in the folk tradition.
3. Explain how music can be used as a tool in social movements.

Teaching Time: 1 to 1½ class periods.

Materials and Preparation: Obtain copies of the lyrics and, if possible, the music for one or more songs of the labor movement, as well as several songs popular during the civil rights movement. The song "Ludlow Massacre" by Woody Guthrie is particularly appropriate; "We Shall Overcome" and "Keep on Walkin'" are excellent examples of civil rights songs. A good source for such songs is *The Ballad of America: The History of the United States in Song and Story,* by John Anthony Scott (Carbondale, IL: Southern Illinois University Press, 1983). Obtain recordings of the works of Bob Dylan ("The Times They Are A-Changin'" and "Blowin' in the Wind"); if these are not available, you might substitute recordings by Joan Baez, Peter, Paul and Mary, Simon and Garfunkel, or others who sang antiwar songs or songs about the disaffection of youth in the 1960s.

Procedure:

1. Ask students, as a class or in small groups, to brainstorm a list of all the situations in which they hear music. Some possibilities include when listening to the radio; as background in movies; as part of church services; as background in stores, elevators, and other public places.
2. Ask students to think about how music is used in each situation—for enjoyment, to set a mood, to worship, to inspire or unite people, and so on. Are any of the uses negative (e.g., to incite violence, encourage drug use)?
3. Tell the students that in the 20th century, music has played a part in inspiring and uniting people involved in a number of social and political movements. Tell students that black musician Bernice Reagon developed an entirely new vision of music as a result of her participation in the civil rights movement. Read the passage below written by Reagon. Discuss with students what Reagon means by such descriptions as "an instrument with which you can drive a point." You may wish to share some background information on Reagon with students during this discussion (see "Teacher Background Information").

continued

Figure 13.5   Sample lesson: Music and movements (Giese, Parisi, and Singleton 1990)

The Civil Rights Movement changed my view of music. It was after my first march. I began to sing a song and in the course of singing changed the song so that it made sense for that particular moment. Although I was not consciously aware of it, that was one of my earliest experiences with how my music was supposed to function. This music was to be integrative of and consistent with everything I was doing at that time. . . .

I fell in love with that kind of music. I saw to define the music as something you listen to, something that pleases you, is very different from defining it as an instrument with which you can drive a point. In both instances, you have the same song. But using it as an instrument makes it a different kind of music.

I now believe that black music exists in every place where Black people run, every corner where they live, every level on which they struggle. We have been here a long while, in many situations. It takes all that we have created to sing our song. I believe that Black musicians/artists have a responsibility to be conscious of their world and to let their consciousness be heard in their songs.

4. Divide the class into small groups and give each group one set of the songs you have copied. The groups are to read through the songs, determine what movement each song was a part of, and decide to whom each song was addressed. What techniques (such as repetition, humor, pathos, defiance) do the songs use to make their points?

5. Allow time for the groups to report on their songs to the class. You may share information about Guthrie from the "Teacher Background Information" during this discussion.

6. Play the recording of sixties music you brought to class. Allow students to discuss the songs in their small groups, or conduct a whole-class discussion. What movement were these songs part of? To whom were they addressed? What techniques were used? What was the quality of the singing? Does the quality of singing affect the power of the message?

7. Encourage students to research other songwriters who have written about social or political problems including such contemporary musicians as Tracy Chapman, John Cougar Mellencamp, U2, Queen Latifah, and Bruce Springsteen.

Teacher Background Information: Bernice Reagon was a college student in Albany, Georgia, in the 1960s, when she became involved in the civil rights movement. One of the original Freedom Singers of the Student Nonviolent Coordinating Committee (SNCC), Reagon went on to receive a doctorate in oral history from Howard University. A consultant and field researcher in black music for the Smithsonian Institution, Reagon was one of the founders of the singing group Sweet Honey in the Rock. In 1989, she received a MacArthur award—often called a "genius grant" because it is given to outstanding people who do not apply for the award—to pursue her work.

Woody Guthrie was born in Oklahoma in 1912. His first songs were of the Dust Bowl and the people made homeless by its ravages. He went on to write songs about dozens of issues. In 1940, he organized a group called the Almanac Singers, which also included Pete Seeger. Guthrie was disabled for years before his death, but he inspired many other musicians. His son Arlo is also a folk musician.

Each student should be assigned a specific number of people to be surveyed. Students should be briefed on survey etiquette. Potential respondents should be approached politely and asked if they would have time to respond to a brief survey; the purpose should be explained in a few words. If someone says no, students should not try to change his or her mind. Those who consent should be thanked.

Working with a math teacher to help students analyze their data and present them effectively may be helpful, though probably not necessary. Students should also be encouraged to consider the limitations of their data.

ACTIVITY   ### Designing a Survey Project

Identify a unit taught in a geography course at the high school level. How could you use a survey activity in this unit? If you think a survey of students' attitudes would be more appropriate, draft such a survey and develop some questions you would use to stimulate discussion of the results. If you think a student-conducted survey would be more appropriate, describe the issues on which the survey would focus. How would you help students develop a useful questionnaire? In either case, how would you link the survey with the content of the unit?

Oral History

Oral history is the process of collecting information through tape-recorded interviews with people who have firsthand knowledge of particular past events or issues. Oral histories can provide a source of information for social studies classes, but, perhaps more important, students can also *do* oral history. This activity offers several benefits: It engages students in learning about the past, it provides personal information about issues that may give students deeper insight than secondary sources, and it develops a broad range of skills, including speaking, listening, and analyzing.

Oral history projects can be useful for a variety of purposes. They can help students explore how national or international events affected the people in your community. Students can use them to prepare histories of local institutions or events. They can be used to explore topics in community history/politics. Oral histories can also be valuable in exploring social history—changes in child-rearing practices, education, food preparation, and the like.

Before a teacher undertakes an oral history project, students need background information on the era or topic to be explored. Some of that information can be gained through reading other oral histories, which will acquaint students with the form of oral histories and provide a basis for later substantive comparison with the recollections of their interviewees.

A second useful preparatory step is demonstrating the oral history process by conducting an oral history interview in class. Students can help prepare for the interview by determining the purpose of the interview, generating questions that will tap into the knowledge of the interview subject, and creating follow-up questions to keep the memories flowing. Tape-record the interview as you conduct it. You may then spend a follow-up period analyzing the tape; this will be especially valuable in illustrating how careful listening to the responses can help the interviewer revise or create new follow-up questions. Don't be afraid to point out instances in which a better follow-up question would have elicited more information.

Before students embark on their own interviews, acquaint them with the general guidelines for conducting an interview given in Figure 13.6 and provide release forms for the interviewees to sign. The release form should grant the school permission to use the contents of the interview for educational or scholarly purposes. Be sure all students have access to adequate tape-recording equipment.

As a class, determine the purpose of the interviews and work together to generate possible questions or topics for inquiry. Students may feel more comfortable conducting their first interviews with relatives or close acquaintances. Even role playing interviews with classmates may be good preparation for some classes. Sources for interviewees include the local historical society, articles in the local newspaper, nearby colleges or universities, and local chapters of such organizations as the VFW, NAACP, DAR, or Gray Panthers.

Following the interviews, students should analyze the information gathered, using such questions as

- How reliable is the memory of my interview subject?

- Into what context—local, national, or international—does this interview fit?

- How do this person's recollections and opinions fit with those of others who were interviewed? with information from other kinds of sources?

1. Pick a quiet place in which to conduct the interview.
2. Ask the person you are interviewing to sign the release.
3. Test your equipment before you begin the interview.
4. At the beginning of the tape, state your name, the name of the person you are interviewing, and the date.
5. After the interview, label each tape with your name and the subject's name, the date, and the number (if more than one tape).

Figure 13.6   Guidelines for conducting an oral history interview

The tapes created by the students can become part of a school oral history library on which future classes can draw in conducting such projects.

ACTIVITY **Using Oral Histories**

Locate one of the following oral histories. Read several selections on a particular topic. How do the memories of the various interviewees vary? What additional questions do the excerpts raise? How might you go about structuring an oral history activity that pursued those questions?

- *Voices of Freedom: An Oral History of the Civil Rights Movement*, by Henry Hampton (New York: Bantam Books, 1990).

- *Hard Times, Division Street America, The Good War*, or other works by Studs Terkel (New York: Pantheon).

- *Nam: The Vietnam War in the Words of the Soldiers Who Fought There*, by Mark Baker (New York: Berkeley Books, 1981).

- *In Black and White: Voices of Apartheid*, by Barbara Hutmacher (London: Junction Books, 1980).

- *Unforgettable Fire*, by Japan Broadcasting Corporation (New York: Pantheon, 1977).

- *Voices from the Holocaust*, by Sylvia Rothchild (New York: New American Library, 1981).

- *And Justice for All: An Oral History of the Japanese American Detention Camps*, by John Tateishi (New York: Random House, 1984).

- *Navajo Stories of the Long Walk Period*, by Broderick Johnson (Tsaile, Ariz.: Navajo Community College Press, 1973).

- *Mexican Voices/American Dreams: An Oral History of Mexican Immigration to the United States*, by Marilyn Davis (New York: Henry Holt, 1990).

Field Experiences

Field experiences can make what students are learning in class more concrete and real. Field experiences may include standard field trips (e.g., visiting a water treatment facility), observation at public meetings (e.g., attending a public hearing on land use), and opportunities for actual field study (e.g., gathering data at a landfill).

To be successful, field experiences require careful preplanning, in-class preparation, and debriefing. Once you have decided on a site, make an appointment and visit it yourself. Anticipate problems and think about possible solutions. Discuss your plans with the school principal and obtain all necessary permissions from the site owner, the school administration, and the parents. Be sure that you have adequate help to supervise students.

Before you embark on the field study, prepare the students. Be sure that they understand the objectives of the field experience and how it fits into the current unit of study. Provide guidance if you want students to gather data through field notes, photographs, or other means. Having students work in groups during field experiences often proves successful. Immediately before leaving the classroom, make sure students have all the materials needed.

During the field experience, circulate among groups. Show enthusiasm and participate in activities. Help students focus on the environment by using all their senses. Ask questions to help students observe and make comparisons.

Be sure to allow time after the field experience for class discussion and follow-up. Examine with students what they observed and learned, how it relates to the in-class activities they had been doing before the field experience, and what questions remain to be answered. Follow-up visits or interviews, exhibitions of pictures taken on the trip along with other information gathered, or independent investigations of a similar kind may be planned as a means of extending the field experience.

ACTIVITY

Designing Field Experiences

Divide the class into seven small groups, assigning each group one of the social sciences or history. Each group is to design a field study related to a topic that might be taught in its discipline. The group should describe the field study site, the purpose of the field study, and how it relates to classroom activities. Share your group's work with the rest of the class. Do any of the field studies seem to involve more work by the teacher than they are worth? How might they be redesigned to provide a better cost-benefit ratio?

Concept Mapping

Concept maps are diagrams or graphic representations of meaningful relations between concepts. By using concept mapping, teachers can make explicit links between knowledge, help to identify concepts that are missing or poorly linked in the students' knowledge structure, and promote connections between the prior knowledge the students bring into the classroom and the new knowledge presented there (Novak and Gowin 1984).

Concept maps can take a variety of forms; there is no right or wrong way to prepare such a figure. Their use in instruction is usually traced to Hanf (1971), who placed a central idea in the center of a notepad and put subsidiary concepts in concentric circles around it. Maps can be used before classroom instruction to make existing knowledge and concepts of class members explicit; they can be drawn by individual students as a way to classify knowledge or as a prewriting exercise; a post-instruction map can be drawn for the class and compared with the preinstruction maps (see Figure 13.7, a map drawn by a class after reading about Washington, D.C.).

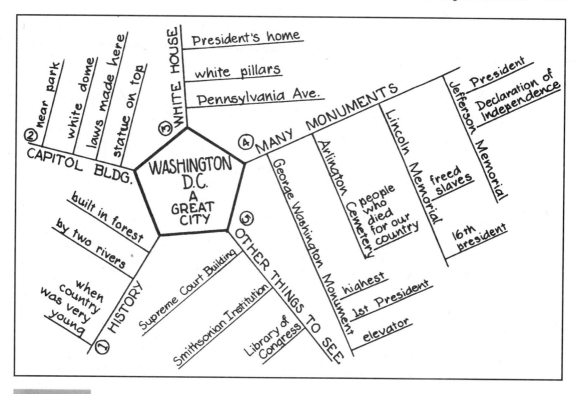

Figure 13.7 Completed class map for Washington, D.C. *Source: From J. Heimlich and S. Pittelman,* Semantic Mapping: Classroom Applications *(Newark, Del.: International Reading Association, 1986). Reprinted with permission of Joan Heimlich and the International Reading Association.*

Research has shown that concept maps can have positive effects on learning. Berkowitz (1986) trained students to generate graphic maps of concepts such as the nation. Groups trained in this way were compared with groups that studied maps for the concept of nation produced by others and to groups that practiced question-answering from the text or rereading procedures. On the average, a student who generated his or her own concept map showed significant advantage in recalling information over a student who studied the concept maps produced by others or who studied the passage without graphic representations. This occurred even though many maps produced by students were incomplete or not entirely accurate.

When teaching students how to construct concept or semantic maps (Jones, Pierce, and Hunter 1989), it is a good idea to present a completed semantic map for students to examine in some detail before they are asked to construct their own; in examining the map, students should consider how such a graphic representation might be useful to them. The teacher may need to explain the utility of the procedure in enhancing understanding of text material. The teacher might then model for students how such a map is completed, either by using the sample or by constructing another. This modeling should involve the use of framing questions, such as, What was the goal? What was the strategy for reaching the goal? What were the outcomes? or What things are being compared? How are they similar? How are they different? Teachers, using a "think-aloud" method, can help students by demonstrating that confusion stops and starts and mistakes are part of the process rather than a sign of failure.

We suggest that students constructing their first concept maps work first as a whole class and then in small groups, sharing their maps, explaining how and why they created the maps as they did, and providing feedback to each other. Throughout this process, the teacher should provide coaching, helping students understand that planning and revision are crucial parts of the process. Finally, students should be given opportunities to practice on their own, with teachers providing feedback on their work.

It is important to note that students will have very different styles of creating semantic or concept maps. Teachers should be tolerant of differences while still pointing out errors in connections, and the like.

Case Study Approach

The case study approach involves providing students with hypothetical or real situations in which there is a conflict or a dilemma. Students then follow a systematic procedure to analyze the facts of the case, reach and support a decision, and weigh the consequences of that decision. A case study requires students to ask questions, define elements important to a situation, analyze, synthesize, compare and contrast elements, and make judgments. The students are, in short, practicing all levels of thinking.

The steps in a case study activity are generally as follows:

Step 1: Review of the facts   This includes distinguishing between facts that are relevant and important to the case and those that are irrelevant or unimportant. It should also include identifying what important facts are missing.

Step 2: Investigation of issues/arguments   This step involves identifying the issue or issues central to the conflict, developing arguments in support of various positions, and evaluating those arguments.

Step 3: Reaching a decision   In this step, students synthesize the various arguments to make and support a decision. If the case being analyzed was a real one, they should compare their decision with the one reached by the court or any other decision-making body in the real case.

Although the case study approach is most commonly used in law-related education, it can be applied to a variety of topics. In fact, the strategy can be implemented any time there is an issue or conflict situation to be considered. Economics teachers could use it to have students consider the conflict between promoting aviation while protecting the safety of passengers, for example. Teachers conducting a study of a science-related social issue could use it to examine instances when policymaking bodies have acted on such issues as location of a landfill, transportation of hazardous waste, or construction of a nuclear power plant. The approach can also be used with story segments, in which students decide what action should be taken next by the characters in a story.

The case study approach requires the teacher to serve in several capacities—diagnostician, discussion leader, and "climate-maker." The last may be the most difficult for teachers. To develop a favorable classroom atmosphere in which to use the case study approach, the teacher must refrain from dominating class discussion by repeating, commenting on, or asking questions of the same respondent following each remark. Rather, questions and comments should be redirected to other members of the group or class. Biases of the instructor regarding a case should be contained; when they are expressed, they should clearly be open to class review and analysis.

Using a fishbowl technique may help the teacher ease into the roles required in using the case study approach. The fishbowl involves dividing the class into four smaller groups in which the students go through the first two steps in the process—reviewing the facts and analyzing arguments. For the decision-making step, one representative from each group is selected to discuss the case, sitting in the middle of the class. A vacant fifth seat is placed with the group of four so that anyone wishing to enter the discussion temporarily could take the fifth seat.

ACTIVITY ## Using the Case Study Method

The following is a case study on ethical choices for social studies professionals. Read the case. Then use the case study techniques just described to reach a decision in the case.*

Betty Knowles, a seventh-grade teacher in a suburban district, is teaching a unit on the contemporary Middle East. A segment of the unit deals with social mores, including a study of the social roles of women in traditional cultural groups of Saudi Arabia. The children learn about the cultural significance of veiled faces, women's subservient behavior before men, the role of women in the home, and their limited educational and professional opportunities. Prior to this unit, the class has discussed contemporary social issues in the United States, including the women's movement and the Equal Rights Amendment.

When the roles of Arabian women are discussed, both boys and girls express shock and dismay. Ms. Knowles tries to point out the cultural context of the traditions in Saudi Arabia, but admits to the class that it is hard for her to express the Saudi point of view objectively because of her own sense of the importance of women's choices.

*Excerpted from P. B. Joseph, "Ethical Choices for Social Studies Professionals," *Social Education,* January, 1989. © National Council for the Social Studies. Reprinted by permission.

Two days later, the principal informs Ms. Knowles that the parents of two girls in the class have complained that their daughters feel uncomfortable with the critical tone of the classroom discussions of Saudi Arabia because their families believe that women should center their lives on the home and that higher education for women should not be a primary goal in this or in any country. The parents demand that the teacher present a sympathetic view of their understanding of the role of women. The principal concludes the discussion with Ms. Knowles by asking: "What are you going to do about this situation?" (Joseph 1989).

Issues

- One of the principles in the NCSS Code of Ethics states: It is the ethical responsibility of social studies professionals to cultivate and maintain an instructional environment in which the free contest of ideas is prized. Has Ms. Knowles violated that principle?

- If Ms. Knowles attempts to camouflage her values, will the goal of that ethical principle be realized?

- Does the teacher have the right to allow her ideas to be heard freely?

- Should social studies professionals make provisions for conservative or anti–social-change points of view?

- Is a critical treatment of another culture an example of moral inquiry or a display of an ethnocentric attitude?

• • •

Write a case description of an ethical dilemma that a secondary student might face. Develop some questions about the case that would help students analyze it in the way that you analyzed the preceding case.

Role Plays and Simulations*

Role playing can be an effective technique for focusing on the process of decision making and alternatives for conflict resolution. Role playing enables students to understand that others have points of view that are different from their own. It also enables students to learn appropriate behavior in a variety of settings.

Successful role playing depends on the establishment of a genuinely receptive atmosphere, based upon the teacher's belief that all individuals have the capacity to solve their problems. To maintain that atmosphere, students should be permitted to make mistakes and learn from them.

The peer group can also affect the success of role playing. Too often, young people are stereotyped by their classmates in a way that tends to be self-fulfilling or

---

*Adapted from A. Gallagher, *The Methods Book* (Chicago: Law in American Society Foundation, 1979). Used by permission of the author.

stifling in a role-playing situation. Yet a child can learn to alter his or her behavior once new approaches have been introduced and practiced. A student's stereotypic classroom image should not be matched with a role of similar characteristics.

Teachers should not be discouraged if role playing appears to fail the first few times they use it. Everyone tends to be uncomfortable with a new strategy, and role playing is one of the more demanding ones. Students will likely demonstrate this discomfort either by acting silly or by being unwilling to participate. They need a great deal of support and encouragement in the beginning. Initial role-playing activities should be simple, but they should become increasingly more complex if role playing is to be more than an exercise in dramatics.

Here are some guidelines to follow in using a role play:

- Present the problem or situation. Be sure to give students adequate information to play their roles convincingly. Specify how much elaboration of the roles is expected or acceptable.

- Assign roles or solicit volunteers. An entire class may participate even if there are only two roles. Arrange the students in pairs or use trios, with the third student acting as observer.

- Get the class involved as quickly as possible. Don't spend too much time on the introduction.

- Role reversal can be a useful device when students appear unsympathetic to the opposing viewpoint or when a student has been stereotyped by peers.

- Vary role-playing activities. Students will tire of the same routine.

Discussion of the role play should either be integrated with the activity or follow it immediately. Any significant lapse of time between role playing and the debriefing will dilute the value of the activity. The following questions may be useful in focusing the follow-up discussion:

- Were the plays realistic?
- Was the problem solved? If so, how? If not, why not?
- What were the alternative resolutions?
- Is this situation similar to anything you have personally experienced?
- How did you feel playing the role?
- If you repeated the role play, would you do anything differently?

Role plays are often a component of simulations, which allow students to experience vicariously a process that might otherwise be inaccessible to them. Simulations also allow students to experience processes and situations without risk. Students can practice decision making and even make mistakes in judgment without suffering serious consequences. Simulations are excellent reinforcers of skills or concepts with which students are already familiar. In addition, they provide a good change of pace.

Simulations are especially effective in recreating the process used in making decisions, either in history or currently. Special types of simulations that are commonly used in social studies are mock trials, moot courts, and mock legislative hearings. Simulations that help students understand economic concepts are also useful.

Note that simulations usually involve both role playing and small-group work. If students do not have experience with these techniques, teachers would be wise to do some role plays and small-group exercises before attempting a simulation.

Simulations seem to run more smoothly if the following stages are used:

Preparation   Break the simulation down by outlining the steps and allocating time periods for each. Organize the classroom to suit the simulation, including rearranging furniture if necessary. Preteach the simulation to a small group if the directions are complicated.

Playing   Introduce the simulation briefly by outlining the rules and procedures. All students should have some assignment in every part of the simulation. For example, in a mock trial, all students may assist in the preparation of the cases, but there may not be enough active roles in the trial for everyone. Those students not participating should be asked to observe for specific criteria or to act as reporters, observing and writing stories or preparing newscasts following the trial.

Debriefing   This usually consists of a follow-up discussion or another technique that helps students absorb and analyze what has happened. It is the most important stage of the simulation. First, the room should be rearranged in its usual setting. Second, a short one-page worksheet with questions designed to elicit reactions about the simulation will help to focus the discussion. It also helps to calm everyone down after what can sometimes be a chaotic and noisy experience. Then conduct small- and large-group discussion, using questions that isolate the purposes of the simulation. Be sure to relate the simulation to the students' previous learning.

A few precautionary notes are in order. Some simulations require extensive teacher preparation. Teachers must ask themselves: "Is it worth it?" Some simulations involve competition. Teachers should be sure that students understand the purpose of the simulation and that "losing" the simulation does not mean students learned less or were less successful. Finally, students may view simulations as unrealistic, and some of them are. Teachers should try to relate the concepts and principles of the simulation to real-life experiences.

A special form of simulation is the computer simulation. The computer can make simulations more realistic and effective by providing increased sophistication, access to databases, inclusion of random events, branching, and reinforcement. However, all computer simulations are not created equal; before choosing one, teachers should work through it to be sure it meets their needs.

Student Writing

According to Glynda Ann Hull (1989), writing research in the past fifteen years

> *has moved us some distance, then, from thinking about writing just as a product, of students as having or not having the right stuff, and . . . of pedagogy as the marking and correcting of products. . . . We've learned to think of writing as a complex cognitive process; of students as possessing immature, incomplete, or perhaps flawed representations of that process . . . and of pedagogy as providing instruction on the process and occasions to experience it. I can hardly overstate the significance of this work. (p. 109)*

As a pedagogical strategy, writing is a tool for developing meaning and discovering appropriate forms for communicating meaning. To learn to write, students must have frequent opportunities to engage in the process. Although some of those opportunities may be brief (e.g., a short informal writing break during a lecture), students do need to understand that writing takes time and often involves the help of collaborators who respond to style, content, and inventiveness. Students need opportunities to write for audiences that are less anxiety-producing than teachers—and the experience of writing for a variety of audiences is valuable in and of itself.

Perhaps most important, students must see and practice writing as a process. In fact, writing consists of several subprocesses—prewriting, drafting, and revising—which occur recursively, with the "writer stopping to plan in the midst of transcribing a paragraph or beginning to revise before she even has a word on the page" (Hull 1989, 107). For instructional purposes, the subprocesses may be broken into the following stages:

- Exploring, in which students discover topics and ideas
- Shaping, in which they find a context and form for their writing
- Drafting, which is the act of composing ideas into words
- Sharing topics, ideas, drafts, and rewrites with others to receive feedback
- Revising, in which students rethink and organize their thoughts
- Publishing, or the opportunity to "show off" a finished work

Writing should be seen not only as a process but also as a means to the ends of communicating and making meaning. Many of the exercises students do in the name of writing are schoolbound; that is, they have no analogs in the world beyond school. "Writing tasks will be authentic in the sense I'm after," says Hull, "when they give writers reasons for communicating" (pp. 121–22). By way of note, our suggestion that you keep a journal during this course is predicated at least in part on using the writing process as an aid to thinking, making meaning, and communicating.

Social studies teachers can use writing tasks to engage students with the subject matter and tap into their knowledge about the subject. Simple freewriting exercises, in which students simply think on paper in response to a stimulus of some kind, are excellent ways to prepare for in-class discussion; what students write gives them some ideas to bring to the discussion. A writing activity following a discussion allows those students who are shy or intimidated by more gregarious students to consider important questions.

Writing assignments should be made in developmental stages, starting with short papers and working up to longer pieces. Many students will see the teacher as the main or most important provider of feedback on their writing; thus, you will have to expend some effort giving validity to peer review, an important element of process writing. One way to introduce the notion of peer review is by conducting a demonstration in which the teacher and two coached students role play a peer-review session. Following the role play, the whole class can discuss the process, examining the reasons for its use and students' feelings about both giving and receiving critical comments.

Some teachers who have developed writing programs believe that groups of three work best for providing feedback. Others suggest that groups ranging in size from two to five students can be effective. Generally, the groups should be heterogeneous. For specific writing assignments, the teacher should provide questions that will help students focus their suggestions and comments. Such questions will keep responders from focusing only on grammar, spelling, and punctuation (which should be attended to after content has been discussed). For example, Neubert and McNelis (1986) suggest the following questions for an assignment in which students are writing letters to their congressperson advocating streamlining of the legislative process.

- Did the letter give at least three convincing reasons for the necessity of streamlining the legislative process?
- Are the reasons logically sequenced?

Neubert and McNelis go on to describe how responses would be provided within the peer group:

> *Each student member takes a turn at being the focus writer to which the other group members respond. The writer reads his or her work aloud, while the responders listen . . . [and] . . . follow along using copies of the writer's material. This oral reading allows the reader to hear the material in a different "voice" and to recognize where changes would be appropriate. It also gives the responders an opportunity to hear the entire work.*
>
> *The author then examines the writing silently while the responders make notations in answer to the focus questions, using the PQP form—praise, question, polish.*
>
> *Praise: What is good about the writing? What should not be changed?*
>
> *Question: What do you not understand?*
>
> *Polish: Suggest specific improvements without actually making the changes for the author. (p. 57)*

This method provides both positive reinforcement and constructive suggestions for change. Of course, the writer is free to use or disregard the suggestions, but even considering them forces the writer to think about the work in a new way.

Focus on Your Own Writing

Incorporating writing into the social studies curriculum requires effort by both teachers and students. The teacher's attitude toward developing a writing program is likely to be influenced by his or her own feelings about writing and his or her sense of competence as a writer.

Free-write for three minutes, focusing on your own feelings about writing. Do you feel competent as a writer? How might you enhance your self-confidence in using writing as an important part of your instructional program?

Team with two other students and share your thoughts on the subject. You do not need to read what you have written—simply talk about the ideas you developed.

Within the next two weeks, work with these two students again, this time sharing your writing and getting and giving feedback. Use the PQP technique. How effective do you find the technique? How might you refine it for use with students?

Research Projects

Research projects or papers are a standard in social studies classes, often used to culminate a unit, semester, or year of study. Group research projects can even be the foundation for an entire unit. Research can give students a feel for the work of social scientists and historians, as well as experience delving into one subject in depth. If treated as an extension of a process writing program, the research project can reinforce writing skills as well. With appropriate support, students can not only learn a great deal from their research efforts, but also enjoy the process and have a product that can be shared with others in the class, school, or community.

Before students begin a research project, they should have an idea of the steps involved. These may be described in a teacher-prepared guide (in which due dates for various intermediate steps can be set), or one of the many available research handbooks could be assigned. Generally, these are the steps in the process:

- Selecting a topic
- Identifying a research strategy and the resources available
- Gathering information
- Analyzing information
- Organizing information
- Reporting results

A critical step in making research enjoyable is selecting an appropriate topic. The topic should, of course, be germane to the course, but it should also interest and have personal meaning for the student. Students may need assistance discovering links between their interests and research topics. For example, a government student who is interested in rap music may not immediately think of the First

Amendment as a relevant research topic. A sports-minded student in the same class could research how the Consumer Products Safety Commission makes decisions about protective equipment.

Formulating the topic in the form of a question is a good idea for several reasons. First, it helps maintain the detective analogy. It will also focus the purpose of the research and help students evaluate whether their topic is too general or too specific. A topic that is too general will take longer to research and write about, and the resulting product may be unfocused. A topic that is too specific may be difficult to research and yield little more than a yes or no answer.

The teacher should be specific about the kinds and number of resources students will be expected to use. Do you want them to use primary resources? human resources? Are encyclopedias acceptable as references? Should they conduct surveys or other original studies? Your decisions about these questions will depend on the abilities of your students and your purposes in assigning the research project. Being explicit about your expectations will be helpful to students. It will also be helpful to alert the librarian or media specialist to the research project so he or she can be prepared to provide assistance.

As students gather their information, it is a good idea to schedule some class time in which problems can be discussed. Students may need assistance, for example, in determining how to analyze conflicting information. Here are some questions that may help students deal with such conflicts:

- Does the conflict involve facts or opinions?
- Are facts up to date? Are opinions based on up-to-date facts?
- What is the source of the fact or the opinion? Is this person qualified to write about the topic? What is he or she trying to achieve in writing about the topic?

Many alternatives for reporting information are available, and different students may find various approaches more appealing. Of course, if one of your goals in assigning the project is giving students practice in presenting information orally, it is appropriate for everyone to give oral reports. If, however, your goal is to encourage in-depth exploration of a topic, students may be allowed to choose the form of report. Among the possibilities are written reports; individual oral reports or panel discussions; slide shows, posters, murals, collages, or other artistic presentations; dramatic or musical presentations; and videotape presentations. Students who present other than standard written reports should be aware of the criteria that will be used to evaluate their presentations.

Writing and presentation of dramatic works can be especially good learning experiences, since such works involve several ways of showing the results of research (i.e., through scenery, the language used by characters, and the development of the story); dramas can also encourage historical empathy, an objective that is sometimes difficult to attain. Working with the English and art teachers to provide some guidance to students in plot and scene development, characterization, and set design and construction may be helpful. With assistance, students may be able to match the focus of their research with dramatic forms of the time under study; for example, George Chilcoat (1988) suggests using the "Living Newspaper" dramatic form developed by the Federal Theatre project as the basis for students' projects on the Depression and the New Deal.

Panel discussions can be particularly effective when students have participated in group research projects. They provide opportunities for practicing oral expression without putting undue pressure on any one group member. The following procedures have been used effectively in structuring panel discussions.

- The moderator introduces the topic, and the panelists present their views and opinions about the issue or topic, with each panelist given a set amount of time.

- The panelists discuss the issue or topic with each other, asking questions and reacting to the views and opinions of other panel members. Again a time limit should be established.

- The moderator closes the discussion and provides a summary.

- The moderator then calls for a forum period, during which members of the class may participate by addressing questions to various panel members or by voicing their views and opinions.

The video term paper, which is also most appropriate for group projects, may have the special benefit of being suitable for sharing with the community. With local-access channels provided by cable companies, well-produced video programs on topics of local or general interest may have a ready-made market. Community forums at the school provide another mechanism for disseminating high-quality media projects developed by students. Furthermore, through the process of developing a media project, students may become more aware of how the media influence public opinion.

Community Service/Action

The past several years have seen increasing interest in learning through community service/action projects. Such projects not only put students' classroom learning into action but also involve students in continued learning by doing and giving.

Although many community service/action programs are co-curricular (that is, not part of any specific subject area), the connections with social studies are numerous. First, such programs clearly contribute to the development of informed citizens, a primary goal of the social studies. Research indicates that they also enhance social development. Furthermore, learning through community-based activities can strengthen and deepen students' understanding of many of the concepts introduced in the social studies. For example, by working with government and volunteer agencies, students can learn about decision making, as well as the operation of bureaucracies (political science). By assisting in programs for the homeless, students can learn more about the causes and effects of poverty (sociology and psychology).

Research by Hedin and Conrad (1981) indicates that successful community service/action programs have the following characteristics:

- The service performed is valuable and deemed worthwhile for the community and for the students.
- The service provides opportunities for students to be depended upon.
- The service includes tasks that challenge and strengthen students' critical thinking skills.
- The service provides students with opportunities to make decisions.
- Students and adults work together on the service project.
- Students are given an opportunity to reflect on the experience.

Although reflection activities are too often neglected because of time or other scheduling constraints, the reflection phase is probably the most important phase in ensuring that students learn from their experience. The following are some ideas for encouraging students to connect the service experience with other learning and to integrate what has been learned on a personal level (Johnson 1991). First, ask questions that encourage students to reflect on the experience. Examples might include:

- What incident provided me with learning that I consider to be very important?
- What ideas that we had studied in the classroom applied to this experience? How did this experience change my thinking?
- What do I know about myself from this experience?
- What do I know about others? my community? the world?
- Would I return to volunteer at this site? What would I want to do the same? differently?

Allow time for students to talk or write about their responses to these questions. They may write short articles or journal entries in whatever form is most comfortable for them.

Another reflection strategy is to allow students to role-play situations from the service experience and then reflect upon the significance of their experience. This may be particularly effective if there were aspects of the service experience that troubled or confused students.

Reflection could also be encouraged by having students document a service project with pictures and design a newsletter to interest others in service activities. Articles written collaboratively by students to describe pictures they have drawn or taken give students a chance to reflect collectively on the experience.

ACTIVITY   Designing a Community Service Project

Select a community in which you might teach following graduation. Gather information about the community from local sources, including the newspaper, Chamber of Commerce, city government, and so on. Construct a community profile; then use the profile to identify at least two community service projects that would involve valuable work by students; write a paragraph describing each project and how it would relate to the social studies curriculum.

How might you use the construction of a community profile with secondary students? What would students learn from developing such a profile? How could they use the profile in other kinds of activities?

Reflecting on the Chapter

In your journal, write a vignette describing your social studies classroom five years from now. Tell what strategies you are using, as well as the content, skills, and attitudes you are teaching. How does the vignette reflect the metaphor of the student–teacher relationship you created at the beginning of the chapter?

References

Aronson, E., et al. *The Jigsaw Classroom*. Beverly Hills, Calif.: Sage Publications, Inc., 1978.

Barber, B. *Strong Democracy: Participatory Politics for a New Age*. Berkeley and Los Angeles: University of California Press, 1984.

Berkowitz, S. "Effects of Instruction in Text Organization on Sixth Grade Student's Memory for Expository Reading." *Reading Research Quarterly* 21 (1986): 166–78.

Beyer, B. K. *Inquiry in the Social Studies Classroom*. Columbus, Ohio: Charles E. Merrill, 1971.

Bloom, B., ed. *Taxonomy of Educational Objectives, Handbook I: Cognitive Domain*. White Plains, N.Y.: Longman, 1956.

Brooks, J. G., and M. G. Brooks. *In Search of Understanding: The Case for Constructivist Classrooms*. Alexandria, Va.: Association for Supervision and Curriculum Development, 1993.

Chilcoat, G. W. "The `Living Newspaper' as a Teaching Strategy." *Social Education* 52, no. 6 (1988): 439–43.

Cornbleth, C. *How-To-Do-It: Using Questions in Social Studies*. Washington, D.C.: National Council for the Social Studies, 1977.

Engle, S. H. "The Commission Report and Citizenship Education." *Social Education* 54, no. 7 (November/December 1990): 431–34.

Engle, S. H., and A. S. Ochoa. *Education for Democratic Citizenship*. New York: Teachers College Press, 1988.

Gall, M. D. "Synthesis of Research on Teachers' Questioning." *Educational Leadership* (1984): 40–47.

Gallagher, A. *The Methods Book*. Chicago: Law in American Society Foundation, 1979.

Giese, J. R., L. S. Parisi, and L. R. Singleton, eds. *A Humanities Approach to U.S. History: Activities and Resources for Secondary Teachers*. Boulder, Colo.: Social Science Education Consortium, 1990.

Guilford, J.P. "The Structure of Intellect." *Psychological Bulletin* 53 (1956): 267–93.

Hanf, M. "Mapping: A Technique for Translating Reading into Thinking." *Journal of Reading* 14, no. 4 (1971): 225–30.

Hedin, D., and D. Conrad. *Executive Summary of the Final Report of the Experiential Education Evaluation Project.* Minneapolis: Center for Youth Development and Research, University of Minnesota, 1981.

Hull, G. A. "Research on Writing: Building a Cognitive and Social Understanding of Composing." In *Toward a Thinking Curriculum: Current Cognitive Research*, ed. L. B. Resnick and L. E. Klopfer. Alexandria, Va.: Association for Supervision and Curriculum Development, 1989.

Johnson, D. W., and R. Johnson. *Learning Together and Alone: Cooperative, Competitive, and Individualistic Learning.* Englewood Cliffs, N.J.: Prentice Hall, 1987.

———. *Cooperation and Competition: Theory and Research.* Edina, Minn.: Interaction Book, 1989.

———. "Social Skills for Successful Group Work." *Educational Leadership* (January 1990): 29–33.

Johnson, J., ed. *CCSS Newsletter: Special Issue on Community Service* (Winter 1991).

Jones, B. F., J. P. Pierce, and B. Hunter. "Teaching Students to Construct Representations." *Educational Leadership* (January 1989): 20–25.

Joseph, P. B. "Ethical Choices for Social Studies Professionals." *Social Education* (January 1989): 55–57.

Kagan, S. "The Structural Approach to Cooperative Learning." *Educational Leadership* (January 1990): 12–15.

Lockwood, A. L., and D. E. Harris. *Reasoning with Democratic Values: Ethical Problems in United States History.* New York: Teachers College Press, 1985.

McCaslin, M., and T. L. Good. "Compliant Cognition: The Misalliance of Management and Instructional Goals in Current School Reform." *Educational Researcher* 21, no. 3 (April 1992): 4–17.

Neubert, G. A., and S. J. McNelis. "Improving Writing in the Disciplines." *Educational Leadership* (April 1986): 54–58.

Newmann, F. M. *Clarifying Public Controversy: An Approach to Teaching Social Studies.* Boston: Little, Brown, 1970.

Novak, J., and D. B. Gowin, *Learning How to Learn.* New York: Cambridge University Press, 1984.

Oliver, D. W., and J. P. Shaver, *Teaching Public Issues in the High School.* Boston: Houghton Mifflin, 1966.

O'Neil, J. "Making Sense of Style." *Educational Leadership* (October 1990).

Powell, J. C. "The Constructivist Approach to Teaching in Action." In *Teaching about the History and Nature of Science and Technology: Teacher's Resource Guide*, Draft. Boulder, Colo.: Social Science Education Consortium; Colorado Springs: BSCS, 1994.

Public Issues Series. Boulder, Colo.: Social Science Education Consortium, 1988–1993.

Rowe, M. B. "Wait Time: Slowing Down May Be a Way of Speeding Up!" *Journal of Teacher Education* 37, no. 1 (1986): 43–50.

Slavin, R. E. "Student Teams and Achievement Divisions." *Journal of Research in Education* 12 (1978): 39–49.

———. *Cooperative Learning*, 2nd ed. Washington, D.C.: National Education Association, 1987.

————. "Research on Cooperative Learning: Consensus and Controversy." *Educational Leadership* (January 1990): 52–55.

Wilen, W., and J. White. "Interaction and Discourse in Social Studies Classrooms." In *Handbook of Research on Social Studies Teaching and Learning*, ed. James P. Shaver. New York: Macmillan, 1991.

Woolever, R. M. "A New Framework for Developing Classroom Questions." *Social Education* (October 1987): 407–10.

CHAPTER

14

USING INSTRUCTIONAL MATERIALS

Laurel R. Singleton

ACTIVITY LIST

• • •

ACTIVITY

Culture in a Bag

Before your class meets, select three items that represent you and the culture in which you grew up. Place the items in a bag and bring them to class.

All the members of your class should place their bags on a table. Each person should then select one bag to analyze, trying to infer as much as possible about the person who selected the items and the culture in which he or she was raised. As a class, discuss the inferences you made, as well as the questions raised.

Next, consider the kinds of materials selected by the class members. What kinds of materials (e.g., artifacts, autobiographies, documents, photographs) were most common? Why? If these kinds of materials represent people and cultures well, would they be useful instructional materials? Why or why not? How often, in your experience, are these materials used in social studies classrooms? What kinds of materials are used most often? Why do you think this is true?

In your journal, write your thoughts on the most commonly used instructional materials and reasons for their use.

INTRODUCTION

Teachers have access to a wide range of instructional materials, materials that can convey information, engage students, structure complex classroom activities, and involve students with the latest technologies. As you begin teaching, you will find curriculum materials extremely important, since you simply will not have time in your first few years of teaching to develop top-notch materials for every unit of every course you teach. Certainly, many teachers do develop most of their own materials, but over the span of several (if not *many*) years.

Because you will rely on prepared instructional materials, we recommend that you spend some time now thinking about what kinds of materials you will use to meet particular instructional purposes. This chapter is intended to help you think through those issues, as well as issues related to selecting materials. To provide a starting place for learning about the actual materials available, the chapter ends with a list of publishers who produce creative social studies resources. We also recommend that you take advantage of opportunities to attend the National Council for the Social Studies conference, held in November each year, or the conferences of its regional or state affiliates. Such conferences feature exhibits of materials, as well as sessions and workshops in which ideas and materials are shared.

TEXTBOOKS AND OTHER PRINT MATERIALS

According to research (Armento 1986), commercially published textbooks are the most widely used type of instructional material in social studies classrooms, despite the numerous criticisms of them. Among the problems various critics have cited are the emphasis on breadth of information (often trivial) rather than depth; the lack of coverage of women and minorities or presentation of those groups in a stereotypic fashion; turgid writing styles; failure to make connections between present and previous learning; lack of scholarly integrity; too much emphasis on attractive graphics or other marketing features that lack instructional value; low-level questions; and, in general, an "inconsiderate" writing style that does not help students understand and construct meaning.

Given this long list of serious charges against textbooks, why do teachers continue to use them? Some teachers rely on textbooks to compensate for lack of information on their own parts. Others find the structure provided by the text useful in organizing their courses. Still others believe that parents expect their children to be using textbooks, much as they did when they were students.

Despite their problems, we would not argue that textbooks are "evil" and should never be used. Rather, we would caution beginning teachers against "over-reliance on the indiscriminate, routine, and mindless use of textbooks and their questions" (Turner 1989, 58). We suggest that teachers view the textbook as a resource on which they can draw, not as the source or organizer of the curriculum or course.

The following guidelines or suggestions may prove useful in deciding when and how to use textbooks:

- Be thoroughly familiar with the text. Be aware of the text's strengths and weaknesses and plan accordingly. Don't assign students to read sections or answer questions that you have not read yourself; they may not be worth students' time.

- Develop files of material that you can use to update dated portions of the text. The files might include newspaper clippings, magazine articles, visuals, documents, and the like.

- Combine use of the textbook with use of other materials and a variety of active learning strategies.

- Never assign text-reading and question-answering without a clear purpose in mind. Purposes that have proven to be effective include helping students practice specific skills, preparing students for future lessons, challenging students to transfer a skill or concept to a new situation, and requiring students to integrate many skills and concepts to create a new response. Cooperative learning strategies can be effective in assigning text-reading and question-answering, as well. For example, each student in a cooperative group might be responsible for answering particular questions and sharing that information with the group.

- Model for students how to read expository text, a task that many find difficult. For example, you might read a passage of text aloud with the class, pausing after each paragraph to explain how you identify the main idea of that paragraph.

- Help students make connections with other learning. Often, use of graphic organizers and elaborating strategies are useful in this regard.

- Teach students to approach texts critically, just as they would other kinds of sources. Too often, students cannot detect an author's explanations or identify the author's perspective (Epstein 1994). One reason may be that students simply do not expect texts to have a perspective—they view them simply as collections of factual information.

In addition to textbooks, many other kinds of print materials are available for use in social studies classes. Among them are supplementary books for students (e.g., Greenhaven Press's *Opposing Viewpoints* series, which presents pro and con arguments from experts on a wide range of contemporary issues); complete instructional units with teaching plans and student materials (e.g., SSEC's *American History Series*, which presents all the material needed for in-depth study of particular events or topics in U.S. history); and prepared simulations (e.g., Interact's *The Scopes Trial*, which provides complete instructions, role cards, and the like for a re-enactment of the famous trial on the teaching of evolution). Such materials can be especially useful, since they often provide engaging teaching strategies and the kinds of in-depth and source material on particular topics that textbooks do not (and cannot) provide. However, like texts, they should not be used without careful review by the teacher.

AUDIOVISUAL MATERIALS

Social studies teachers can make good use of various kinds of audiovisual materials, including slide programs, records/tapes/compact discs, filmstrips, and films/videos. As with textbooks, however, some social studies teachers have earned a reputation for overuse of such audiovisual materials.

You should have a specific purpose in mind when you decide to use an audiovisual program. Audiovisual materials are effective in presenting information that must be experienced visually for understanding (for example, slides of particular landforms), in evoking a strong emotional reaction from students (for example, a film on the Holocaust), and in giving students a sense that they are part of what they are studying (for example, a recording of Martin Luther King, Jr.'s "I Have a Dream" speech). Julie Johnson and Colby Vargas, teachers who have used films in their classrooms, also believe that feature films in particular "dramatize themes and ideas from history and literature in ways that amplify and illuminate these issues for students, sparking their synthesis and higher-order questioning" (Johnson and Vargas 1994). Preview the item you plan to use to make sure that it matches your purpose and that it is suitable for your students.

Before using the material, prepare the class by giving an overview of what they will be seeing and hearing, linking the material to previous learning, and giving students a task to complete while viewing and listening (for example, a list of key questions to find answers to). Often, it is advisable to use materials in a stop-action format; that is, stopping the program in the middle for discussion of specific points.

Following use of the audiovisual program, discuss the task students completed, as well as any questions they have. With films, in particular, you can also help students develop reading and analysis skills by asking such questions as: What was the main idea of this film? What do you think would happen in a sequel to this film? What symbols were used in the film? If time does not allow you to deal with those issues, you might plan for collaborative use of audiovisual materials with a language arts teacher. You may want to give students an opportunity to evaluate the program; you can use that information in deciding whether to use it again.

You need not always use a complete film to reap the benefits of introducing students to a topic in a dramatic way. For example, a history teacher developed a lesson on the impact of industrialization using only the first twenty minutes of Charlie Chaplin's classic film *Modern Times*. Another teacher developed a lesson on freedom of the press, using only a segment of the film *All the President's Men*.

| ACTIVITY |

Using Films in the Classroom

Develop a lesson or unit plan in which you use part of one of the following films to introduce a unit in a U.S. history class:

- *Glory*
- *Dances with Wolves*
- *Presumed Guilty*
- *Driving Miss Daisy*
- *Platoon*
- *Powwow Highway*
- *Do the Right Thing*

COMPUTER SOFTWARE

In the area of relatively new technologies, such as microcomputers, CD-ROMs, and interactive video systems (a videodisc that interfaces with a computer so that access is controlled by the user), social studies teachers have not been known for overuse. Indeed, social studies teachers have been accused of resisting the use of such technologies because of their own lack of familiarity with them, the difficulty of gaining access to the hardware needed, and the lack of quality software. However, as schools get more hardware so that competition for machines decreases and as the quality of software improves, those reasons become less compelling.

Many reasons for using advanced technology in the classroom have been given. Among those particularly relevant to social studies are the following:

- Students learn and develop at different rates, and technology can help the teacher individualize instruction.

- Working with computers often motivates students. The motivation may spring from several different sources, including the ability to produce technology-based art forms and the creation of an audience for student work via networking functions.

- Citizens of the future must be proficient in accessing, evaluating, and communicating information, including information from resources outside the classroom. Computers provide access to such information, as well as tools for processing it and communicating the results.

- Citizens of the future need to be able to solve complex problems. Computers provide tools to allow them to do so.

- Students must feel comfortable with the tools of the Information Age. (Peck and Dorricott 1994)

How can computers be used in social studies? Several general uses of microcomputers as aids to teaching and learning are described in the next few paragraphs:

Drill and Practice   This is the most mundane use of computers and also the easiest type of program to create. Programs falling into this category include those involving geographical location of nations and continents, capitals of states or nations, and so on.

Tutorials   These programs use a sequence of question (computer)-response (student)-feedback (computer). Programs of this type include those on how to read a map, how a bill becomes a law, and so on.

Demonstration   Demonstration often incorporates many special capabilities of the computer, such as high-resolution graphics, multicolored diagrams, and sound effects. The computer can be used to demonstrate such system interactions in the social sciences as the circular flow diagram of a market economy, the evolution of geological strata, the time flow of underlying and immediate causes of a historical event, and the dynamics of a social system. Unfortunately, demonstration programs for social studies have been relatively rare.

Simulations   Simulations model situations, allowing students to understand the factors involved and to manipulate variables to determine what the outcome will be. Commercially produced simulations include programs simulating a trip along the Oregon Trail, presidential elections, and decisions about the environment.

Information Storage and Retrieval   For the social studies, information retrieval and analysis may be the most promising use of the microcomputer. At the most basic level, dates, people, and places can be stored for retrieval by students. For example, information about states, regions, or countries can be stored, and students can retrieve information that would enable them to compare and contrast. At a more sophisticated level, voting patterns, results of attitude surveys, economic data, and the like can be stored and retrieved by students doing research or responding to questions requiring analysis. With the use of CD-ROM or videodisc, photographs, taped interviews, historical film footage, and other visual images can become part of the database available to students. In using such materials, teachers should be careful that historical events do not become decontextualized, mere snippets of "news from the past" not related to other events, before or after.

Instructional Games   Instructional games are usually simulations that involve competition with another student or the computer. Topics of instructional games include getting from point A to point B by the shortest and quickest route (map-reading skills), solving a mystery (logic and problem solving), and war games.

As with any teaching tool, you should have a clear purpose in mind when using computer-based materials, prepare students for use of the material, and carefully debrief the activity. Debriefing is particularly important when using computer simulations or instructional games. Although students often become highly involved in such computer-based activities, they are unlikely to learn from them without having the opportunity to reflect on the experience. John Chiodo and Mary Flaim (1993) suggest a four-step process:

1. Reviewing the facts gained in the simulation
2. Making inferences about what happened in the simulation
3. Analyzing/transferring the experience to the real world
4. Developing generalizations and drawing conclusions

For each stage, you should prepare questions to stimulate thinking and discussion.

Today, one of the computer-related topics receiving attention is how teachers and students might benefit from getting on the "information superhighway," either through the Internet or through other networking systems. Many teachers are excited about the access to information that Internet provides, as well as the possibilities for linking classrooms of students around the world through computer networks. In fact, a number of teachers are already taking advantage of these opportunities (see, for example, Pawlowski 1994). Although many states are currently developing plans to give schools access to Internet, much remains to be done before widespread use of Internet is a reality in most secondary classrooms (Pearlman 1994).

PRIMARY SOURCE DOCUMENTS

Chapter 11 provided a rationale for classroom use of primary sources, as well as some guidelines for use in analyzing primary sources. The almost limitless kinds of sources available can, of course, be used in classes besides history. For example, census records could be useful in sociology, economics, and geography courses, and the personal correspondence of a president or a legislator could be used in political science classes.

When students begin using such sources, they may need help in differentiating primary sources (documents written at or near the time of an event by a person who witnessed the event, a drafting committee of a document, a poet, etc.) and secondary sources (documents put together after an event based on the evidence of others rather than on firsthand experience), as well as assistance in analyzing the document. As they grow more proficient in use of primary source documents, they can be introduced to more specialized techniques of analyzing particular kinds of sources.

ACTIVITY

Using Primary Sources

Below is a sampling of potentially useful primary sources. Each student in your class should select one type of source, find an example of such a source in the library, evaluate the reliability of the source, write a question you would ask the author if you could talk to him or her, and describe how the source might be used in two social studies courses.

- Personal correspondence
- Autobiography
- Texts of court decisions, trial transcripts, court records
- Classified government documents
- Laws, statutes, ordinances
- Testimony before government bodies
- Eyewitness accounts
- Advertising
- Household records, such as checkbooks, receipts, and recipes
- Memorabilia, such as postcards or baseball cards
- Diaries and journals
- City directories
- Maps
- Songs
- Fiction or poetry

VISUALS

Photographs, posters, artwork, cartoons, and other visuals can all be useful teaching tools. One use of such visuals is simply to stimulate student interest. For example, before beginning a lesson on propaganda, the teacher might display several World War II posters, turning the classroom into an "art gallery." Students could be allowed some time to view and enjoy the posters. When students have returned to their seats, the teacher might ask students which posters they liked best and why; through this discussion, students could begin developing a list of the characteristics of effective propaganda.

Visuals can also be used as a source of information. As with other kinds of primary sources, students will need analysis skills to gather and evaluate material from visual materials. For example, the following questions present a framework for analyzing persuasive visuals, such as political cartoons and posters.

- List all the objects in the visual.
- Which of the objects on your list are symbols?
- What do you think each symbol means?
- Describe the action taking place.
- Record three important words or phrases used.
- Explain how the visual images support the printed message.
- What makes the visual appealing and why? (Consider the use of color, shape, and dominant and subordinate features as well as the relationship of the images to the printed word.)
- Interpret the message of the visual.
- Who might have developed the visual and why?

Analyzing Visuals

Use the questions above to analyze a political cartoon from today's newspaper. How could you use such an activity in a secondary social studies class?

ARTIFACTS

Artifacts offer a rich resource for learning about another culture or time period through hands-on, inquiry learning. Artifacts are, however, only as effective as the strategies teachers employ for using them in the classroom. Use of artifacts as a "teacher's show and tell" makes them no more effective than an illustrated lecture.

Students who are using artifacts for the first time might simply be asked to look at an article to determine what it is. This may be a special challenge when dealing with historical items that have no contemporary analogs. Encourage students to examine any writing on the object, to determine what the object is made of, and to see how the parts of the object work together. All of these can provide clues to the object's function. It may sometimes be impossible to determine what an object was used for; that may be frustrating to some students, but it also opens up their thinking to more possibilities.

Examination of a collection of items can be organized as a scavenger hunt. Give students a list of items to find, for example:

- Find one traditional toy.

- Find three eating utensils.

- Find an item that shows that Japanese kids and American kids have similar interests.

Although students should be encouraged to form hypotheses based on the artifacts they examine, one pitfall of using artifacts representing other cultures is that students may use the limited number of artifacts available to form or confirm stereotyped impressions, particularly if the teacher has a large number of items representing traditional culture. To help students recognize stereotypes, form hypotheses, and appreciate the importance of testing hypotheses, divide the class into small groups and give each group several traditional items. Have each group develop hypotheses about the culture that produced the items. Next give each group contemporary items from the same culture and have them hypothesize about the culture that produced these items. Inform students that the two sets of items represent the same culture. How would students change their hypotheses to reflect that information? What problems do students see in characterizing a culture based on limited data?

A second problem in using artifacts is that they are not readily available from commercial sources. Museums, historical societies, and antique shops may be able to provide access to historical artifacts. Many teachers who travel develop their own collections of artifacts. If you begin collecting artifacts, it is important to keep the notion of balance in mind. Include a balance of the traditional and modern, culturally unique and culturally universal, valuable and mundane. Balance in the collection will help students develop balanced views of the culture or the time period represented. If you have access to a large number of artifacts from a culture or a time period, you may wish to organize them into trunks by categories: young people, home life, sports/recreation, the arts, and so on.

NEWS MEDIA

Social studies teachers can teach both *about* and *through* the news media. Because Americans, and young people in particular, spend so much time watching television, cite television as the primary source of their information about current events, and are influenced by what they hear and see on television, learning to use television appropriately is especially important for students.

As a teaching and communication tool, television does a number of things well (Miekle 1988, 363):

- Tells stories
- Shows and demonstrates things that otherwise could not be seen
- Goes places that could not otherwise be visited
- Provides living role models
- Illustrates concepts in visual metaphors
- Captures phenomena in human and emotional context
- Presents compelling graphics that model and facilitate thought processes

You can probably think of examples of each of these characteristics, from C-SPAN to *Sesame Street* to *48 Hours* to dramatic programs.

In learning to use television, students should approach it as they would any other source; that is, they should evaluate the reliability of the information, look for corroboration from other sources, try to determine the motivations of the people producing the television programming, and so on. Ongoing monitoring or comparative analysis of television with other news media can help students test and refine their hypotheses about the reliability of information gained from various types of television programming.

Newspapers and newsmagazines can also be sources of information and objects of study. Many daily newspapers in large cities have education programs, designed for use with their newspaper; the weekly newsmagazines also offer such programs. Although the materials offered by these programs can be very useful, it is wise to remember that they are generally affiliated with the organization's marketing department.

ACTIVITY

Science and Technology in the News

Divide your methods class into three groups. One group will use the analysis form in Figure 14.1 to conduct a content analysis of daily newspapers' coverage of science and technology, the second group to analyze television news programs, and the third to analyze weekly newsmagazines. Agree on an analysis period of several days or a week.

After the analysis is complete, discuss the results as a large group. What generalizations can you develop on the basis of your analysis? Which medium covered the topic best? How did you define best—in terms of quantity, accuracy, agreement with your own point of view? Do the news media show the effects of science and technology on society? How do the news media influence the way the public thinks

Use this form to record the amount of attention devoted to issues related to science and technology by _____ during the period _____ .				
Publication or broadcast date	*% of time/space devoted to science/ technology*	*Science/ technology issues covered*	*Was coverage positive, negative, or balanced?*	*Was the effect of science and technology on society covered?*

Figure 14.1   News media analysis form

about science and technology? How would you improve coverage of issues related to science and technology by newspapers? television? newsmagazines?

• • •

How might you change this activity for use in a secondary classroom? What objectives would it help you achieve? How would you relate the activity to other learning?

QUANTITATIVE DATA

The importance of quantitative data to understanding the world through a social science perspective was clearly demonstrated in Part Two of this book, particularly in the chapters on psychology and economics. Thus, numerical data become one of the tools of the social studies teacher.

Many students may not, however, have the skills or understandings necessary to analyze quantitative data. Hartoonian (1989) has identified the following quantitative concepts necessary to use data in the social studies:

- Statistics: The theory and method of analyzing data to study and compare underlying patterns and relationships, to accept or reject hypotheses, and to aid in making decisions about empirical observations.
- Probability: The estimate of the likelihood of an event's occurrence.
- Ratio: The relation between two numbers or two magnitudes of the same kind.
- Percent: An amount or quantity commensurate with a number of units in proportion to 100.
- Index number: Any of a series of numbers indicating the quantitative changes in a given statistical aggregate over time.
- Central tendency: The central points in a distribution. Three measures of central tendency are the mean (the sum of the raw scores divided by the number of cases), the median (that point in a distribution of scores with 50 percent of the cases on each side of it), and the mode (the most frequent score).
- Dispersion: The variability in a distribution. Two measures of dispersion are range (the difference between the highest and lowest scores) and standard deviation (a measure of how much scores are spread out around the mean).

How many of these concepts are you familiar with? How many can you use readily? One of the difficulties some social studies teachers face in teaching with quantitative data is their own lack of confidence in analyzing such data. You may find that working together with a mathematics teacher to plan lessons or units using quantitative data will increase your confidence, as well as providing the math teacher with some "real-world" data for use in his or her class.

ACTIVITY **Using Census Data**

Use the data in Figure 14.2 to answer questions 1–4.

1. Which columns present ratios?
2. Which column presents a percentage?
3. Which two columns present measures of central tendency?
4. What is the range in population for the years shown on the table?

• • •

Year	Population (in thousands)	Places of 50,000 or More persons	Median Age	Males per 100 Females	Non-Agricultural Workers per 100 Agricultural Workers[1]	High School Graduates		Average Number of Persons per Household
						Percent of Persons Age 17 or Over	Percent of Persons Age 25 or Over	
1790	3,929	0		104[2]				5.79
1800	5,308	1	16.0[2]	104[2]				
1810	7,240	2	16.0[2]	104[2]				
1820	9,638	3	16.7	103				
1830	12,866	4	17.2	103				
1840	17,069	5	17.8	104	29			
1850	23,192	10	18.9	104				5.55
1860	31,443	16	19.4	105				5.28
1870	39,818	25	20.2	102	94	2.0		5.09
1880	50,156	35	20.9	104	125	2.5		5.04
1890	62,948	58	22.0	105	155	3.5		4.93
1900	75,995	78	22.9	104	180	6.3		4.76
1910	91,972	110	24.1	106	206	8.6		4.54
1920	105,711	145	25.3	104	290	16.3		4.34
1930	122,775	192	26.4	103	366	28.8		4.11
1940	131,669	200	29.0	101	433	49.0	24.5	3.67
1950	150,697	233[3]	30.2	99	711	57.4	34.3	3.37
1960[4]	179,323	333[3]	29.5	97	1,418	63.4	41.1	3.33
1970	203,302	396[3]	28.0	95	2,684	75.8	52.3	3.14
1980	226,546	463[3]	30.0	95	3,437		66.5	2.75

[1]1840 data included all persons, all ages; 1870–1930, persons age 10 and over; 1940–1960, persons age 14 and over; and 1970–1980, persons age 16 and over.
[2]White only.
[3]Using current urban definition.
[4]Denotes first year for which figures here include Alaska and Hawaii.

Figure 14.2 Historical census data of the United States. *Sources: Bureau of the Census.* Historical Statistics of the United States, Colonial Times to 1970; 1987 Statistical Abstract; 1980 Census of Population, Vol. 1, Chapter A 1960, 1970, 1980 Census of Housing, Vol. 1, Chapter A; 1940 Census of Population.

Create an activity for secondary students using this data table. Specify the course in which the activity would be used and how it would connect with other learning in that course. The activity should teach at least one quantitative concept.

Reflecting on the Chapter

In your journal, write a vignette describing your social studies classroom five years from now. Tell what materials and strategies you are using, as well as the content, skills, and attitudes you are teaching.

References

Armento, B. "Research on Teaching Social Studies." In *Handbook of Research on Teaching*, 3rd. ed., ed. M. C. Wittrock. New York: Macmillan, 1986.

Chiodo, J. J., and M. L. Flaim. "The Link between Simulations and Social Studies Learning: Debriefing." *The Social Studies* 84, no. 3 (1993): 119–21.

Epstein, T. L. "*America Revised* Revisited: Adolescents' Attitudes Towards a United States History Textbook." *Social Education* 58, no. 1 (January 1994): 41–44.

Hartoonian, H. M. "Social Mathematics." In *From Information to Decision Making*, ed. M. A. Laughlin, H. M. Hartoonian, and N. M. Sanders. Washington, D.C.: National Council for the Social Studies, 1989.

Johnson, J., and C. Vargas. "The Smell of Celluloid in the Classroom: Five Great Movies that Teach." *Social Education* 58, no. 2 (February 1994): 109–13.

Mielke, K. W. "Television in the Social Studies Classroom." *Social Education* (September 1988).

Pawlowski, B. "How I Found Out about the Internet." *Educational Leadership* 51, no. 7 (April 1994): 69–73.

Pearlman, R. R. "Can K–12 Education Drive on the Information Superhighway?" *Education Week* 13, no. 35 (May 25, 1994): 48, 38.

Peck, K. L., and D. Dorricott. "Why Use Technology?" *Educational Leadership* 51, no. 7 (April 1994): 11–14.

Turner, T. N. "Using Textbook Questions Intelligently." *Social Education* (January 1989): 58–60.

Sources of Creative Social Studies Materials

Addison-Wesley Innovative Division
2725 Sand Hill Road
Menlo Park, CA 94025

Agency for Instructional Technology
1111 West 17th Street
Box A
Bloomington, IN 47402

Alarion Press, Inc.
Box 1882
Boulder, CO 80306

American Bar Association
750 North Lake Shore Drive
Chicago, IL 60611

Anti-Defamation League of B'nai B'rith
823 United Nations Plaza
New York, NY 10017

Broderbund Software
500 Redwood Boulevard
Novato, CA 94968

Brown Publishing-ROA Media
2460 Kerper Boulevard
Dubuque, IA 62001

Bureau of the Census
Data User Services Division, Room 306WP
Washington, DC 20233

Center for Civic Education
5146 Douglas Fir Road
Calabasas, CA 91302

Center for Research and Development
in Law-Related Education
2714 Henning Drive
Winston-Salem, NC 27106

Center for Teaching International Relations
University of Denver
Denver, CO 80208

Chelsea Curriculum Publications
1974 Sproul Road, Suite 400
Broomall, PA 19008

Choices Education Project
Box 1948
Providence, RI 02912

Close Up Foundation
44 Canal Center Plaza
Alexandria, VA 22314

Cloud Associates/Publishing
Box 39016
Phoenix, AZ 85069

Cobblestone Publishing
7 School Street
Peterborough, NH 03458

Constitutional Rights Foundation
601 South Kingsley Drive
Los Angeles, CA 90005

C-SPAN in the Classroom
4000 North Capitol Street, NW
Washington, DC 20001

Didatech
3812 William Street
Burnaby, BC V5C 3H9 Canada

Dushkin Publishing Group
Sluice Dock
Guilford, CT 06437

Educational Activities
Box 392
Freeport, NY 11520

Educational Insights, Inc.
19560 South Rancho Way
Dominguez Hills, CA 90220

Educators for Social Responsibility
23 Garden Street
Cambridge, MA 02138

Encyclopedia Brittanica
425 North Michigan Avenue
Chicago, IL 60611

Fearon Education
500 Harbor Boulevard
Belmont, CA 94002

Foreign Policy Association
729 Seventh Avenue
New York, NY 10019

Good Apple
Box 299
Carthage, IL 62321

Greenhaven Press
Box 289009
San Diego, CA 92198

Guidance Associates
Box 3000
Mt. Kisco, NY 10549

Instructional Resources Corporation
1819 Bay Ridge Avenue, Suite 160
Annapolis, MD 21403

Interact
Box 2006
Lakeside, CA 92040

Jackdaw Publications
Box 503
Amawalk, NY 10501

Learning Enrichment, Inc.
105 Moody's Run
Williamsburg, VA 23185

Lerner Publications Company
241 First Avenue North
Minneapolis, MN 55401

Media Materials, Inc.
1821 Portal Street
Baltimore, MD 21224

Micromaps Software
Box 757
Lambertville, NJ 08530

Minnesota Educational Computing
Corporation
3490 Lexington Avenue
Saint Paul, MN 55126

National Archives & Records Administration
7th and Pennsylvania Avenue, NW
Washington, DC 20408

National Center for History in the Schools
UCLA
Moore Hall 231
405 Hilgard Avenue
Los Angeles, CA 90024

National Council on Economic Education
1140 Avenue of the Americas
New York, NY 10036

National Geographic Society
17th & M Streets, NW
Washington, DC 20036

National Women's History Project
7738 Bell Road
Windsor, CA 95492

NewsCurrents/Knowledge Unlimited
Box 52
Madison, WI 53701

Opportunities for Learning, Inc.
20417 Nordhoff Street
Chatsworth, CA 91311

PBS Video
1320 Braddock Place
Alexandria, VA 22314

Perfection Learning
1000 North Second Avenue
Logan, IA 51546

Population Reference Bureau, Inc.
1875 Connecticut Avenue, NW, Suite 520
Washington, DC 20009

Scholastic Inc.
730 Broadway
New York, NY 10003

Scott, Foresman & Company, Goodyear
Books
1900 East Lake Avenue
Glenview, IL 60025

Tom Snyder Productions, Inc.
80 Coolidge Hill Road
Watertown, MA 02172

Social Issues Resource Series
Box 2348
Boca Raton, FL 33427

Social Science Education Consortium, Inc.
Box 21270
Boulder, CO 80308-4270

Social Studies School Service
10200 Jefferson Boulevard
Culver City, CA 90232

Stanford Program on International & Cross-
Cultural Education
Littlefield Center, Room 300
300 Lasuen Street
Stanford, CA 94305-5013

Sunburst Communications
39 Washington Avenue
Pleasantville, NY 10570

The World Bank
1818 H Street, NW
Washington, DC 20433

World Eagle, Inc.
111 King Street
Littleton, MA 01460-1527

Worldview Software
786 North Broadway, Suite 4009
Hicksville, NY 11801

World Wise
4 West Wheelock Street
Hanover, NH 03755

Zaner-Bloser Publishing
Box 16764
Columbus, OH 43216

Zero Population Growth, Inc.
1400 16th Street, NW, Suite 320
Washington, DC 20036

Zephyr Press
Box 66066-A
Tucson, AZ 85728

CLASSROOM ASSESSMENT

Laurel R. Singleton

ACTIVITY LIST

• • •

Survey and paired discussion, p. 408

K-W-L (know–want to know–learned) prereading strategy, pp. 410 and 428

Planning a unit and assessment criteria, p. 414

Critiquing a performance assessment, p. 418

Designing a portfolio assignment, p. 422

Writing an essay test, p. 424

Role playing, p. 431

Journal writing, p. 432

ACTIVITY

Reaction Statements

Use the following scale to indicate your reaction to each statement below.

SA–Strongly   A–Agree   N–No   D–Disagree   SD–Strongly
  Agree   Opinion   Disagree

_____ In American schools, assessment and testing are virtually synonymous.

_____ Multiple-choice tests can measure higher-order thinking skills adequately.

_____ The most important part of assessment is teaching students to evaluate their own work.

_____ The teacher's goal should be to make assessment as value-neutral as possible.

_____ My own work as a student has usually been fairly assessed.

When you have marked your responses, compare your answers with those of another student. For each statement where your positions differ, try to persuade your partner to change his or her mind.

After ten minutes, join with another pair and repeat the discussion process with the new pair of students.

What perceptions of assessment did your discussions reveal? What value positions affected your discussions? What emotional responses seemed to be important? How do you think your own experiences as a student will affect the way in which you assess student learning in your classroom?

INTRODUCTION

When you visualize yourself as a teacher, how much time do you imagine spending on assessment? According to a recent study, teachers spend as much as 20 to 30 percent of their professional time on assessment-related tasks, including designing, developing, selecting, administering, scoring, recording, reporting, evaluating, and revising such items as daily assignments, tests, quizzes, observations, and discussions (Stiggins 1988). Another study indicated that teachers make decisions on how to interact with students at the rate of one decision every two to three minutes (Shavelson and Stern 1981); those decisions are based on the teacher's assessment of how much learning is occurring, what actions are facilitating learning, and what might be hindering it.

Clearly, assessment is integral to teaching. Classroom assessment serves a number of interrelated functions: (1) to determine needs and establish baseline information for later comparison, (2) to identify problems and make needed changes in instruction, and (3) to determine to what extent teachers and students have reached their objectives. Assessments at other levels, such as districtwide or statewide assessment programs, have still other functions, including generating information for use in program improvement and providing a basis for sorting students for various purposes (e.g., college admissions). National educational standards are currently being developed; these standards will be used as the basis for a national assessment that will determine how well we are meeting our educational goals as a nation. When we examine the uses to which assessment data are put at all levels, we cannot escape the fact that what and how we assess are driven by our educational purposes.

Because of the relationship between purposes and assessment, assessment is a value-laden process (Archbald and Newmann 1988, 1). When asked what beginning teachers should know about evaluation, Richard Stiggins responded that they should, among other things, be aware that assessment is "an interpersonal act with personal antecedents and personal consequences" (Stiggins 1991, 9).

Recognizing these attributes of assessment, teachers can strive to develop an assessment plan that reflects their clearly articulated goals, is as fair to students as possible, and provides useful information for students, parents, and the teacher. This chapter provides a brief introduction to some of the information teachers will need to develop such a plan. The next section looks more closely at the relationship between assessment and educational purposes, examining common problems related to assessment and identifying characteristics of authentic assessment. The following section looks at a range of assessment methods, emphasizing in particular some of the newer techniques, such as portfolios and performance assessments. The final section provides a few tips for communicating assessment information to parents and students.

This chapter is not a substitute for a course in assessment. None of the topics we cover is dealt with in depth, and there are many topics we do not deal with at all. We highly recommend a course in evaluation to all prospective teachers to help them gain the skills they need to assess every student equitably and in a manner that informs learning and teaching.

ACTIVITY   **Identifying What You Know and Want to Know about Assessment**

Divide a sheet of paper into three columns. In the first column, make notes about what you already know about classroom assessment. In the second column, write questions about classroom assessment that you want to have answered. Leave the third column for answering the questions in the second column and noting other things you learn while working through this chapter. You can add to the second and third columns throughout your work with the chapter.

ASSESSMENT AND EDUCATIONAL PURPOSES

Classroom assessment should identify how well students and teachers have met their goals and assist them in improving their knowledge and abilities. The traditional ways in which students' learning has been assessed—primarily multiple-choice and other forms of "objective" tests—have been criticized for a wide variety of shortcomings in fulfilling those functions. According to Doug Archbald and Fred Newmann (1988, 1), "Most traditional assessment indicators communicate very little about the quality or substance of students' specific accomplishments. . . . The type of learning actually measured is often considered trivial, meaningless, and contrived by students and adult authorities." Although a teacher may emphasize higher-level thinking in the classroom, if his or her tests emphasize recall of factual information, students will get the message about what kind of learning is truly most important to the teacher.

When educators do attempt to use multiple-choice tests to measure higher-level thinking, great inferences must usually be made in interpreting test scores. That is, the multiple-choice exam is an indirect test that evaluates less abstract, more observable features of performance that are believed to be linked to the abstract skill; a classic example is the use of tests of vocabulary knowledge to make inferences about verbal aptitude (Fredericksen and Collins 1989).

The process involved in moving from educational goal to exam question illustrates the inferences that must be made. Consider a broad goal of developing students' commitment to democratic values. The teacher first translates that goal into instructional objectives that he or she believes, when taken together, will help achieve the goal. Those objectives might include being able to describe how the Bill of Rights came into being, to list the rights covered in the Bill of Rights, and to give examples of their application in everyday life and their interpretation by the courts. The teacher then develops a list of indicators presumed to indicate that the objectives have been achieved and writes test items based on those indicators. Thus, the test items might include questions that asked students to select from four arguments for inclusion of a Bill of Rights in the Constitution the one *not* made by the Anti-Federalists, to select the correct definition of *due process of law*, to select the answer that best summarizes the Supreme Court's reasoning in the *Hazelwood* student press case. This test rests on the assumption that those items measure achievement of the broad goal of developing commitment to democratic values, an assumption that requires many inferences indeed.

Multiple-choice items have also been criticized for other reasons. Lorie Shepard points out that "although multiple-choice questions can elicit important conceptual distinctions from students, tests composed entirely of such items do not measure a respondent's ability to organize relevant information and present a coherent argument" (Shepard 1989, 5). Multiple-choice tests require passive selection of responses rather than construction of an answer; in doing so, they promote the idea that there are right and wrong answers to all questions (Mitchell 1992, 15).

The conditions under which traditional tests are given are not based on real-life contexts in which knowledge is used or applied. They tend to be highly time-constrained, with great priority placed on secrecy, another practice that has been roundly criticized. According to Ruth Mitchell, "Keeping tests secret is demeaning; it is also unnecessary" (Mitchell 1992, 83).

As Mitchell continues, she highlights how concerns over secrecy exemplify the differences between traditional views of assessment and new views of what has come to be called authentic assessment: "If, however, students know what will be in the examination ahead of time and know the standards by which they will be judged, nothing is secret and no one will trip over nonessentials. Students can also get involved in assessing their own work, which should be the ultimate aim of any educational assessment."

Students' active involvement in assessment is one feature of new views of assessment. Teachers' assessment plans should help students develop the skills and habit of the "reflective self-evaluation that is inseparable from pursuing virtually any kind of worthwhile work" (Wolf 1989, 35). Student involvement includes knowing the tasks to be performed and the criteria to be used in judging success, as well as understanding the value of the tasks and criteria and being able to apply them to their own and others' work.

Hart (1994) highlights another key feature of authentic assessment—testing what we care about, essential learning outcomes, rather than those that are nonessential or trivial. As Grant Wiggins points out, "To design an authentic test, we must first decide what are the actual performances we want students to be good at and must pay careful attention to what we mean by evidence of knowing." He continues:

> *Mastery is more than producing verbal answers on cue; it involves thoughtful understanding as well. And thoughtful understanding implies being able to do something effective, transformative, or novel with a problem or complex situation. . . . Knowledge is thus displayed as thoughtful know-how—a blend of good judgment, sound habits,*

Figure 15.1   How does this drawing reflect the differences between authentic assessment and more traditional assessment? *Source: Tom Teague. Used by permission of Tom Teague.*

responsiveness to the problem at hand, and control over the appropriate information and context. Indeed, genuine mastery usually involves even more: doing something with grace and style. (Wiggins 1989, 705)

At the most fundamental level, advocates of authentic assessment call for a change in the relationship between assessment and instruction; Gene Maeroff describes the desired relationship as a "synergy of instruction and assessment in which each complements the other to raise learning to new levels" (Maeroff 1991, 274). When students know what tasks they will be asked to complete and how their work will be judged, assessment can promote and direct students' learning.

Several educators have used sports, the performing arts, and debate as analogies to illustrate the desired relationship between instruction and evaluation. The athletic or debate coach and the music teacher aim through their teaching to improve performance in a realistic setting; the coach or teacher and the students interact as they evaluate the performance; and the "test" of learning occurs repeatedly, not just once or twice, allowing teacher and learner to observe patterns of success or failure.

What kinds of assessment tasks in social studies will fulfill the same function as the soccer game, the debate, or the concert? According to Archbald and Newmann (1988, 1–3), the tasks must be "worthwhile, significant, and meaningful—in short, authentic." These authors provide three criteria for judging whether tasks are authentic:

1. They must require disciplined inquiry. Disciplined inquiry depends on substantive and procedural knowledge, aims to develop in-depth understanding rather than mere exposure, and moves beyond acquisition of knowledge produced by others to assembling and interpreting information, formulating ideas, and making critiques.

2. They must require integration of knowledge, tapping students' understanding of and ability to create theories, designs, arguments, etc., rather than to repeat fragments of knowledge.

3. They must have value beyond evaluation; that is, the tasks or their results should have aesthetic or utilitarian value apart from determining competence. Meeting this requirement may involve the production of discourse, objects, or performances. It is likely to require flexible use of time and collaboration among students.

Moving toward the type of authentic assessment described by the educators we have cited in this section often requires changes in classroom conditions. The work of Jane Heckley Kon and Giselle Martin-Kniep highlights both the relationship between classroom conditions and authentic assessment and the difficulty that can occur in changing teacher and student roles. In piloting new ways of assessing geographic knowledge and skills, Kon and Martin-Kniep (1992, 96) found that some students had difficulty getting started on what they perceived to be unusual tests.

They wanted to go directly to answers rather than reflecting on the problem. Unless reflection and problem solving have been stressed as classroom values, it may be difficult for students to show these habits of mind in an assessment.

Rieneke Zessoules and Howard Gardner (1991, 61) suggest that to help students learn from the assessment process, teachers should design assessment so that

- Students tackle project work regularly and often.
- Students judge their own work at all stages and in relation to other works.
- Students collaborate and converse with others.
- Students can distinguish a real audience for their work.
- Students reflect on their learning over time.
- Students understand the standards defining improvement.

Like students, teachers may find developing new ways of thinking about teaching, learning, and assessment difficult. Their changing role in the process may be uncomfortable at first. The attractions of the traditional forms of assessment have been their ease of use and their contribution to classroom control (see Chapter 2). To move beyond those forms, teachers may have to sacrifice some convenience and comfort in order to nurture in students complex understandings relevant beyond school walls (Zessoules and Gardner 1991).

ACTIVITY

Matching Desired Outcomes and Assessment Criteria

Among the *National Standards for Civics and Government* (1994) is the following standard:

> *Students should be able to evaluate, take, and defend positions on what the fundamental values and principles of American constitutional democracy are and their importance to the maintenance of constitutional democracy.*

The fundamental values listed in the framework are the public or common good; individual rights, including life, liberty, and the pursuit of happiness; justice; equality; diversity; truth; and patriotism. The fundamental principles of American constitutional democracy are popular sovereignty and constitutional government, including the related principles of rule of law, separation of powers, checks and balances, minority rights, separation of church and state, power of the purse, federalism, and civilian control of the military.

With a partner, use the unit-planning guide in Chapter 4 to begin sketching out an outline for a unit for a ninth-grade civics course that would address this objective (you may focus on particular values or principles from the list rather than addressing all of them). What kinds of learning activities would you use? How would you build in opportunities for students to reflect on their work? What would be the best evidence that students had a "reasoned commitment" to the values or principles on which your unit focused? How might you gather such evidence, keeping in mind Archbald and Newmann's criteria for authentic assessment tasks? How would you communicate to students the standards by which you would judge their progress?

As you began thinking about instructional and assessment tasks, did they seem similar? If so, it is not surprising: when both instruction and assessment are aimed at complex understandings, assessment tasks resemble learning tasks.

METHODS OF ASSESSMENT

Teachers use a wide range of assessment measures, including students' daily work, observations of student behavior, questionnaires, interviews, teacher-made tests, standardized tests, performances, portfolios, and much more. The appropriate method for a particular purpose depends on the match with the objectives or outcomes being assessed, the time the teacher has to develop and use the assessment, the reliability and validity of the method or instrument, and the value of the information generated for students, parents, and teachers. In this section, we deal with only a few of the methods of assessment, looking first at performance assessments and portfolios, then at various types of tests, attitude measures, and finally at observations of student behavior.

Performance Assessment

Performance assessments involve evaluating students' work through authentic tasks intended to require their use of what they have learned as they might use it in "real-life" applications. An example of a performance assessment for a ninth-grade local history class might be the following:

> *You must complete an oral history based on interviews and written sources and then present your findings orally in class. The choice of subject matter is up to you. Some examples of possible topics include: your family, running a small business, substance abuse, a labor union, teenage parents, and recent immigrants.*
>
> *Create three workable hypotheses based on your preliminary investigations and four questions you will ask to test out each hypothesis. (Wiggins 1989)*

The teacher evaluates students' findings using a set of criteria (called a rubric) known to students in advance. Optimally, models of work at all levels of performance (benchmarks) would be available for student use in preparing their projects and in evaluating their own work, a key element of performance assessment. The public presentation and defense of the work helps ensure that mastery is genuine.

Because performance assessments do not decontextualize what is learned as many tests do, they provide better evidence of a student's ability. Furthermore, because they are more authentic intellectual activities than most tests, they are more likely to interest and motivate students.

In designing a performance assessment, the teacher thinks of the knowledge to be tested as a "tool for fashioning a performance or product. The essential material of a course must be a necessary means to a successful performance end" (Wiggins 1992, 27). In identifying those performance ends, the teacher considers what kinds of tasks, achievements, or roles all students should be able to master; what genuine mastery of each of these tasks would look like; and what characteristics would best discriminate between various levels of mastery (Wiggins 1992, 26). These are not easy tasks. Their successful completion depends on the teacher's clear understanding of the purposes for teaching particular material and a commitment to objectives far beyond mere acquisition of knowledge.

Wiggins (1992, 28–29) provides the following guidelines for designing performance assessment tasks:

- Contextualize the task; that is, provide enough detail so the task does not feel contrived and the standard of performance is apparent.

- Design tasks that are "meaningful," involving genuine use of knowledge and skills in an engaging and thought-provoking manner.

- Be sure the task is a performance and not a drill; that is, the tasks must require use of knowledge in higher-order thinking.

- Refine the tasks by comparing them with models and scoring criteria that you develop to judge student work.

Wiggins suggests that job roles are a useful way for teachers to think about designing performance assessments. For example, students might be asked to act as museum curators designing museum exhibits or competing for grant money. A scored discussion of a public isssue is another possible performance assessment, as are settings that simulate government bodies in which advice concerning policy decisions is given. For example, Mitchell (1992) suggests that the model used in the national bicentennial competition on the Constitution could be used by teachers for evaluation purposes. In this model, panels of students "testify" before Congress regarding constitutional issues. Students know what some of the questions will be beforehand, but other questions are spontaneous.

The California Assessment Program for high school history, which is assessing knowledge as well as skills in critical thinking, group participation, and oral and written communication, uses a similar setting. Working in small groups, students use document packets to focus on a task such as the following:

Next month, heads of state and foreign secretaries will gather to discuss the future of Europe in light of the reunification of Europe. Your group advises the France desk at the State Department and is holding a preliminary session to discuss the topic.

Action 1: Read and share ideas from documents in your folder. Confer about what you have learned in world history that relates to this topic.

Action 2: Prepare a brief statement about aspects of historical events that would influence the policy of France toward reunified Germany. Outline what this policy might be. . . . Be ready to present your group's statement orally to the entire class and to answer questions from the evaluator or other students. (Bartlett 1992, 102)

Following completion of this group task, students individually write articles on the topic.

In developing scoring criteria for performance assessments, teachers should focus on what is most important in completing the task, what have been called the primary traits necessary to achieving the goal of the task; for example, primary traits might include clarity of expression, creativity, depth of understanding or thoroughness, consideration of multiple perspectives, and focus or coherence (Fredericksen and Collins 1989, 29–31). Students can participate in analyzing the tasks and developing the criteria, a process that will give them a sense of ownership and a deeper understanding useful in learning to evaluate their own work. Also key to this process is the availability of models of work at all levels, but particularly outstanding work.

The following is an example of a performance assessment task and scoring criteria designed to measure the students' ability to demonstrate empathy for Americans during the Civil War period.

Assignment: Do one of the following:

1. *Write a diary as though you were the mother of two sons during the Civil War, one fighting for the North and one for the South. Attach a statement about what you think was hardest for this mother.*

2. *Create a play about a family in the Civil War, where the action revolves around the decision of a member of the family to join the army. Attach a commentary about how the members of the family are like and unlike families you know.*

Criteria for scoring:

1. *Accurately uses information from the historical period (no evidence of anachronisms).*

2. *Uses sufficient detail to create a sense of what it was like for people who lived at the time under study.*

3. *Draws out relationships or comparisons between that period and the present.*

4. *Uses affective language in dealing with the experiences of people in history and today. (Diez and Moon 1992, 39–40)*

Performance assessments should be administered in as authentic a manner as possible; that is, students should have the time and access to resources that they would have in facing such a problem in a real-life context.

Following the task, students should receive feedback on both their performance and their self-evaluation of the performance (Jamentz 1994). Self-evaluation is a skill that must be taught and reinforced. By modeling (i.e., evaluating his or her own performance), the teacher can help students understand both how self-evaluation is done and its benefits.

ACTIVITY   ## Critiquing a Performance Assessment

Ms. Johnson teaches an eighth-grade civics class. For several years, she has had students do individual research papers on gains and setbacks in achieving equal rights and opportunities for all Americans. This year, she decided to have students create products other than traditional research papers. She assigned students to take the roles of editors for a special edition of a national newsmagazine. Each student is to design a page that features one turning point in the effort to achieve equality in the United States. Ms. Johnson was not sure how to assess the magazine pages but eventually came up with the scoring rubric presented in Figure 15.2.

With a group of classmates, discuss Ms. Johnson's assignment and scoring rubric. Do you think this is an authentic task? What important outcomes does it assess? Do the criteria on the scoring sheet discriminate between various levels of mastery? Why or why not? How would you improve the task and the scoring rubric?

Portfolios

Teachers who approach writing as a process developed the portfolio as a device for assessing students' growth in writing. Portfolios are currently being adapted for use in many other curriculum areas, including social studies, but they retain the essential characteristics of evaluating growth in a process of learning. A portfolio is a collection of student work that demonstrates the student's experiences and achievements. Some teachers call these collections "process-folios" to indicate that the work included is not necessarily finished but was selected to show development of the student's thinking. By emphasizing development and growth rather than end products only, portfolios allow teachers to emphasize the importance of the processes of learning, thinking, and reflection.

Although the teacher may establish a list of the kinds of materials to be included in the portfolio, student participation in selection of the actual items to be included is a critical part of portfolio development. Students should also be able to justify their selections. Through the processes of selection and justification, students take responsibility for both their learning and its assessment and become more reflective and better able to critique their work (Mitchell 1992).

A social studies portfolio may include a wide range of items, including group assignments and team ideas, teacher comments, student writings, student reflections,

Performance Assessment: Searching for Equality Posters

1. Historical accuracy of description of event and its cause(s).

Exemplary: Who, what, when, and where are explained in historical context; relevant group(s) affected are identified; relevant details are included.

Proficient: Who, what, when, where are stated in minimal historical context.

Unsatisfactory: Only minimal information is included.

Comments:

2. Clarity of writing and analysis.

Exemplary: Event is characterized as a setback or progress toward equality; analysis is supported by reasons; connections to present are made; correct spelling, correct punctuation.

Proficient: Event is characterized as a setback or progress toward equality; few reasons to support analysis are given; no connection to the present is made; some grammar errors.

Unsatisfactory: No analysis; writing is unclear.

Comments:

3. Neatness and creativity.

Exemplary: Shows much evidence of planning—centered titles, borders; uses symbols to convey ideas; main idea is easily understood by viewer.

Proficient: Poster is somewhat "cluttered."

Unsatisfactory: Mistakes not corrected; poster is very "cluttered"; no evidence of planning is apparent.

Comments:

4. Personal reflection.

Exemplary: Takes and communicates a clear position reflecting on the importance of fairness and equality in society; statement builds upon analysis.

Proficient: Personal reflection is not obvious; does not flow from analysis.

Unsatisfactory: No personal statement is given.

Comments:

Figure 15.2   Scoring rubric for research activity

data gathered and analyzed by the student, problems and investigations, individual and group projects, rough drafts and polished products, a biography of a work, and creative expressions related to social studies topics. High-tech materials (e.g., videotapes or laser discs) can be combined with more traditional print products. Work included should be dated and annotated with the student's reasons for including the item. Adams and Hamm (1992, 104) suggest the following as examples of items students might be asked to pick for inclusion in their portfolios.

- A sample that reflects a problem that was difficult for you, work that shows where you started to figure out the problem, and a sample that shows you reached a solution
- A sample that shows you learned something new
- A sample of work in which you need to keep searching for ideas
- Two items of which you are proud
- One example of a comical disaster

In selecting materials to be included in their portfolios, students should be aware of the purpose of the portfolio and the standards that the teacher will use to make judgments about it. When you begin using portfolios, you may find that your purposes evolve over the course of the year. That is fine, as long as you keep students apprised of how your thinking is developing; indeed, sharing these changes with students can be a model for reflection and self-critique. Students should have the opportunity to change their own thinking, eliminating items from the portfolio and substituting others as their evaluation of their work evolves.

To maximize benefits from creating their portfolios, students should see models of completed portfolios and have the opportunity to talk with others about how they are developing their collections of work. As a beginning teacher, you may not have a collection of portfolios to present to students; however, you might present a portfolio you have constructed for a class or ask other teachers if they have portfolios you can share with your class. Asking other teachers for assistance will also give you the opportunity to exchange ideas on the use of portfolios, benefiting from other teachers' experiences.

Although specific evaluation criteria will depend on the purposes the portfolios are designed to achieve, identifying criteria as clearly as possible is important. The following example should help to clarify how criteria might be specified.

Ms. Parenti teaches a senior elective on public policy issues. At the beginning of the semester, students select three issues they will study as a group, spending about four weeks on each issue; individual students or groups of students will then select a fourth issue for study and presentation to the group. One of the class requirements is compilation of a portfolio, which is to include, at a minimum, the following items:

- An initial position statement on the three issues selected by the group for study, including what the student perceives each issue to be, his or her initial position on the issue, and why he or she thinks the issue is worthy of study.

- A personal position paper on each of the three issues, written at the end of the group studies. The paper is to explain the issue, the student's position on the issue, and the evidence supporting that position.

- A reflection on how the student's approach to the issues changed as a result of class interaction, evidence, and other factors.

- A creative work (poem, artwork, etc.) on the issue that the student found most difficult to grapple with.

- A plan for approaching the issue to be studied in small groups or individually, including a justification for choosing the issue, an initial formulation of the issue, and a list of evidence that may be helpful in addressing the issue.

- A biography of the small group or individual project, explaining how the actual project varied from the plan and why, the challenges the student confronted, and how he or she resolved them.

- Recommendations for improving the course based on the student's self-evaluation.

Criteria for evaluating the portfolios include the following:

- Understanding of the issues. Students should state the issue or problem under study as a series of public or private decisions and should identify the conflicting value positions that underlie opposing views. Students should identify and present relevant evidence to support their own views.

- Clarity of presentation. Arguments should be well organized and presented coherently and in sufficient detail to allow the reader to follow the student's thinking. Where appropriate, data should be gathered and presented in an appropriate format.

- Technical vocabulary. Students should show increasing ability to use the technical vocabulary for analyzing public issues taught by the teacher.

- Use of analogies. Students should show increasing ability to use analogies to clarify their positions on the issues.

- Meta-cognition. Students should be able to explain the strategies they used in addressing an issue, evaluating those that were effective and those that were not. They should show awareness of their increasing use of particular strategies as the semester progressed.

- Reflection. Students should be able to use their self-evaluations to make concrete suggestions for improving the course.

Developing a Portfolio Assignment

Return to a unit that you planned in conjunction with an earlier chapter. Develop a portfolio assignment for the unit that will help students reflect on growth and changes in their thinking. The assignment should include items that require students to use knowledge from the unit to solve a problem. Develop criteria for judging the merit of students' work in compiling the portfolio.

Trade assignments with another student and provide each other with feedback on the assignment and the criteria. Which items do you think would be especially helpful to students? For which items is it more difficult to understand the value? What other items might you suggest? Are the evaluation criteria clear? Can the students use the criteria to guide their work? Can the criteria be applied fairly?

Tests

Teachers have long used essay tests to evaluate students' ability to analyze, apply, evaluate, and synthesize course material. Essay tests also provide students with opportunities to demonstrate their ability to select, organize, and summarize information.

As they must in designing other types of evaluations, teachers creating an essay test must think carefully about what they want to accomplish, identify the objectives they are assessing, and make sure that the question is related to those objectives in a way that can be defined in terms of expected student behavior. The question should have a clear focus in order to give students some ideas for how to begin framing a response. Similarly, a clear focus will help the teacher specify criteria for grading. The criteria should be shared with students so they can plan and organize their time.

The following is an example of a question that might be used in a science/technology/society unit on acid rain. The question has a clear focus and specifies criteria for grading.

> *Mary is going to hike into a lake in the Oregon Cascades. Fifteen years earlier, Mary had been to the same lake to conduct a study for the Oregon Fish and Wildlife Commission. At that time the lake was a typical high mountain lake surrounded by coniferous trees on three sides and some alders, birches, and maples on the more level, meadow side of the lake. The lake had been a favorite fishing spot for her father and grandfather, producing many shrimp-fed rainbow trout. She learned that crawfish from the lake were good bait for the fish.*
>
> *Describe the changes you think might have occurred in the plants and animals of this environment if acid rain had significantly affected the area. Make specific references to the assigned reading to support your hypotheses.*
>
> *The following criteria will be used to evaluate your response:*
> *1 point will be given if your response is clear and well organized.*
> *1 point will be given if the response is logically supported by specific references to the background reading.*

2 points will be given if the response shows "in-depth" thought, that is a careful and thorough consideration of the possible effects that acid rain might have had on this environment. (Fielding and Fiasca 1987)

Recently, some educators have begun referring to performance-based tests. These tests appear to be variations of the essay test in which the questions require use of knowledge in a manner similar to its use in the kinds of performance assessments discussed earlier. For example, Jane Heckley Kon and Giselle Martin-Kniep (1992, 95) developed three performance-based questions for assessing students' geographic knowledge and skills. The first asked students to plan a two-day camping trip in a specific geographic area; the second called for preparing an evacuation plan for residents of a small community in response to an oil tanker fire near the city marina; the third problem involved deciding whether to develop a coalfield on a hypothetical island. For all three exercises, students were given maps and other forms of data and asked to use that information to develop a plan or take a position.

Although the conventional wisdom has been that essay questions are easier to write than multiple-choice items, constructing well-thought-out questions with evaluation criteria does take time, as does scoring students' responses.

The ease of scoring has been one of the primary factors making multiple-choice tests the most common form of test in American schools. Other commonly used forms of objective tests (those that can be scored with little or no subjective judgment) are short-answer tests, true-false tests, and matching tests. These tests are most often used to assess content knowledge or attainment of such skills as distinguishing fact from opinion or reading a graph. Thus, teachers should be wary of overreliance on so-called objective tests, since they will send students the message that lower-level thinking, primarily recall, is what is valued.

Multiple-choice tests do have their advocates, who argue that such tests can be used to assess higher-order thinking. Certainly, multiple-choice items can be designed to assess more than simple recall. For example, the following item is intended to assess students' ability to evaluate sources of information or recognize bias.

Which one of the following sources of information on the environmental effects of industrial pollution is likely to be most objective?

A. The President of Selpo Manufacturing, which is located on the banks of the Hudson River.

B. A report prepared by a panel of university scientists, industrial engineers, and government researchers.

C. A position paper prepared by the Union for Free Enterprise, an organization dedicated to decreasing government regulation of business.

D. A mother whose daughter experienced serious health problems after swimming in a polluted lake. (Fielding and Fiasca 1987)

Teachers should be aware, however, that interpreting the results of such tests always depends on inferences based on the assumptions that underlie the questions. For example, the question above depends on shared assumptions about self-interest and objectivity; further, a correct answer to the question does not guarantee that a student could actually recognize bias in a document produced by any of these sources, although that is the inference made when a correct answer is said to show the ability to recognize bias. A better test of whether students can identify bias would be having them actually evaluate several documents on a topic.

When teachers do choose to use objective tests, the questions asked should be matched with instructional objectives; that is, even when testing recall of factual information, the questions should target the information believed to be most important in meeting course goals. Objective tests should also have the following characteristics (Psencik and Grigar n.d.):

1. Clarity. Ambiguity should be avoided, and directions should be clear.

2. Consistency. Items and responses should be worded in the same form throughout the test.

3. Accuracy. The desired answers should be correct ones, and the distractors (wrong answers) should indeed distract. The effects of guessing should be minimized by keeping distractors approximately similar in length, plausible, and grammatically congruent with the question. Response patterns should be avoided.

4. Avoidance of racial, socioeconomic, religious, or sexual bias. All the knowledge and skills needed to answer the questions correctly should have been taught in the unit or course.

5. Representativeness. The test items should be written to sample adequately the learning outcomes of the course or unit.

6. Emphasis on content and methodology. The test items should be written to measure student mastery of the content and learning strategies covered in the course or unit.

Asking another teacher to review test items—and the correct responses—is a good idea. Often, another reader may identify problems that the test-writer does not notice. After giving a test, ask for reaction from students and consider their response seriously in planning future tests.

ACTIVITY   **Writing an Essay Test**

Pick a lesson or unit plan you developed earlier in this course. Write a clearly focused essay question that will assess whether students can use essential learnings from the lesson or unit. Develop scoring criteria to be shared with students.

When you have completed your essay question, trade questions with another student and provide feedback, using the following questions:

- Is the question clearly focused?
- Does it require students to use what they have learned (rather than simply repeating it)?
- Do the criteria evaluate what is most important in showing mastery?
- Are the criteria written so that students could understand and use them?

Attitude Measures

Many goals or outcomes in social studies call for development of particular attitudes or values. Often, assessment of those goals is neglected because they are not used in grading. Yet teachers need assessment information related to student attitudes if they are to improve their teaching in this area.

Survey questionnaires are one technique for assessing student attitudes. When administered before and after instruction, questionnaires can provide diagnostic information, as well as indications of changes that occurred because of instruction.

Items on survey questionnaires can be open-ended, allowing students the chance to express themselves freely. For example, a teacher trying to assess students' attitudes toward politicians might simply ask, "Do you think local politicians are honest?" Open-ended questions may sometimes elicit useful information about student perceptions that you would not otherwise find out. They do, however, take longer for students to answer and for teachers to read.

Questionnaire items can also be closed, providing students with a limited number of responses to choose among. Several different kinds of response formats are available.

Likert scale response formats allow students to indicate their intensity of feeling about something (for example, from strongly disagree to strongly agree or not at all important to very important):

Politicians in our community do not care about high school students' opinions.

Strongly Disagree   Disagree   No Opinion   Agree   Strongly Agree

Semantic differential items ask students to rate their reactions to a person or an idea along a series of continua formed by pairs of adjectives:

I believe politicians are:

Valuable   Worthless

Honest   Dishonest

Unfair   Fair

Checklist items give students a series of statements related to a particular topic. Students can check the responses that apply to them. A checklist can be useful in determining if students have taken particular actions that might indicate commitment to targeted values:

This semester, have you (Check each space that applies):

_____ Read the newspaper at least three times a week?

_____ Discussed public policy issues with family and friends at least twice?

_____ Attended a public meeting, such as a school board meeting or city council meeting?

_____ Voted?

_____ Signed a petition?

_____ Written to a representative?

Rank order scales ask students to put items in order according to perceived importance, frequency, or preference. Rank order scales provide a good means of obtaining feedback on students' responses to class activities:

Rank the class activities in the law unit from 1 to 5, with 1 being the activity you feel you learned the most from, 2 the second most, and so on.

_____ Mock trial

_____ Discussions of cases

_____ Court tour

_____ Textbook

_____ Research project

All questionnaire items should be clearly written, focusing on a single item. For example, an item such as "I liked the law unit because it involved mock trials and case studies" confounds attitudes toward the class with two teaching strategies. Questions should be designed to discriminate among students; that is, if most students are likely to answer a question in the same way (for example, "Would you prefer to play video games or do a social studies research project?"), the question will not provide much useful information. Asking several questions about the same attitude may increase the teacher's confidence that the information gathered is significant.

Projective techniques can also be useful in learning about students' attitudes. Projective techniques allow students to react to an open-ended stimulus in a creative way. Projective techniques include writing stories to match titles, finishing sentences, or finishing stories. An example of each is given here.

Title: The Honest Politician

Sentence Starter: My advice to our city council would be . . .

Unfinished Story: During a lecture on separation of powers, Mr. Arbuckle became ill and left his classroom. Several of the students in the class immediately began throwing paper airplanes and spitwads around the room. Soon, the activity escalated and pencils, erasers, and books were flying through the air. Then three things seemed to happen simultaneously: Paul was hit in the head with a notebook, sending his glasses flying across the room and giving him a bloody nose, Cindy (who had been using the time to work on her algebra homework) stood up to sharpen her pencil and caught an eraser as it whizzed by her head, and the principal walked into the classroom. "Cindy," he demanded, "what's going on here?"

What happened next?

As with other forms of assessment, students should understand the purposes of attitude measures. For students to feel comfortable responding honestly to attitude measures, they must believe that their answers will not have negative consequences, either on their grades or in their interactions with the teacher. To gain their trust, teachers may want to allow students to respond anonymously. Note, however, that if pretests and posttests are being used, some method of matching students' tests is needed. A student-administered numbering system may be a possible solution that will also increase student confidence in the teacher's trustworthiness.

Classroom Observations

Teachers have always relied on their own observations of students' classroom behavior to make judgments about instruction and, sometimes, about performance. Most teacher observations are not systematic, and conducting systematic observations of every student would be extremely difficult (if not impossible) to do. However, two strategies can make classroom observations more systematic and useful to the teacher. First, students can be taught to observe each other's abilities in such areas as discussion skills, cooperative learning, and group communication. Second, observers (whether the teacher or students) can focus on a group rather than on individuals.

In both of these cases, a checklist of behaviors is a useful observation tool. The checklist can be developed by the teacher or by students and teacher working together. Steps in developing a checklist include identifying what is to be assessed, listing the behaviors or characteristics to be observed, and then sequencing the items logically. Figure 15.3 provides an example of a checklist used in observing group process skills. With checklist in hand, students designated as observers can sit outside a group and identify whether group members are functioning as intended.

If feasible, it may on occasion be instructive to videotape the class and then analyze the tape with the students. This process allows you to highlight examples of skills or processes that you want students to develop. Students may initially find this tech-

	Yes	*No*	*Can't tell*	*Comments*
1. Group members check to make sure everybody is clear about what the group is trying to accomplish.	——	——	————	————
2. Each group member participates.	——	——	————	————
3. Group members engage in constructive give-and-take.	——	——	————	————
4. The group sticks to its task.	——	——	————	————
5. The group works without interfering with other groups.	——	——	————	————
6. The group checks its progress toward accomplishing its goals and modifies its processes, if needed.	——	——	————	————
7. The group records and summarizes what it has accomplished.	——	——	————	————

Figure 15.3   Group skills checklist. *Source: Fielding and Fiasca 1987. From G. Fielding and M. Fiasca,* Personal and Social Issues in Science: Lessons from the Classroom, *Oregon State System of Higher Education, 1987. Used by permission.*

nique somewhat threatening, but if the teacher makes it clear that his or her skills are also open for comment and critique, students may find the process more engaging!

ACTIVITY

Assessing Your Learning

Return to the three-column sheet of things you knew, wanted to know, and learned about assessment. How would you assess your own learning? Do you think you are ready for the ultimate performance assessment—evaluating the progress of your students? In what areas do your assessment knowledge or skills need further development?

This strategy, developed by Donna Ogle (1986), is called the K-W-L technique (for *k*now, *w*ant to know, and *l*earned). The strategy is intended to encourage conceptual change by activating the learner's existing knowledge structures, providing a context for reading and other learning activities, and encouraging the learner to compare and contrast new information with existing knowledge. Do you think this activity was successful in meeting those ends with respect to your own learning? How might you use a similar activity with secondary students?

COMMUNICATING ASSESSMENT INFORMATION TO PARENTS AND STUDENTS

Providing Feedback to Students

The primary purpose of providing feedback to students is to help them improve their performance. Thus, decisions about what is shared with students and how it is shared should be based on answers to these questions:

- What information will help the student improve performance?
- How can I present that information in the most helpful way?

As student self-evaluation comes to play an important part in classroom assessment plans, communication with students about their performance necessarily becomes ongoing and essential. As students develop their self-evaluation skills, one of the teacher's most important roles will be that of coach, helping them assess what they have done and reflect on how they might improve. Often, informal "rehashing" of a test or performance can be very helpful to students in developing insights about their learning.

Teachers may also want to schedule more-formal conferences with students to discuss such topics as behavior patterns or characteristics (e.g., perserverance, lack of concentration) that are affecting learning and how far the student has progressed toward obtaining particular objectives or outcomes. To assess progress, teachers must first have established and made public milestones that indicate various levels of achievement; such milestones provide criteria by which students can judge their own progress, as well as benchmarks for you to use in discussing needed improvements. Discussions with students should include identifying areas in which students need help and designing experiences to meet those needs. Carrying through on those plans will reinforce the students' belief that assessment activities are designed to help them, rather than judge or punish them.

Keep in mind that the feedback process should be a two-way communication; that is, students should have the opportunity to provide the teacher with feedback as well. Teachers may also gather information that will help them improve their teaching through careful listening to students' self-evaluation. Areas about which you may be able to gather information include the aspects of the social studies curriculum most helpful to students, the quality of the learning environment, preconceived ideas or schema that are resistant to change, and what was engaging or motivational for students. Such information can be critical in helping plan new experiences, restructure experiences, and even contribute to long-range revision of the social studies program.

In setting up student conferences, be sure to allow enough time for a meaningful two-way discussion. Check for understanding throughout the discussion so that you are sure you are communicating clearly and that you are hearing the student's comments. Although doing so is sometimes difficult, try to arrange for the conferences to be held at a time when and in a place where you will have the student's attention and the student will have yours.

Communicating with Parents

Communication with parents has several purposes, including informing parents of their children's progress, exchanging information that will help both teacher and parents assist students in improving performance, and enlisting parental support for the social studies program. These purposes suggest an important guideline to keep in mind in communicating with parents. Be an active listener; parents may provide useful information both directly (e.g., by giving suggestions on ways of presenting information that work well with their child) or indirectly (e.g., by indicating skepticism about affective goals, a skepticism that may affect the student's willingness to undertake certain kinds of work).

In planning any kind of communication, be sensitive to the needs of families—language differences, inability to read, or scheduling problems, for example. Also be sensitive to the fact that, unfortunately, many parents had unhappy experiences during their own school years and may be uncomfortable, distrusting, or defensive in dealing with their students' teachers. Thus, it is especially important to take steps to develop parents' trust and make them comfortable in their dealings with you.

One crucial step is ensuring that parents are physically comfortable. Before a parent conference, set up a comfortable place for parents to sit; they should have ample room to look at students' work. Organize the information you are going to share with parents into broad categories so they do not feel overwhelmed with details that do not seem to have any coherence. Make sure to have dated examples of students' work available. Firsthand evidence of a student's performance and achievement in a particular area will help parents be more objective in evaluating their child's growth and give them greater insight into the goals of the social studies program.

When parents arrive for the conference, try to put them at ease with welcoming comments, but do not spend too much time on small talk. Parents who are nervous about what you may have to tell them about their child will not enjoy the delay.

In sharing information with parents, avoid educational jargon. Such language is off-putting at best and, at worst, may reinforce parents' negative stereotypes of teachers and schools. If parts of your grading or evaluation policy are mandated by the school or district, make that clear to parents.

Begin your sharing of information by explaining the major projects or units of study students have undertaken and how student learning has been evaluated. Present positive information first. Give examples that support your points regarding student growth and areas for continued improvement. Allow time for parents to examine student work, and encourage them to clarify what you are saying and to provide their own perspectives. If they ask questions you cannot answer, don't try to "fake it." Simply, tell them you don't know but will try to find an answer to their question.

Try to reserve some time at the end of the conference to plan follow-up actions that both you and the parents may take. Be sure to follow through with anything you commit to doing. Failure to do so can negate all your careful preconference planning.

Many of the do's and don'ts for conferences apply to written communication with parents as well. In written communication, getting to the point quickly is especially important, as is a positive or inviting tone. Although the need for notes to parents may be most frequent when students are having problems, sending good news or compliments home is a good practice, too. If you want to establish a regular system of written communication with parents, choose a specified day of the week or month for such communications; copying the memo or letter on a particular color paper may also be helpful.

Special events can also be useful components of your parent communication program. For example, one school sponsored a humanities exposition (Barone 1991). Through twenty-minute presentations that included dramatic productions, media presentations, and oral readings of stories and essays, students demonstrated what they had learned through an interdisciplinary humanities project. Portfolios were also displayed. A middle school teacher assigned her students to create exhibits for a natural history museum exhibition on ancient Egypt. When the exhibition was completed, each student had not only prepared an exhibit but could explain other students' exhibits as well. Parents who attended the "opening" of the exhibition gained a new respect for the depth and breadth of student work, as well as for the high level of student enthusiasm.

Another school offers portfolio evenings (Hebert 1992). After students have reviewed their portfolios with the teacher, they invite their parents to school for a portfolio evening. Six or seven students present their portfolios to their parents each evening. As part of their presentations, students explain why they selected pieces for inclusion in their portfolios, how various pieces showed their growth over the semester or year, the steps they went through in completing a particular project, what they were proud of, and what they believe needed more work. The teacher is available to provide assistance as needed, but student presentation of their work is the focus. Again, parents have gained new respect and understanding for the work students are doing.

| ACTIVITY | ## Role Playing a Parent–Teacher Conference |

You are a seventh-grade geography teacher. You have scheduled an appointment with the parents of Travis, a student who has been having difficulty in your class. He is often inattentive and sometimes disruptive. The first unit of the course focused on map and globe skills; you tested student learning through paper-and-pencil exercises and did not worry about performance assessments. Travis did fairly well on that unit. In the second unit, which focused on Latin America, Travis did not even complete his project, which was to have been a travel brochure for a South American resort. Travis dismissed the project as "a bunch of crap." You want to enlist his parents' help in motivating Travis to improve his performance—and behavior—in your class.

When Travis's parents arrive for the conference, it quickly becomes clear to you that they have somewhat different views on Travis's performance and on education. Travis's mother opens the conference by announcing that Travis has always been a "straight-A student." His father gives her an unpleasant look and comments that schools aren't "what they used to be."

Three students in the class should role-play the remainder of the conference, with the rest of the class members acting as observers and recorders. Following the role play, discuss what was successful from the teacher's point of view. What techniques helped the teacher accomplish his or her goals for the conference? How did the parents feel or react when the teacher used these strategies? What was successful from the parents' point of view? How did the teacher feel when he or she believed the parents were being evasive or defensive? Would the conference be likely to result in any improvements in Travis's performance? Why or why not?

Reflecting on the Chapter

Pick one of the courses you are currently taking. Based on what you have learned in this chapter, how would you assess student learning in the course if you were the professor? How is your plan different from that being used in the course? How do your perceptions of the professor's evaluation plan affect your motivation and the way you approach the course work? Write some thoughts in your journal about how a teacher's assessment plans influence students' motivation and their approach to learning. How will you, as a teacher, assure that your assessment plans have a positive impact on students?

References

Adams, D. M., and M. E. Hamm. "Portfolio Assessment and Social Studies: Collecting, Selecting, and Reflecting on What Is Significant." *Social Education* 56, no. 2 (1992): 103–05.

Archbald, D. A., and F. M. Newmann, *Beyond Standardized Testing: Assessing Authentic Academic Achievement in the Secondary School*. Reston, Va.: National Association of Secondary School Principals, 1988.

Barone, T. "Assessment as Theater: Staging an Exposition." *Educational Leadership* 48, no. 5 (1991): 57–59.

Bartlett, L. D. "Students Successfully Grapple with Lessons of History in Innovative Group Performance Tasks." *Social Education* 56, no. 2 (1992): 101–02.

Diez, M. E., and C. J. Moon. "What Do We Want Students to Know? . . . And Other Important Questions." *Educational Leadership* 49, no. 8 (1992): 38–41.

Fielding, G., and M. Fiasca. *Personal and Social Issues in Science: Lessons from the Classroom.* Monmouth, Oreg.: Oregon State System of Higher Education, 1987.

Fredericksen, J. R., and A. Collins. "A Systems Approach to Educational Testing." *Educational Researcher* 18, no. 9 (1989): 27–32.

Hart, D. *Authentic Assessment: A Handbook for Educators.* Menlo Park, Calif.: Addison-Wesley, 1994.

Hebert, E. A. "Portfolios Invite Reflection from Students and Staff." *Educational Leadership* 49, no. 8 (1992): 58–61.

Jamentz, K. "Making Sure that Assessment Improves Performance." *Educational Leadership* 51, no. 6 (March 1994): 55–57.

Kon, J. H., and G. O. Martin-Kniep. "Students' Geographic Knowledge and Skills in Different Kinds of Tests: Multiple-Choice versus Performance Assessment." *Social Education* 56, no. 2 (1992): 95–98.

Maeroff, G. I. "Assessing Alternative Assessment." *Phi Delta Kappan* 73, no. 4 (1991): 272–81.

Mitchell, R. *Testing for Learning: How New Approaches to Evaluation Can Improve American Schools.* New York: The Free Press, 1992.

National Standards for Civics and Government. Calabasas, Calif.: Center for Civic Education, 1994.

Ogle, D. W. "K-W-L Group Instruction Strategy." In *Teaching Reading as Thinking*, ed. A. S. Palincsar et al. Alexandria, Va.: Association for Supervision and Curriculum Development, 1986.

Psencik, L., and L. Grigar. *Evaluation and Social Studies: Practical Ideas for Classroom Teachers.* Austin: Texas Education Agency, n.d.

Shavelson, R. J., and P. Stern. "Research on Teachers' Pedagogical Thoughts, Judgments, Decisions, and Behavior." *Review of Educational Research* 51, no. 4 (1981): 455–98.

Shepard, L. A. "Why We Need Better Assessments." *Educational Leadership* 46, no. 7 (1989): 4–9.

Stiggins, R. J. "Revitalizing Classroom Assessment: The Highest Instructional Priority." *Phi Delta Kappan* 69, no. 5 (1988): 363–68.

———. "Relevant Classroom Assessment Training for Teachers." *Educational Measurement* 10, no. 1 (1991): 7–12.

Wiggins, G. "A True Test: Toward More Authentic and Equitable Assessment." *Phi Delta Kappan* 70, no. 9 (1989): 703–13.

———. "Creating Tests Worth Taking." *Educational Leadership* 49, no. 8 (1992): 26–33.

Wolf, D. P. "Portfolio Assessment: Sampling Student Work." *Educational Leadership* 46, no. 7 (1989): 35–39.

Zessoules, R., and H. Gardner. "Authentic Assessment: Beyond the Buzzword and into the Classroom." In *Expanding Student Assessment*, ed. V. Perrone, 47–71. Alexandria, Va.: Association for Supervision and Curriculum Development, 1991.

PROFESSIONAL ORGANIZATIONS

ORGANIZATIONS WITH BROAD SOCIAL STUDIES INTERESTS

Social studies teachers will find the following three organizations with broad interests in social studies to be especially helpful in keeping up to date on issues, ideas, and materials in the field.

National Council for the Social Studies (NCSS)
3501 Newark Street NW
Washington, DC 20016
202/966-7840

The primary professional organization in the field of social studies is the National Council for the Social Studies (NCSS). This membership organization, which publishes several journals as well as bulletins on special topics related to social studies education, hosts its annual conference in November. The conference is an excellent way of finding out about new ideas and materials. NCSS also has state and local affiliates that provide a variety of services to their members. Contact NCSS for additional information.

ERIC Clearinghouse for Social Studies/Social Science Education
Social Studies Development Center
Indiana University
2805 East 10th Street
Bloomington, IN 47408
812/855-3838

The social studies/social science clearinghouse in the ERIC (Educational Resources Information Center) system, located at Indiana University's Social Studies Development Center, provides many low-cost information products and a free newsletter. The clearinghouse also provides assistance in finding resources related to particular issues or topics in social studies education.

Social Science Education Consortium (SSEC)
Box 21270
Boulder, CO 80308-4270
303/492-8154

The Social Science Education Consortium (SSEC), which produced this methods text, is a national nonprofit organization dedicated to the improvement of social studies education at all levels. The SSEC undertakes a variety of staff development and curriculum development projects in which teachers can take part. SSEC can also provide assistance in locating organizations that can help teachers in particular curriculum areas.

SPECIALIZED ORGANIZATIONS

Many additional organizations provide assistance to teachers in more focused fields, such as history, geography, global studies, or law-related education. A sampling of such organizations is provided below.

American Bar Association
Special Committee on Youth Education for Citizenship
541 North Fairbanks Court
Chicago, IL 60611-3314
312/988-5735

American Forum for Global Education
45 John Street
New York, NY 10038
212/732-8606

Center for Civic Education
5146 Douglas Fir Road
Calabasas, CA 91302
818/591-9321

Constitutional Rights Foundation
601 South Kingsley Drive
Los Angeles, CA 90005
213/487-5590

Foreign Policy Association
729 Seventh Avenue
New York, NY 10019
212/764-4050

National Center for History in the Schools
University of California at Los Angeles
405 Hilgard Avenue
Los Angeles, CA 90024-1512
213/825-4702

National Council on Economic Education
432 Park Avenue, South
New York, NY 10016
212/685-5499

National Council on Geographic Education
16-A Leonard Hall
Indiana University of Pennsylvania
Indiana, PA 15705
412/357-6290

National Geographic Society
Geography Education Program
17th and M Streets NW
Washington, DC 20036
202/857-7000

National History Day
University of Maryland
0121 Caroline Hall
College Park, MD 20742
301/314-9734

National Institute for Citizen Education in the Law
711 G Street SE
Washington, DC 20003
202/546-6644

Stanford Program on International and Cross-Cultural Education
Stanford University
Littlefield Center, Room 300
Lausen Street
Stanford, CA 94305
800/578-1114

SOCIAL SCIENCE ORGANIZATIONS

Each of the social science disciplines also has a professional organization. Although these organizations focus primarily on scholarship in the social sciences, education is often a secondary interest.

American Anthropological Association
1703 New Hampshire Avenue NW
Washington, DC 20009
202/232-8800

American Economic Association
2014 Broadway, Suite 305
Nashville, TN 37203-2418
615/322-2595

American Historical Association
400 A Street SE
Washington, DC 20003
202/544-2422

American Political Science Association
1527 New Hampshire Avenue NW
Washington, DC 20036
202/483-2512

American Psychological Association
750 First Street NE
Washington, DC 20002-4242
202/236-5500

American Sociological Association
1722 N Street NW
Washington, DC 20036
202/833-3410

Association of American Geographers
1710 16th Street NW
Washington, DC 20009
202/234-1450

Organization of American Historians
112 North Bryan Street
Bloomington, IN 47401
812/335-7311

World History Association
Drexel University
Department of History and Politics
Philadelphia, PA 19104
215/895-2471

Index